FAIRY TAIL

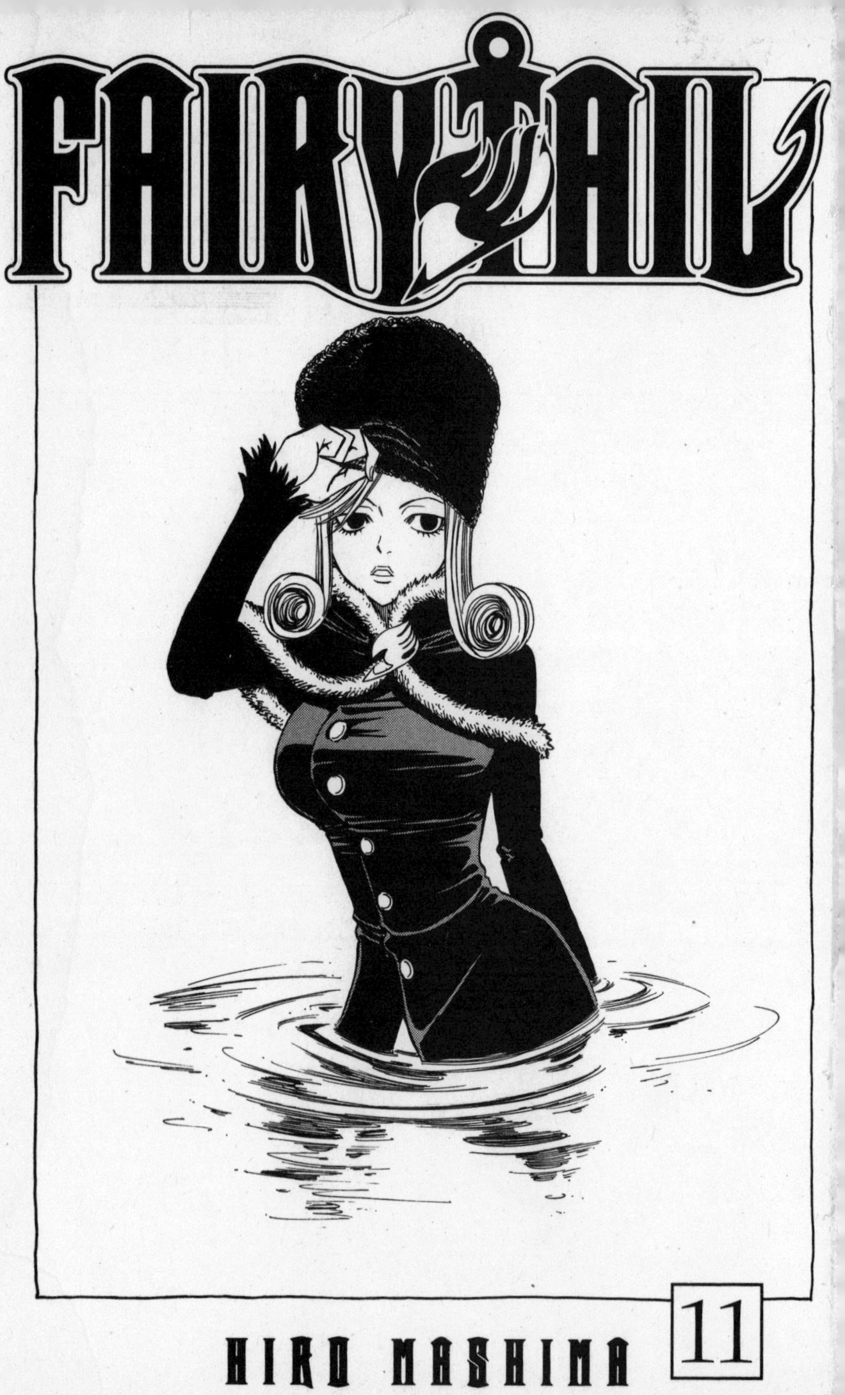

11

HIRO MASHIMA

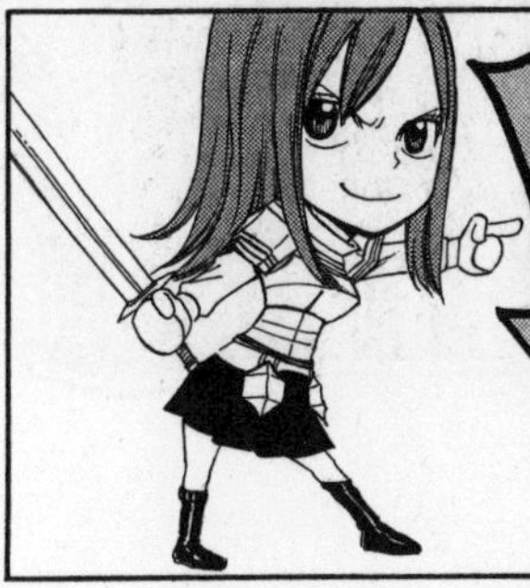

FAIRY TAIL 11

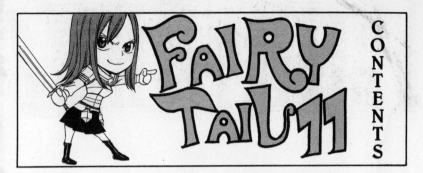

CONTENTS

FAIRY TAIL

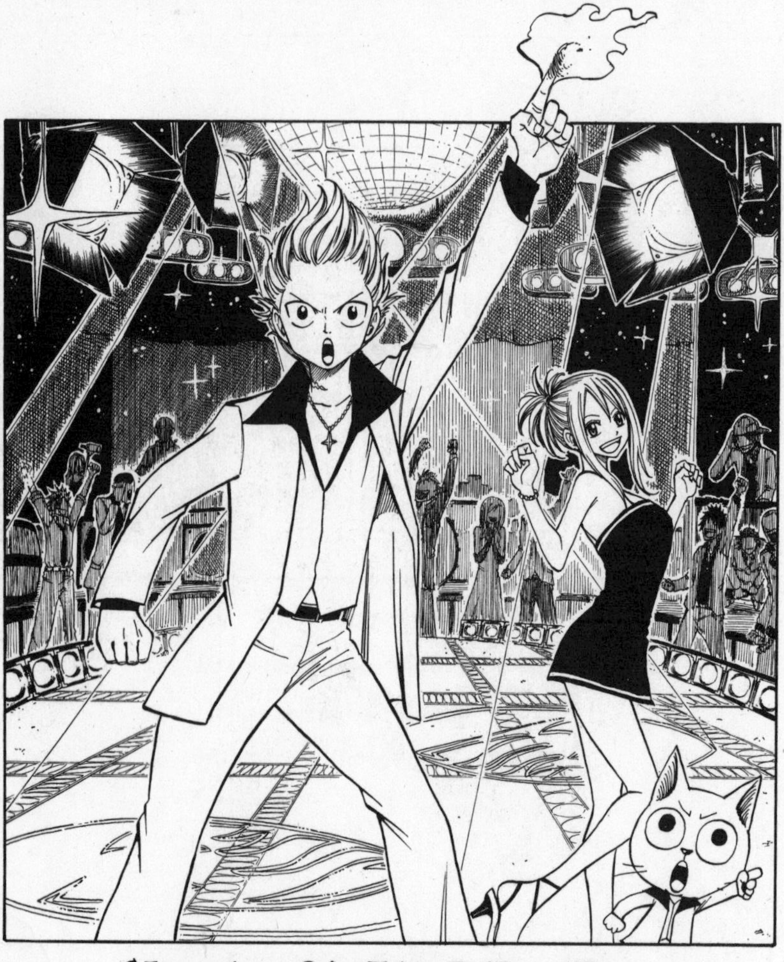

Chapter 83: Find the Way

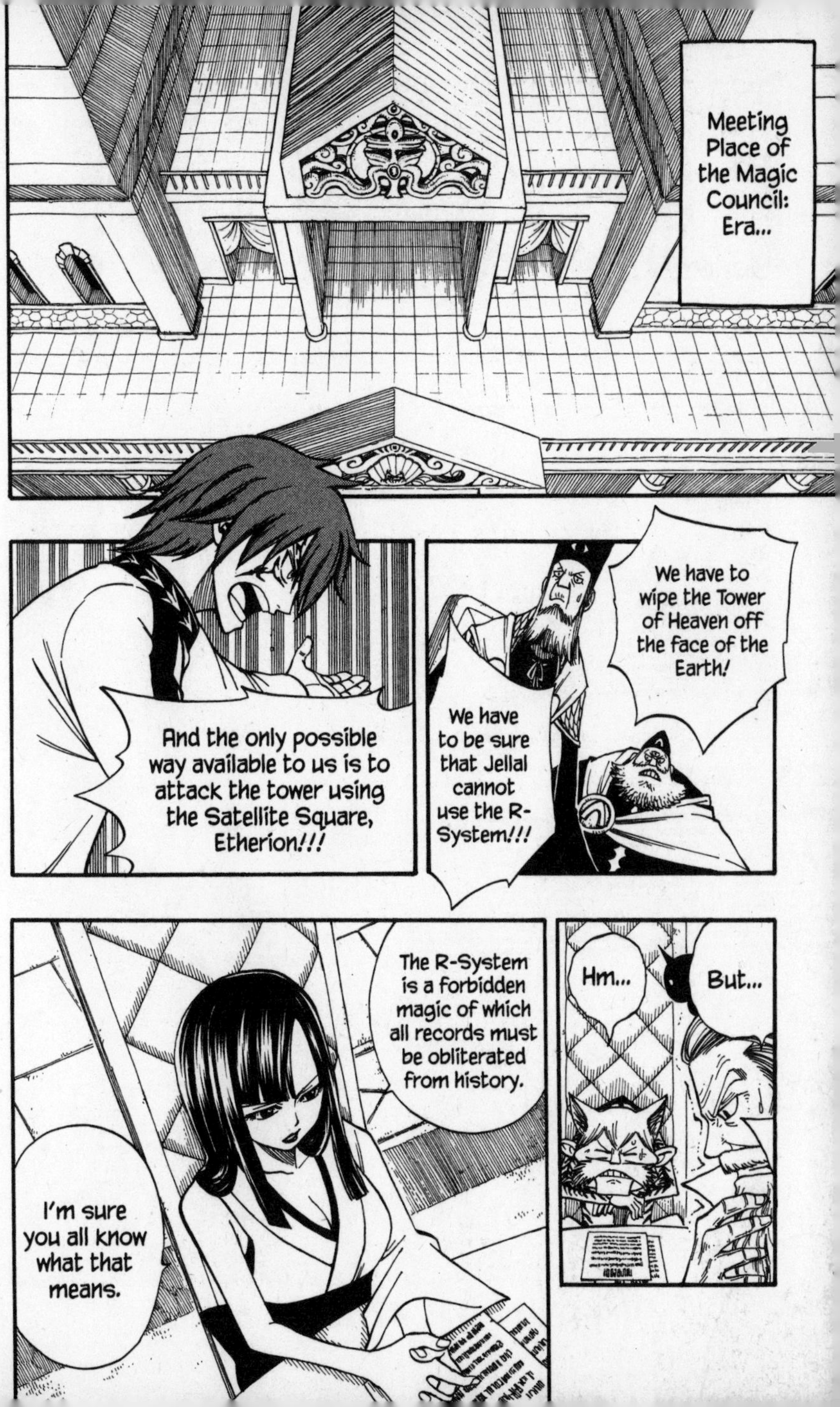
Meeting Place of the Magic Council: Era...
We have to wipe the Tower of Heaven off the face of the Earth!
We have to be sure that Jellal cannot use the R-System!!!
And the only possible way available to us is to attack the tower using the Satellite Square, Etherion!!!
But...
Hm...
The R-System is a forbidden magic of which all records must be obliterated from history.
I'm sure you all know what that means.

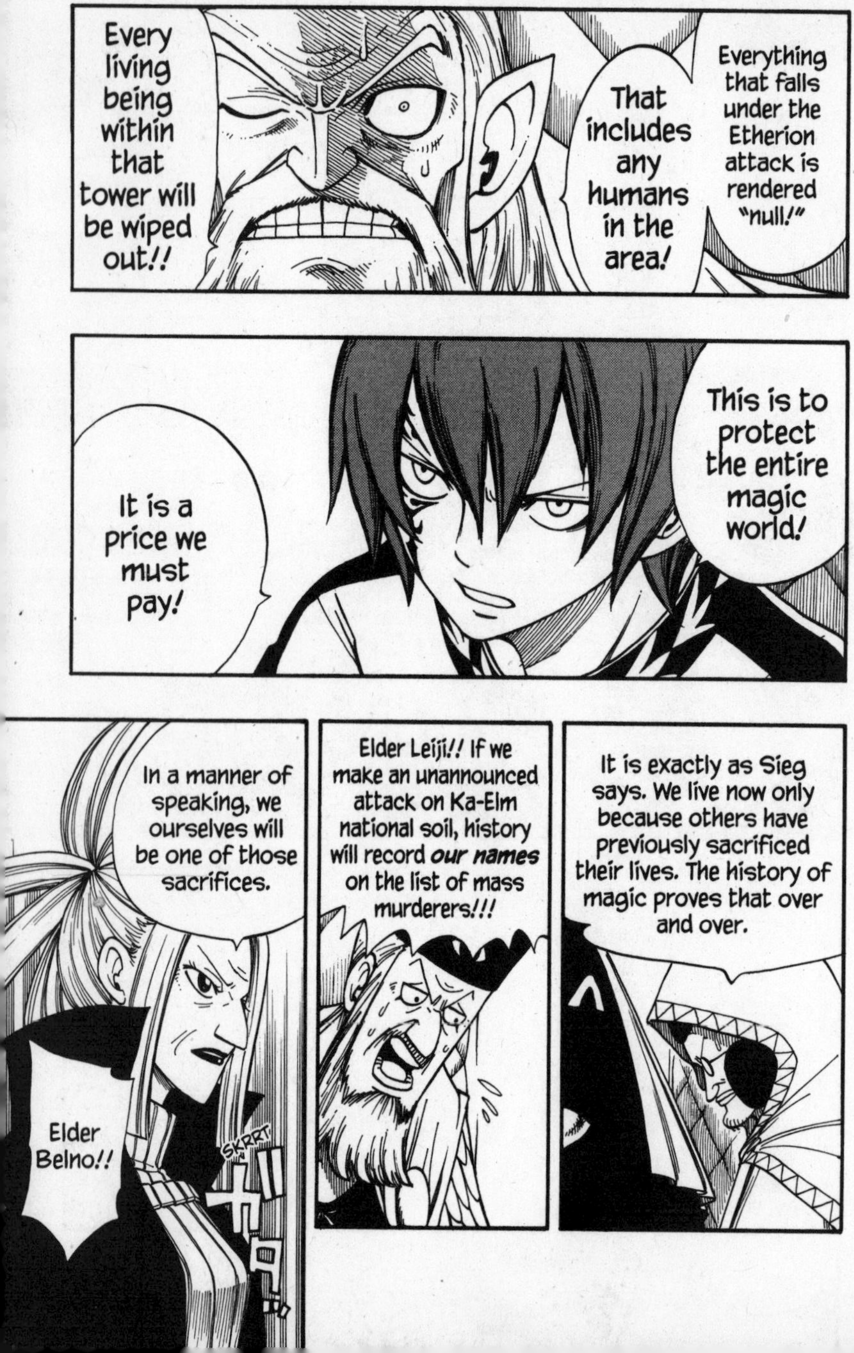
Everything that falls under the Etherion attack is rendered "null!"
That includes any humans in the area!
Every living being within that tower will be wiped out!!
This is to protect the entire magic world!
It is a price we must pay!
It is exactly as Sieg says. We live now only because others have previously sacrificed their lives. The history of magic proves that over and over.
Elder Leiji!! If we make an unannounced attack on Ka-Elm national soil, history will record ***our names*** on the list of mass murderers!!!
In a manner of speaking, we ourselves will be one of those sacrifices.
Elder Belno!!
SKRRT

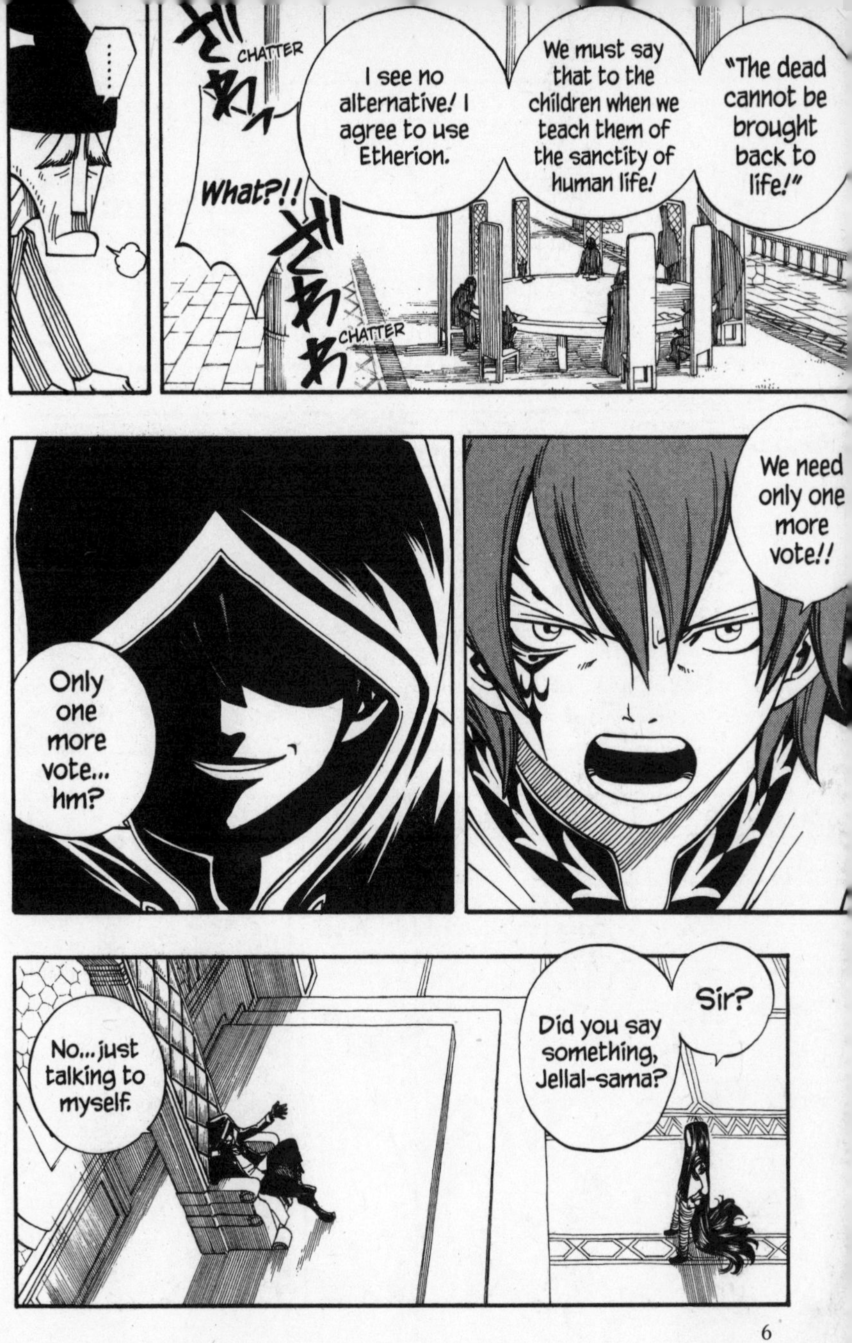
"The dead cannot be brought back to life!"
We must say that to the children when we teach them of the sanctity of human life!
I see no alternative! I agree to use Etherion.
CHATTER
What?!!
CHATTER
......
We need only one more vote!!
Only one more vote... hm?
Sir?
Did you say something, Jellal-sama?
No...just talking to myself.

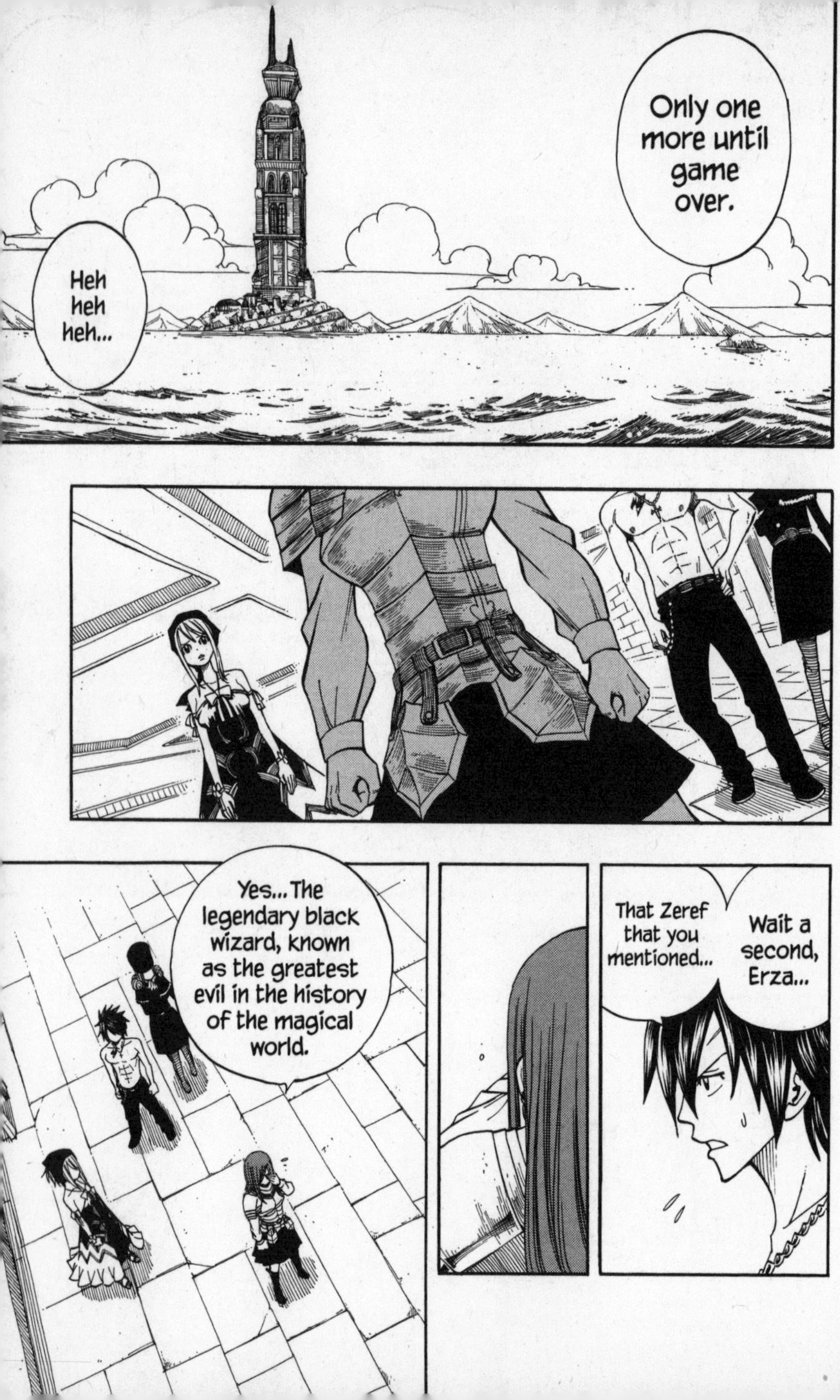
Only one more until game over.
Heh heh heh...
Wait a second, Erza...
That Zeref that you mentioned...
Yes... The legendary black wizard, known as the greatest evil in the history of the magical world.

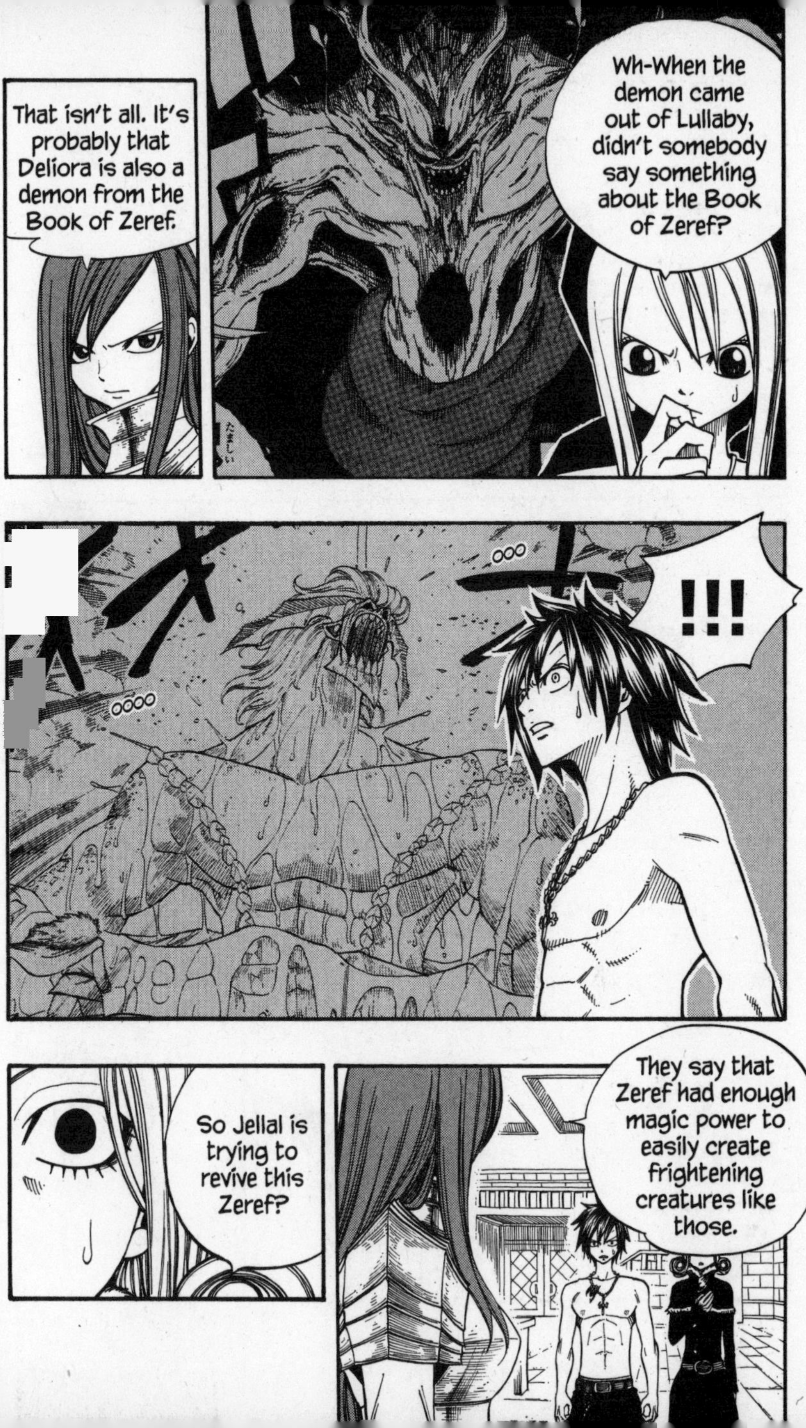
Wh-When the demon came out of Lullaby, didn't somebody say something about the Book of Zeref?
That isn't all. It's probably that Deliora is also a demon from the Book of Zeref.
!!!
ooo
oooo
They say that Zeref had enough magic power to easily create frightening creatures like those.
So Jellal is trying to revive this Zeref?

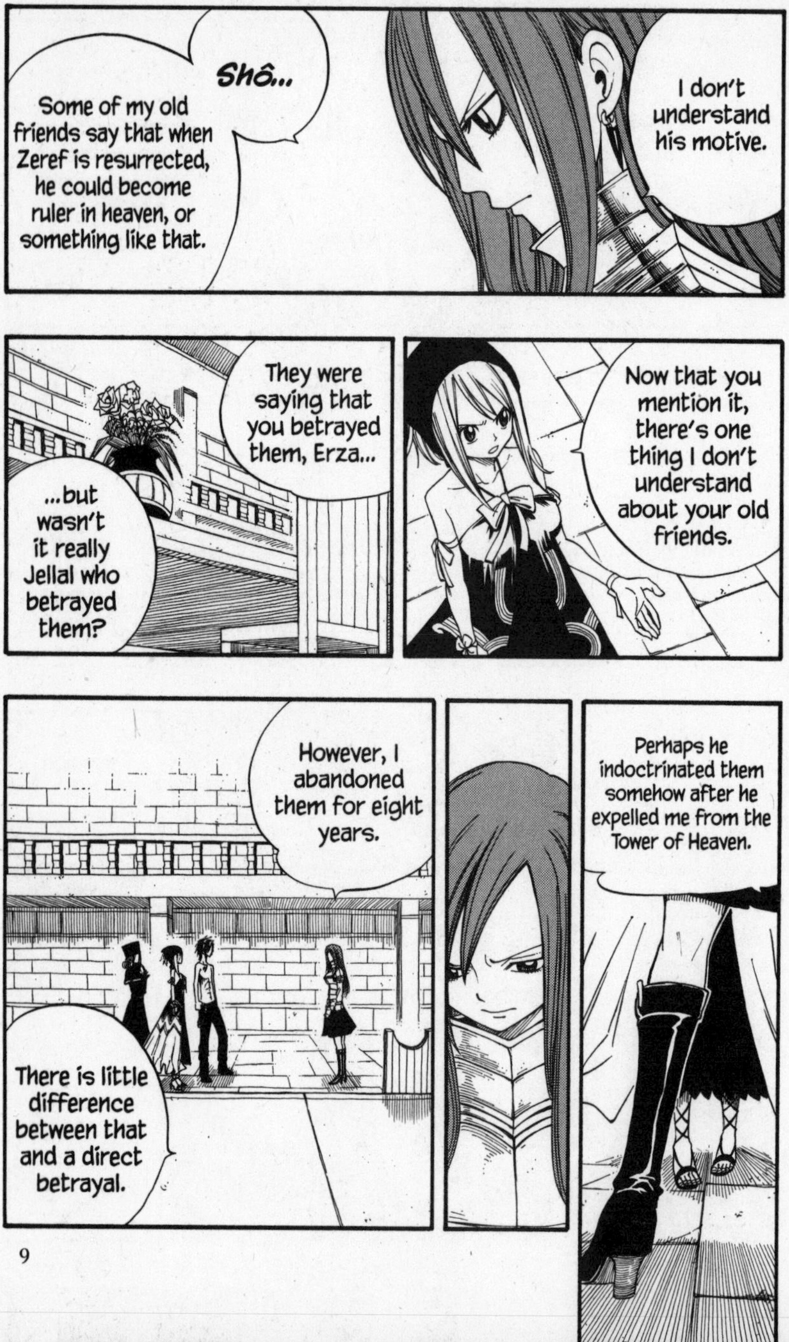
I don't understand his motive.
Shô... Some of my old friends say that when Zeref is resurrected, he could become ruler in heaven, or something like that.
Now that you mention it, there's one thing I don't understand about your old friends.
They were saying that you betrayed them, Erza...
...but wasn't it really Jellal who betrayed them?
Perhaps he indoctrinated them somehow after he expelled me from the Tower of Heaven.
However, I abandoned them for eight years.
There is little difference between that and a direct betrayal.

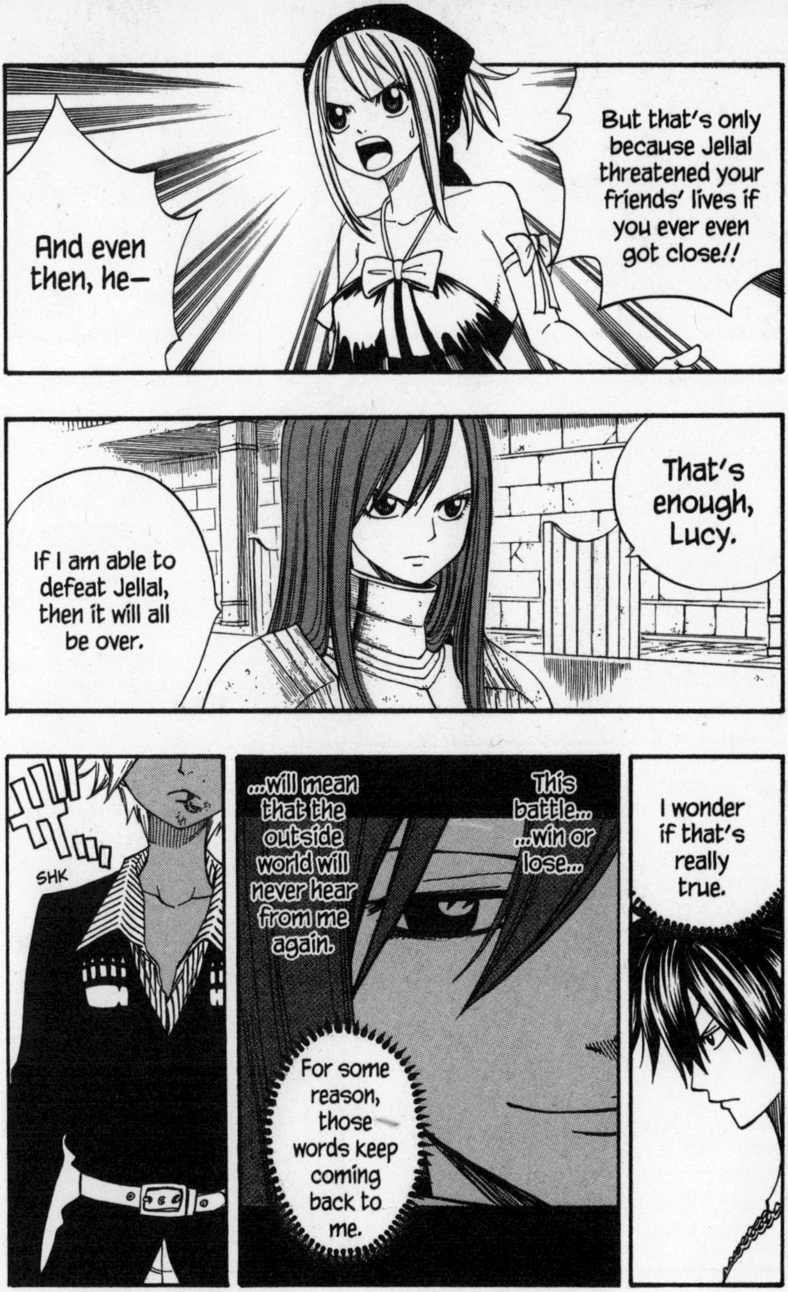
But that's only because Jellal threatened your friends' lives if you ever even got close!!
And even then, he—
That's enough, Lucy.
If I am able to defeat Jellal, then it will all be over.
I wonder if that's really true.
This battle... ...win or lose...
...will mean that the outside world will never hear from me again.
For some reason, those words keep coming back to me.
SHK

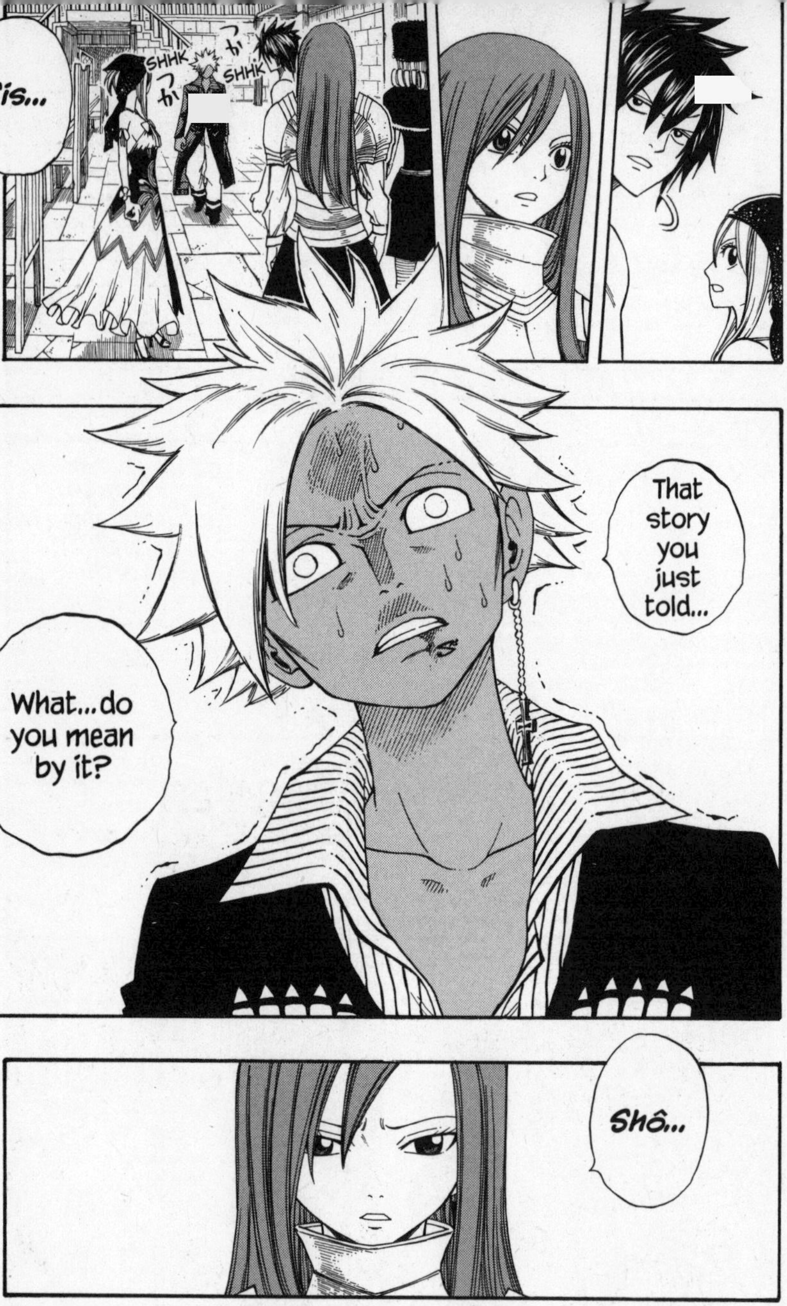
つか
SHHK
SHHK
つか
Sis...
That story you just told...
What...do you mean by it?
Shô...

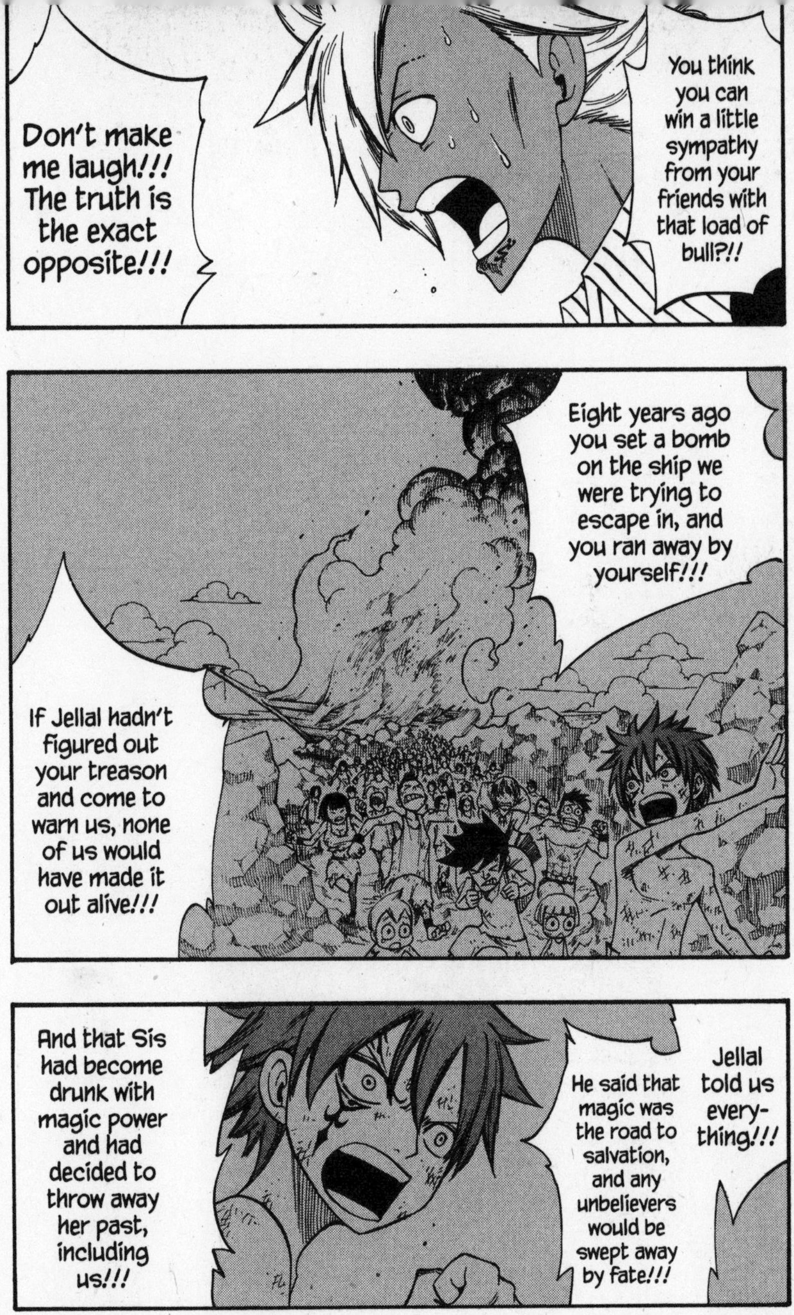
You think you can win a little sympathy from your friends with that load of bull?!!
Don't make me laugh!!! The truth is the exact opposite!!!
Eight years ago you set a bomb on the ship we were trying to escape in, and you ran away by yourself!!!
If Jellal hadn't figured out your treason and come to warn us, none of us would have made it out alive!!!
Jellal told us every-thing!!!
He said that magic was the road to salvation, and any unbelievers would be swept away by fate!!!
And that Sis had become drunk with magic power and had decided to throw away her past, including us!!!

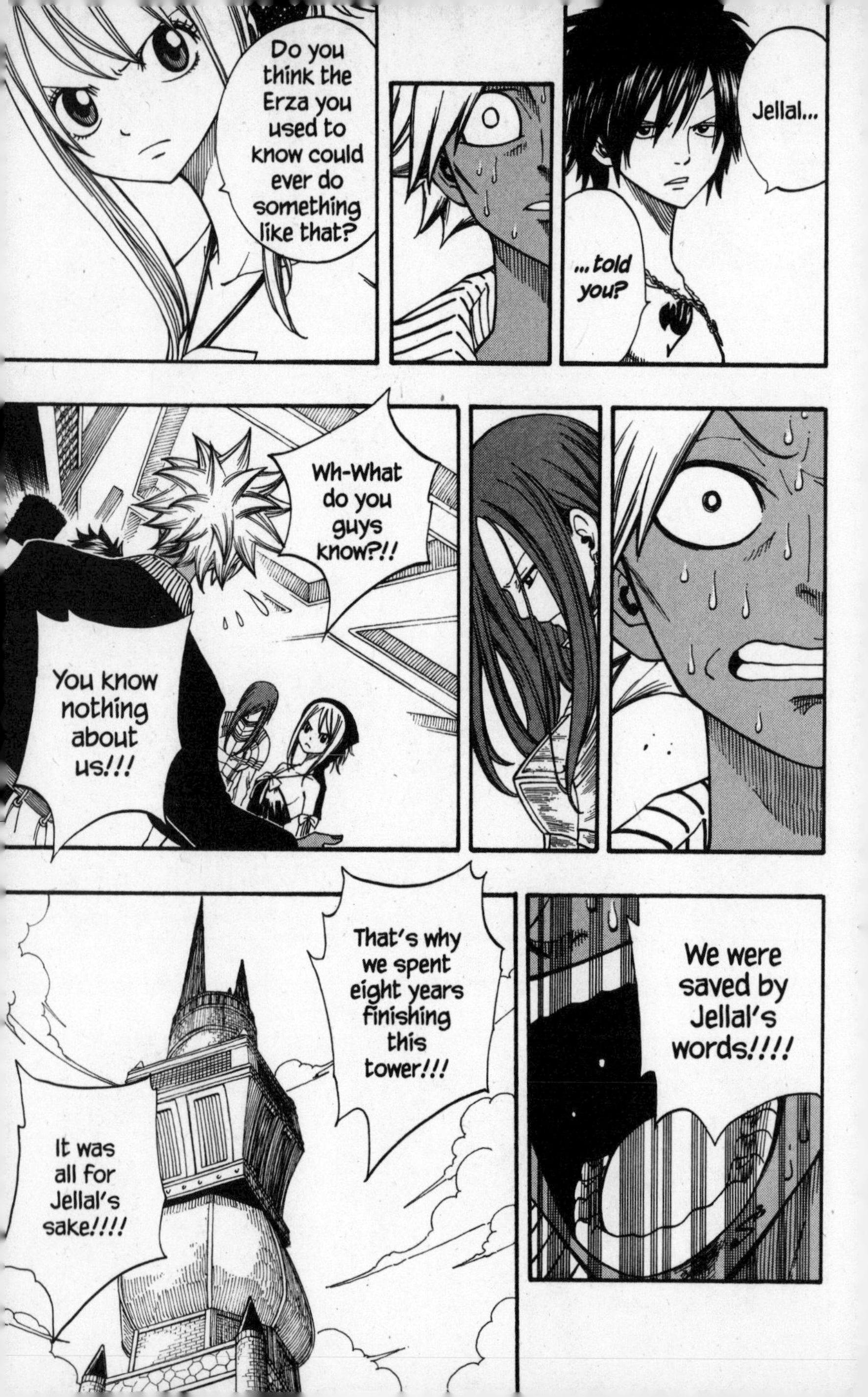
Jellal...
...told you?
Do you think the Erza you used to know could ever do something like that?
Wh-What do you guys know?!!
You know nothing about us!!!
We were saved by Jellal's words!!!!
That's why we spent eight years finishing this tower!!!
It was all for Jellal's sake!!!!

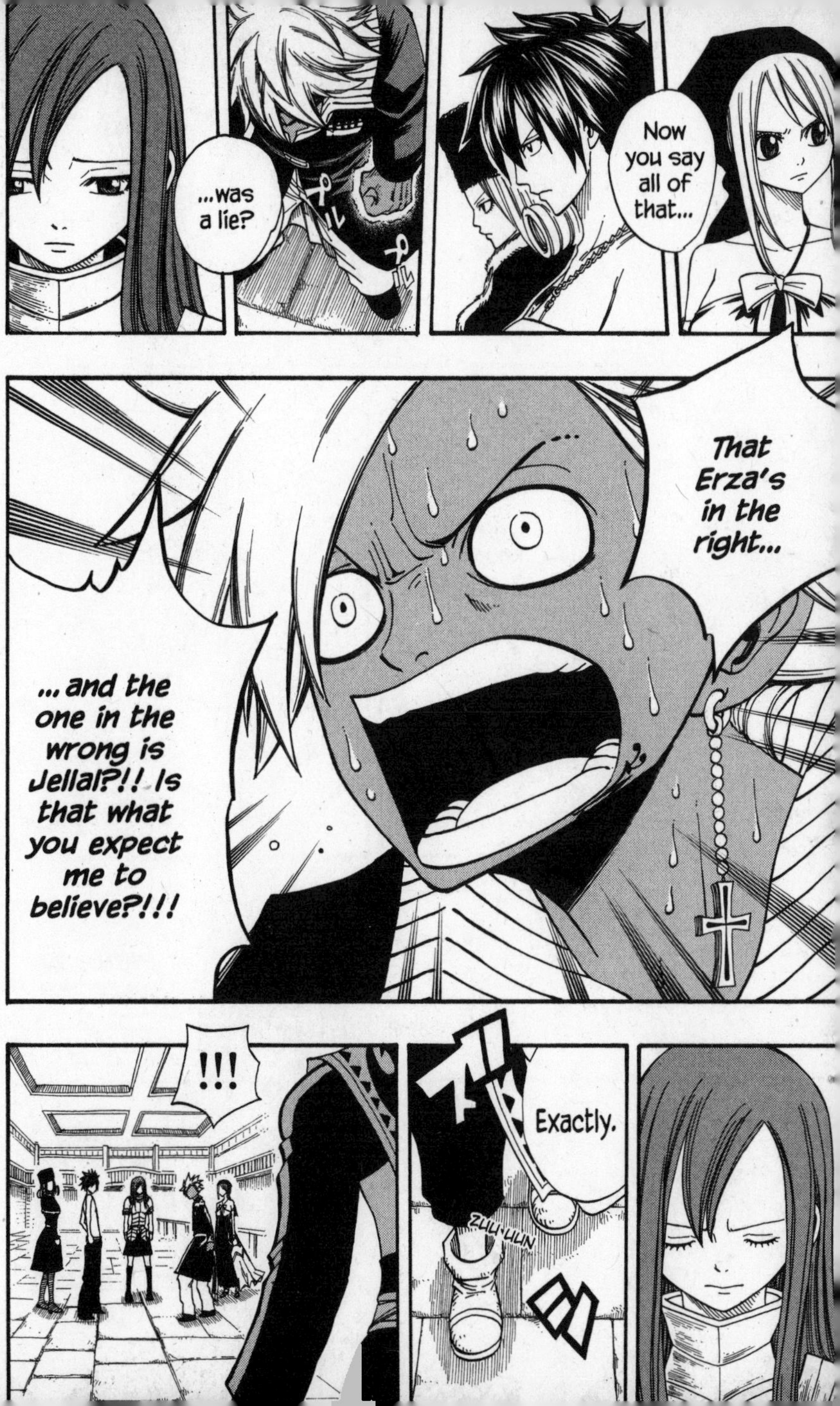
Now you say all of that...
...was a lie?
That Erza's in the right...
...and the one in the wrong is Jellal?!! Is that what you expect me to believe?!!!
Exactly.
ZUU-UUN
!!!

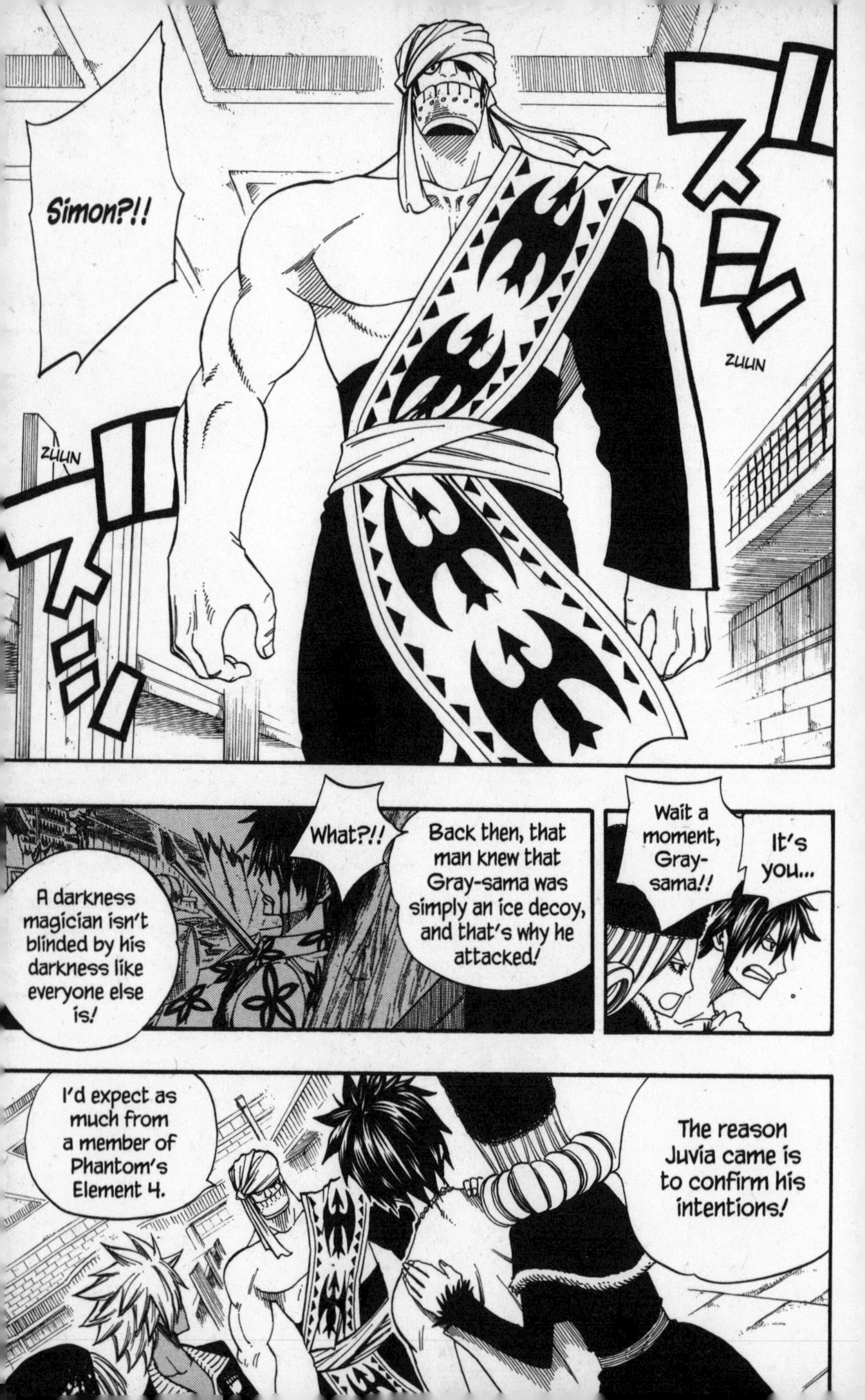

Simon?!!
ZUUN
ZUUN
It's you...
Wait a moment, Gray-sama!!
Back then, that man knew that Gray-sama was simply an ice decoy, and that's why he attacked!
What?!!
A darkness magician isn't blinded by his darkness like everyone else is!
The reason Juvia came is to confirm his intentions!
I'd expect as much from a member of Phantom's Element 4.

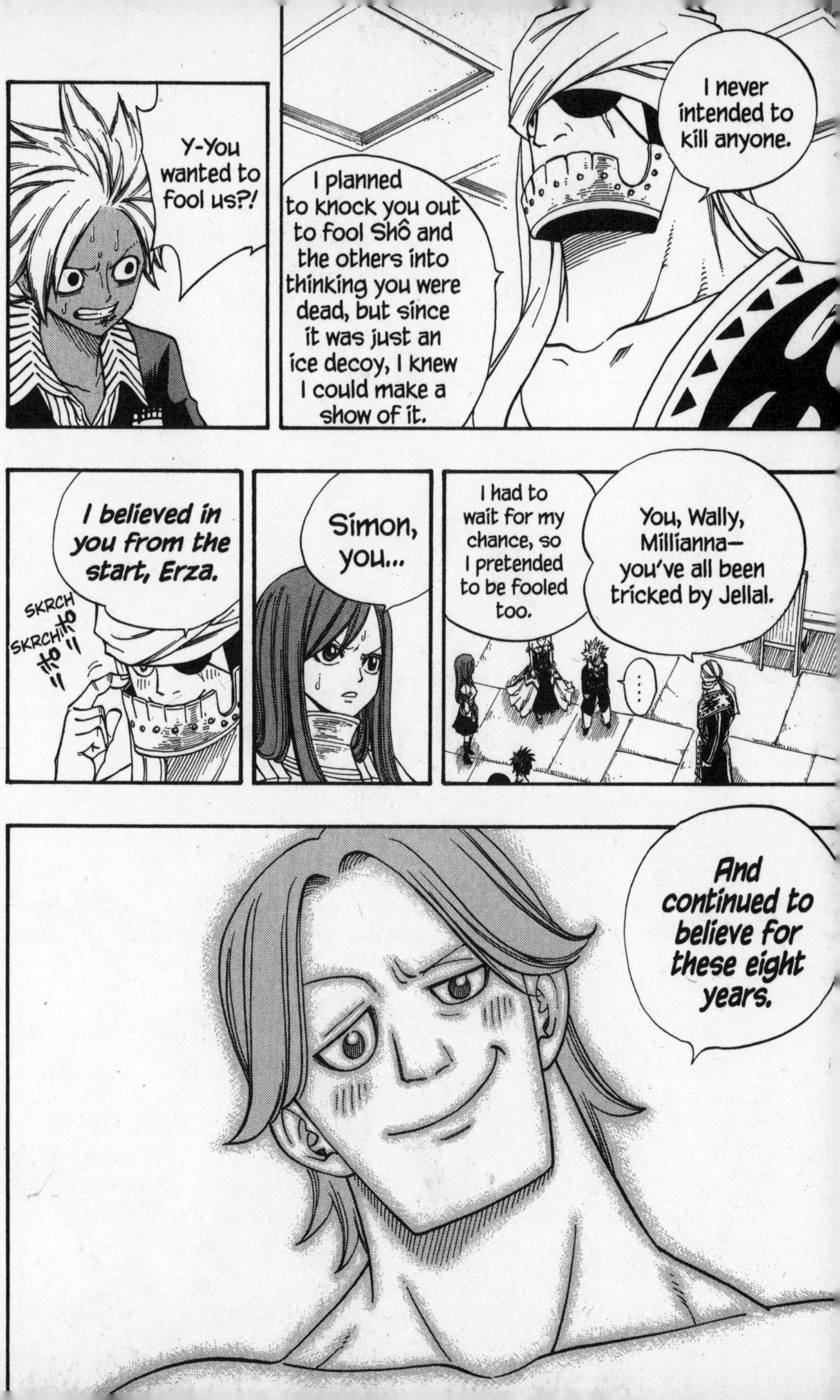
I never intended to kill anyone.
I planned to knock you out to fool Shô and the others into thinking you were dead, but since it was just an ice decoy, I knew I could make a show of it.
Y-You wanted to fool us?!
You, Wally, Millianna— you've all been tricked by Jellal.
I had to wait for my chance, so I pretended to be fooled too.
...
Simon, you...
I believed in you from the start, Erza.
SKRCH
SKRCH
And continued to believe for these eight years.

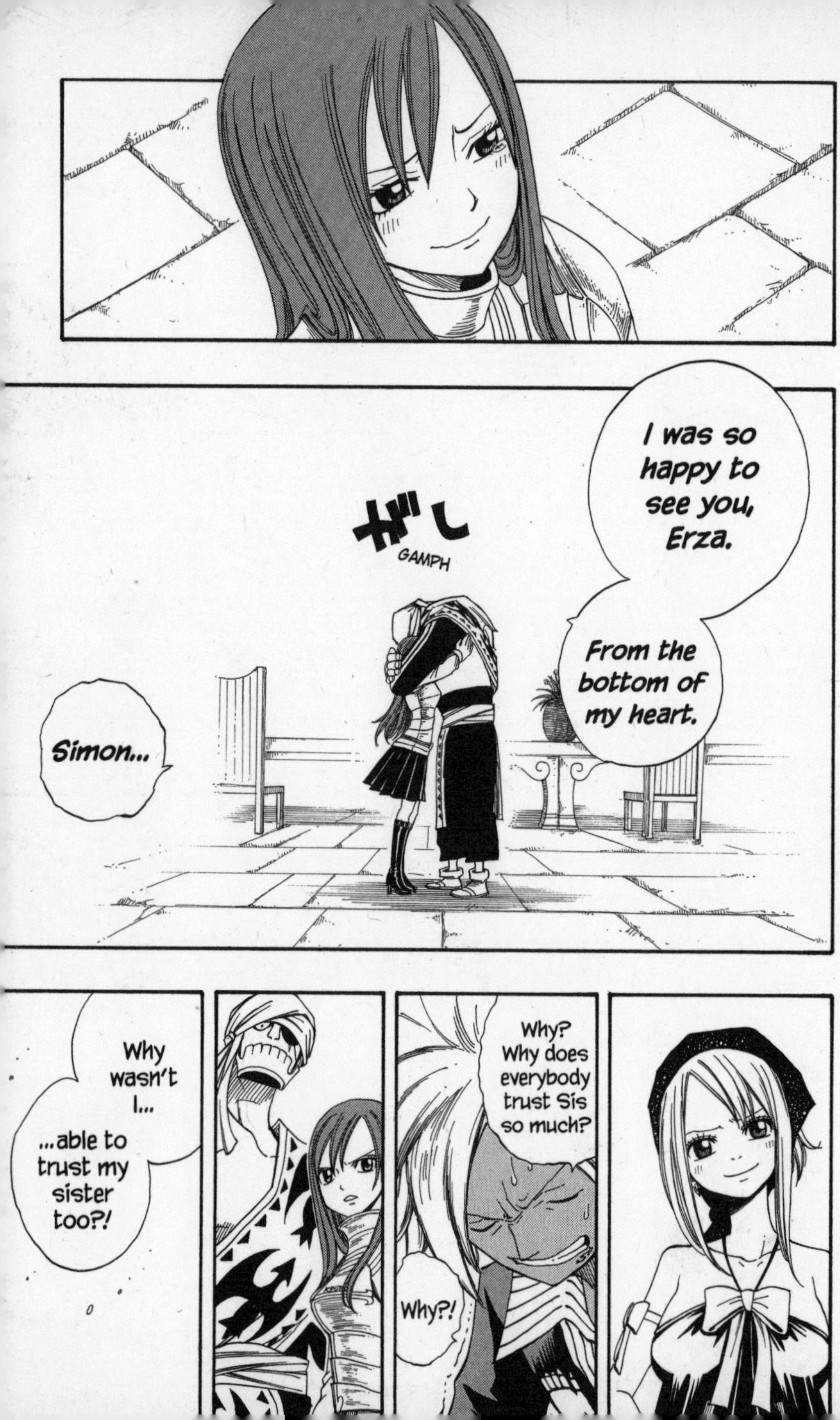
I was so happy to see you, Erza.
From the bottom of my heart.
がし
GAMPH
Simon...
Why? Why does everybody trust Sis so much?
Why?!
Why wasn't I...
...able to trust my sister too?!

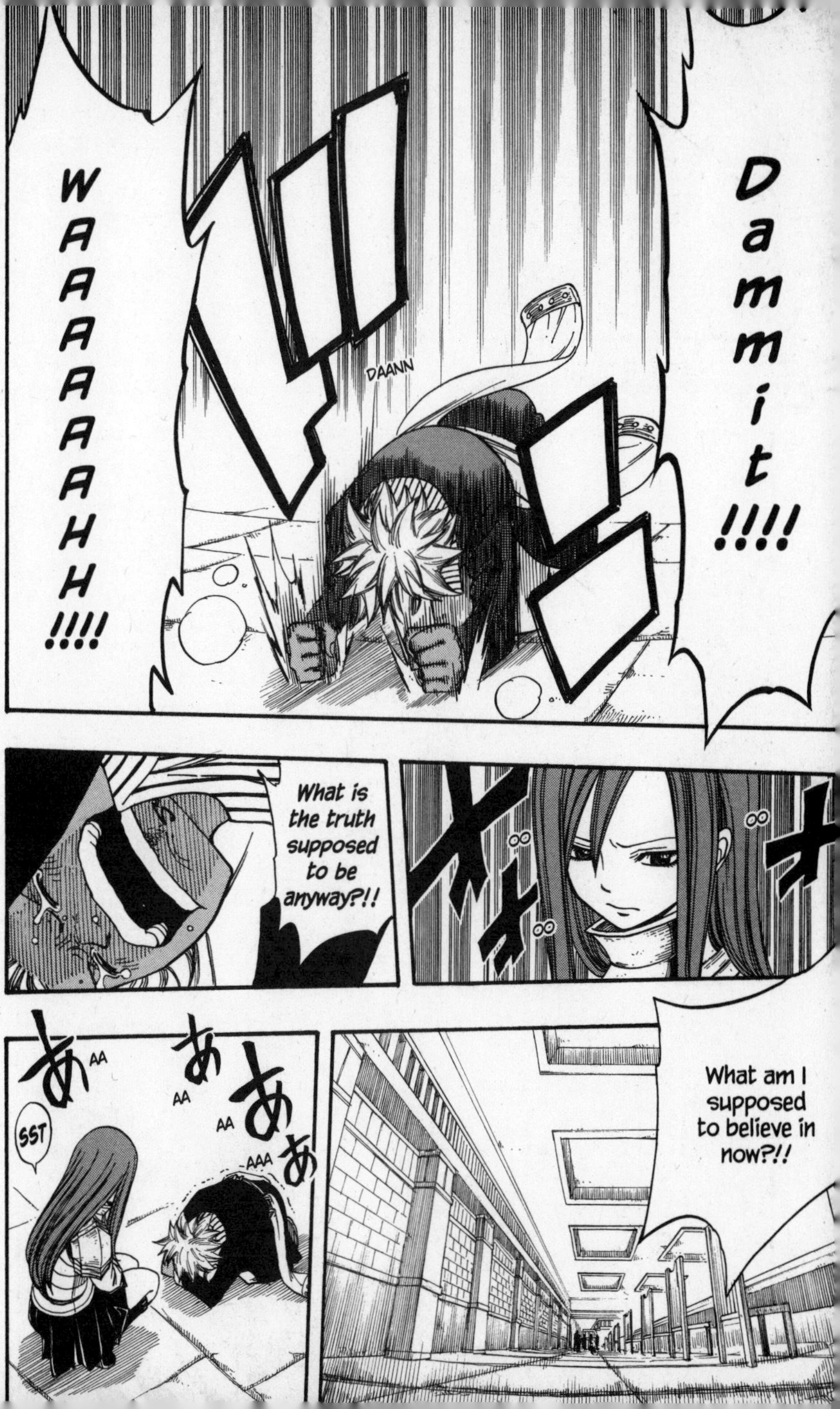
Dammit!!!!
WAAAAAAAHH!!!!
DAANN
What is the truth supposed to be anyway?!!
What am I supposed to believe in now?!!
AA
AA
AA
AAA
SST

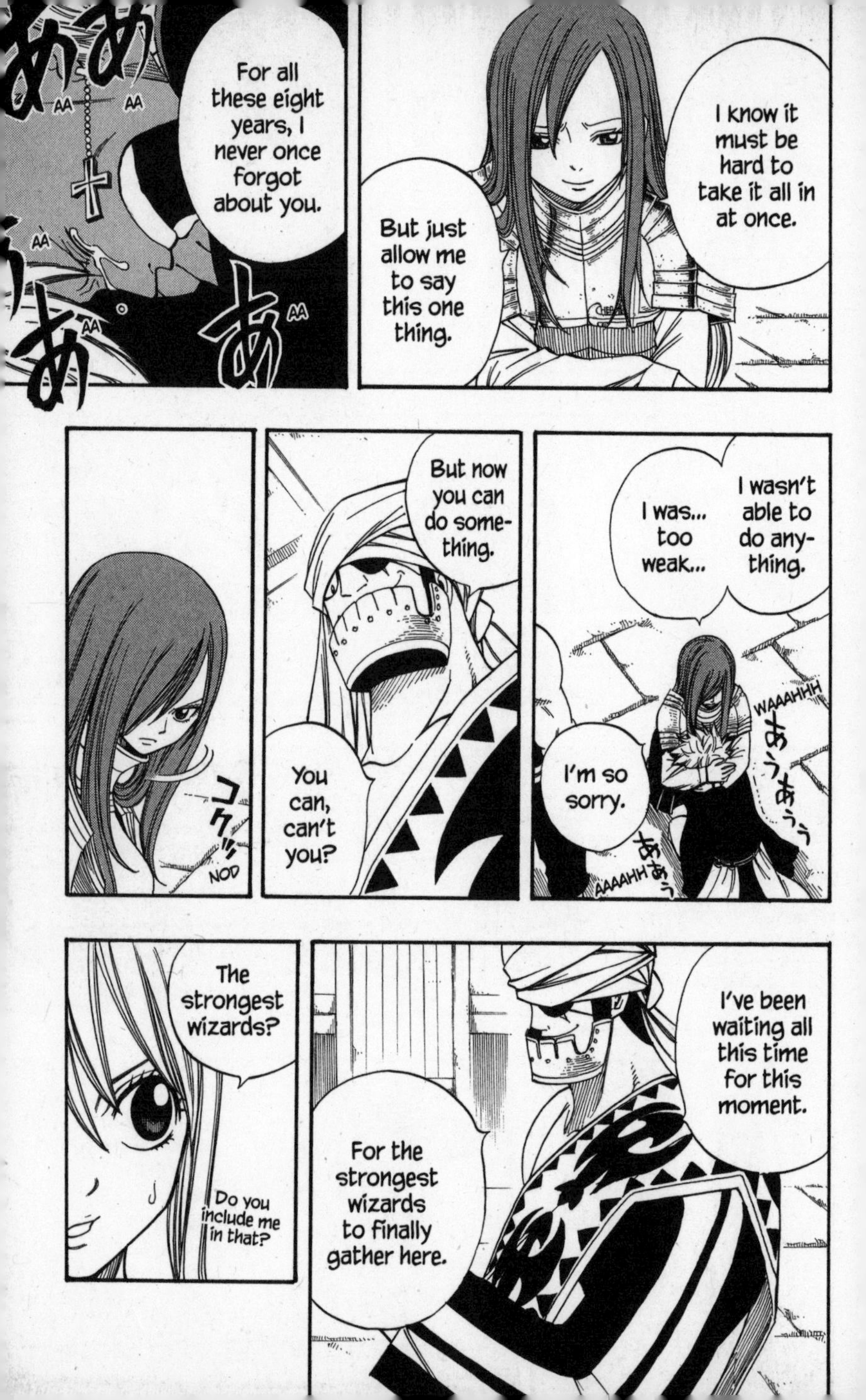

I know it must be hard to take it all in at once.
But just allow me to say this one thing.
For all these eight years, I never once forgot about you.
AA AA AA AA AA
I wasn't able to do anything.
I was... too weak...
I'm so sorry.
WAAAHHH
AAAAHH
But now you can do something.
You can, can't you?
NOD
I've been waiting all this time for this moment.
For the strongest wizards to finally gather here.
The strongest wizards?
Do you include me in that?

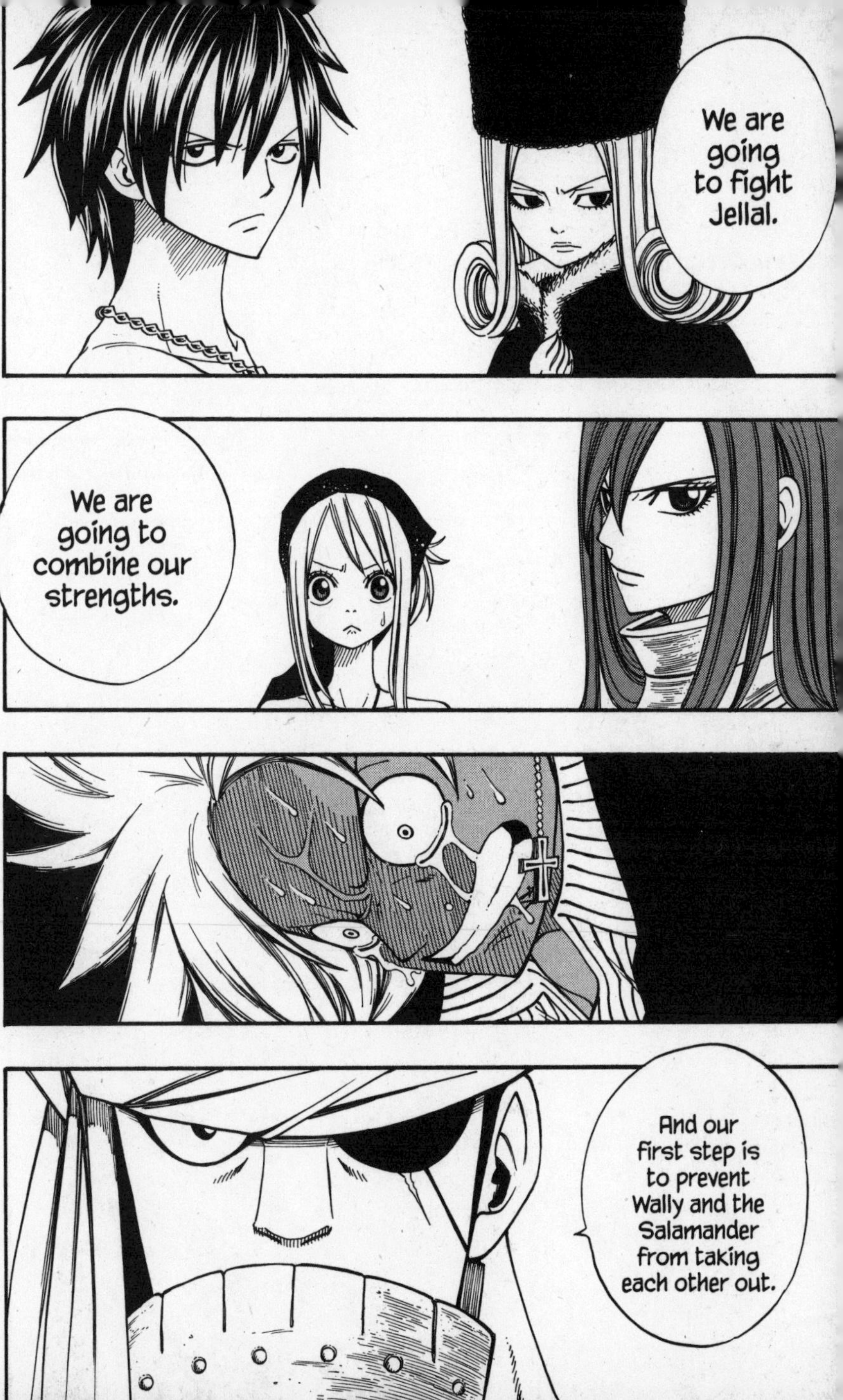
We are going to fight Jellal.
We are going to combine our strengths.
And our first step is to prevent Wally and the Salamander from taking each other out.

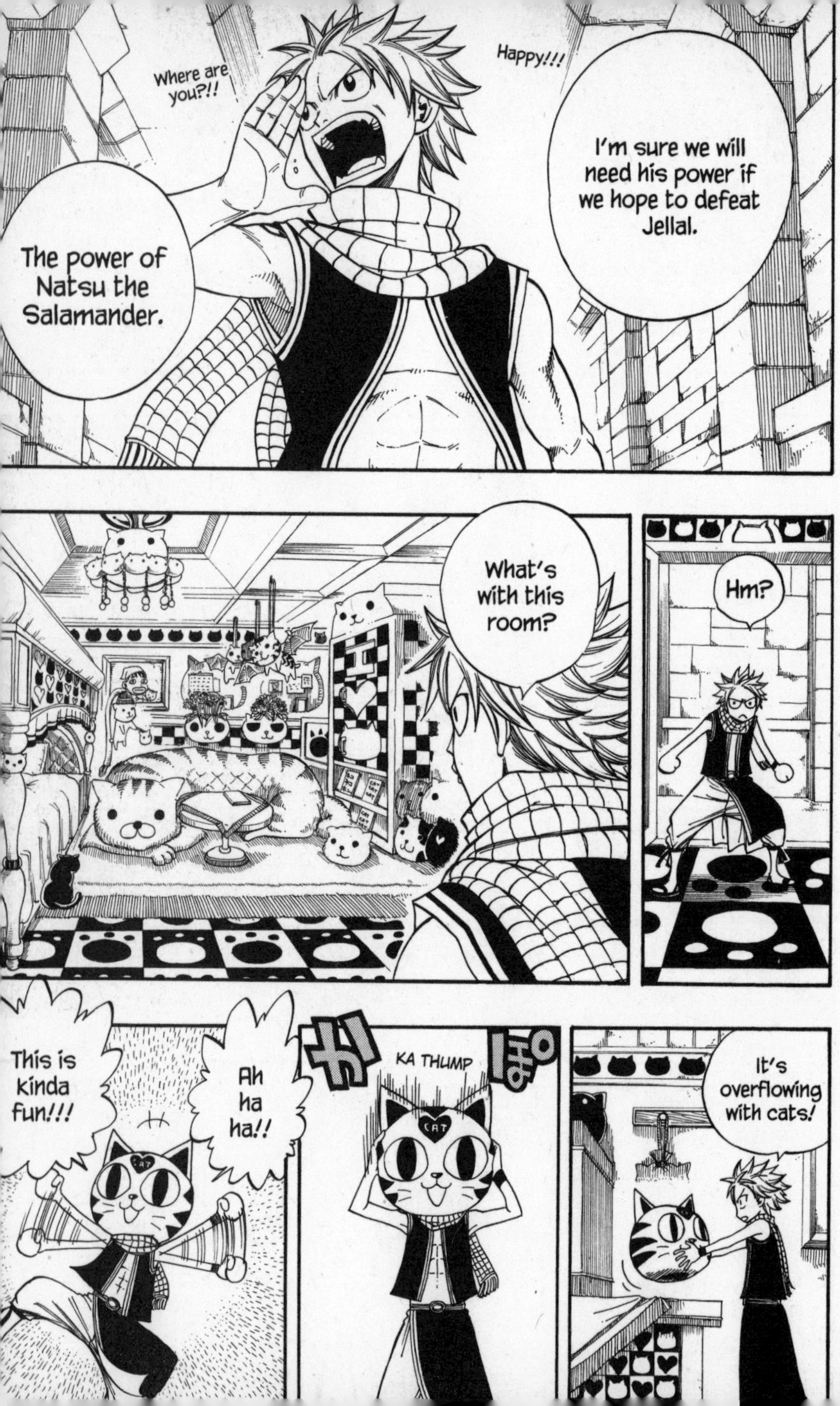

Happy!!!
Where are you?!!
I'm sure we will need his power if we hope to defeat Jellal.
The power of Natsu the Salamander.
Hm?
What's with this room?
It's overflowing with cats!
KA THUMP
Ah ha ha!!
This is kinda fun!!!

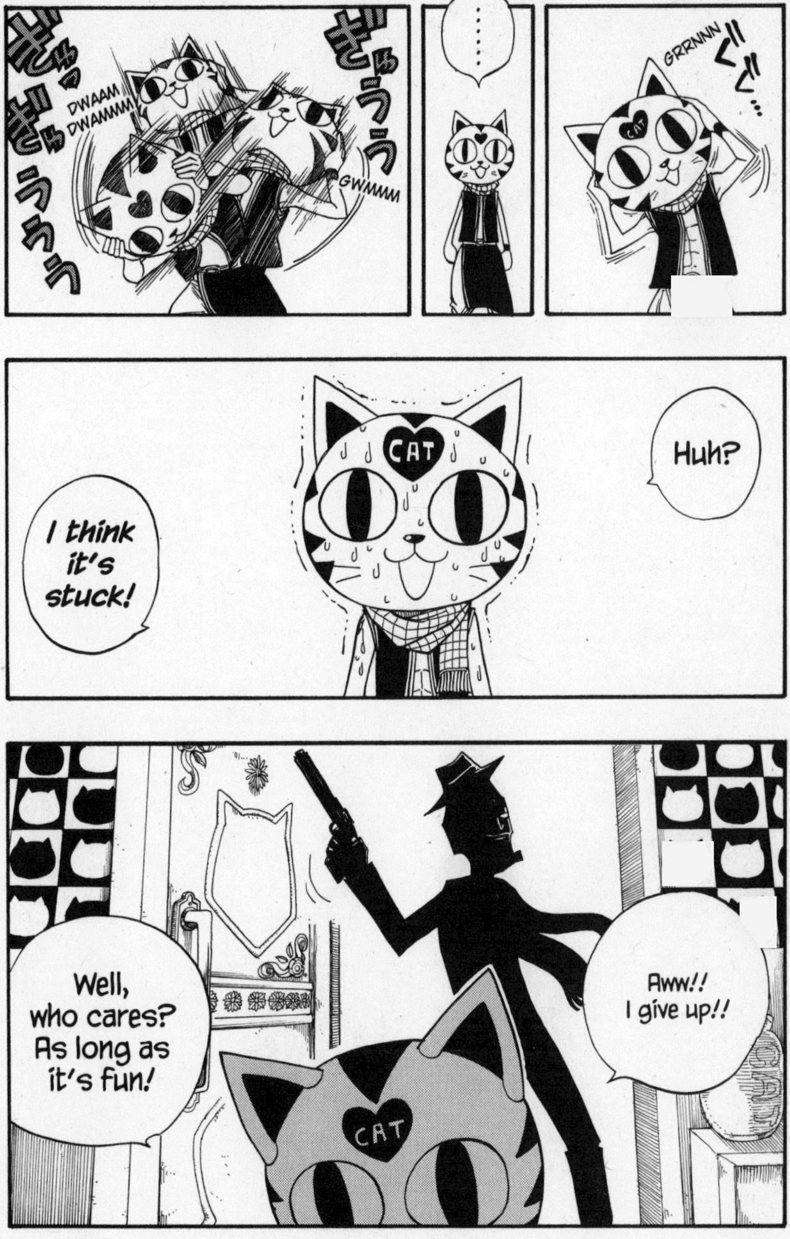
GRRNNN
......
DWAAM DWAMMM
GWMMM
Huh?
I think it's stuck!
Aww!! I give up!!
Well, who cares? As long as it's fun!

FAIRY TAIL

Chapter 84: Natsu-Cat Fight!!

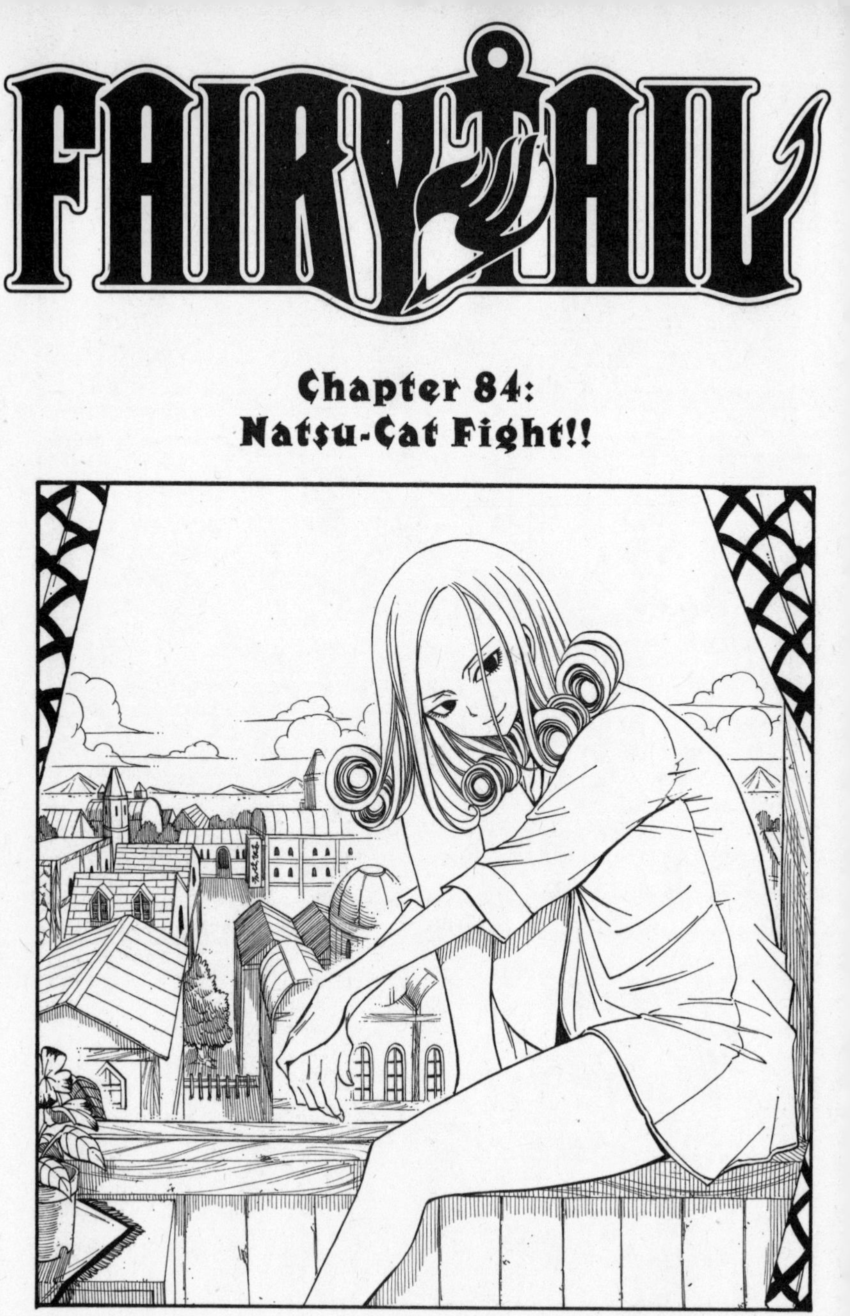

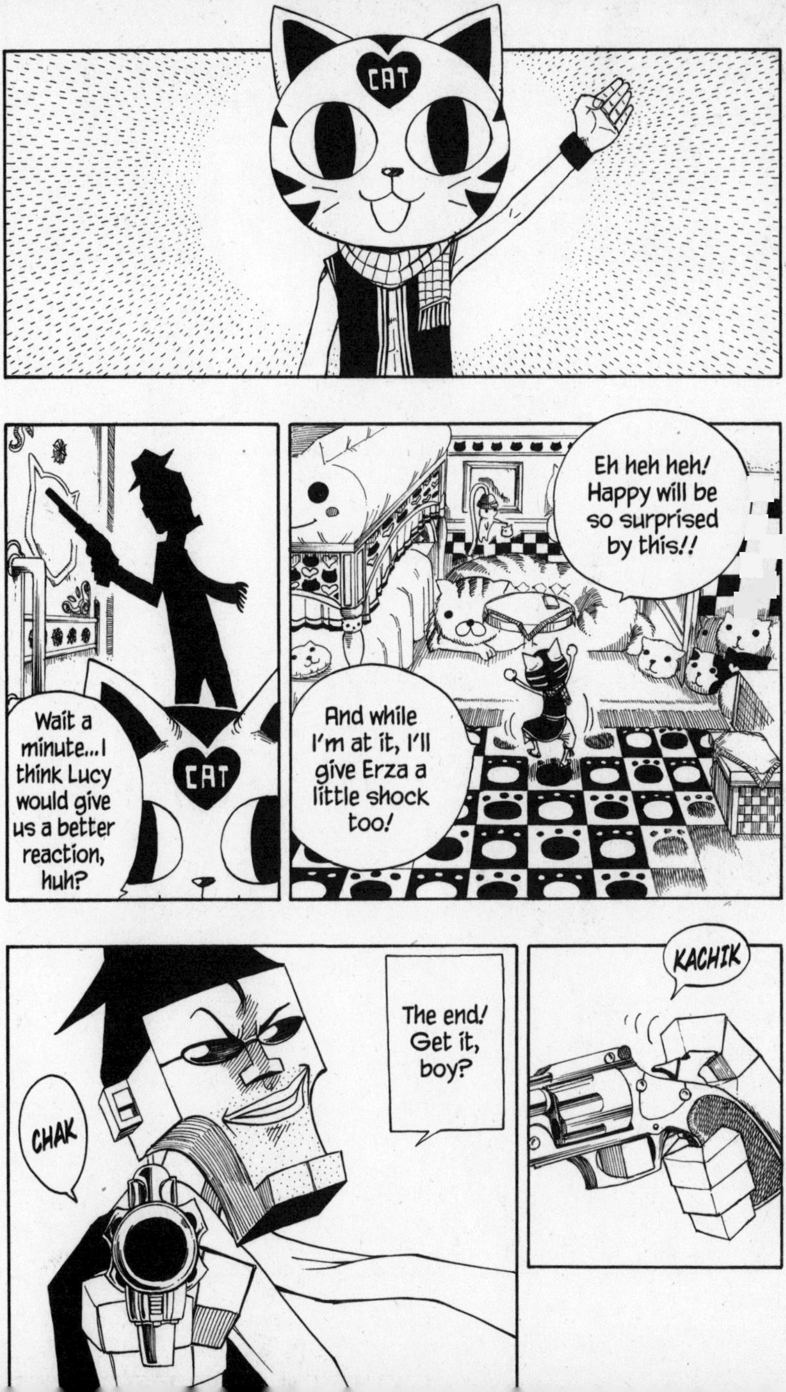
Eh heh heh! Happy will be so surprised by this!!
And while I'm at it, I'll give Erza a little shock too!
Wait a minute...I think Lucy would give us a better reaction, huh?
KACHIK
The end! Get it, boy?
CHAK

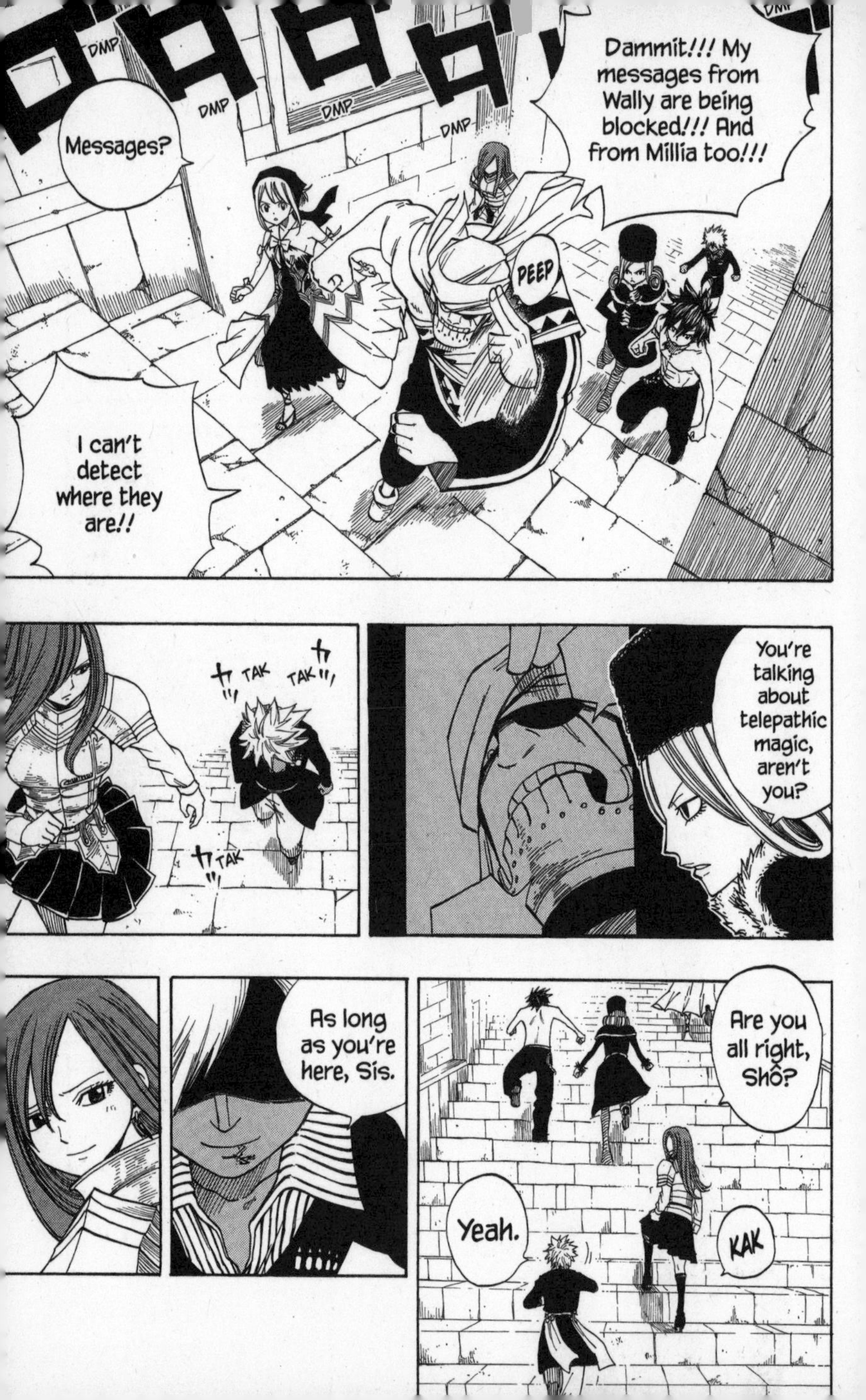
Dammit!!! My messages from Wally are being blocked!!! And from Millia too!!!
DMP
DMP
DMP
DMP
PEEP
Messages?
I can't detect where they are!!
You're talking about telepathic magic, aren't you?
TAK
TAK
TAK
Are you all right, Shô?
KAK
Yeah.
As long as you're here, Sis.

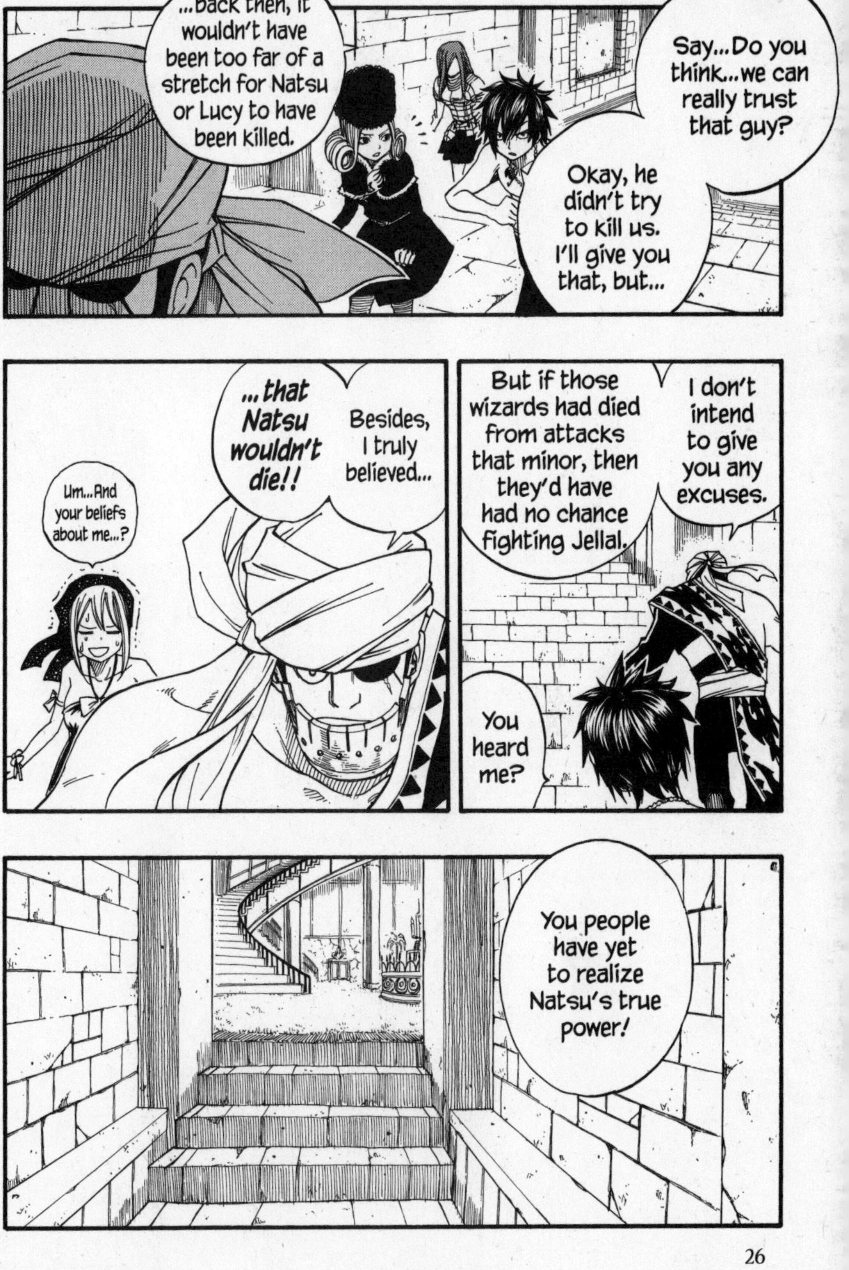
Say...Do you think...we can really trust that guy?
Okay, he didn't try to kill us. I'll give you that, but...
...back then, it wouldn't have been too far of a stretch for Natsu or Lucy to have been killed.
I don't intend to give you any excuses.
But if those wizards had died from attacks that minor, then they'd have had no chance fighting Jellal.
You heard me?
Besides, I truly believed...
...that Natsu wouldn't die!!
Um...And your beliefs about me...?
You people have yet to realize Natsu's true power!

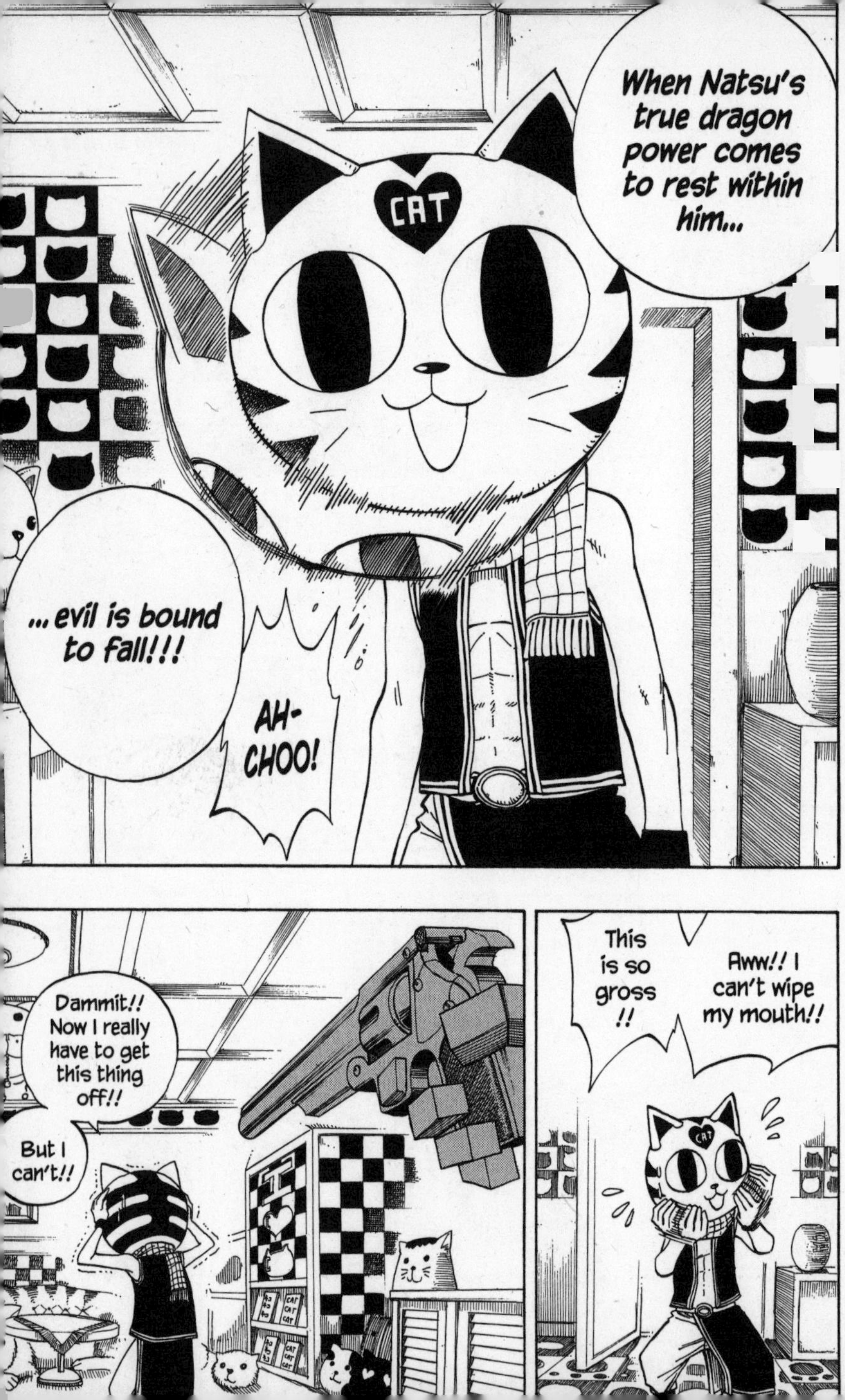
When Natsu's true dragon power comes to rest within him...
...evil is bound to fall!!!
AH-CHOO!
Aww!! I can't wipe my mouth!!
This is so gross!!
Dammit!! Now I really have to get this thing off!!
But I can't!!

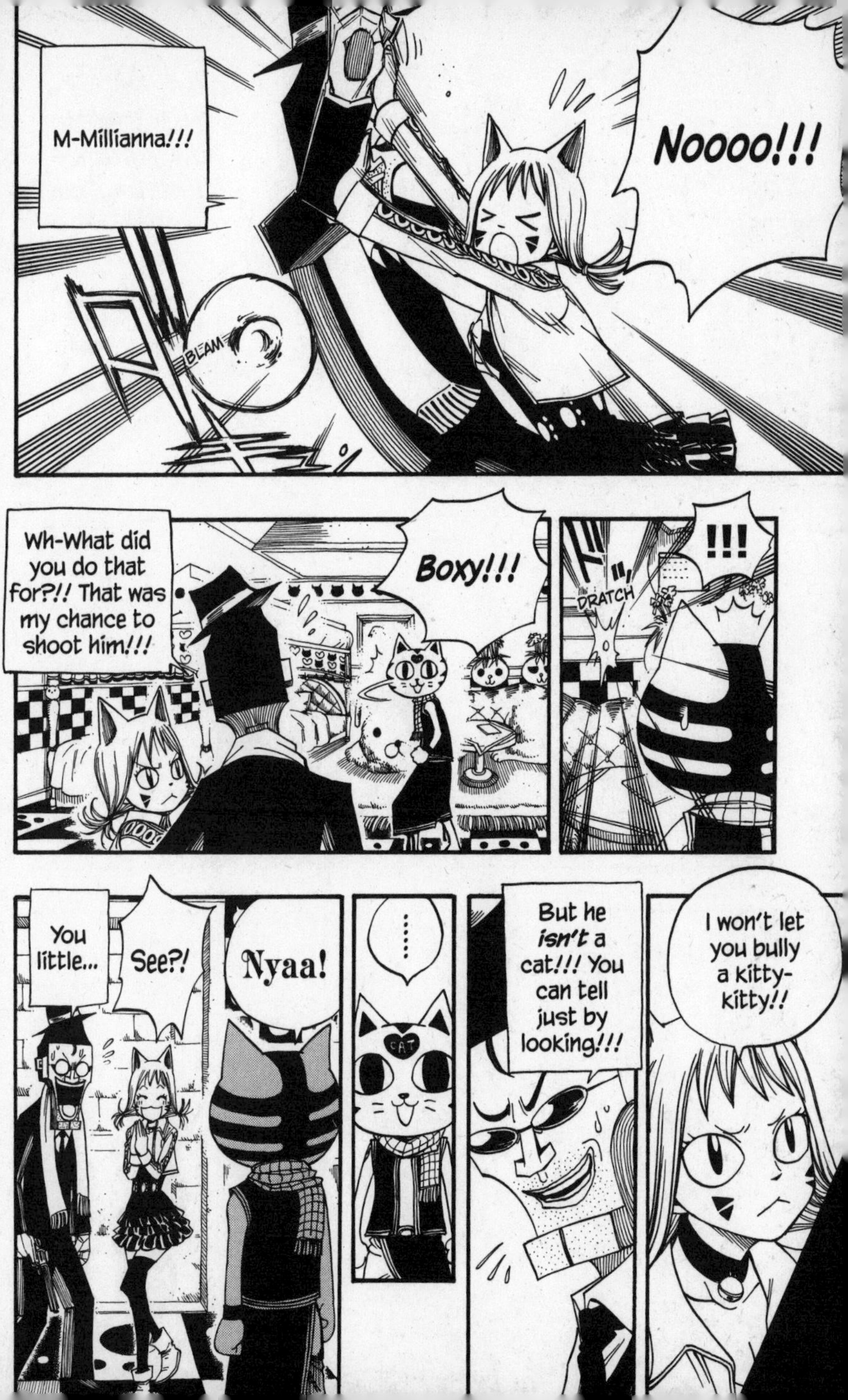
Noooo!!!
M-Millianna!!!
BLAM
!!!
DRATCH
Boxy!!!
Wh-What did you do that for?!! That was my chance to shoot him!!!
I won't let you bully a kitty-kitty!!
But he isn't a cat!!! You can tell just by looking!!!
......
Nyaa!
See?!
You little...

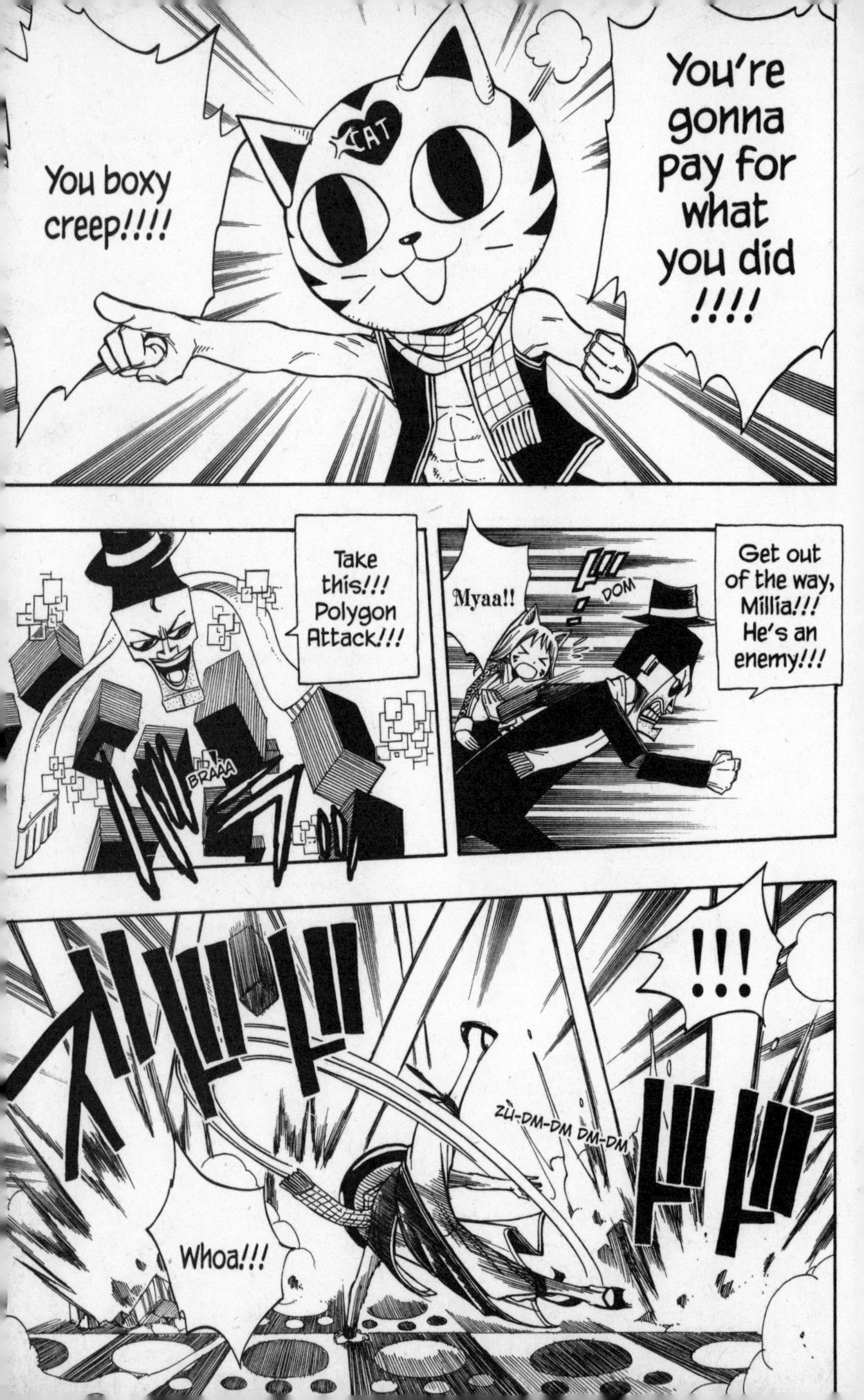
You're gonna pay for what you did!!!!
You boxy creep!!!!
Get out of the way, Millia!!! He's an enemy!!!
DOM
Myaa!!
Take this!!! Polygon Attack!!!
BRAAA
!!!
ZU-DM-DM DM-DM
Whoa!!!

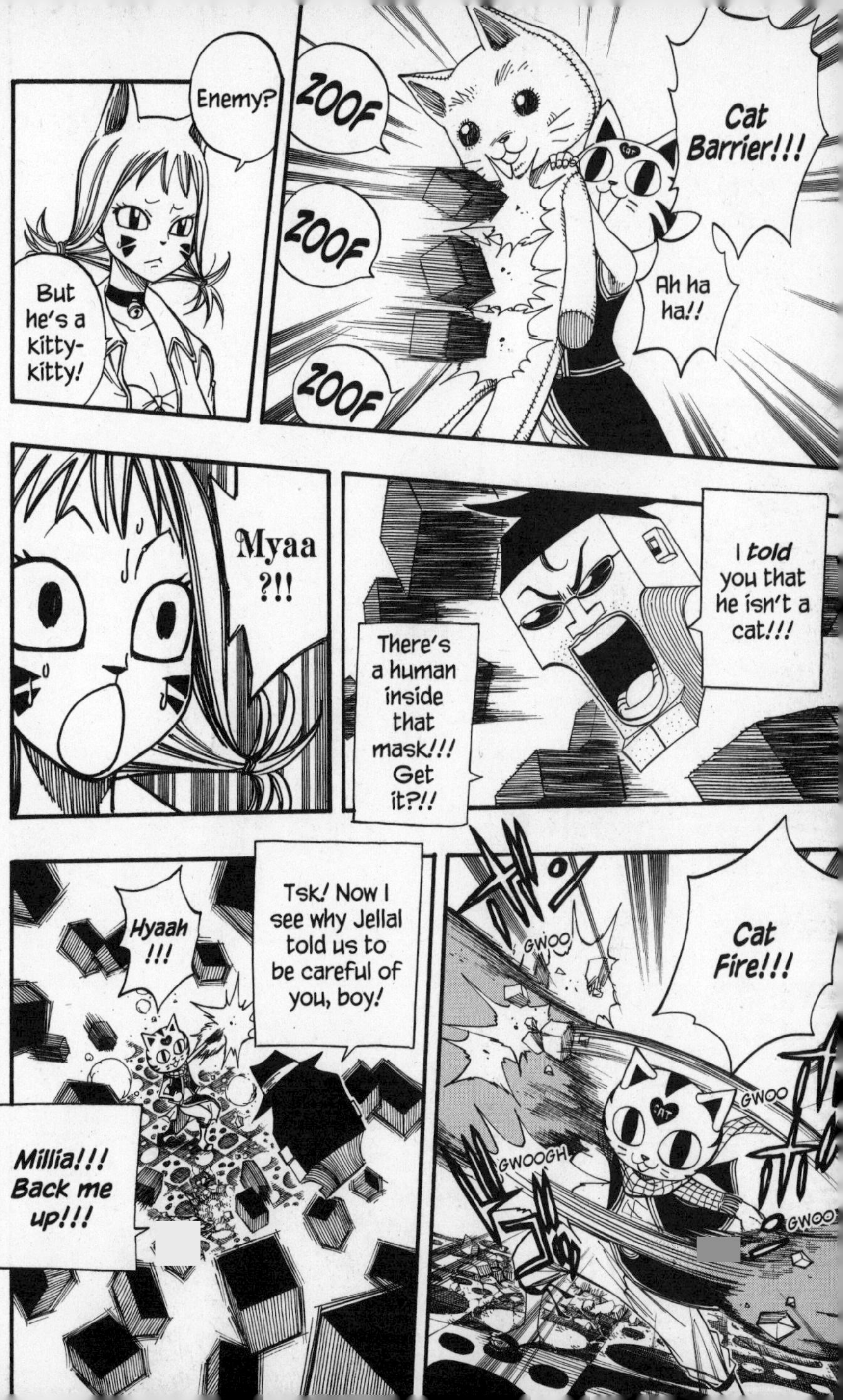
Cat Barrier!!!
Ah ha ha!!
ZOOF
ZOOF
ZOOF
Enemy?
But he's a kitty-kitty!
I *told* you that he isn't a cat!!!
There's a human inside that mask!!! Get it?!!
Myaa ?!!
Cat Fire!!!
GWOO
GWOO
GWOOGH
GWOO
Tsk! Now I see why Jellal told us to be careful of you, boy!
Hyaah!!!
Millia!!! Back me up!!!

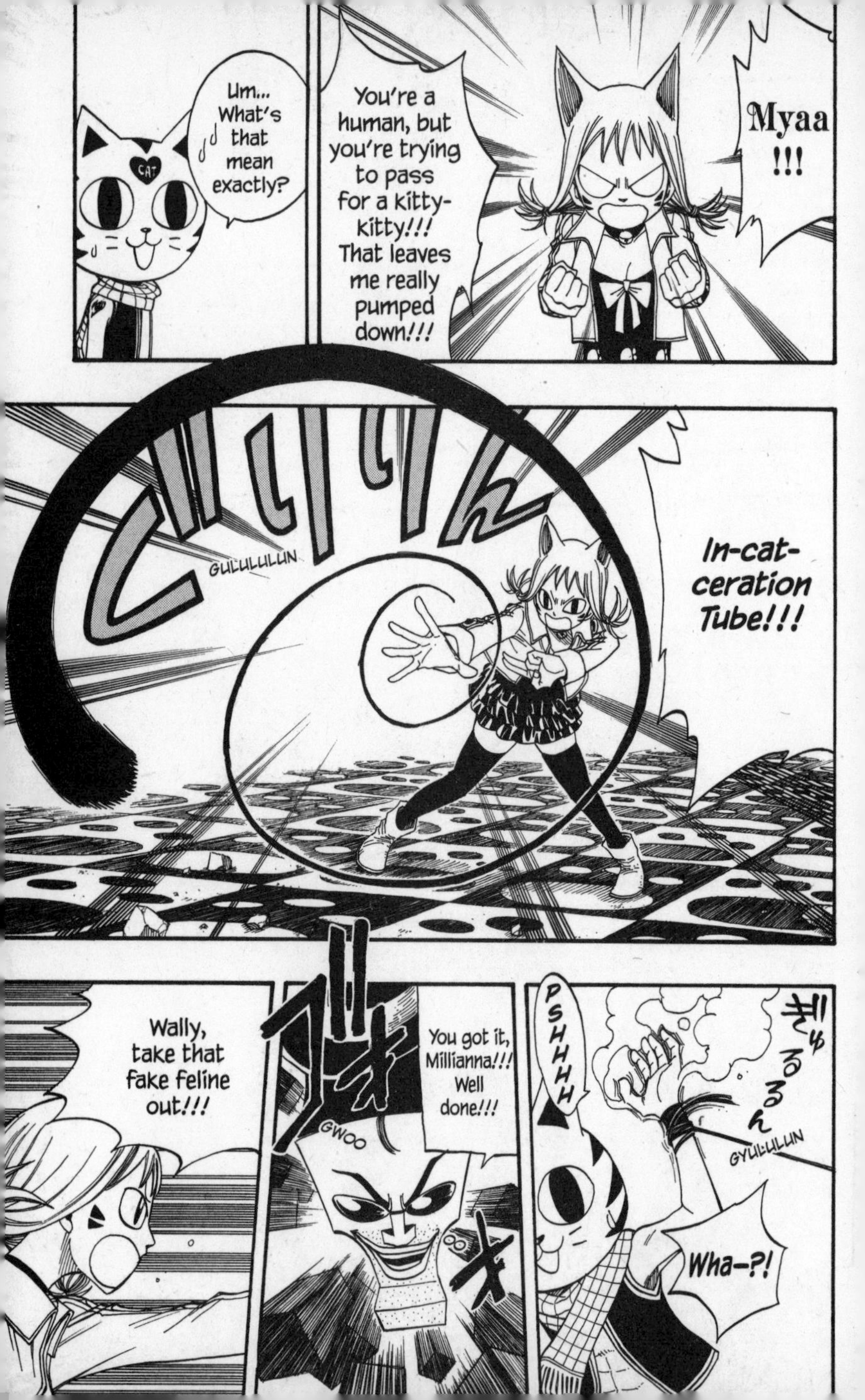
Myaa !!!
You're a human, but you're trying to pass for a kitty-kitty!!! That leaves me really pumped down!!!
Um... What's that mean exactly?
In-cat-ceration Tube!!!
GULULULUN
PSHHHH
ぎゅるるん
GYULULUN
Wha-?!
You got it, Millianna!!! Well done!!!
GWOO
Wally, take that fake feline out!!!

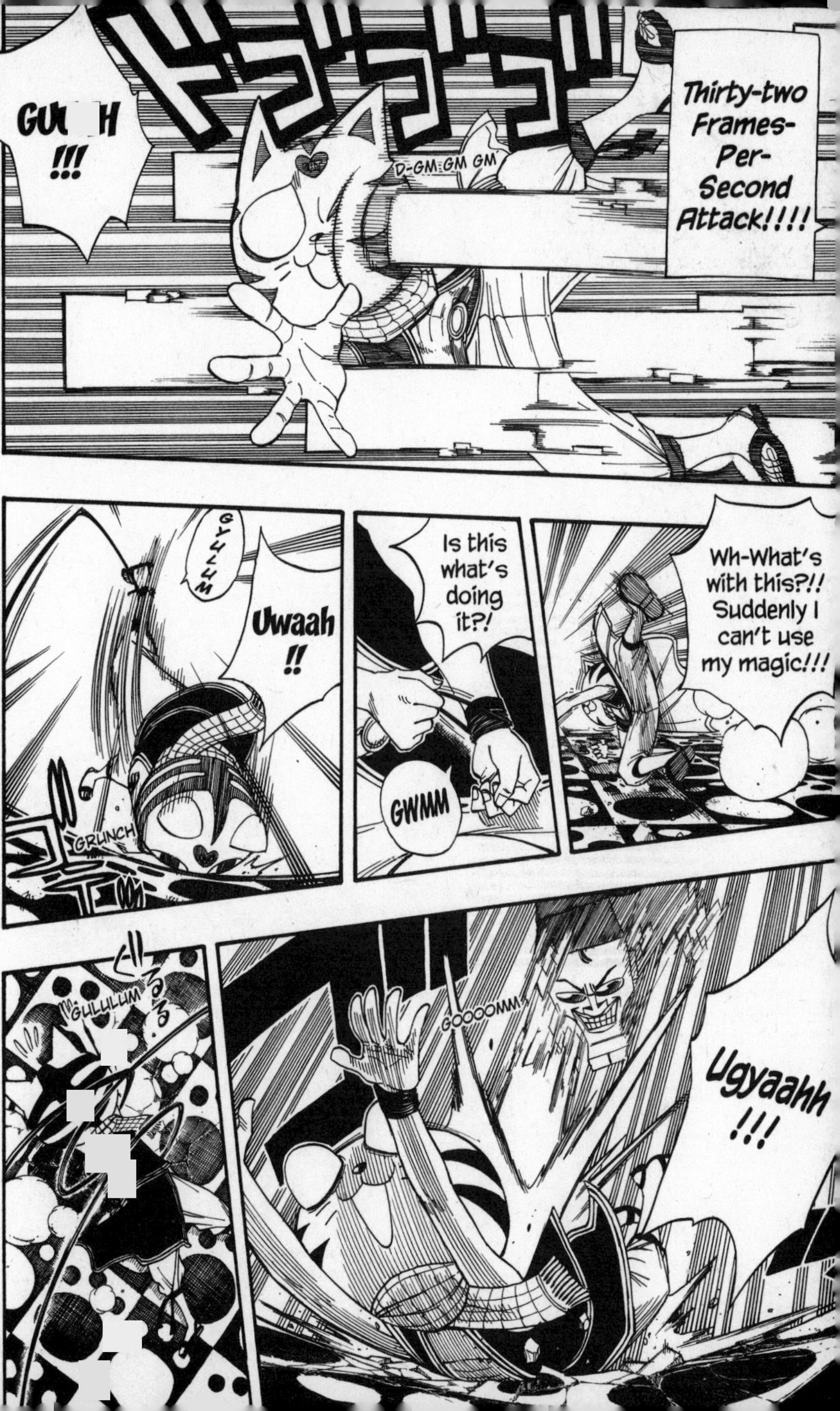

Thirty-two Frames-Per-Second Attack!!!!
D-GM GM GM
ドゴゴゴ
GU H !!!
Wh-What's with this?!! Suddenly I can't use my magic!!!
Is this what's doing it?!
GWMM
GYULUM
Uwaah !!
GRUNCH
Ugyaahh !!!
GOOOOMM
GULULUM

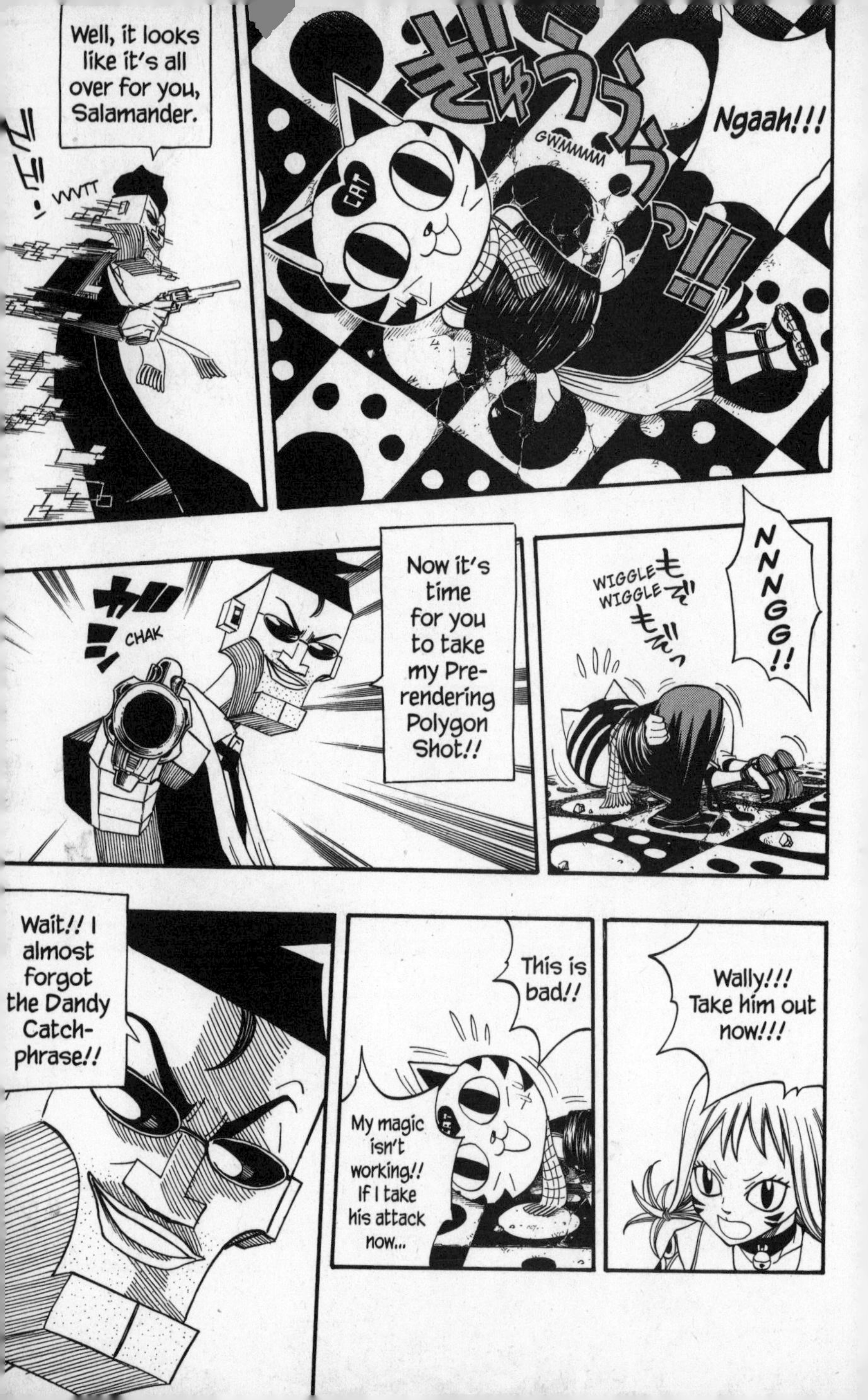
Ngaah!!!
GWMMMMM
Well, it looks like it's all over for you, Salamander.
VVVTT
NNNGG!!
WIGGLE WIGGLE
Now it's time for you to take my Pre-rendering Polygon Shot!!
CHAK
Wally!!! Take him out now!!!
This is bad!!
My magic isn't working!! If I take his attack now...
Wait!! I almost forgot the Dandy Catch-phrase!!

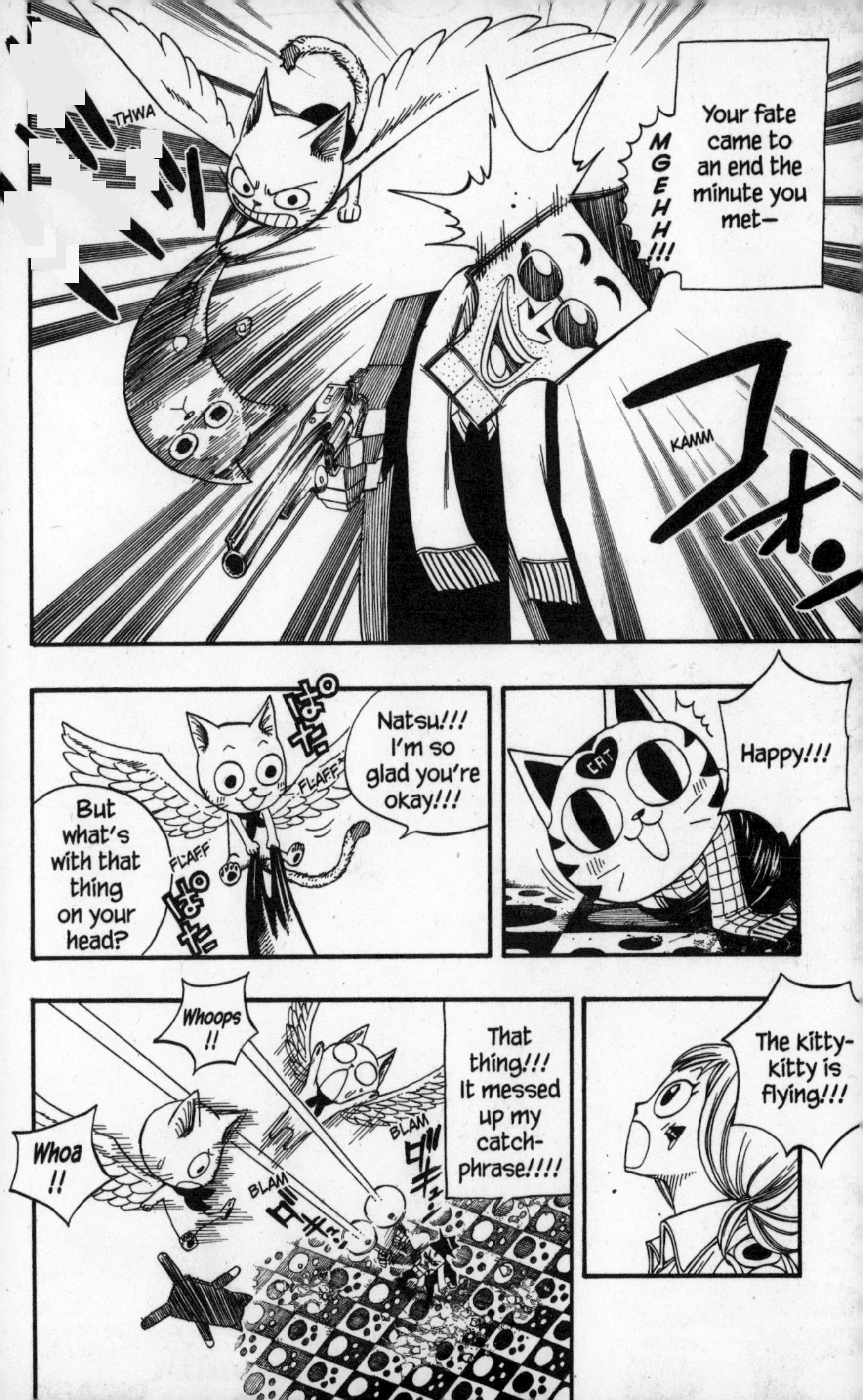
Your fate came to an end the minute you met–
MGEHH!!!
THWA
KAMM
Happy!!!
Natsu!!! I'm so glad you're okay!!!
FLAFF
But what's with that thing on your head?
FLAFF
The kitty-kitty is flying!!!
That thing!!! It messed up my catch-phrase!!!!
Whoops!!
BLAM
BLAM
Whoa!!

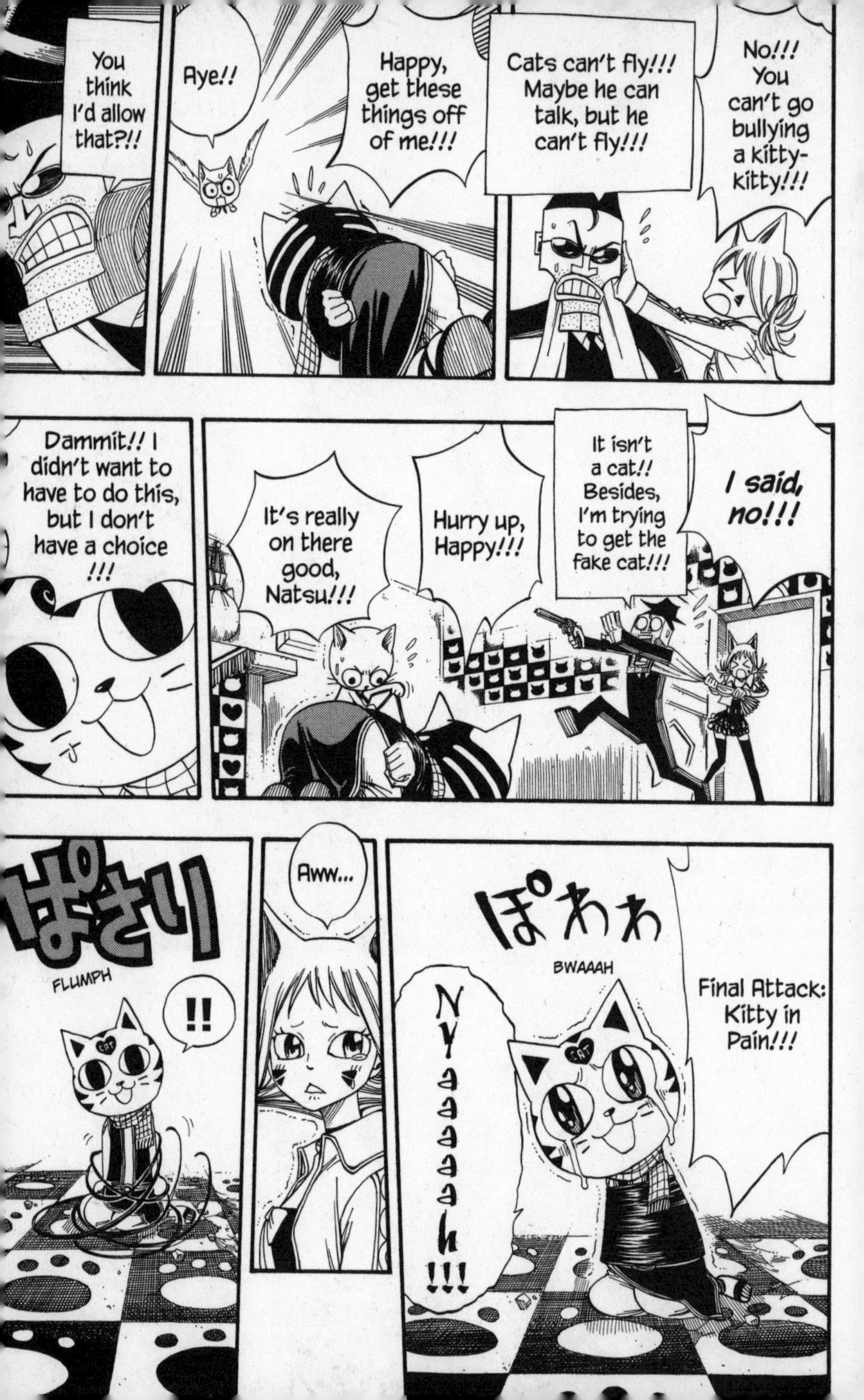
No!!! You can't go bullying a kitty-kitty!!!
Cats can't fly!!! Maybe he can talk, but he can't fly!!!
Happy, get these things off of me!!!
Aye!!
You think I'd allow that?!!
I said, no!!!
It isn't a cat!! Besides, I'm trying to get the fake cat!!!
Hurry up, Happy!!!
It's really on there good, Natsu!!!
Dammit!! I didn't want to have to do this, but I don't have a choice!!!
Final Attack: Kitty in Pain!!!
ぽわわ
BWAAAH
Nyaaaaaah!!!
Aww...
ぱさり
FLUMPH
!!

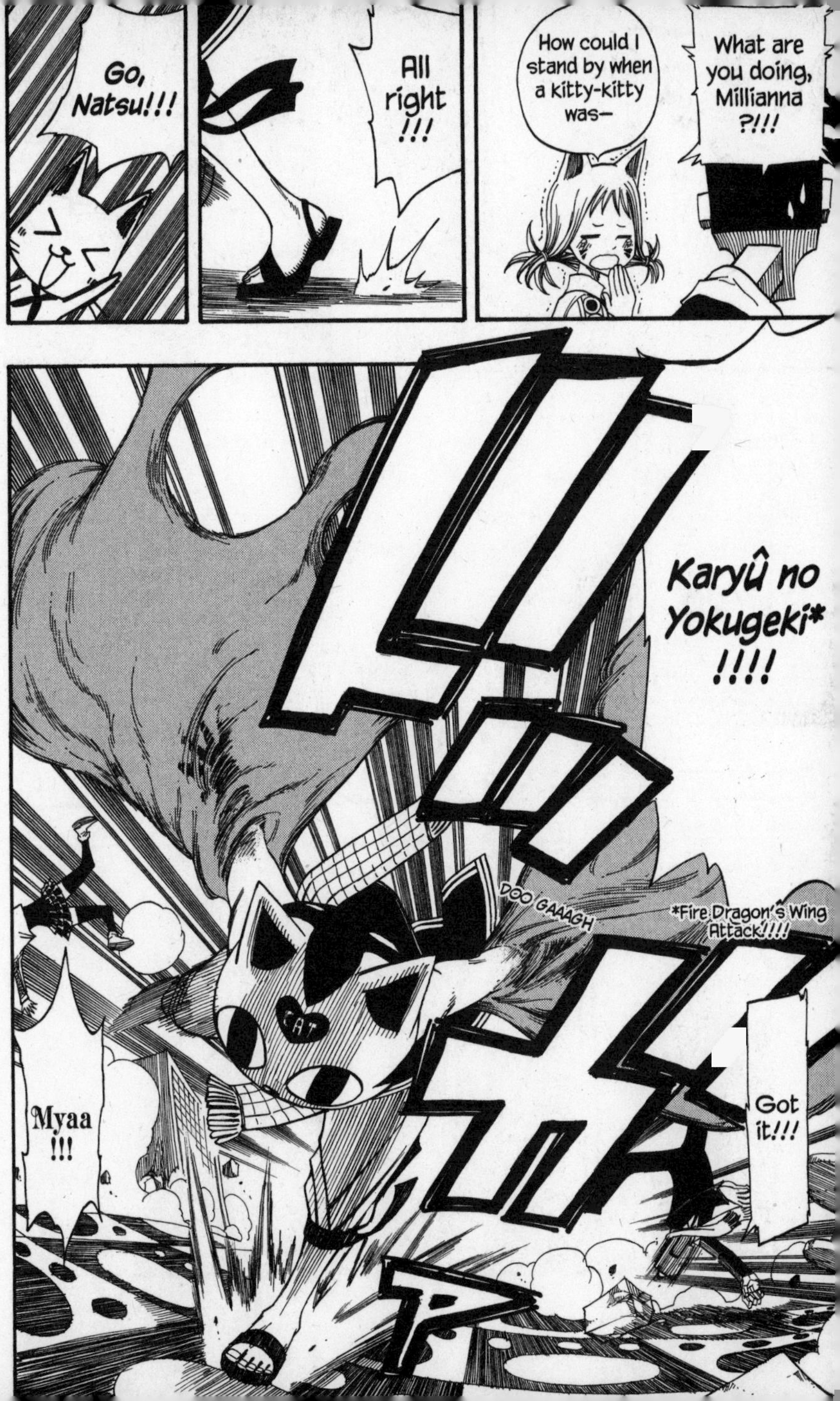
What are you doing, Millianna?!!!
How could I stand by when a kitty-kitty was—
All right!!!
Go, Natsu!!!
Karyû no Yokugeki*!!!!
*Fire Dragon's Wing Attack!!!!
DOO GAAAGH
Got it!!!
Myaa!!!

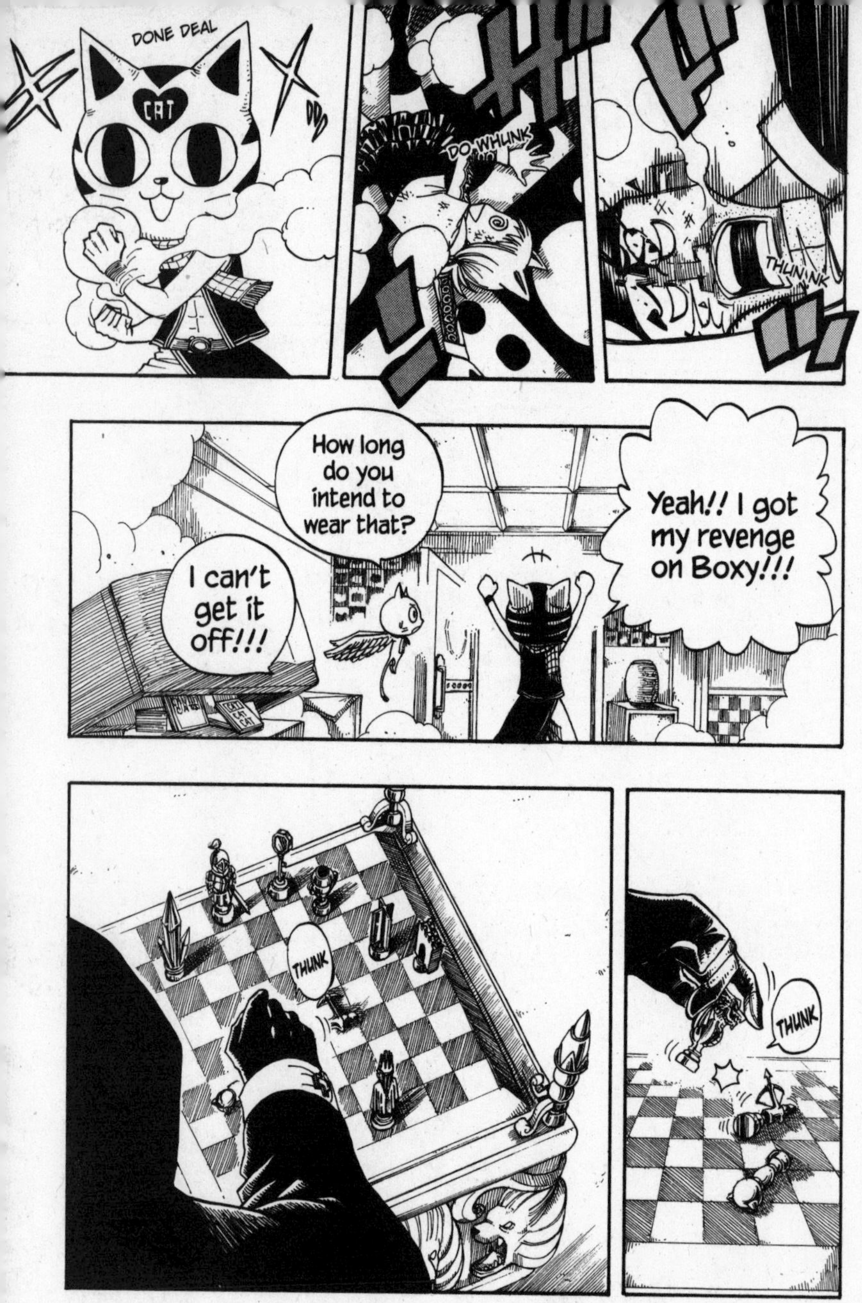
THUN NK
DO WHUNK
DONE DEAL
Yeah!! I got my revenge on Boxy!!!
How long do you intend to wear that?
I can't get it off!!!
THUNK
THUNK

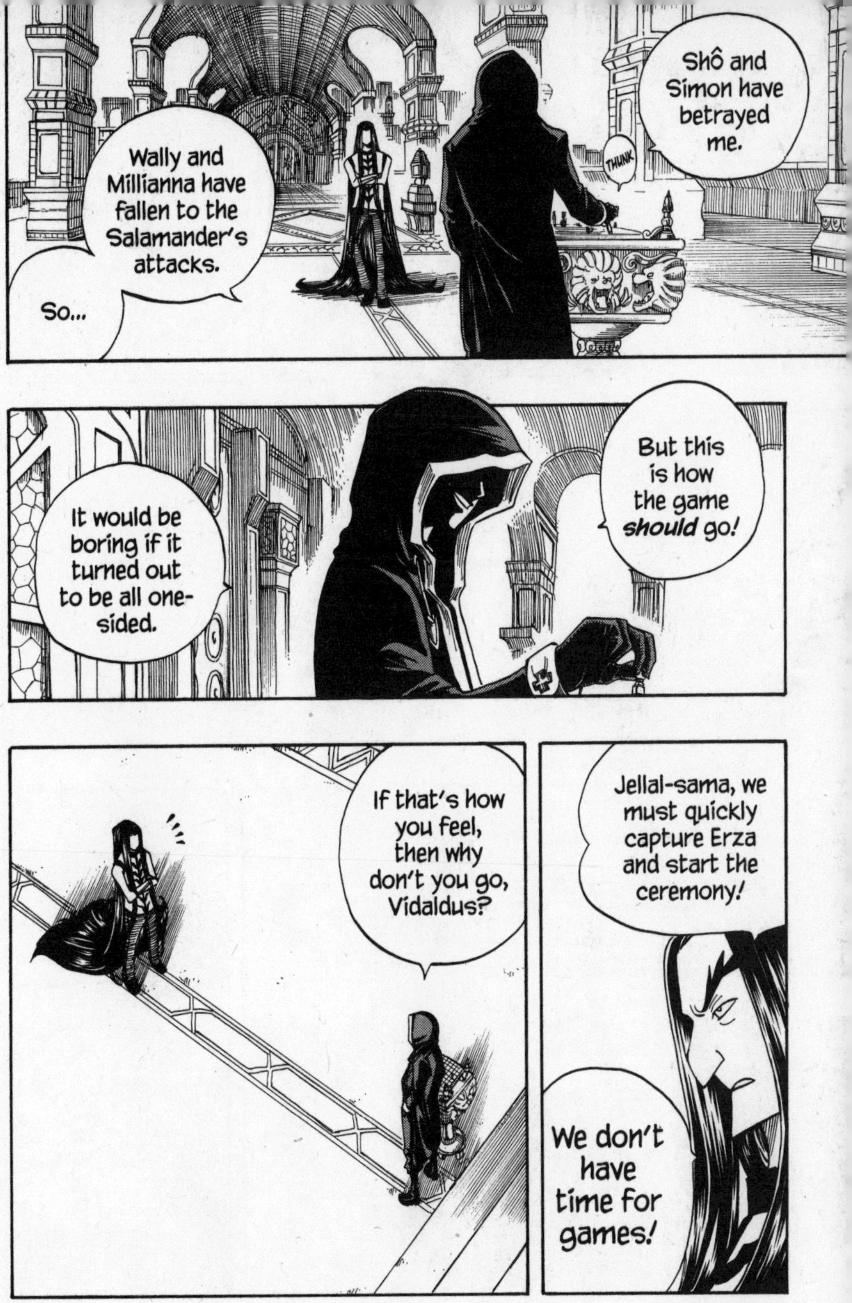
Shô and Simon have betrayed me.
THUNK
Wally and Millianna have fallen to the Salamander's attacks.
So...
But this is how the game *should* go!
It would be boring if it turned out to be all one-sided.
Jellal-sama, we must quickly capture Erza and start the ceremony!
We don't have time for games!
If that's how you feel, then why don't you go, Vidaldus?

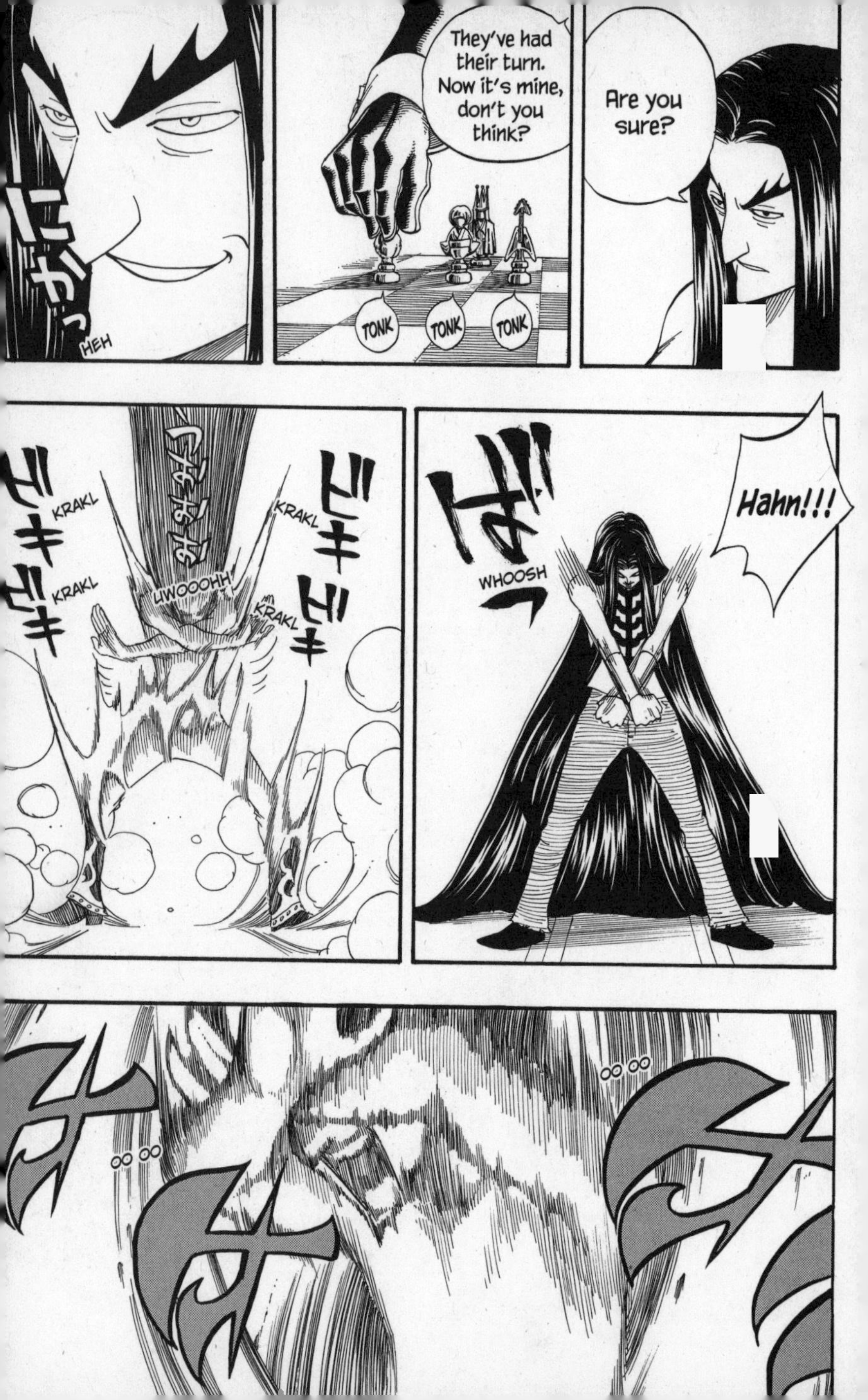
Are you sure?
They've had their turn. Now it's mine, don't you think?
TONK
TONK
TONK
HEH
Hahn!!!
WHOOSH
KRAKL
KRAKL
UWOOOHH
KRAKL
KRAKL

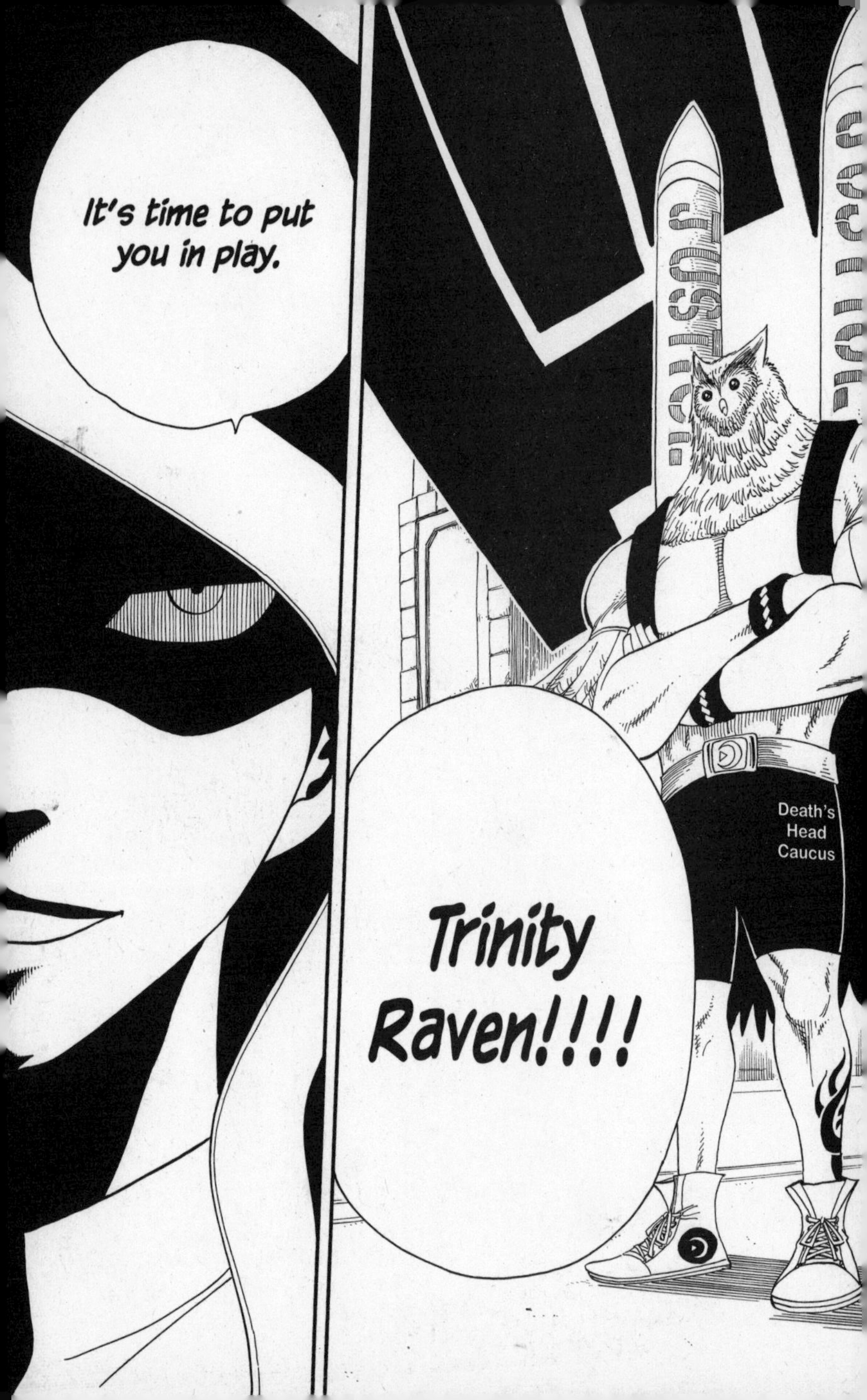
Death's Head Caucus
Trinity Raven!!!!
It's time to put you in play.

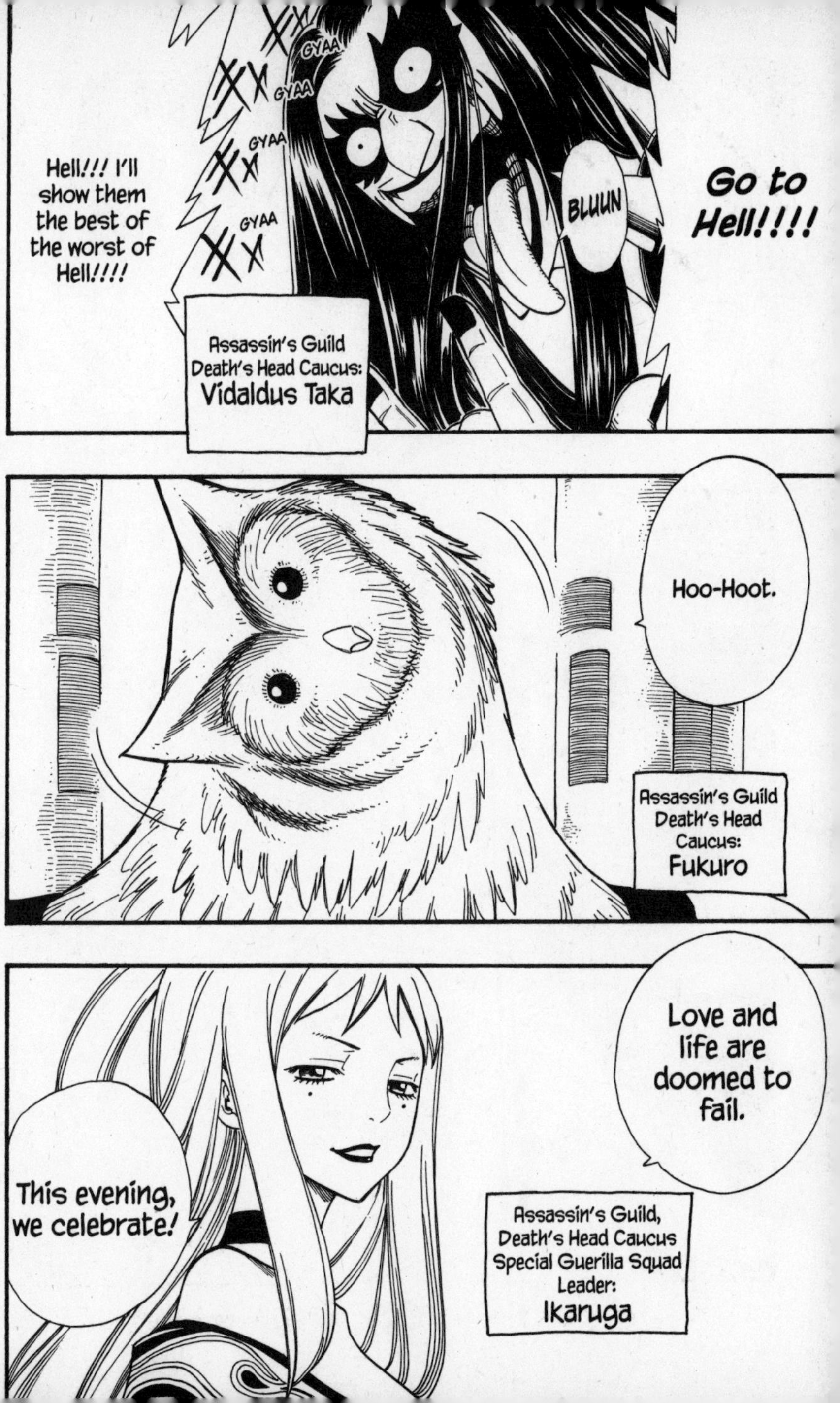
Go to Hell!!!!
BLUUN
GYAA
GYAA
GYAA
GYAA
Hell!!! I'll show them the best of the worst of Hell!!!!
Assassin's Guild Death's Head Caucus: Vidaldus Taka
Hoo-Hoot.
Assassin's Guild Death's Head Caucus: Fukuro
Love and life are doomed to fail.
Assassin's Guild, Death's Head Caucus Special Guerilla Squad Leader: Ikaruga
This evening, we celebrate!

FAIRY TAIL

3.0000J
19000J
OOKA
1000J
7.0000
DA
60.000J
1.0000J
80.0000J
FAIRY TAIL
FILE 1
C.M.A.
FREE

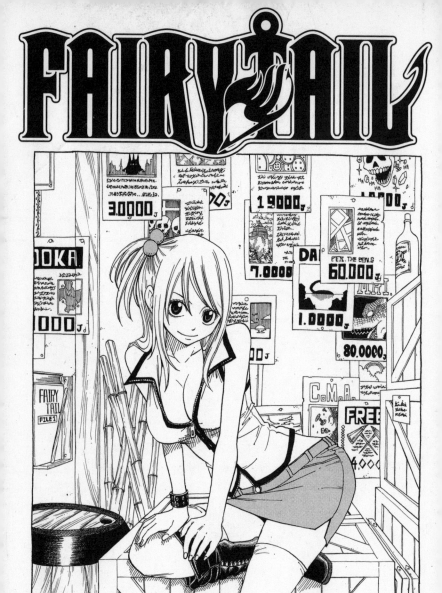

Chapter 85: Heaven's Game

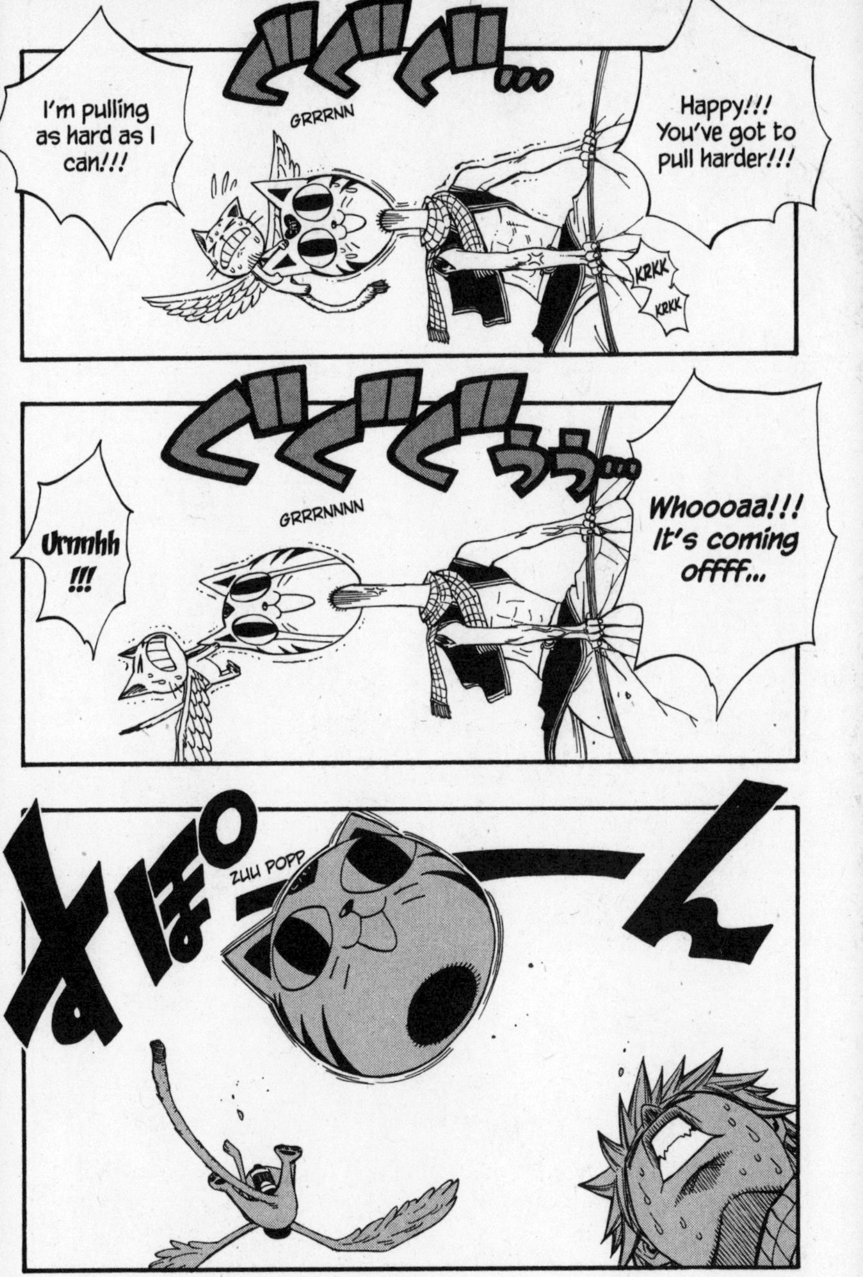
Happy!!! You've got to pull harder!!!
GRRRNN
I'm pulling as hard as I can!!!
KRKK
KRKK
Whoooaa!!! It's coming offff...
GRRRNNNN
Urmhh !!!
ZUU POPP

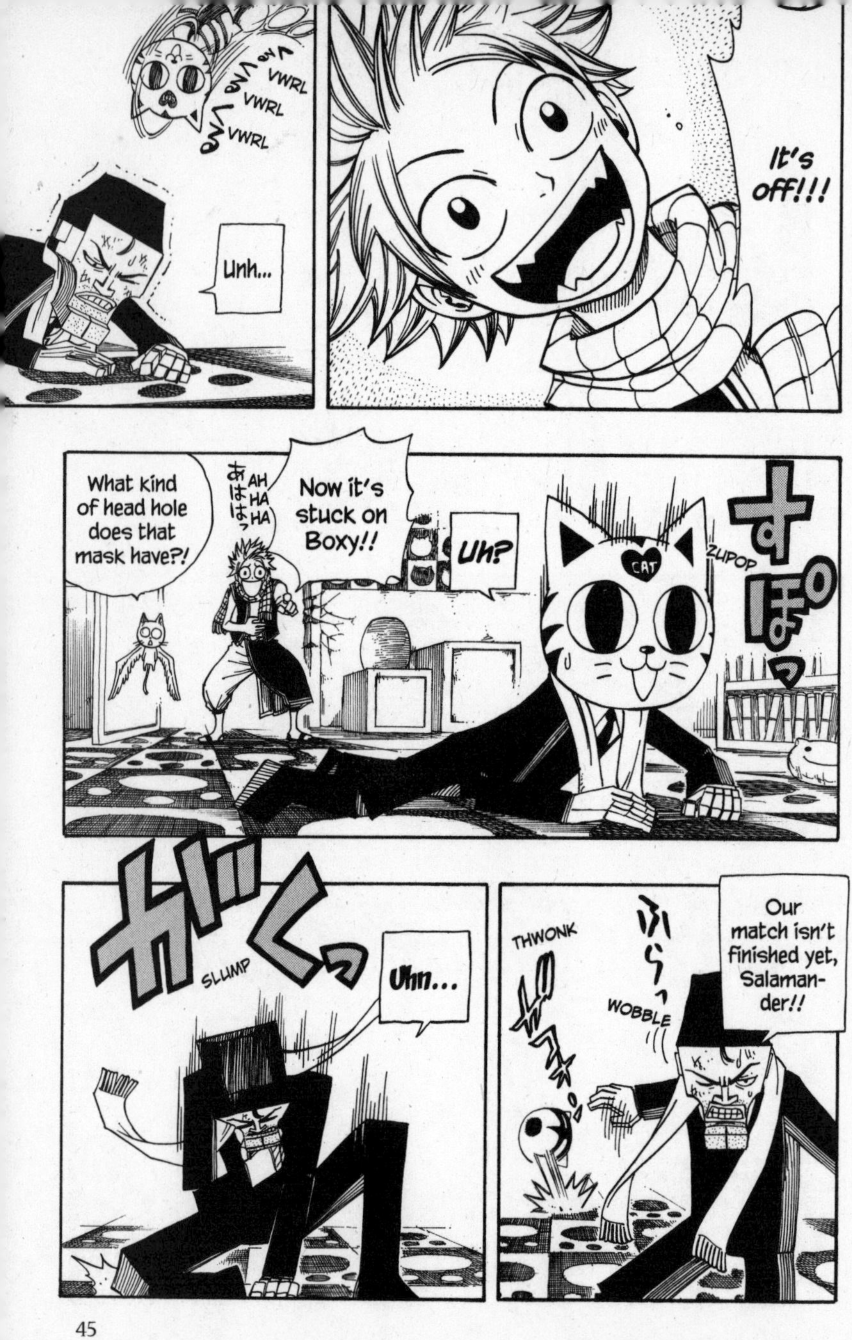
It's off!!!
VWRL
VWRL
VWRL
Unh...
すぽっ
ZUPOP
Uh?
Now it's stuck on Boxy!!
あはは
AH HA HA
What kind of head hole does that mask have?!
Our match isn't finished yet, Salamander!!
ふらっ
WOBBLE
THWONK
Uhn...
がくっ
SLUMP

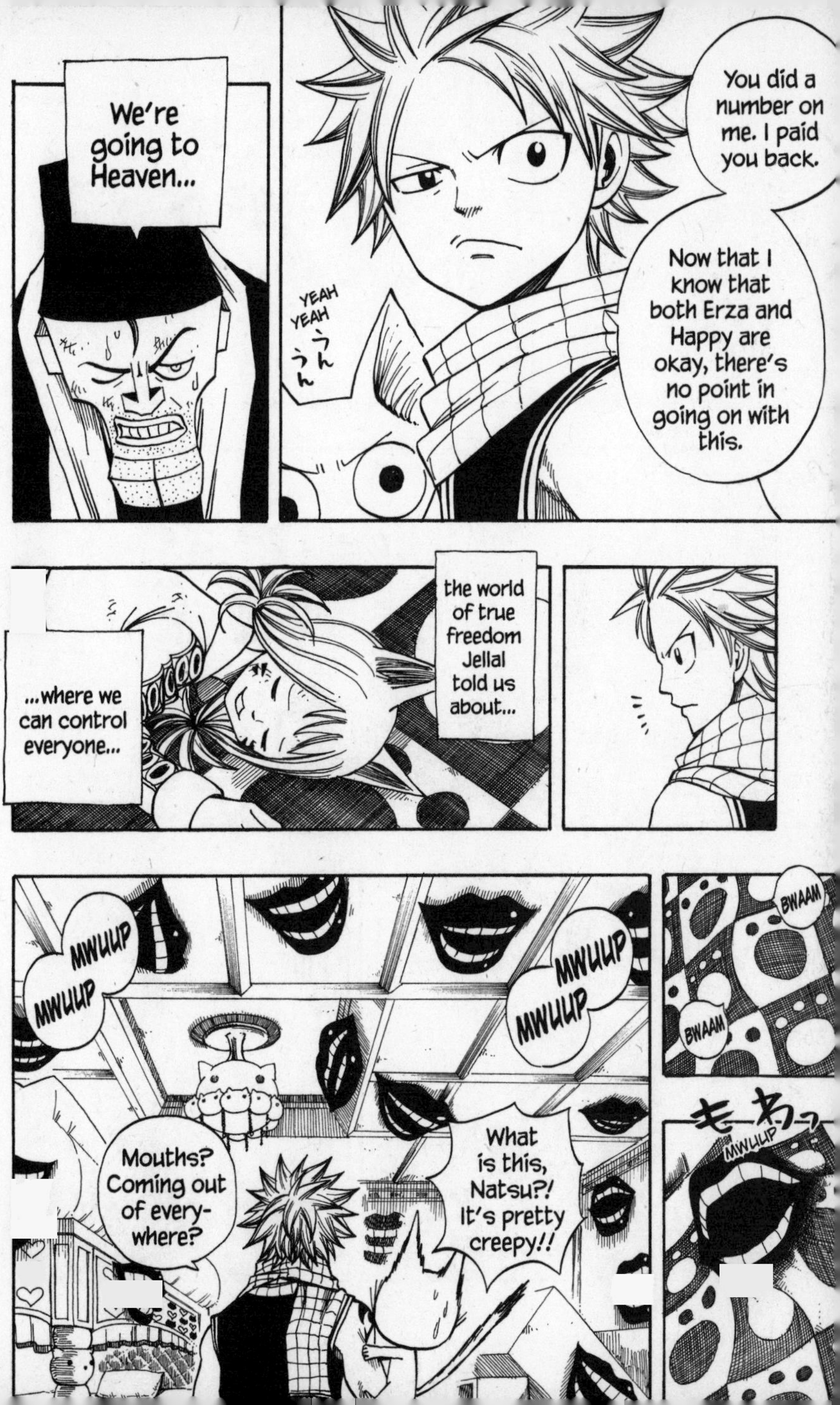
You did a number on me. I paid you back.
Now that I know that both Erza and Happy are okay, there's no point in going on with this.
YEAH YEAH
うん うん
We're going to Heaven...
the world of true freedom Jellal told us about...
...where we can control everyone...
BWAAM
BWAAM
もわっ
MWUUP
MWUUP
MWUUP
What is this, Natsu?! It's pretty creepy!!
Mouths? Coming out of every-where?
MWUUP
MWUUP

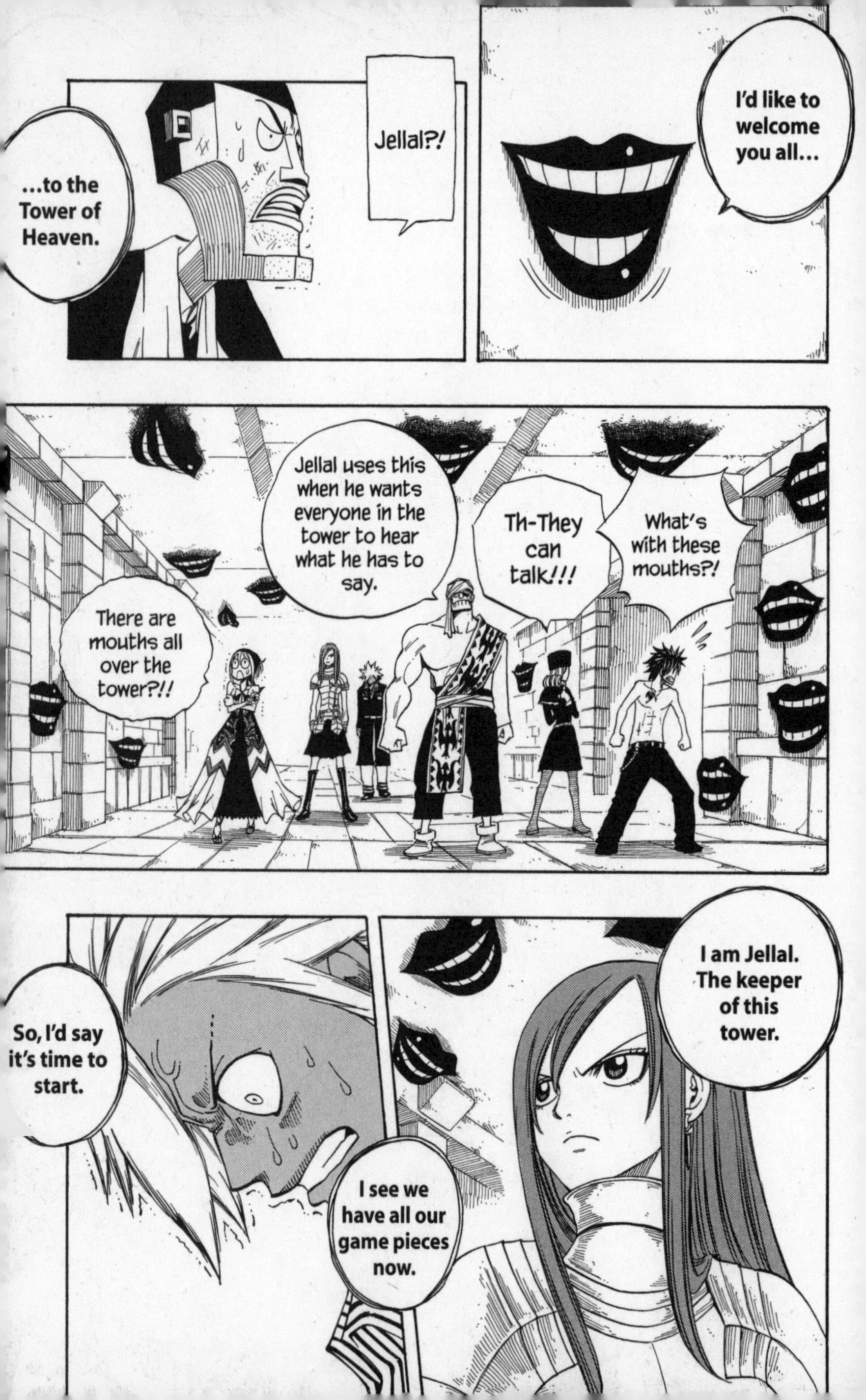
I'd like to welcome you all…
Jellal?!
…to the Tower of Heaven.
What's with these mouths?!
Th-They can talk!!!
Jellal uses this when he wants everyone in the tower to hear what he has to say.
There are mouths all over the tower?!!
I am Jellal. The keeper of this tower.
I see we have all our game pieces now.
So, I'd say it's time to start.

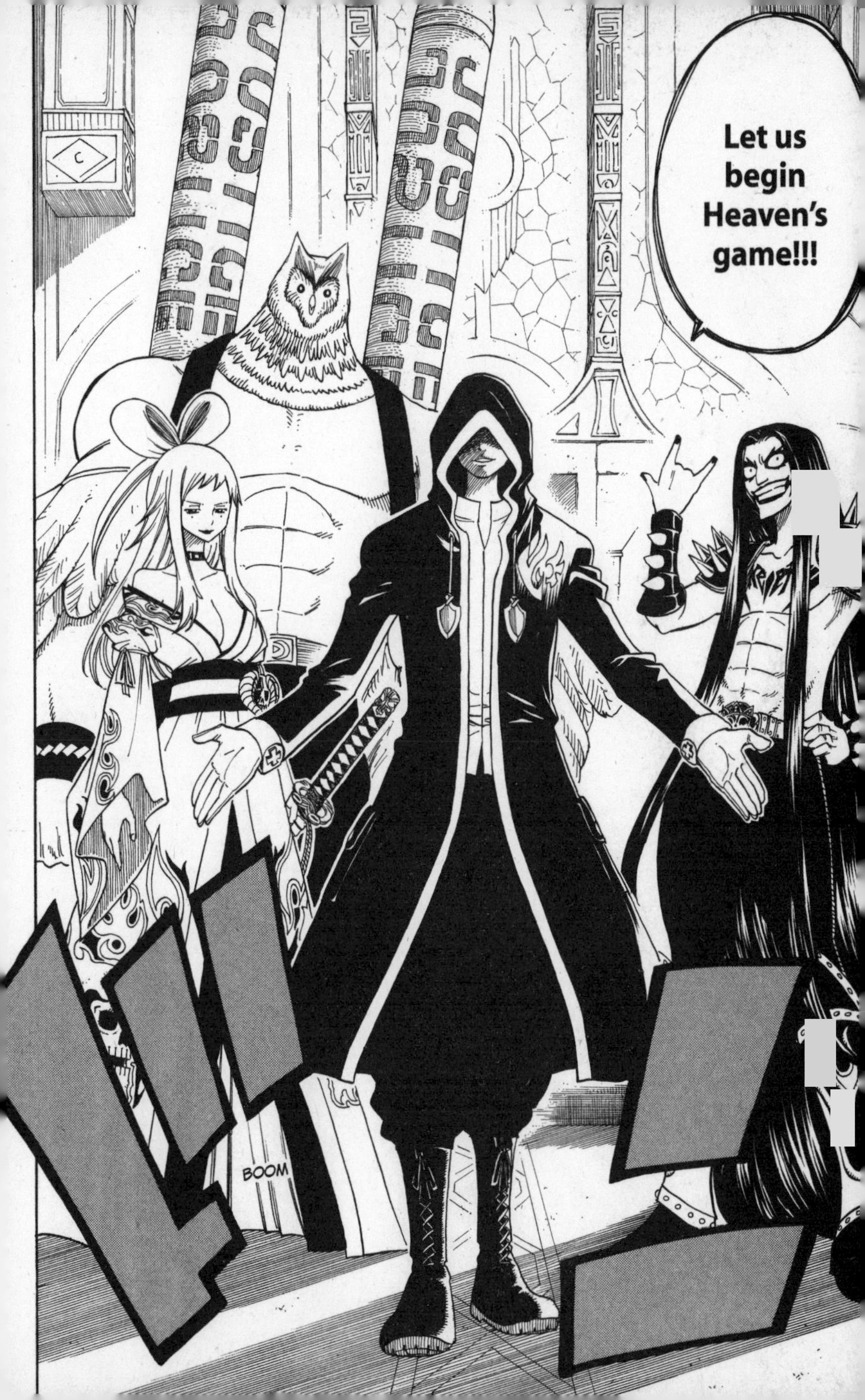
Let us begin Heaven's game!!!
BOOM

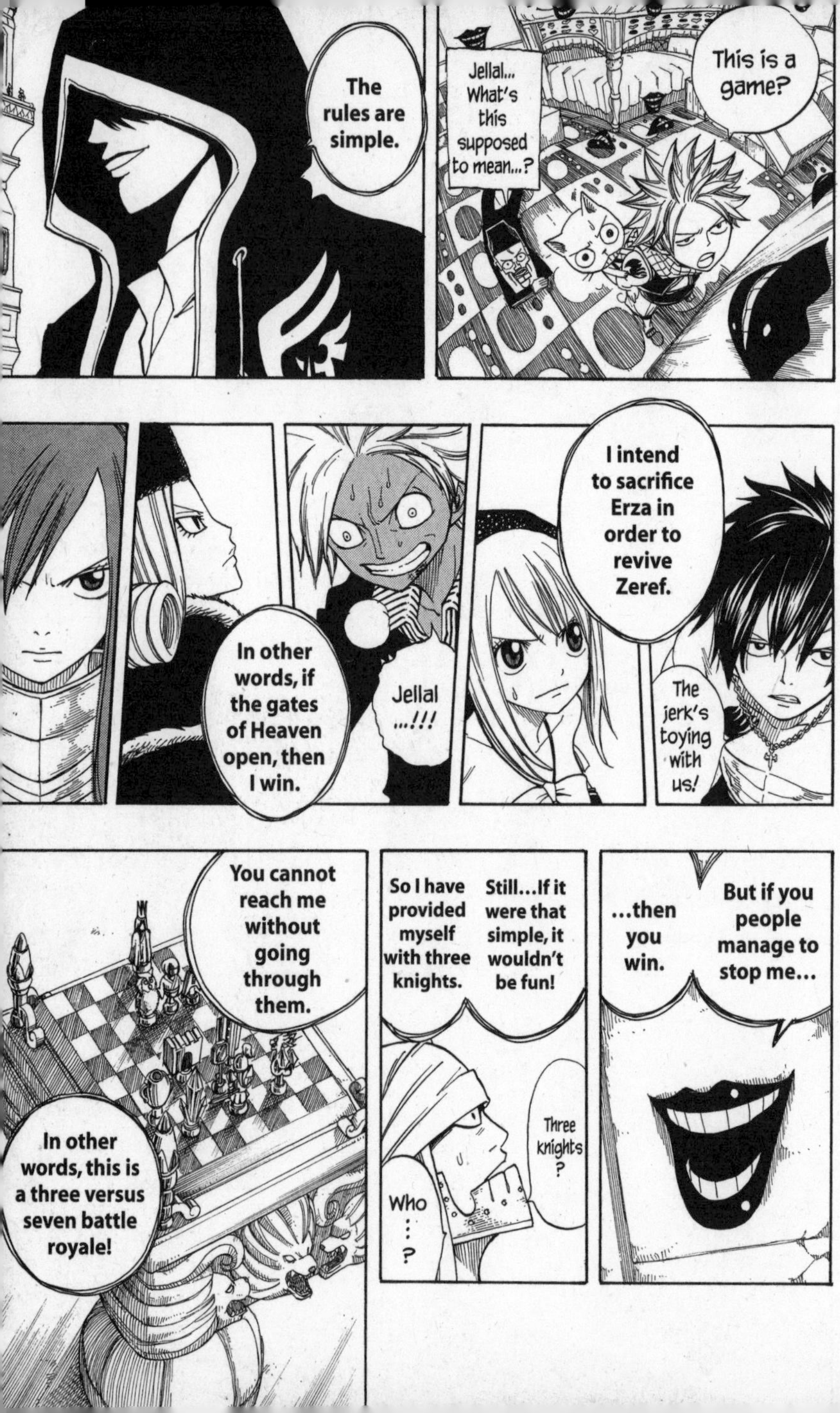
This is a game?
Jellal... What's this supposed to mean...?
The rules are simple.
I intend to sacrifice Erza in order to revive Zeref.
The jerk's toying with us!
Jellal ...!!!
In other words, if the gates of Heaven open, then I win.
But if you people manage to stop me...
...then you win.
Still...If it were that simple, it wouldn't be fun!
So I have provided myself with three knights.
Three knights?
Who...?
You cannot reach me without going through them.
In other words, this is a three versus seven battle royale!

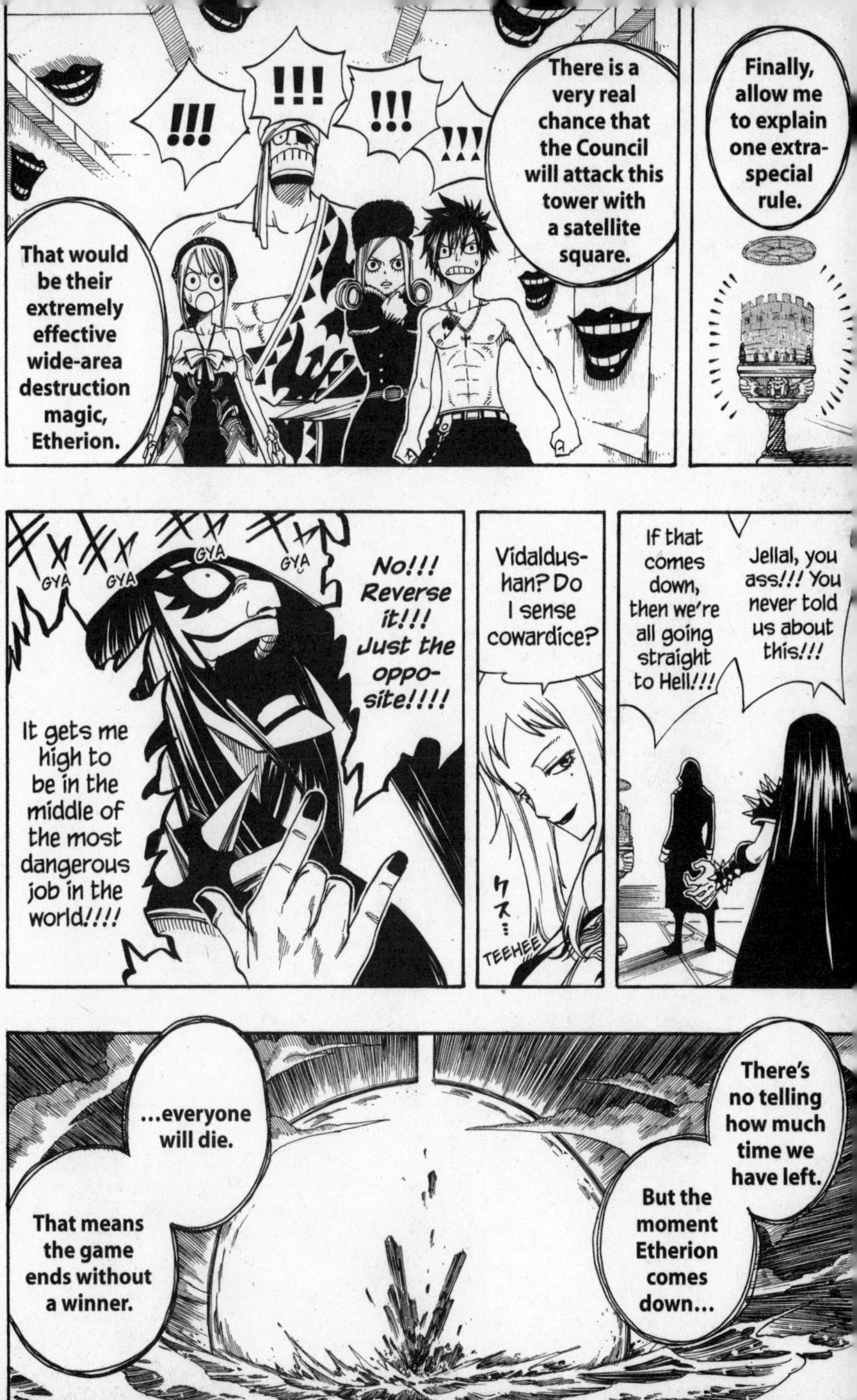
Finally, allow me to explain one extra-special rule.
There is a very real chance that the Council will attack this tower with a satellite square.
!!!
!!!
!!!
!!!
That would be their extremely effective wide-area destruction magic, Etherion.
Jellal, you ass!!! You never told us about this!!!
If that comes down, then we're all going straight to Hell!!!
Vidaldus-han? Do I sense cowardice?
クス…
TEEHEE
GYA
GYA
GYA
GYA
No!!! Reverse it!!! Just the opposite!!!!
It gets me high to be in the middle of the most dangerous job in the world!!!!
There's no telling how much time we have left.
But the moment Etherion comes down…
…everyone will die.
That means the game ends without a winner.

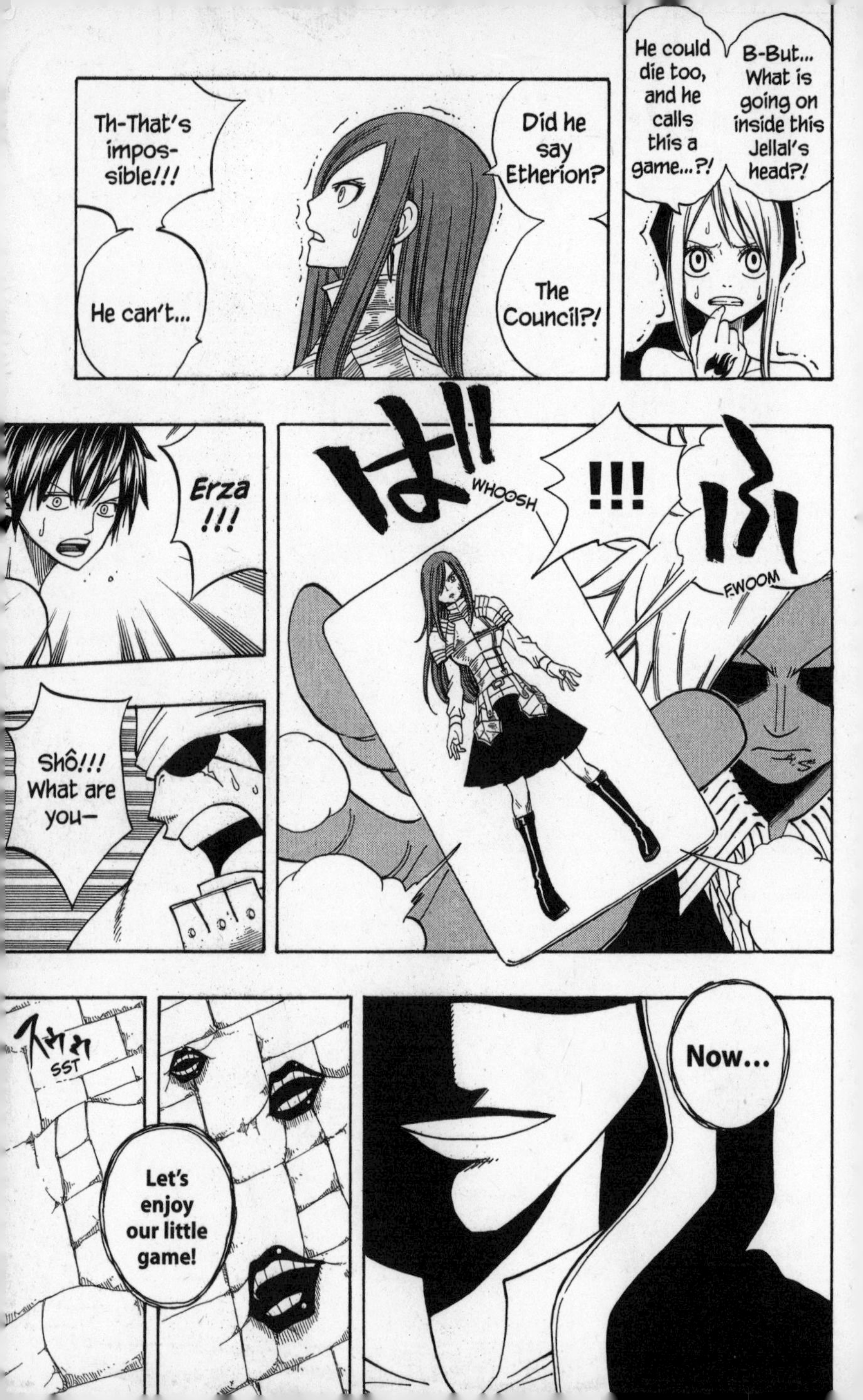
B-But... What is going on inside this Jellal's head?!
He could die too, and he calls this a game...?!
Did he say Etherion?
The Council?!
Th-That's impos-sible!!!
He can't...
FWOOM
!!!
WHOOSH
Erza!!!
Shô!!! What are you—
Now...
SST
Let's enjoy our little game!

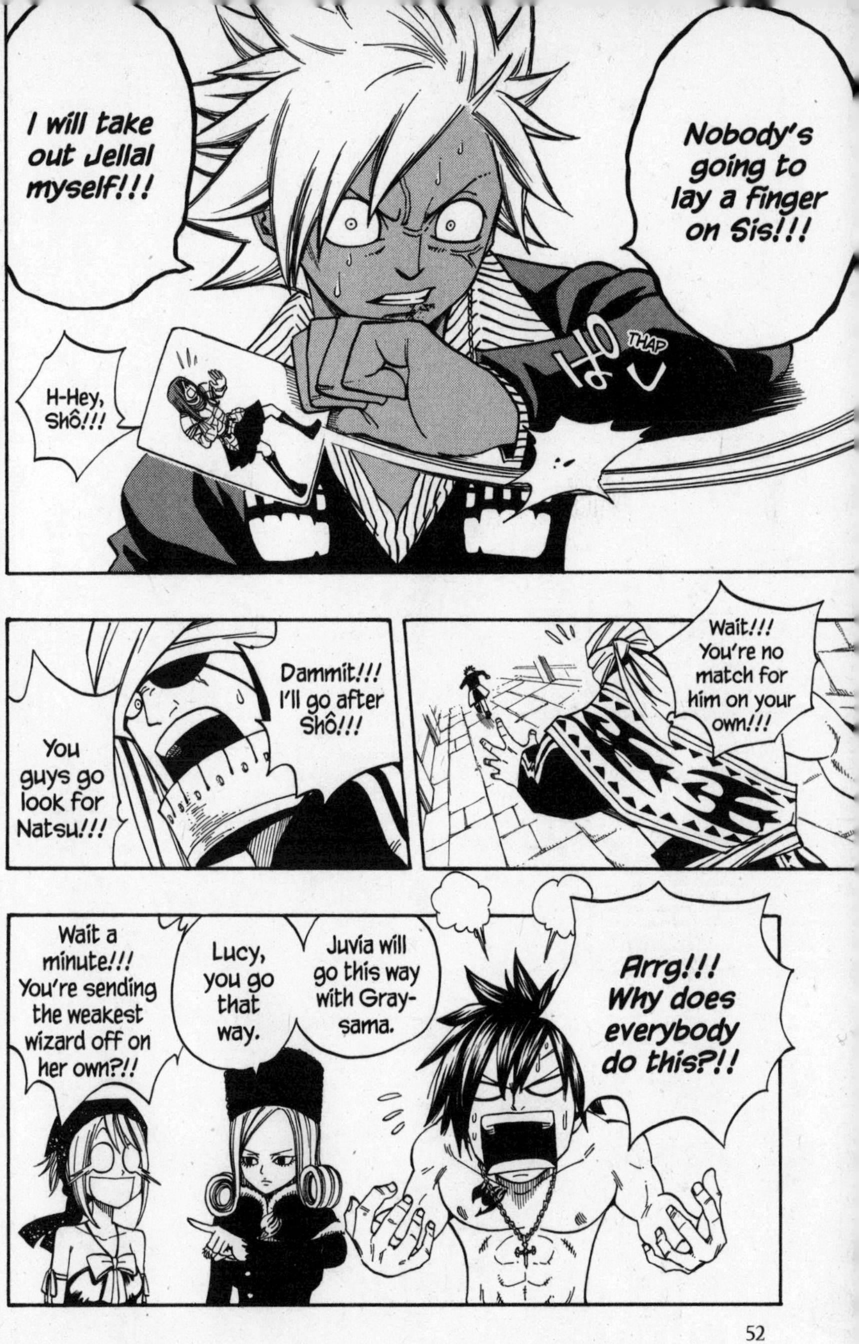
Nobody's going to lay a finger on Sis!!!
I will take out Jellal myself!!!
THAP
H-Hey, Shô!!!
Wait!!! You're no match for him on your own!!!
Dammit!!! I'll go after Shô!!!
You guys go look for Natsu!!!
Arrg!!! Why does everybody do this?!!
Juvia will go this way with Gray-sama.
Lucy, you go that way.
Wait a minute!!! You're sending the weakest wizard off on her own?!!

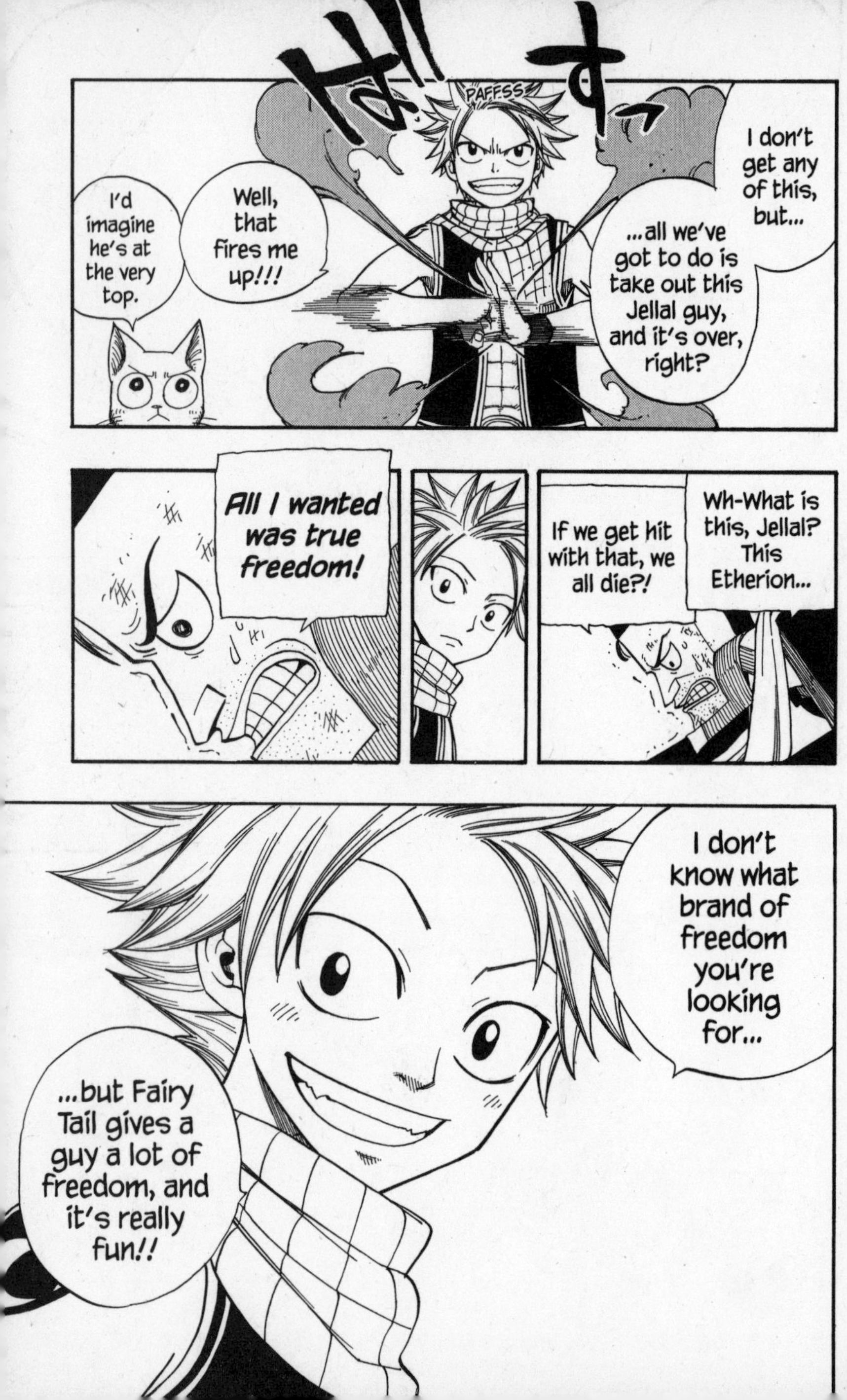
PAFFSS
I don't get any of this, but...
...all we've got to do is take out this Jellal guy, and it's over, right?
Well, that fires me up!!!
I'd imagine he's at the very top.
Wh-What is this, Jellal? This Etherion...
If we get hit with that, we all die?!
All I wanted was true freedom!
I don't know what brand of freedom you're looking for...
...but Fairy Tail gives a guy a lot of freedom, and it's really fun!!

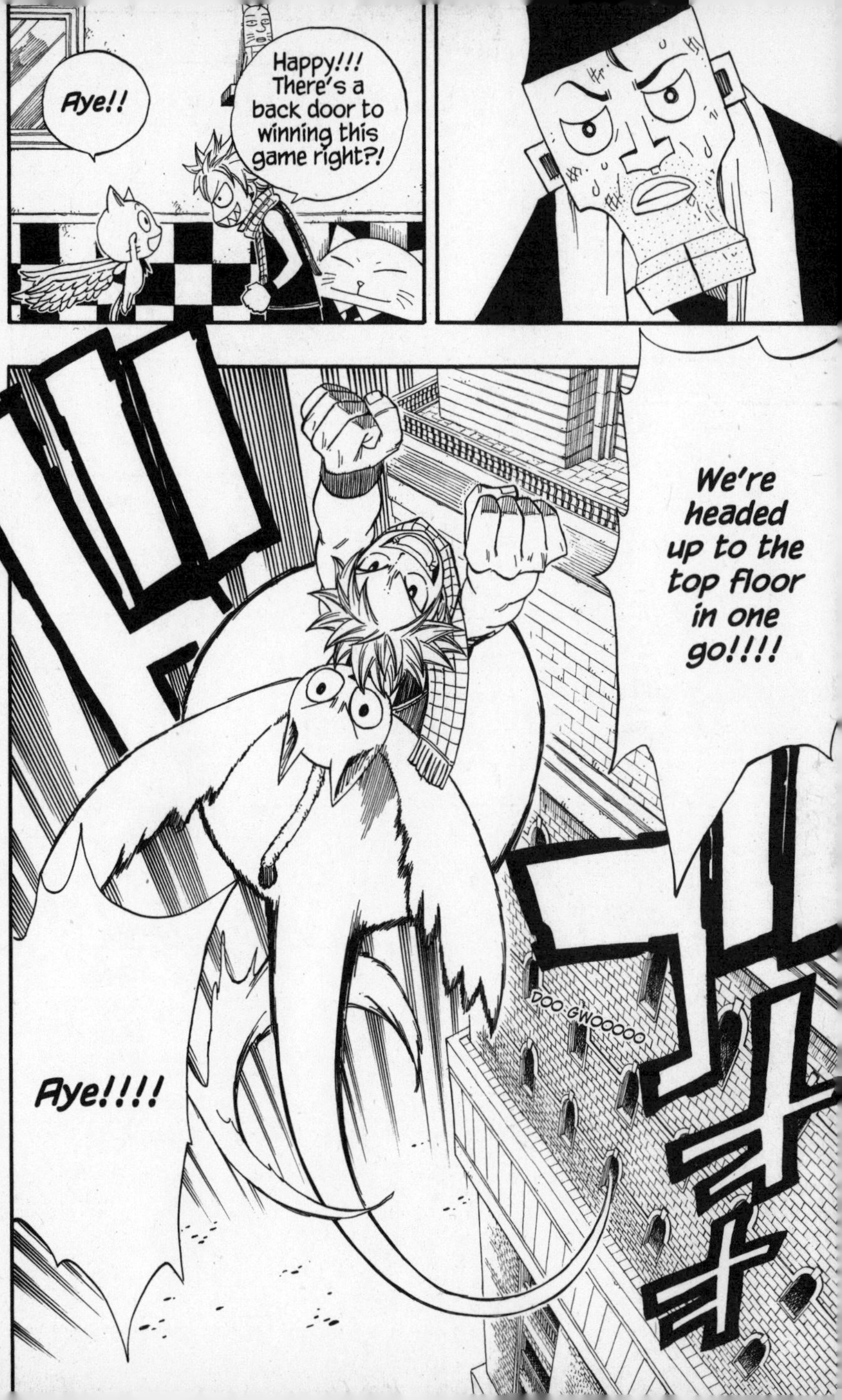
Happy!!! There's a back door to winning this game right?!
Aye!!
We're headed up to the top floor in one go!!!!
DOO GWOOOOO
Aye!!!!

...dandy...

WHUD

...scarf!

That's one...

Salaman-
der...

!!!

GLINT

What's
that?

Some-
thing's
com-
ing this
way!!

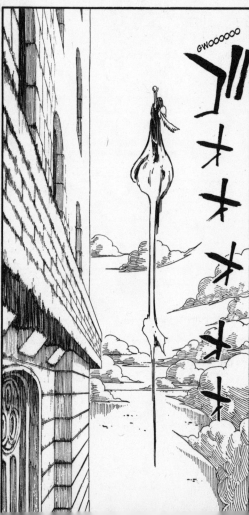

GWOOOOOO

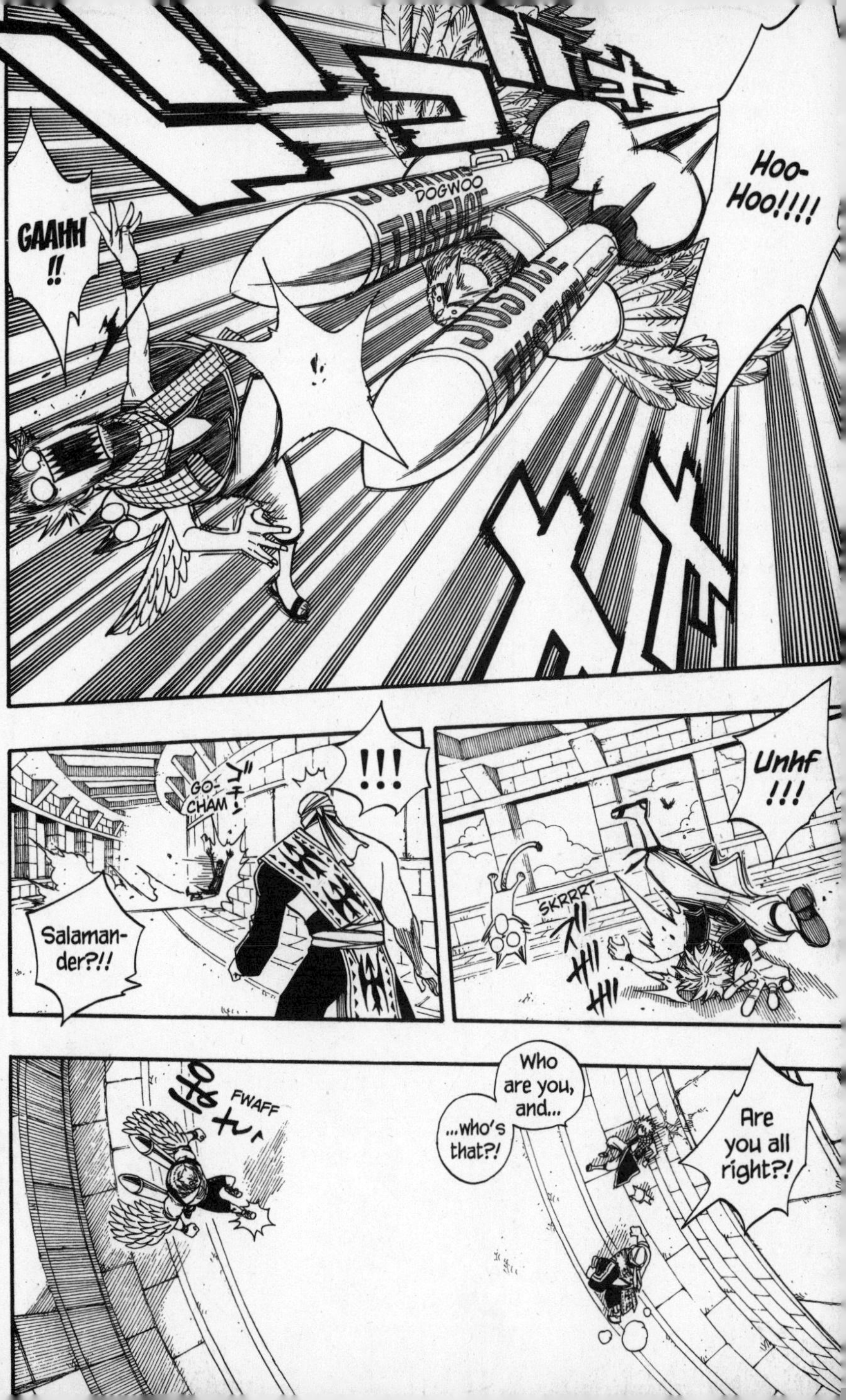
Hoo-Hoo!!!!
DOGWOO
GAAHH!!
Unhf!!!
SKRRRT
!!!
GO-CHAM
Salamander?!!
Are you all right?!
Who are you, and...
...who's that?!
FWAFF

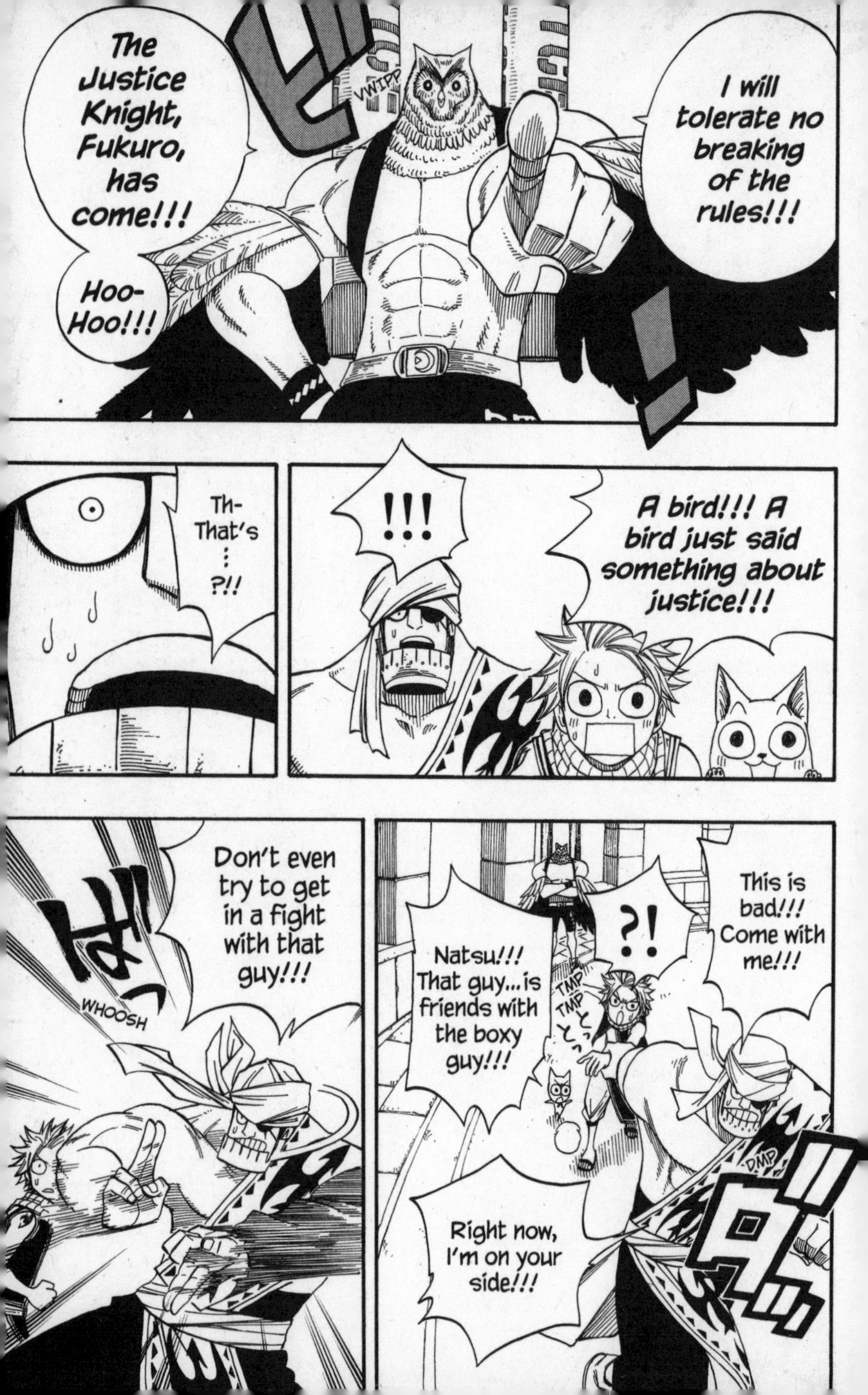

I will tolerate no breaking of the rules!!!
VWIPP
The Justice Knight, Fukuro, has come!!!
Hoo-Hoo!!!
A bird!!! A bird just said something about justice!!!
!!!
Th- That's ...?!!
This is bad!!! Come with me!!!
?!
Natsu!!! That guy...is friends with the boxy guy!!!
TMP TMP
DMP
Right now, I'm on your side!!!
Don't even try to get in a fight with that guy!!!
WHOOSH

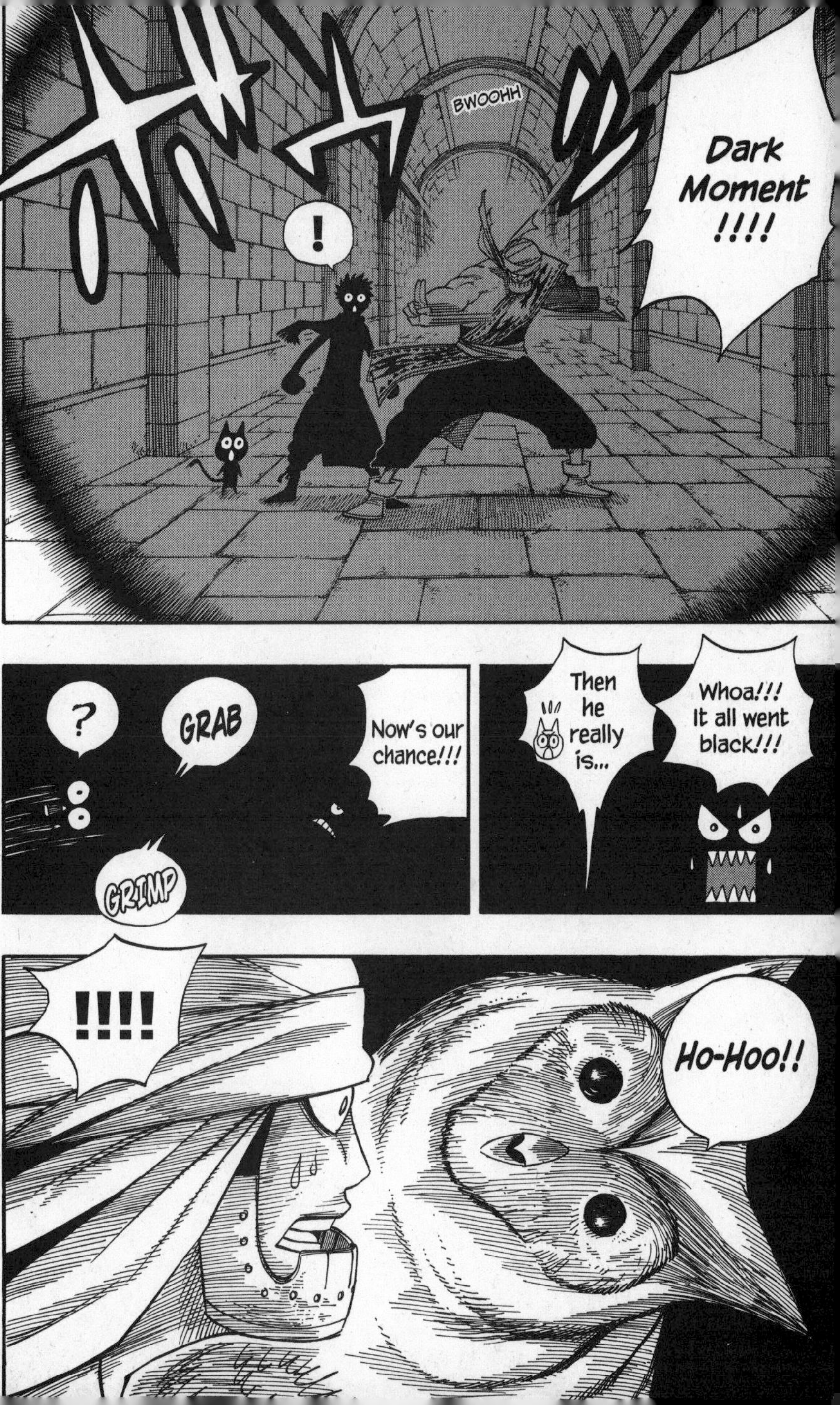
Dark Moment!!!!
BWOOHH
!
Whoa!!! It all went black!!!
Then he really is...
Now's our chance!!!
GRAB
?
GRIMP
Ho-Hoo!!
!!!!

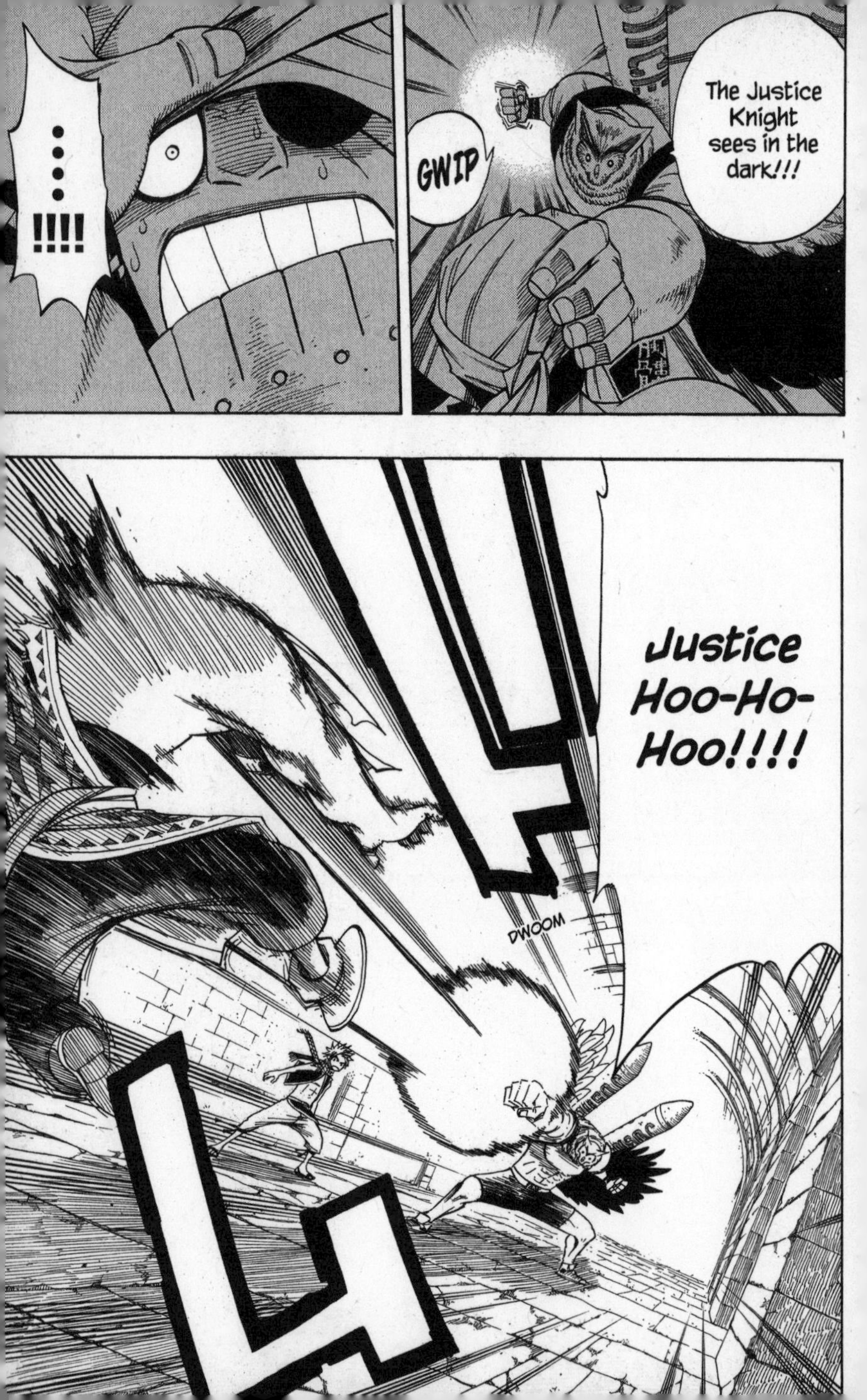
The Justice Knight sees in the dark!!!
GWIP
....!!!!
Justice Hoo-Ho-Hoo!!!!
DWOOM

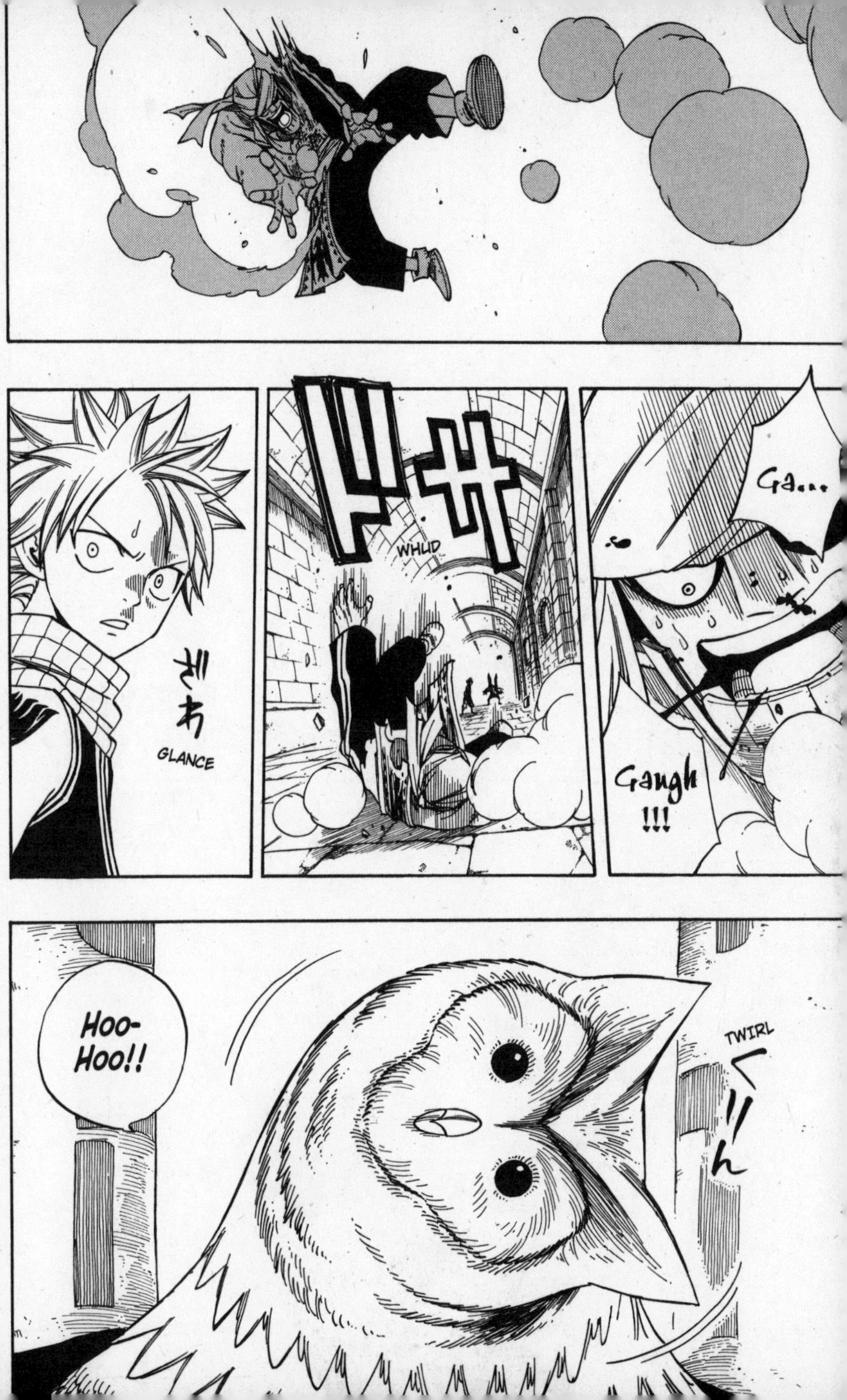

Ga...
Gaugh !!!
WHUD
GLANCE
TWIRL
Hoo-Hoo!!

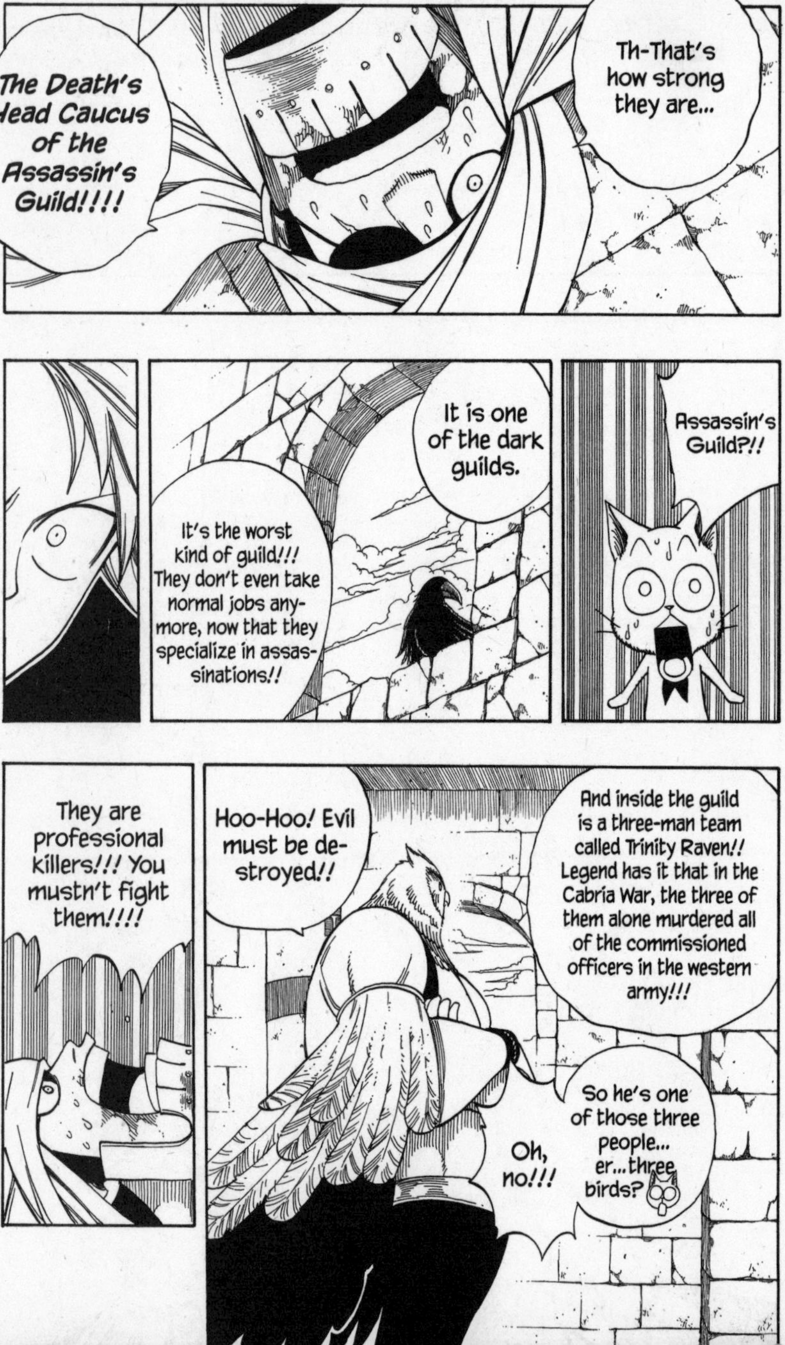
Th-That's how strong they are...
The Death's Head Caucus of the Assassin's Guild!!!!
Assassin's Guild?!!
It is one of the dark guilds.
It's the worst kind of guild!!! They don't even take normal jobs anymore, now that they specialize in assassinations!!
And inside the guild is a three-man team called Trinity Raven!! Legend has it that in the Cabria War, the three of them alone murdered all of the commissioned officers in the western army!!!
Hoo-Hoo! Evil must be destroyed!!
So he's one of those three people... er...three birds?
Oh, no!!!
They are professional killers!!! You mustn't fight them!!!!

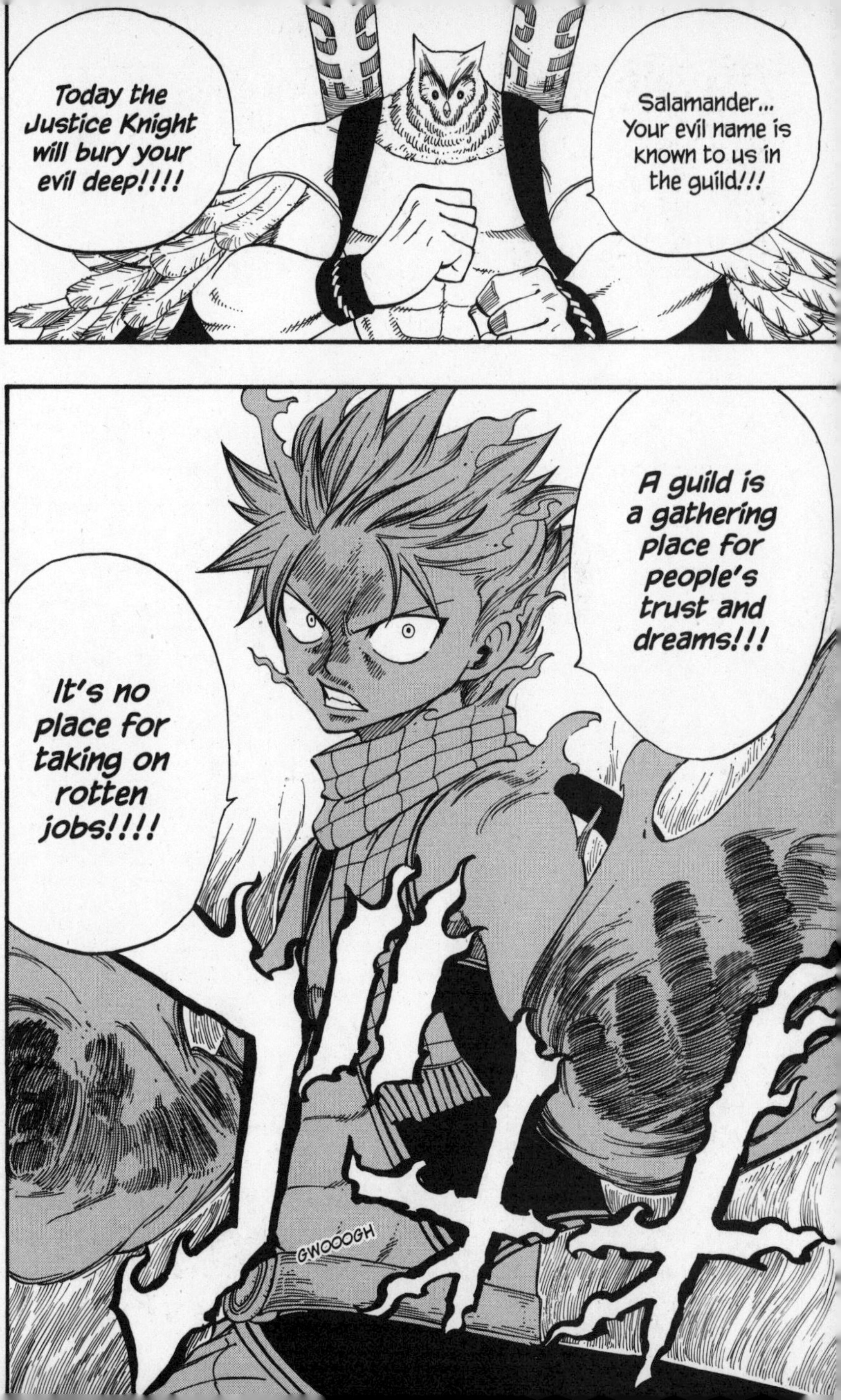
Salamander... Your evil name is known to us in the guild!!!
Today the Justice Knight will bury your evil deep!!!!
A guild is a gathering place for people's trust and dreams!!!
It's no place for taking on rotten jobs!!!!
GWOOOGH

FAIRY TAIL

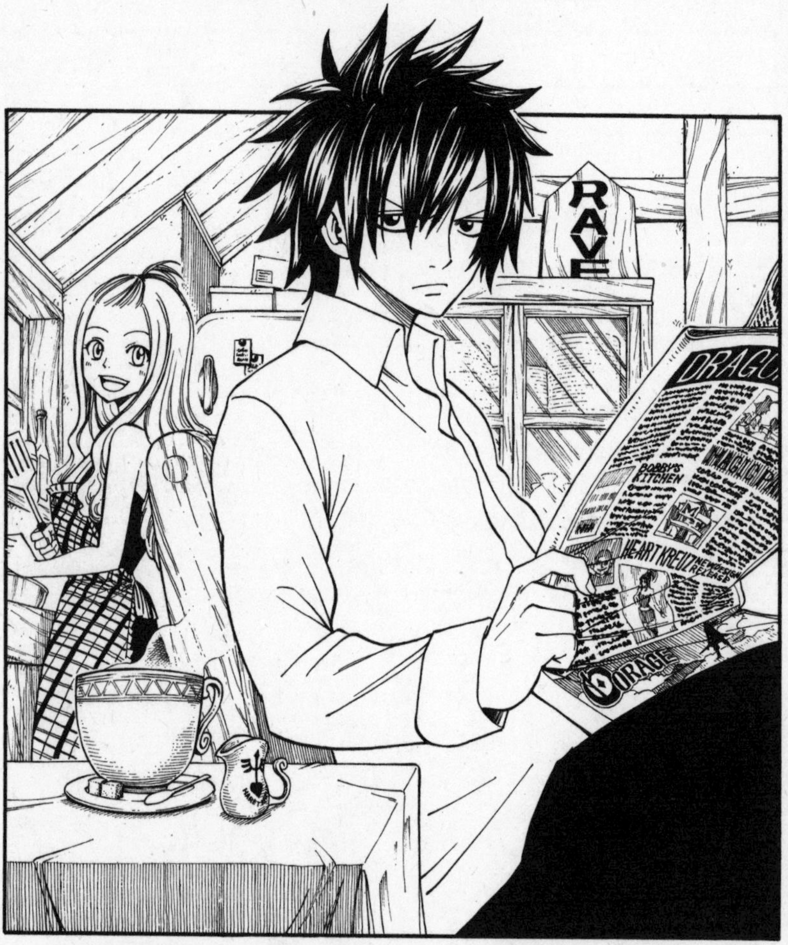
RAVE
BOBBY'S KITCHEN
HEART KREUZ
NEW DESIGN RELEASE
ORAGE

Chapter 86: Rock of Succubus

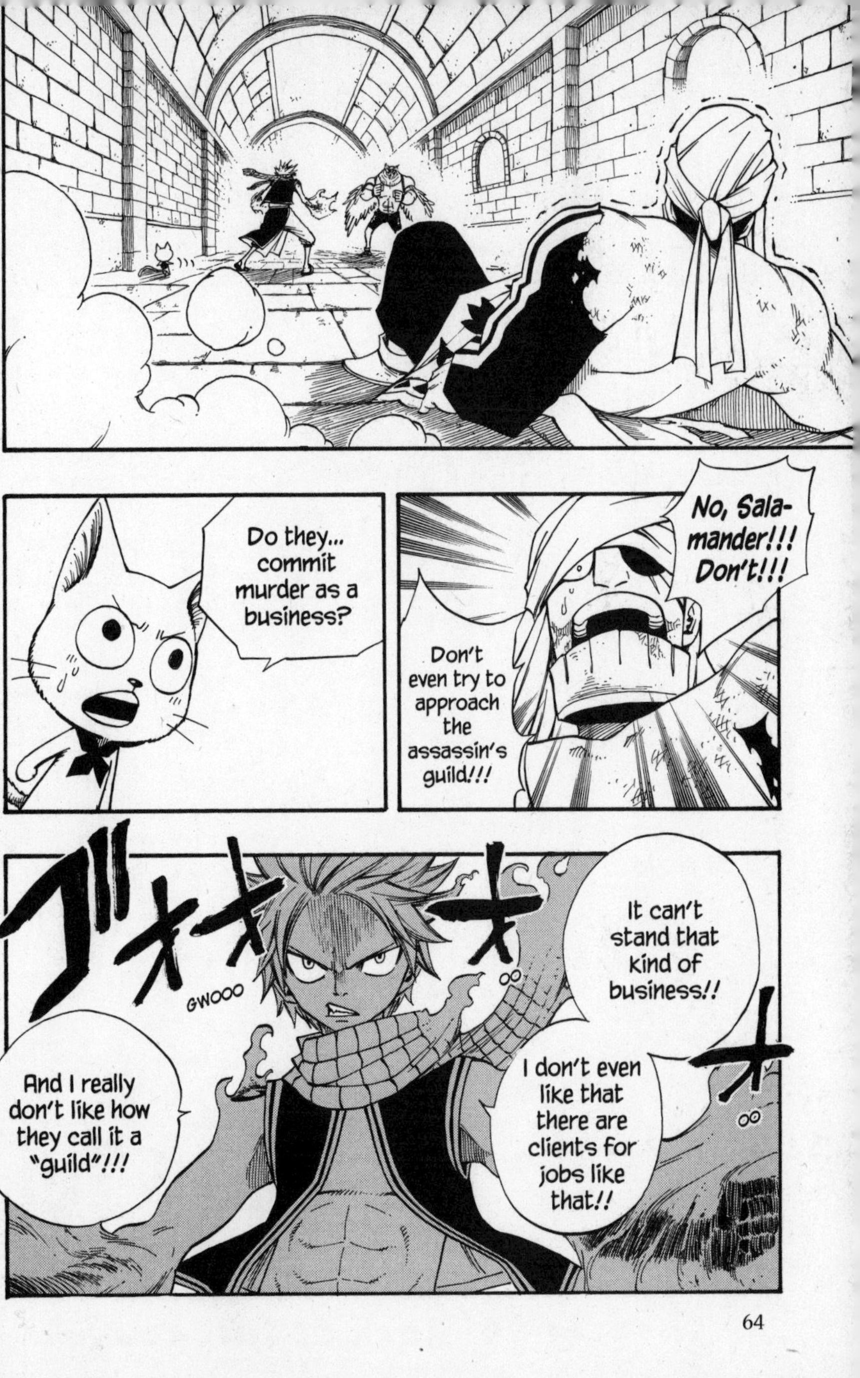
No, Salamander!!! Don't!!!
Don't even try to approach the assassin's guild!!!
Do they... commit murder as a business?
It can't stand that kind of business!!
I don't even like that there are clients for jobs like that!!
GWOOO
And I really don't like how they call it a "guild"!!!

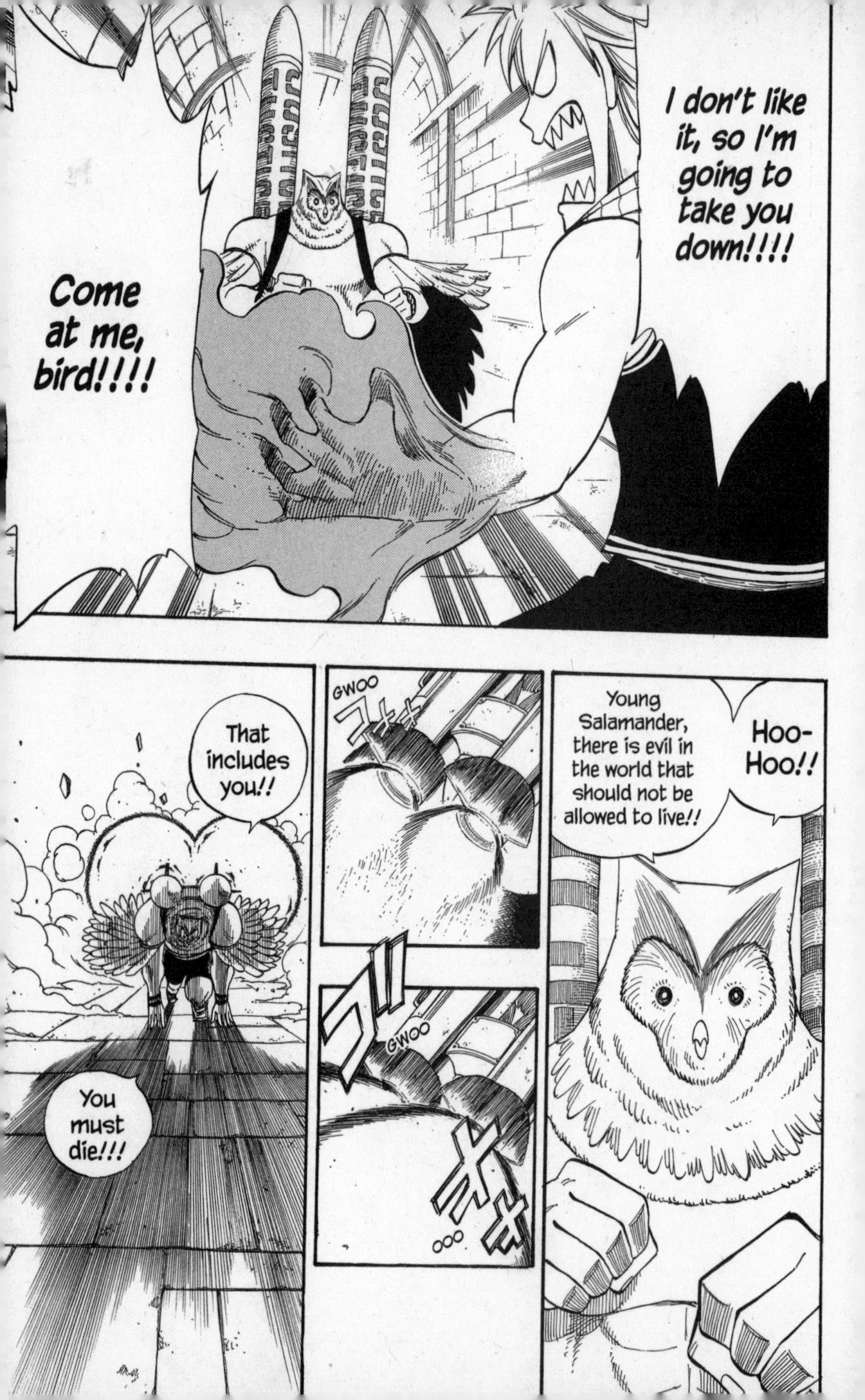

I don't like it, so I'm going to take you down!!!!
Come at me, bird!!!!
Hoo-Hoo!!
Young Salamander, there is evil in the world that should not be allowed to live!!
GWOO
GWOO
ooo
That includes you!!
You must die!!!

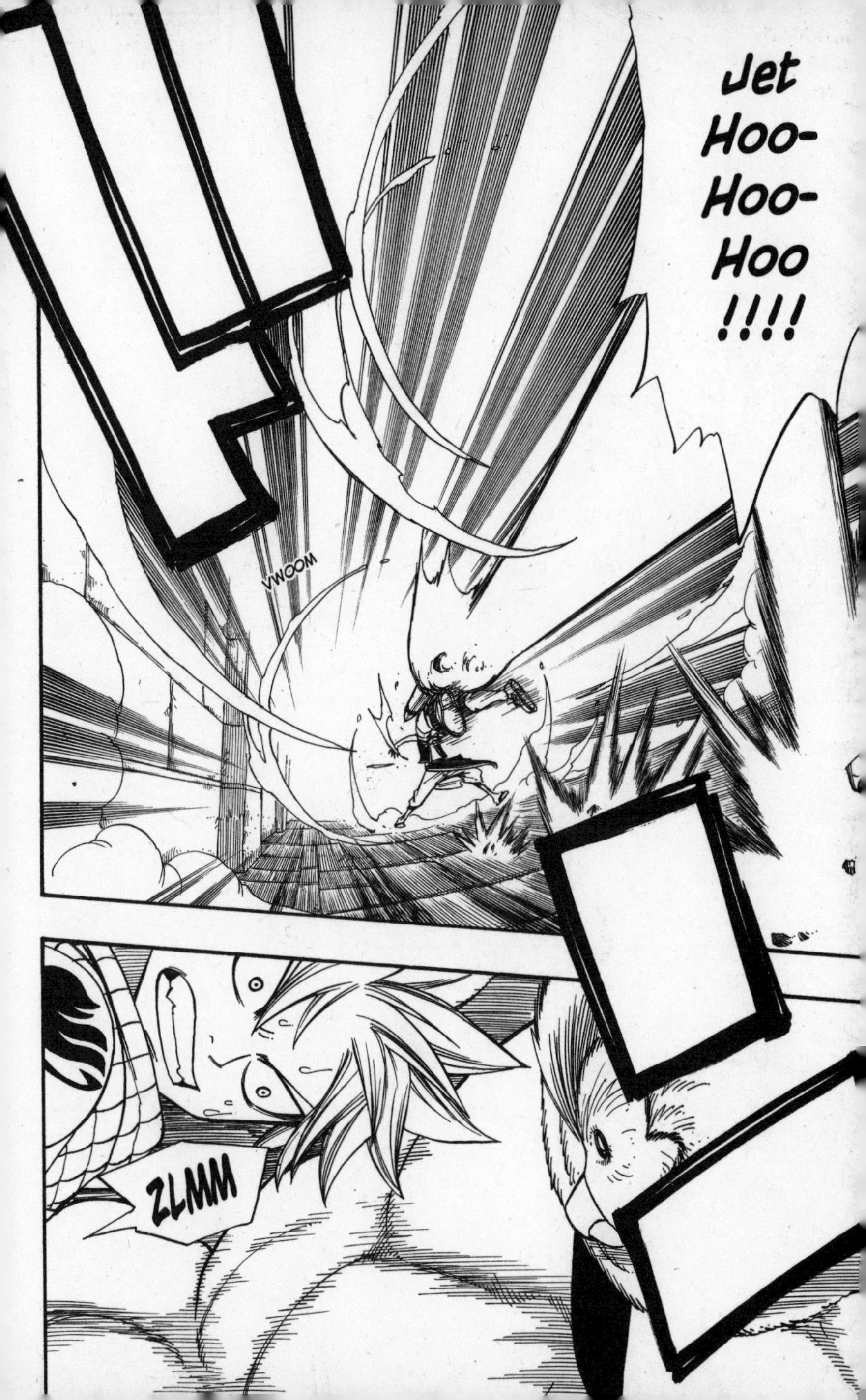
Jet Hoo-Hoo-Hoo !!!!
VWOOM
ZLMM

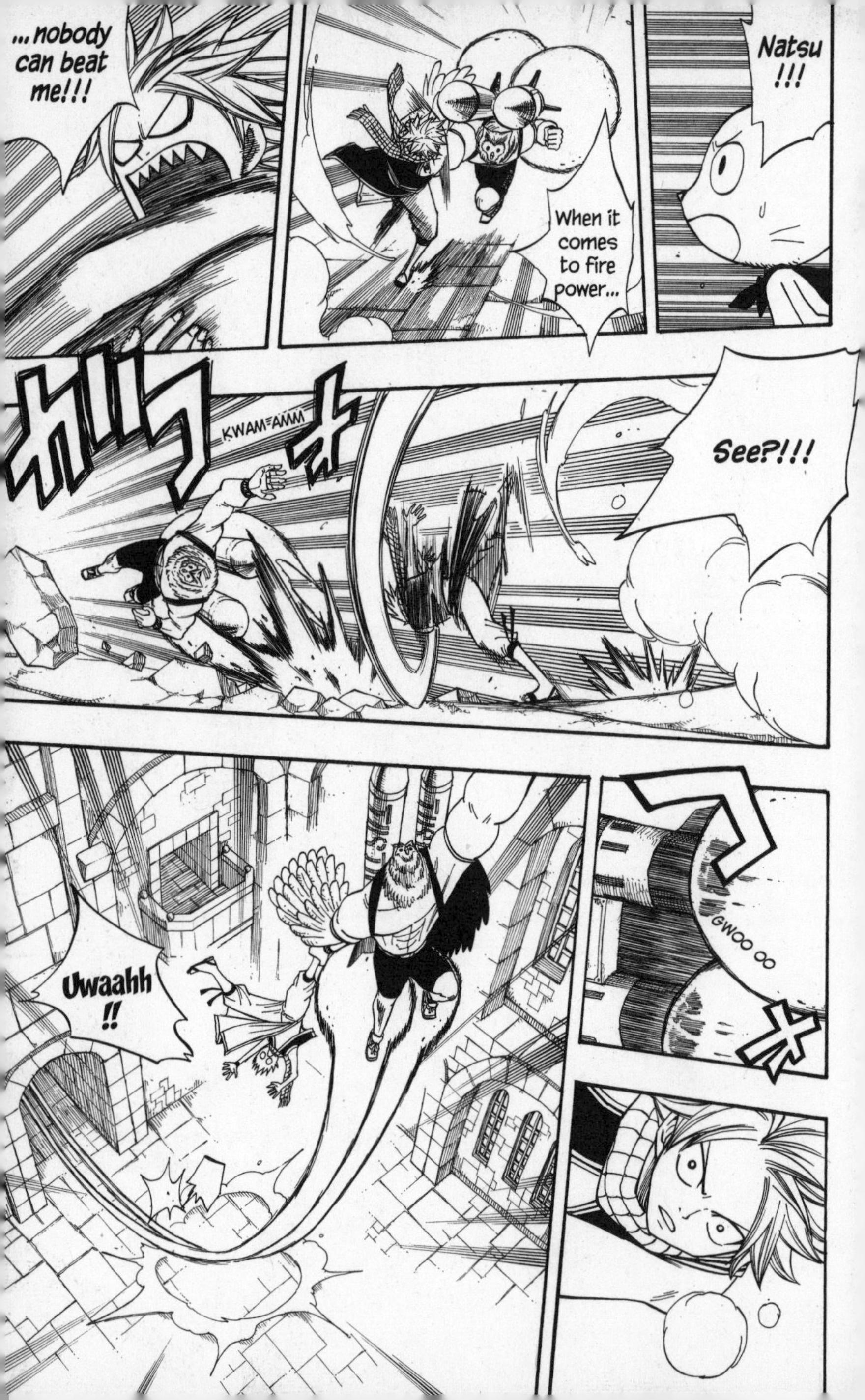
Natsu!!!
When it comes to fire power...
...nobody can beat me!!!
See?!!!
KWAM-AMM
GWOO OO
Uwaahh!!

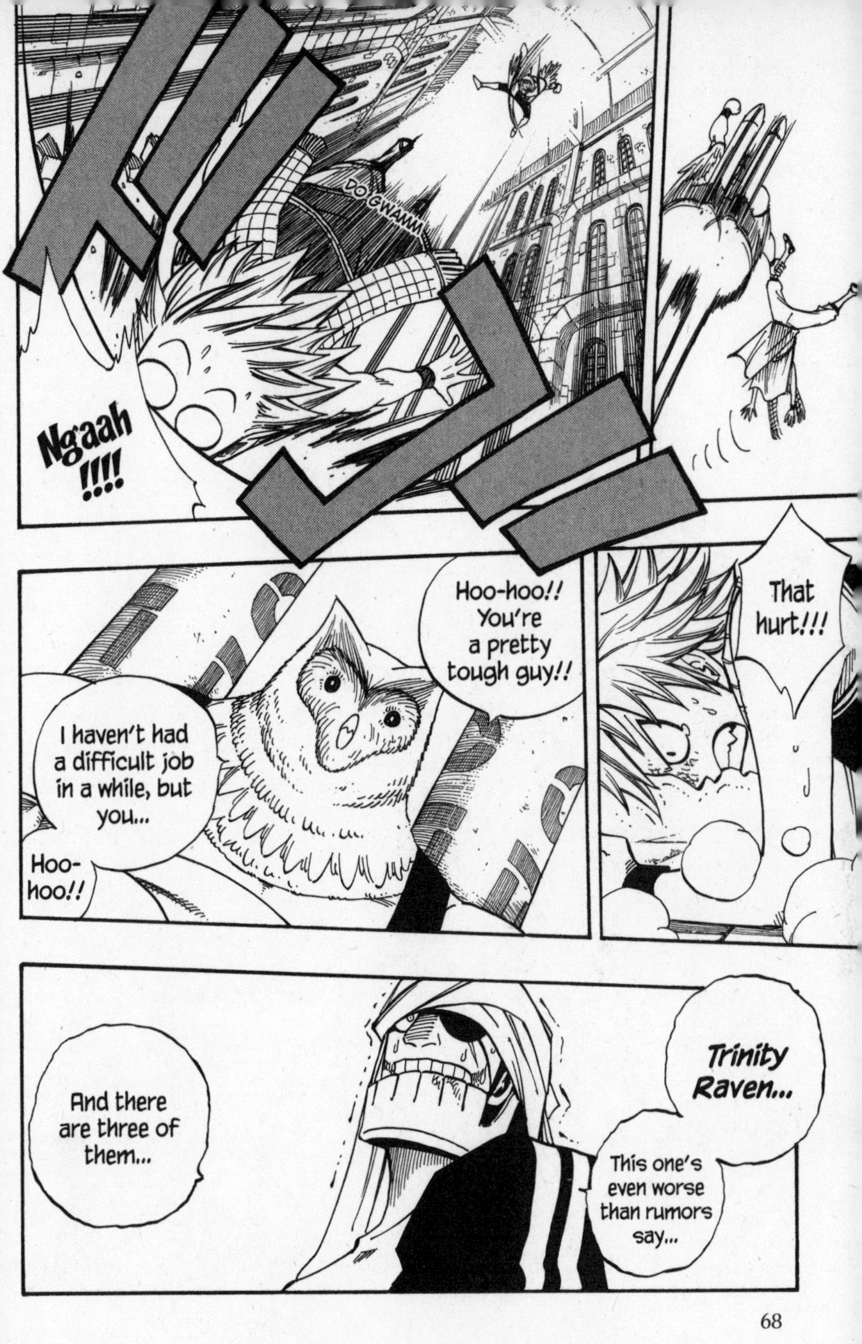
DO-GWAMM
Ngaah!!!!
That hurt!!!
Hoo-hoo!! You're a pretty tough guy!!
I haven't had a difficult job in a while, but you...
Hoo-hoo!!
Trinity Raven...
This one's even worse than rumors say...
And there are three of them...

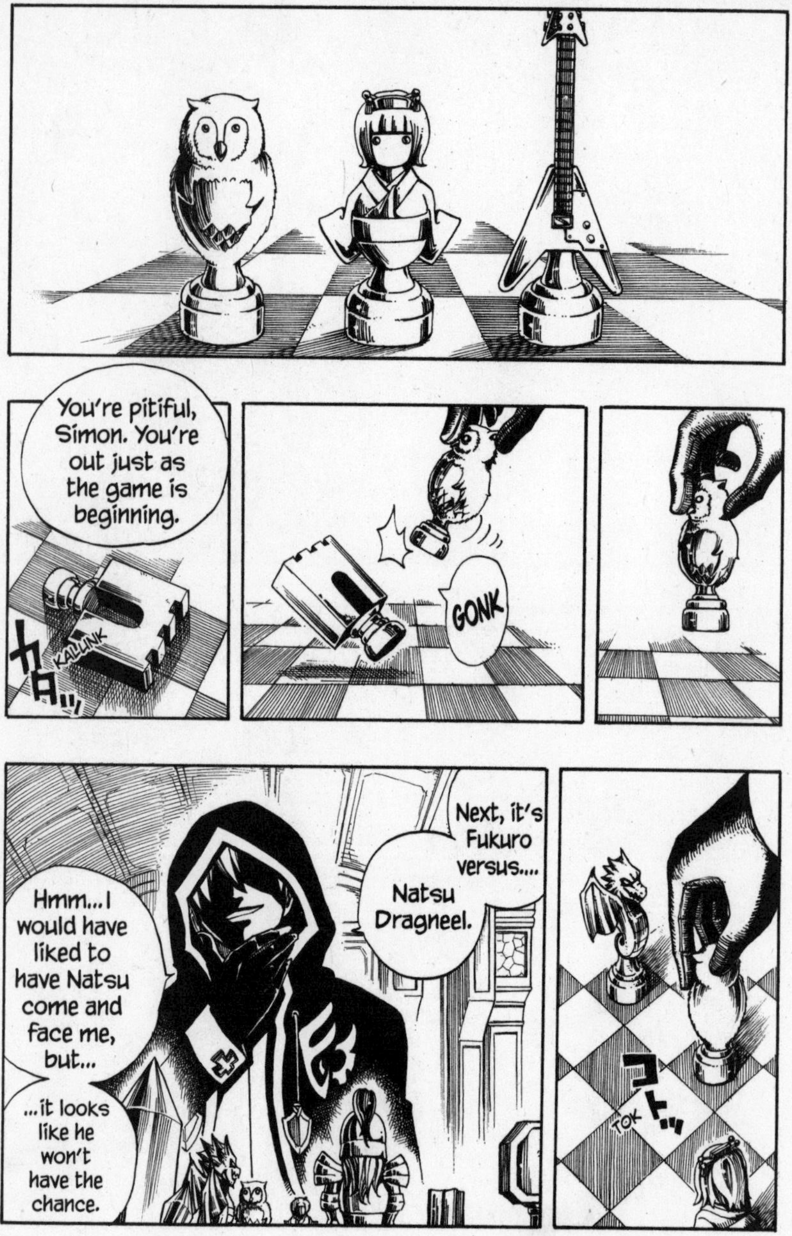
GONK
You're pitiful, Simon. You're out just as the game is beginning.
KALLINK
カタッ
TOK
コトッ
Next, it's Fukuro versus....
Natsu Dragneel.
Hmm...I would have liked to have Natsu come and face me, but...
...it looks like he won't have the chance.

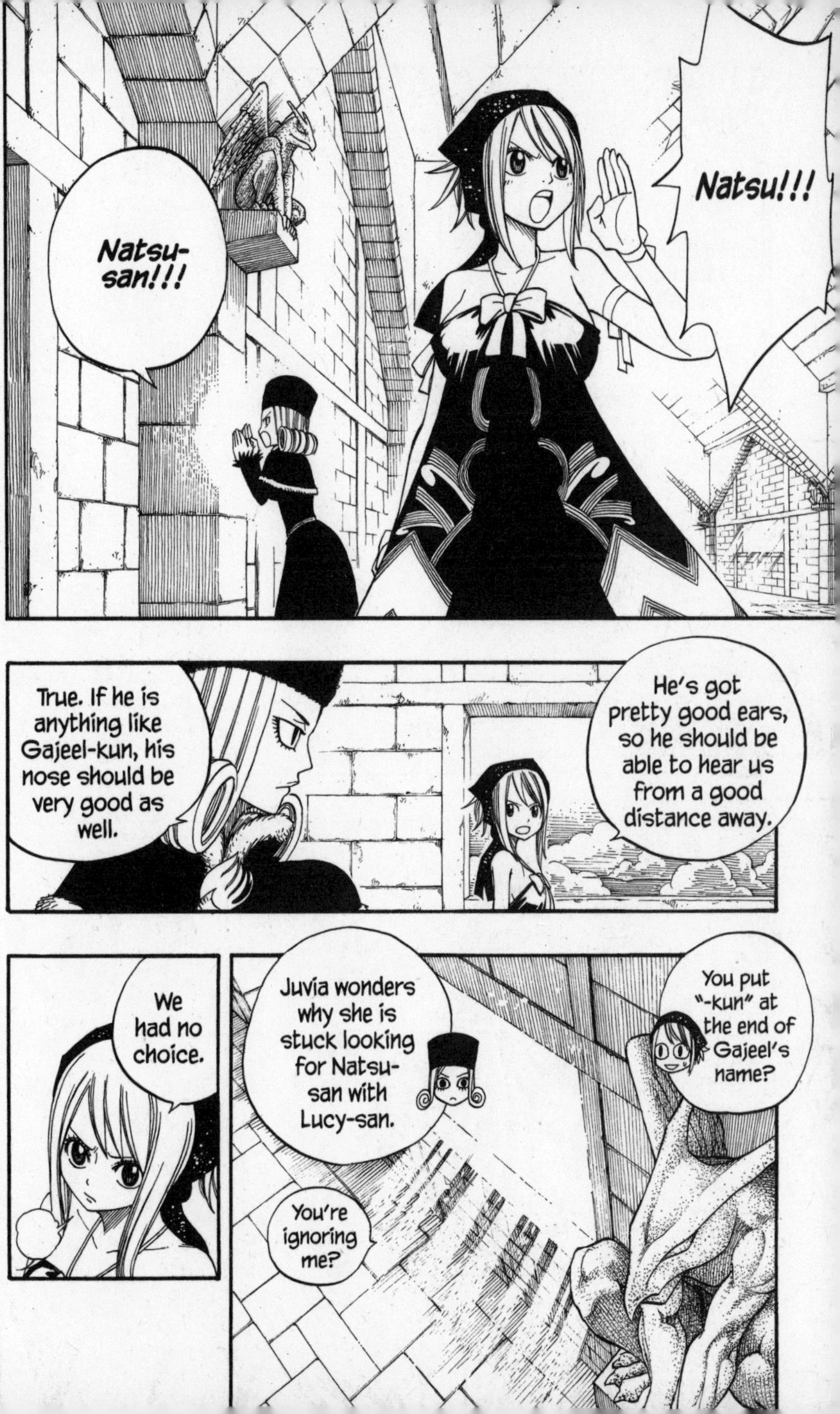
Natsu!!!
Natsu-san!!!
He's got pretty good ears, so he should be able to hear us from a good distance away.
True. If he is anything like Gajeel-kun, his nose should be very good as well.
You put "-kun" at the end of Gajeel's name?
Juvia wonders why she is stuck looking for Natsu-san with Lucy-san.
You're ignoring me?
We had no choice.

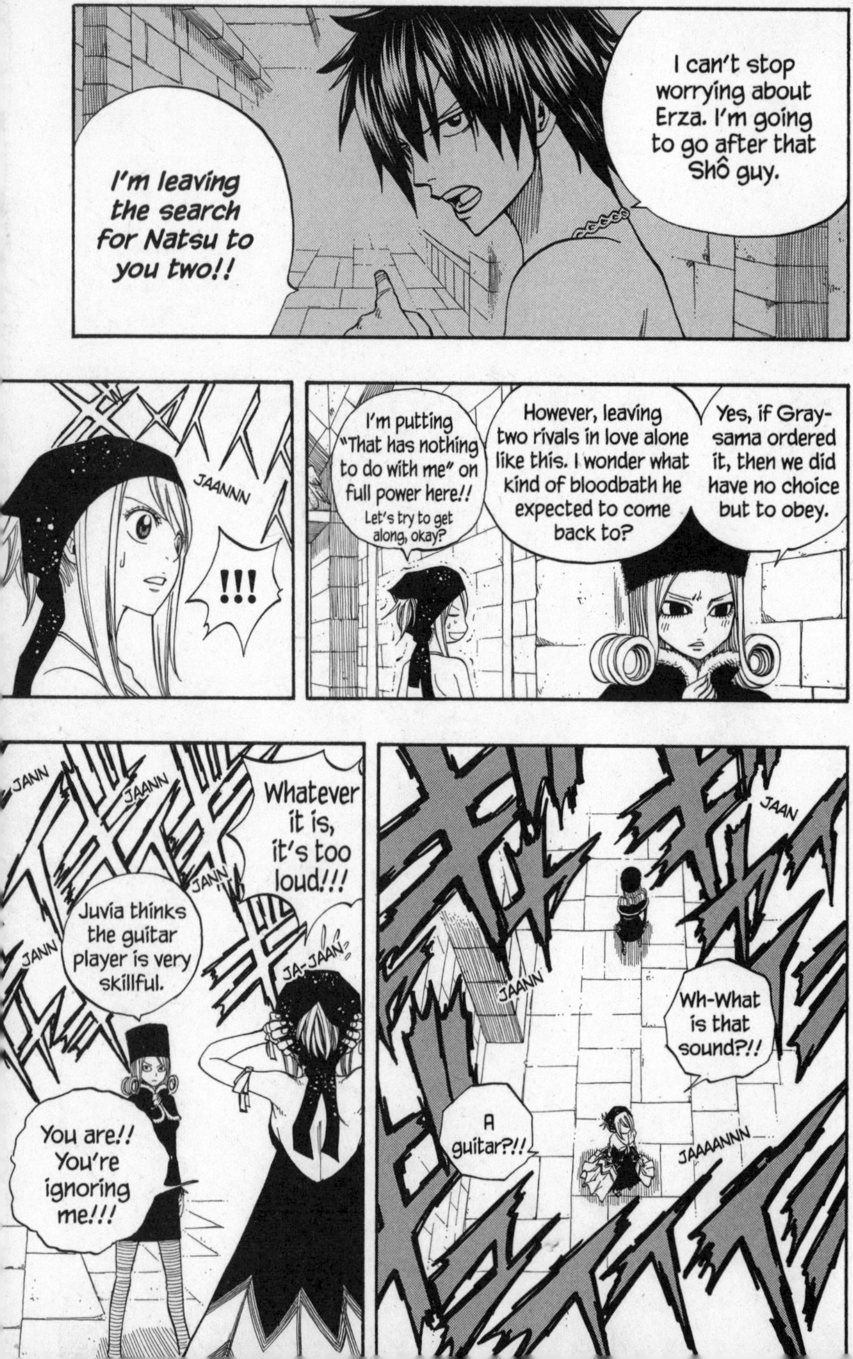
I can't stop worrying about Erza. I'm going to go after that Shô guy.
I'm leaving the search for Natsu to you two!!
Yes, if Gray-sama ordered it, then we did have no choice but to obey.
However, leaving two rivals in love alone like this. I wonder what kind of bloodbath he expected to come back to?
I'm putting "That has nothing to do with me" on full power here!!
Let's try to get along, okay?
JAANNN
!!!
JAAN
Wh-What is that sound?!!
JAANN
A guitar?!!
JAAAANNN
Whatever it is, it's too loud!!!
JAANN
JANN
JANN
Juvia thinks the guitar player is very skillful.
JANN
JA-JAAN
You are!! You're ignoring me!!!

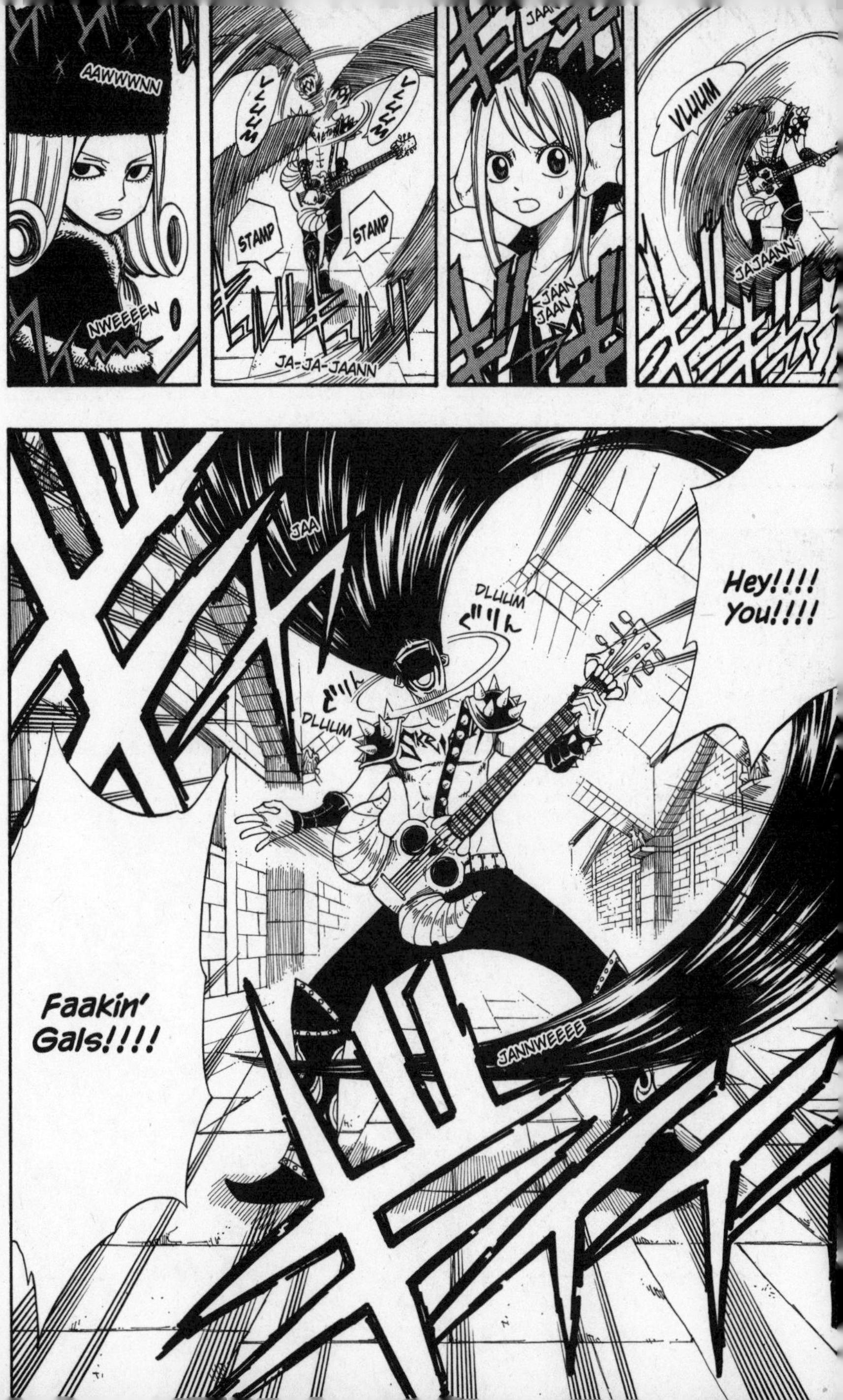
VLUUM
JAJAANN
JAAN
JA'AN JAAN
VLUUM
VLUUM
STAMP
STAMP
JA-JA-JAANN
AAWWWNN
NWEEEEN
Hey!!!! You!!!!
JAA
DLUUM
DLUUM
JANNWEEEE
Faakin' Gals!!!!

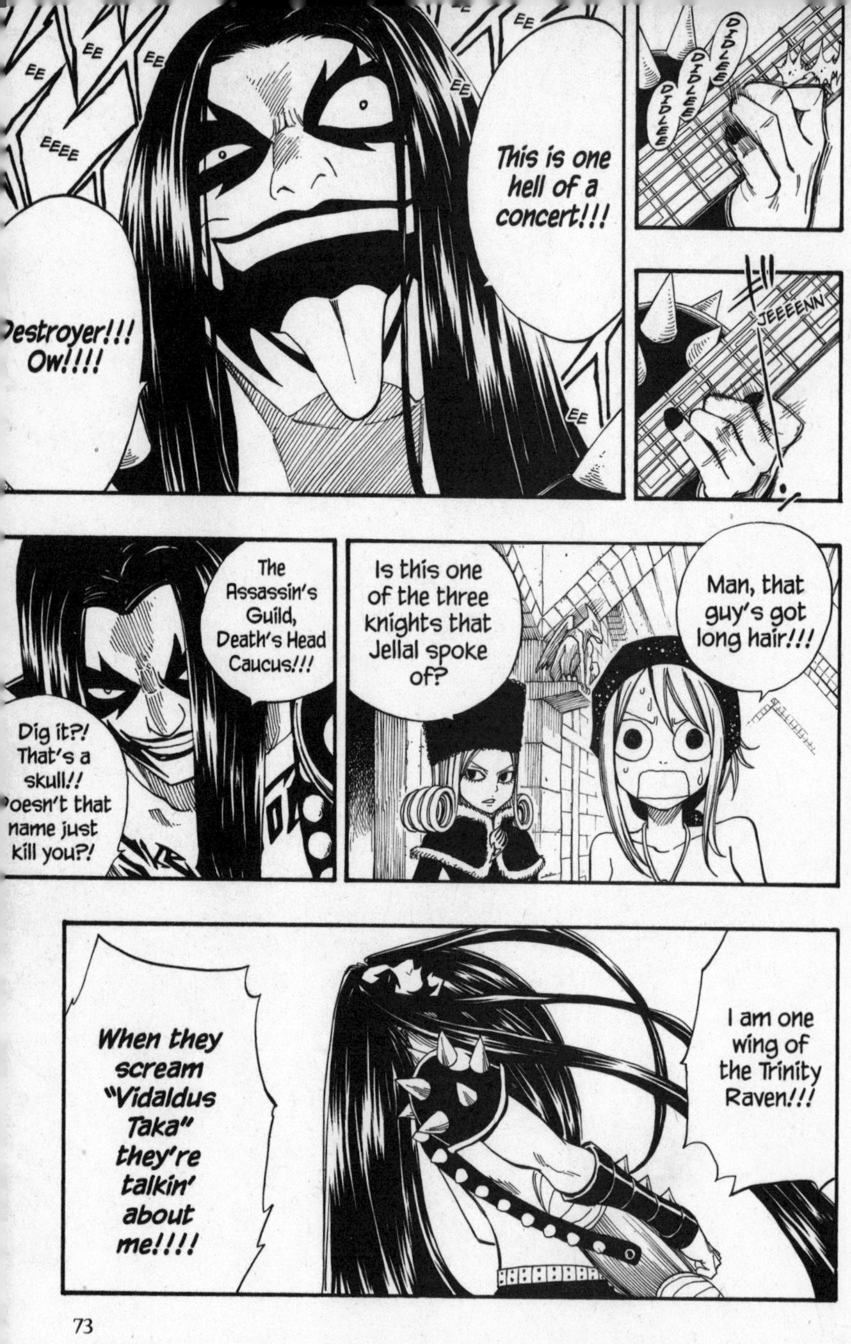
DIDLEE DIDLEE DIDLEE
JEEEENN
EE EE EE EE EE EEEE EE
This is one hell of a concert!!!
Destroyer!!! Ow!!!!
Man, that guy's got long hair!!!
Is this one of the three knights that Jellal spoke of?
The Assassin's Guild, Death's Head Caucus!!!
Dig it?! That's a skull!! Doesn't that name just kill you?!
I am one wing of the Trinity Raven!!!
When they scream "Vidaldus Taka" they're talkin' about me!!!!

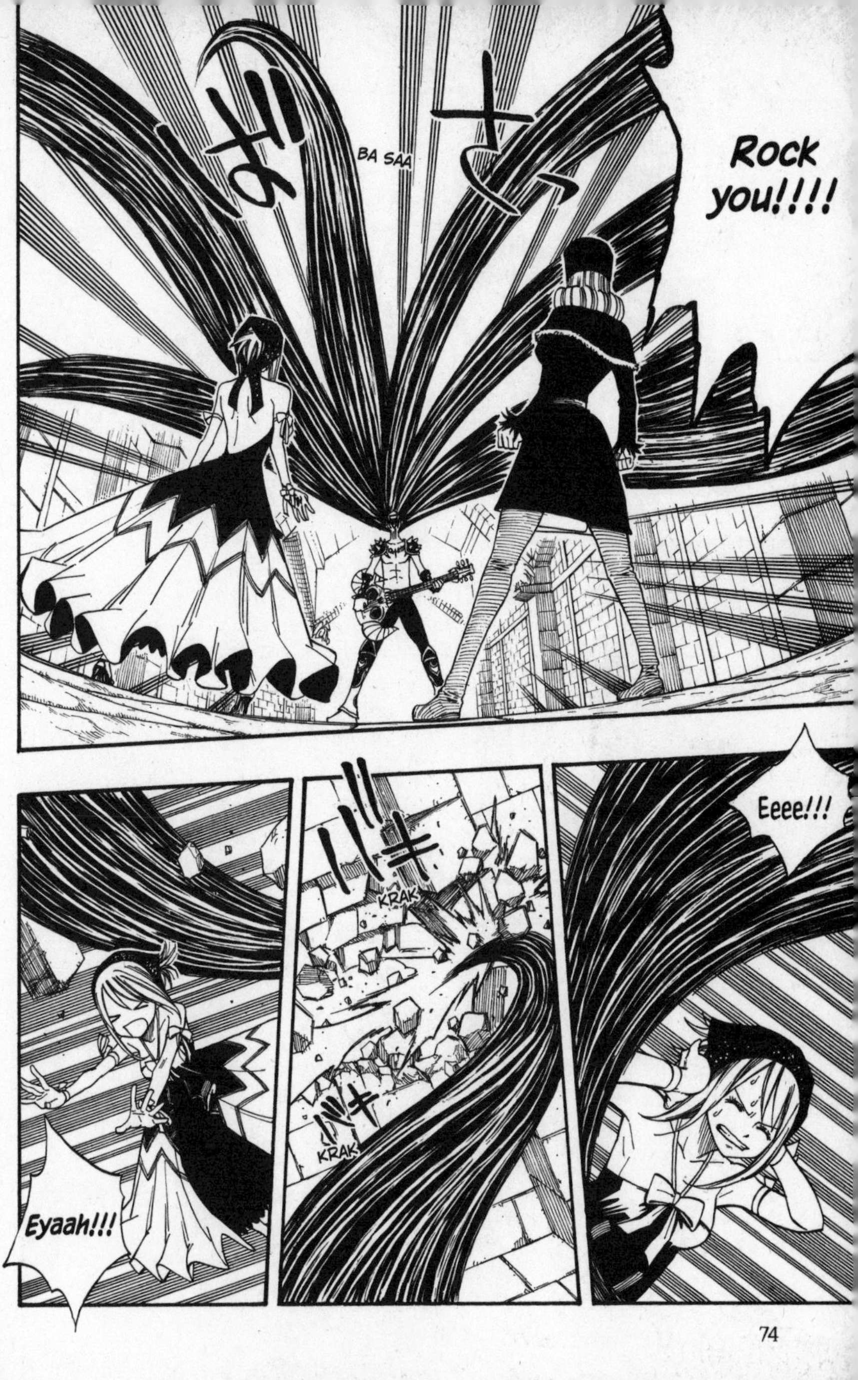
Rock you!!!!
BA SAA
Eeee!!!
KRAK
KRAK
Eyaah!!!

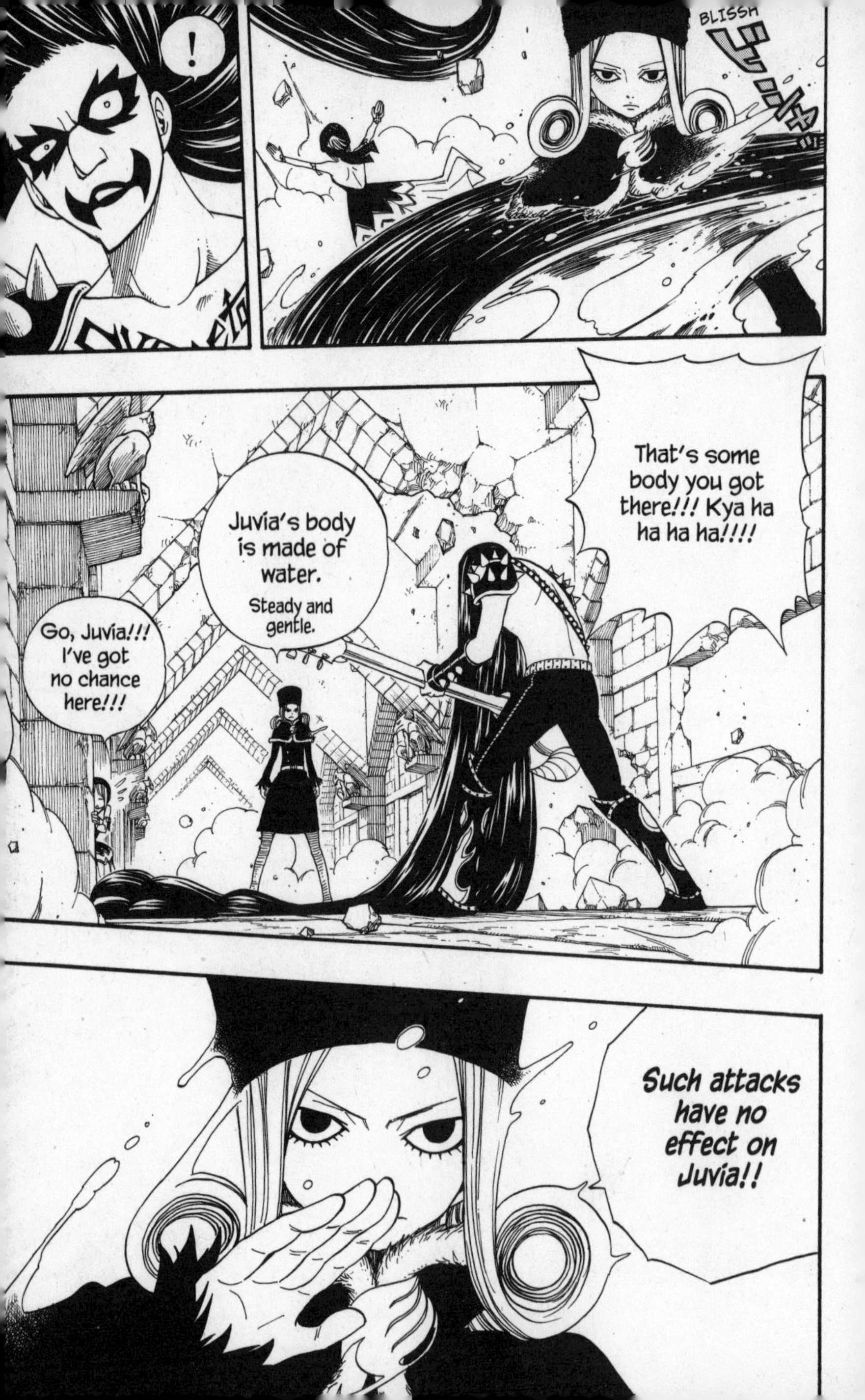
BLISSH
!
That's some body you got there!!! Kya ha ha ha ha!!!!
Juvia's body is made of water.
Steady and gentle.
Go, Juvia!!! I've got no chance here!!!
Such attacks have no effect on Juvia!!

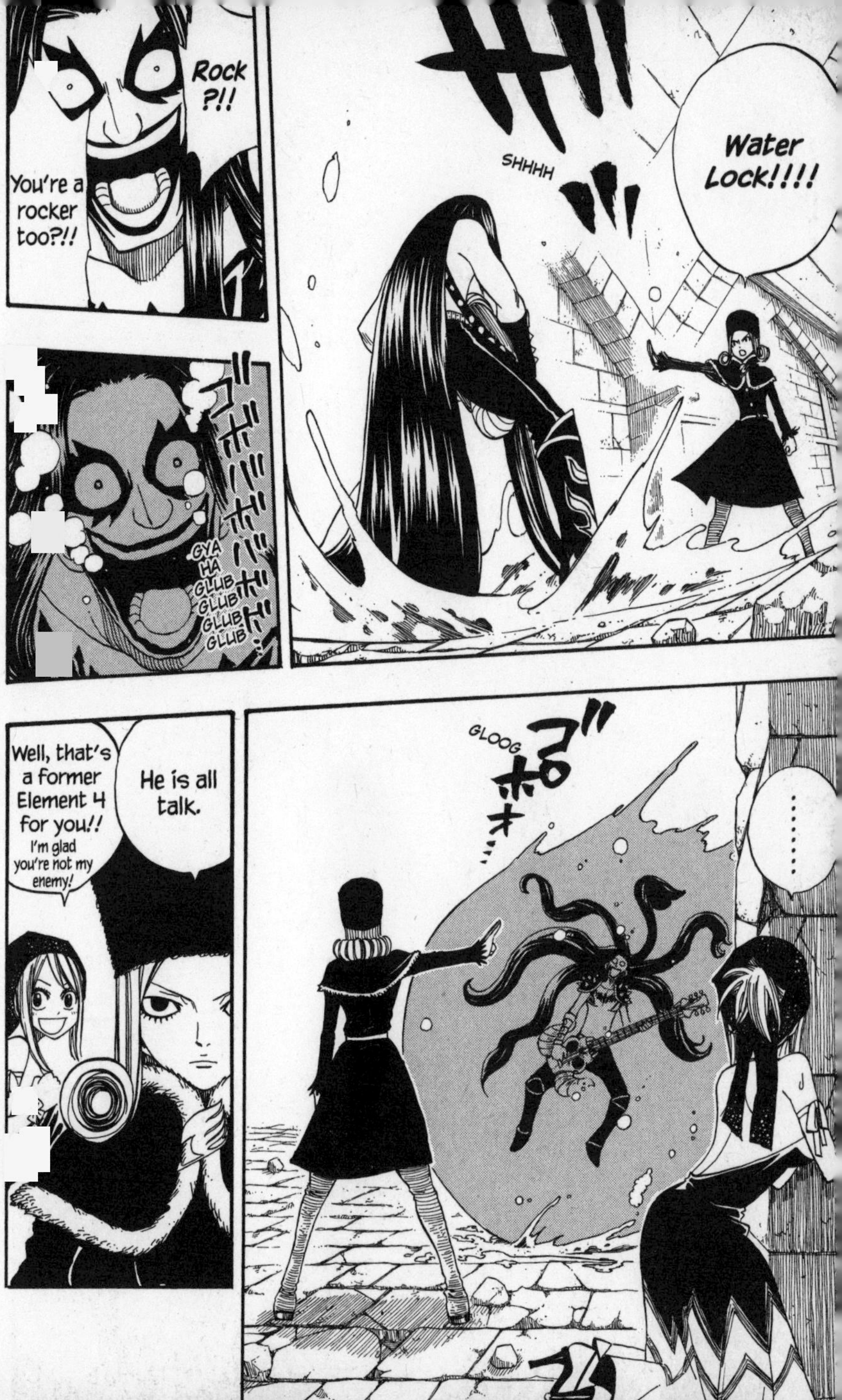
SHHHH
Water Lock!!!!
Rock?!!
You're a rocker too?!!
GYA HA GLUB GLUB GLUB GLUB
GLOOG
......
He is all talk.
Well, that's a former Element 4 for you!!
I'm glad you're not my enemy!

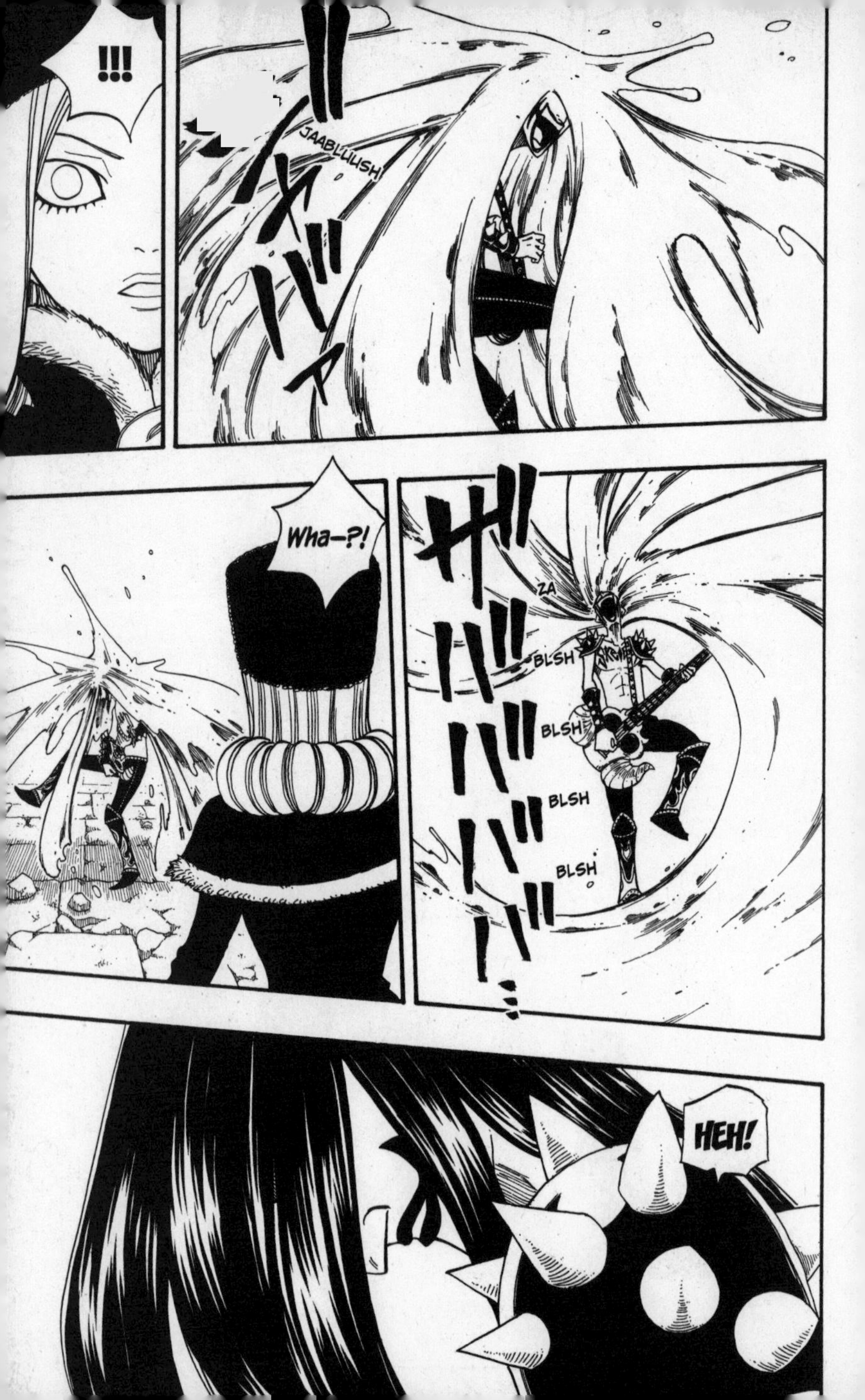
JAABLUUSH
!!!
ZA
BLSH
BLSH
BLSH
BLSH
Wha-?!
HEH!

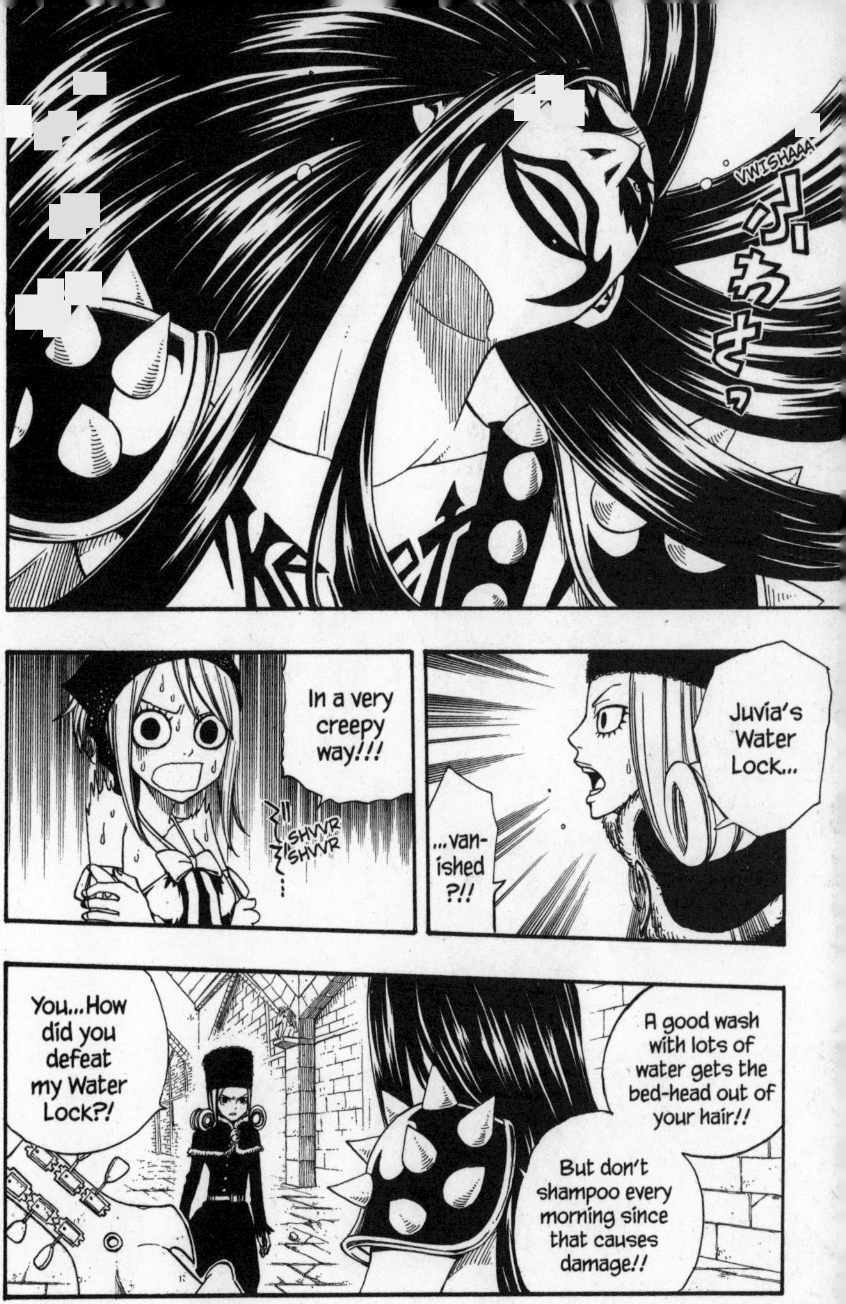
VWISHAAA
ふあさっ
Juvia's Water Lock...
...van-ished?!!
In a very creepy way!!!
SHVVR SHVVR
You...How did you defeat my Water Lock?!
A good wash with lots of water gets the bed-head out of your hair!!
But don't shampoo every morning since that causes damage!!

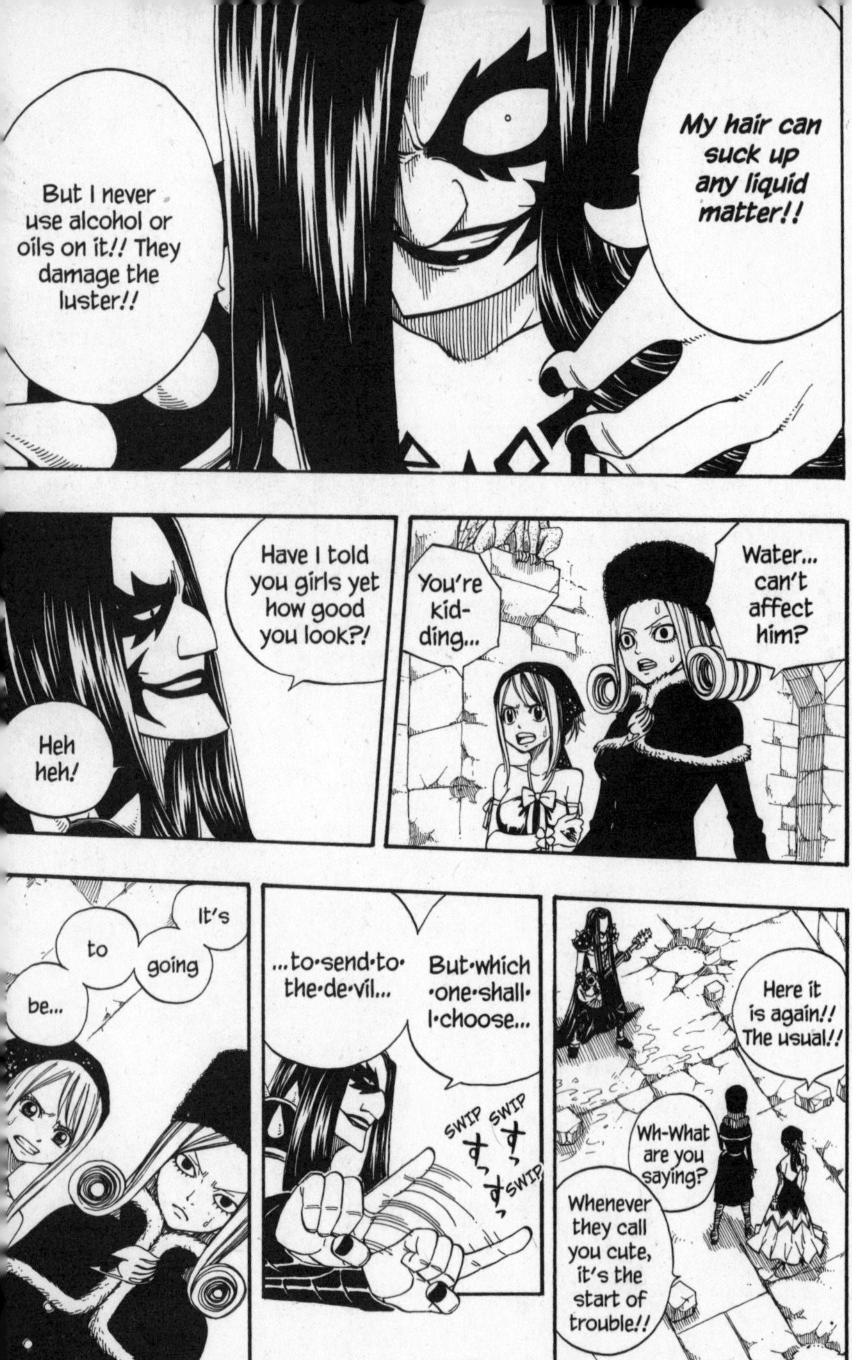
My hair can suck up any liquid matter!!
But I never use alcohol or oils on it!! They damage the luster!!
Water... can't affect him?
You're kid-ding...
Have I told you girls yet how good you look?!
Heh heh!
Here it is again!! The usual!!
Wh-What are you saying?
Whenever they call you cute, it's the start of trouble!!
But·which ·one·shall· I·choose...
...to·send·to· the·de·vil...
SWIP SWIP SWIP
It's going to be...

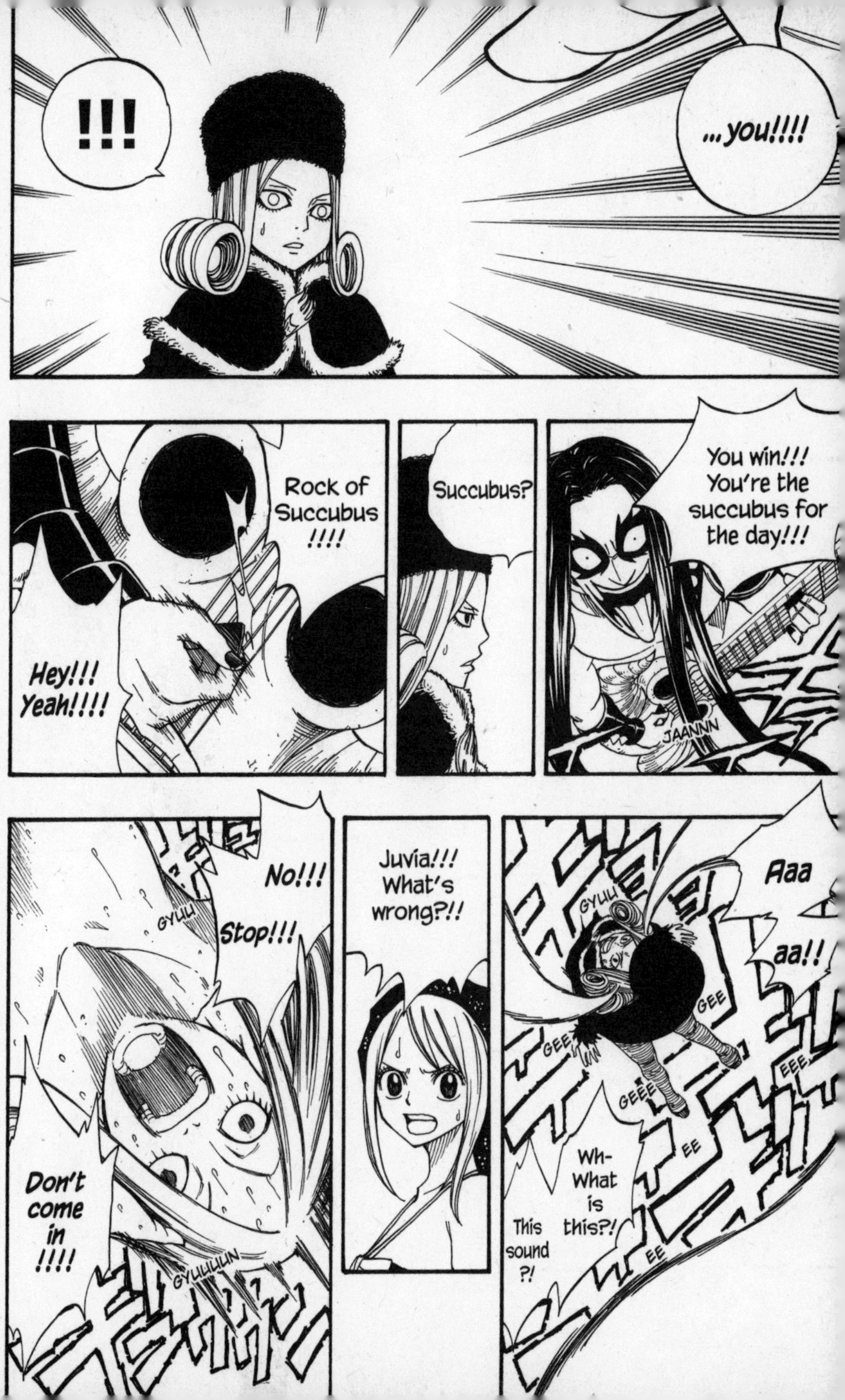
...you!!!!
!!!
You win!!! You're the succubus for the day!!!
JAANNN
Succubus?
Rock of Succubus !!!!
Hey!!! Yeah!!!!
Aaa aa!!
GYUU
GEE
EEE
GEE
GEEE
EE
Wh- What is this?!
This sound ?!
EE
Juvia!!! What's wrong?!!
No!!! Stop!!!
GYUU
Don't come in !!!!
GYUUUUN

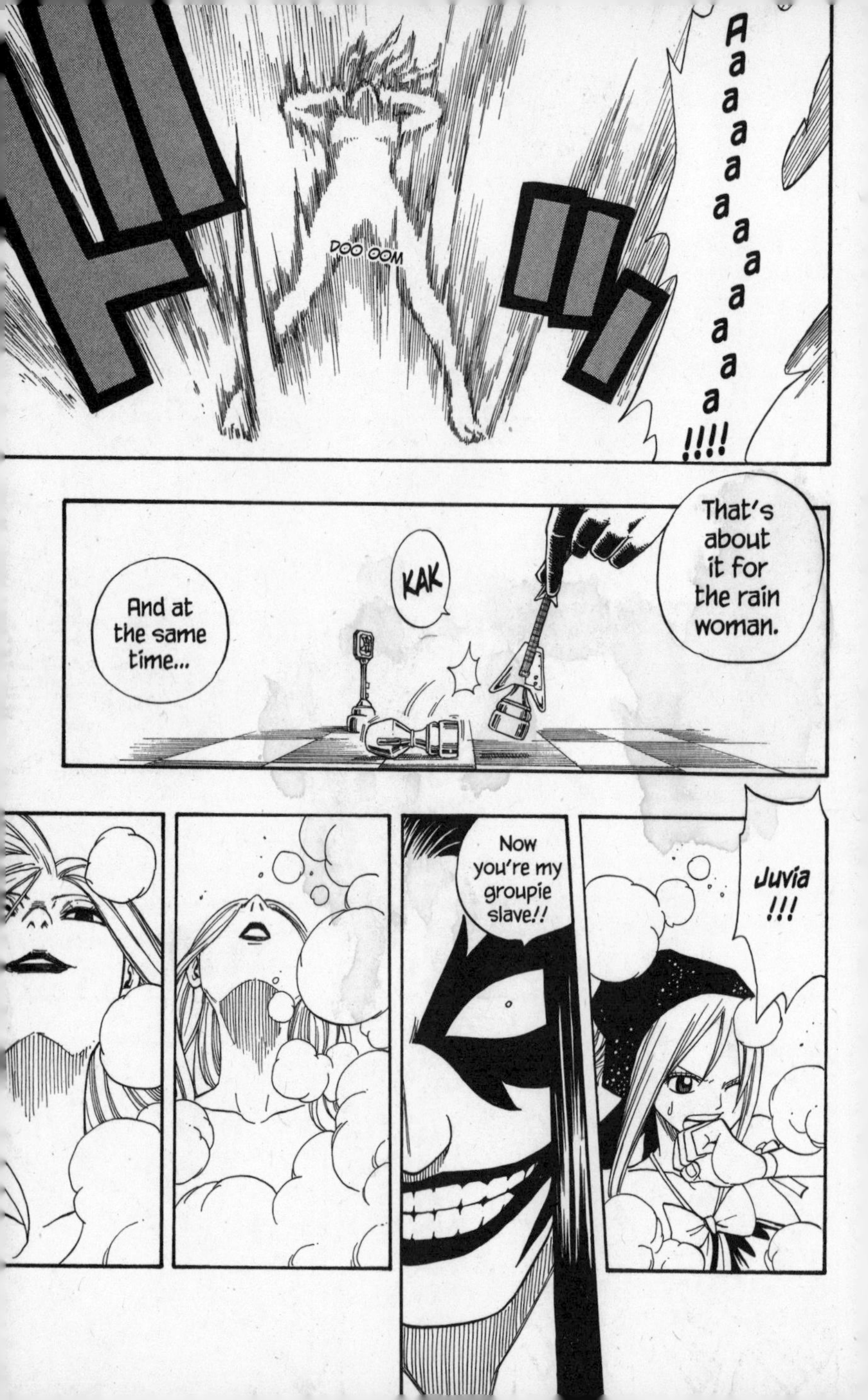
Aaaaaaaaaaaa!!!!
DOO OOM
That's about it for the rain woman.
KAK
And at the same time...
Juvia!!!
Now you're my groupie slave!!

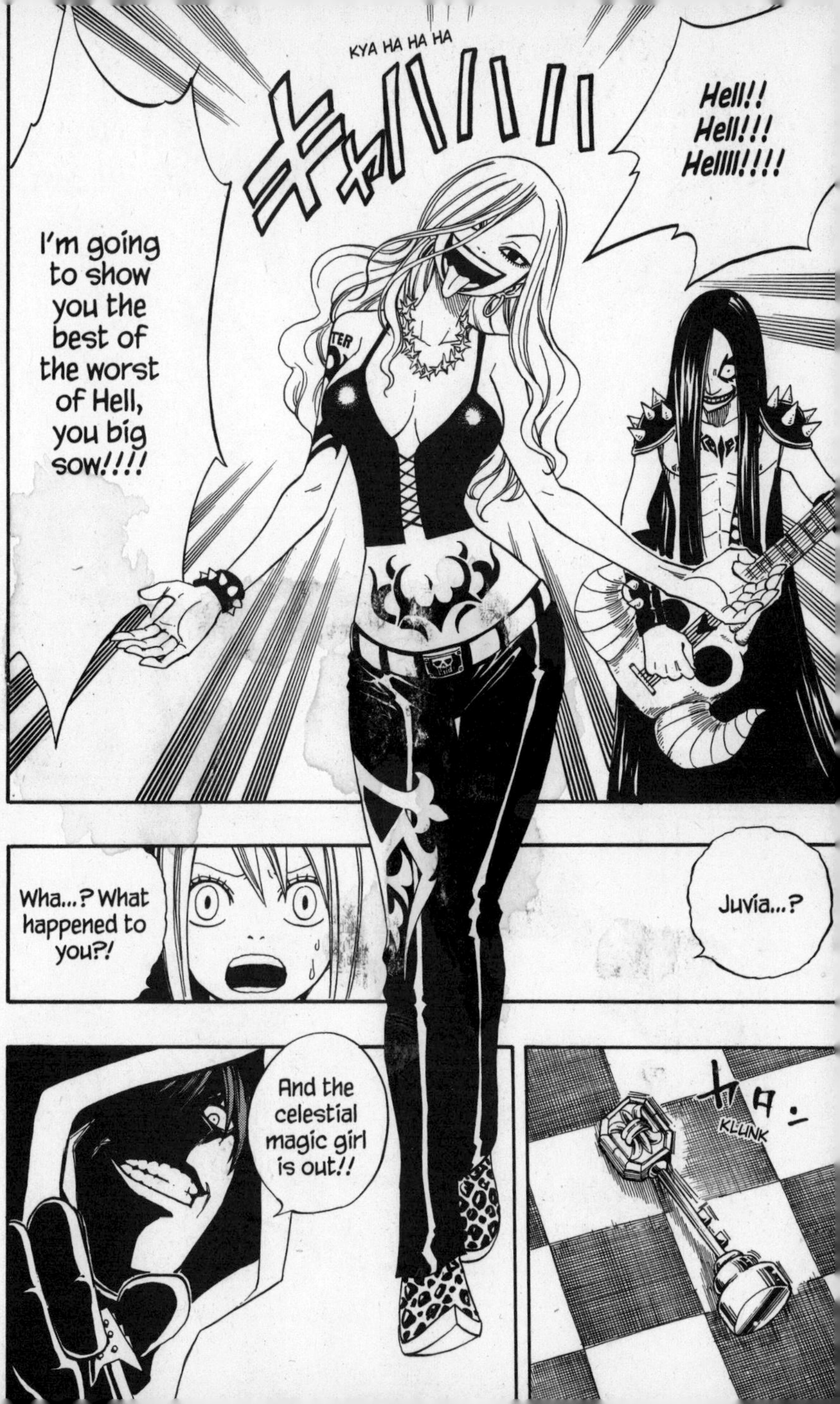
Hell!! Hell!!! Helllll!!!!
KYA HA HA HA
I'm going to show you the best of the worst of Hell, you big sow!!!!
Juvia...?
Wha...? What happened to you?!
KLUNK
And the celestial magic girl is out!!

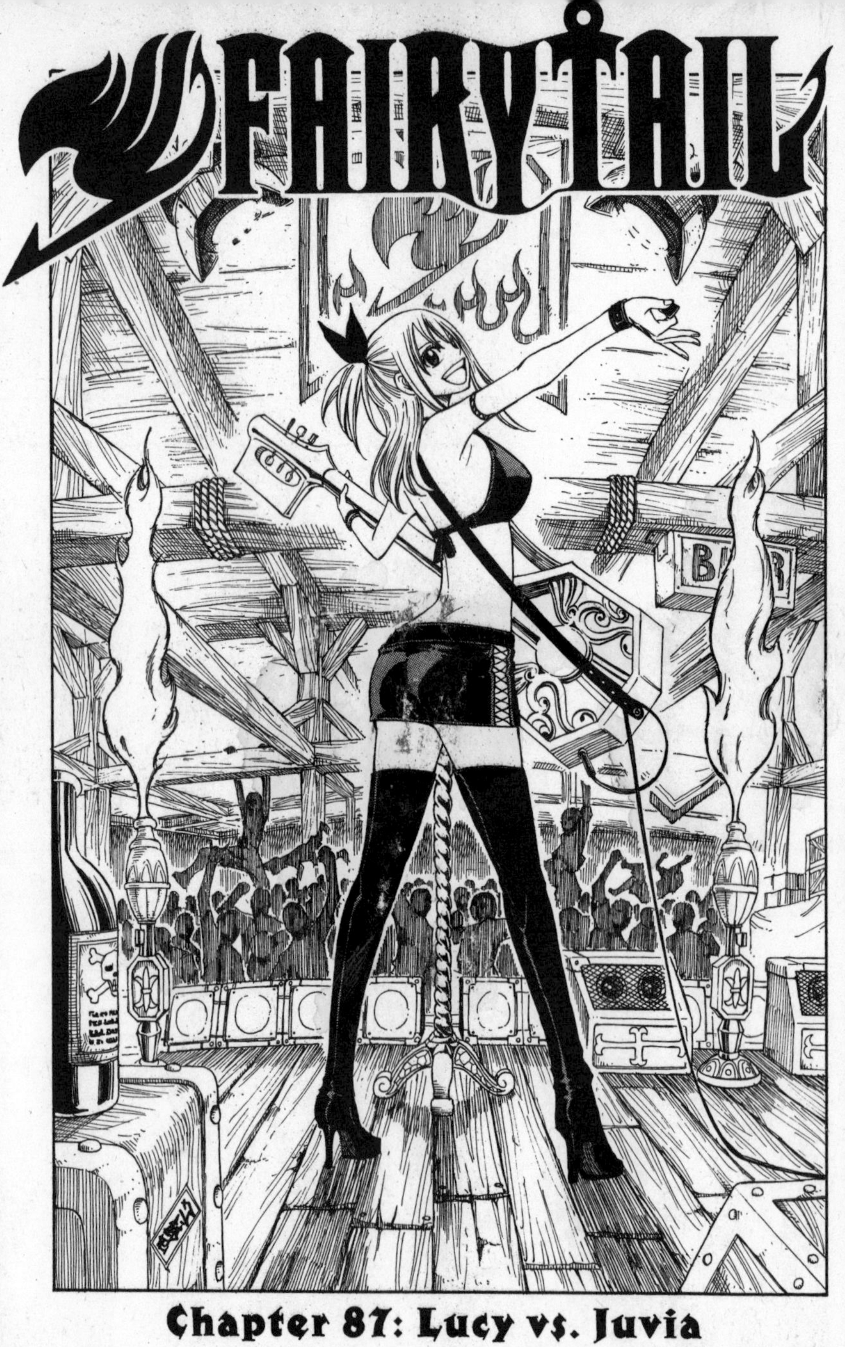
FAIRY TAIL

Chapter 87: Lucy vs. Juvia

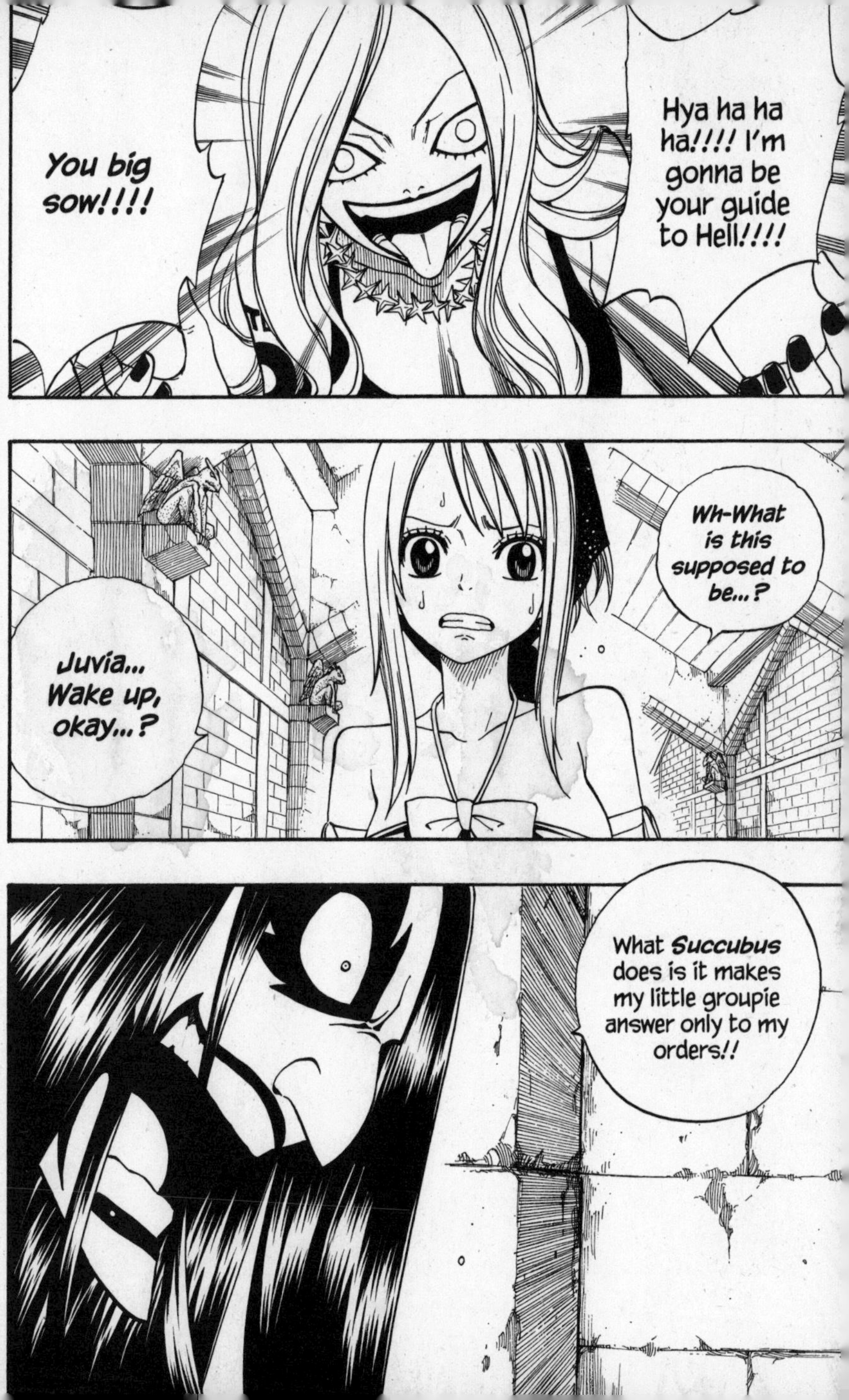
Hya ha ha!!!! I'm gonna be your guide to Hell!!!!
You big sow!!!!
Wh-What is this supposed to be...?
Juvia... Wake up, okay...?
What *Succubus* does is it makes my little groupie answer only to my orders!!

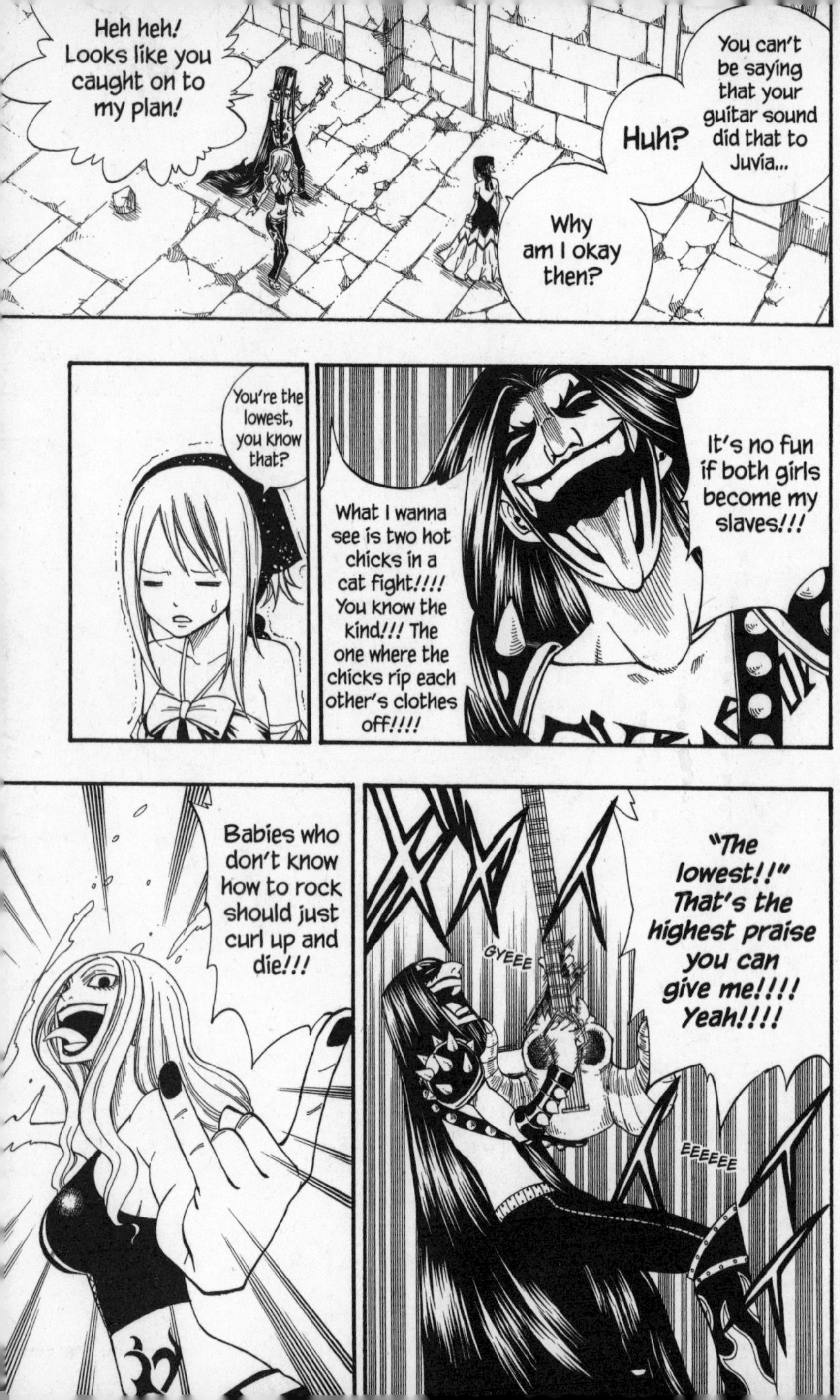

You can't be saying that your guitar sound did that to Juvia...
Huh?
Why am I okay then?
Heh heh! Looks like you caught on to my plan!
It's no fun if both girls become my slaves!!!
What I wanna see is two hot chicks in a cat fight!!!! You know the kind!!! The one where the chicks rip each other's clothes off!!!!
You're the lowest, you know that?
"The lowest!!" That's the highest praise you can give me!!!! Yeah!!!!
GYEEE
EEEEEE
Babies who don't know how to rock should just curl up and die!!!

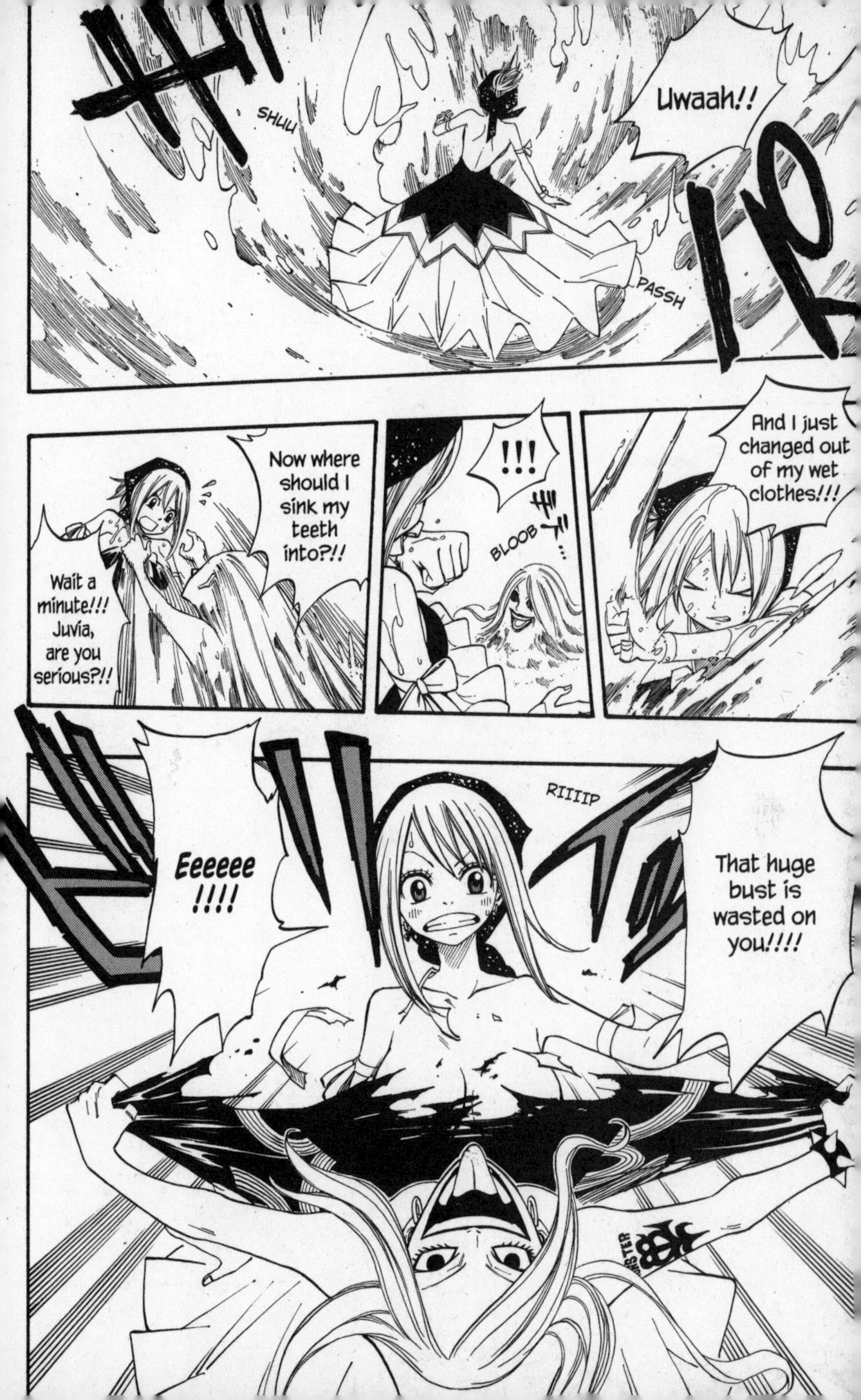
Uwaah!!
PASSH
SHUU
And I just changed out of my wet clothes!!!
!!!
BLOOB
Now where should I sink my teeth into?!!
Wait a minute!!! Juvia, are you serious?!!
That huge bust is wasted on you!!!!
RIIIIP
Eeeeee !!!!

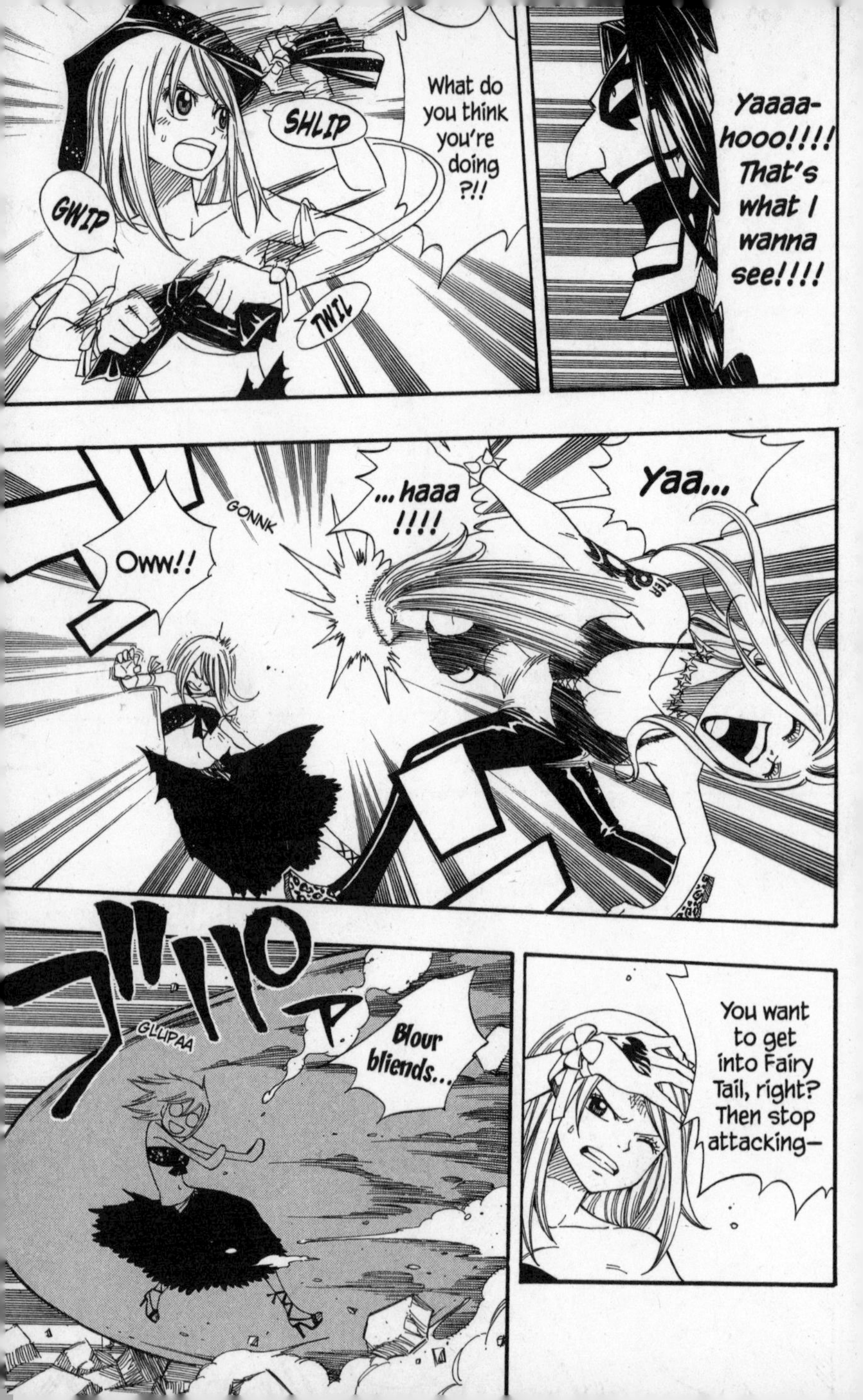
Yaaaa-hooo!!!! That's what I wanna see!!!!
What do you think you're doing?!!
SHLIP
GWIP
TWIL
Yaa...
...haaa!!!!
GONNK
Oww!!
You want to get into Fairy Tail, right? Then stop attacking—
Blour bliends...
GLUPAA

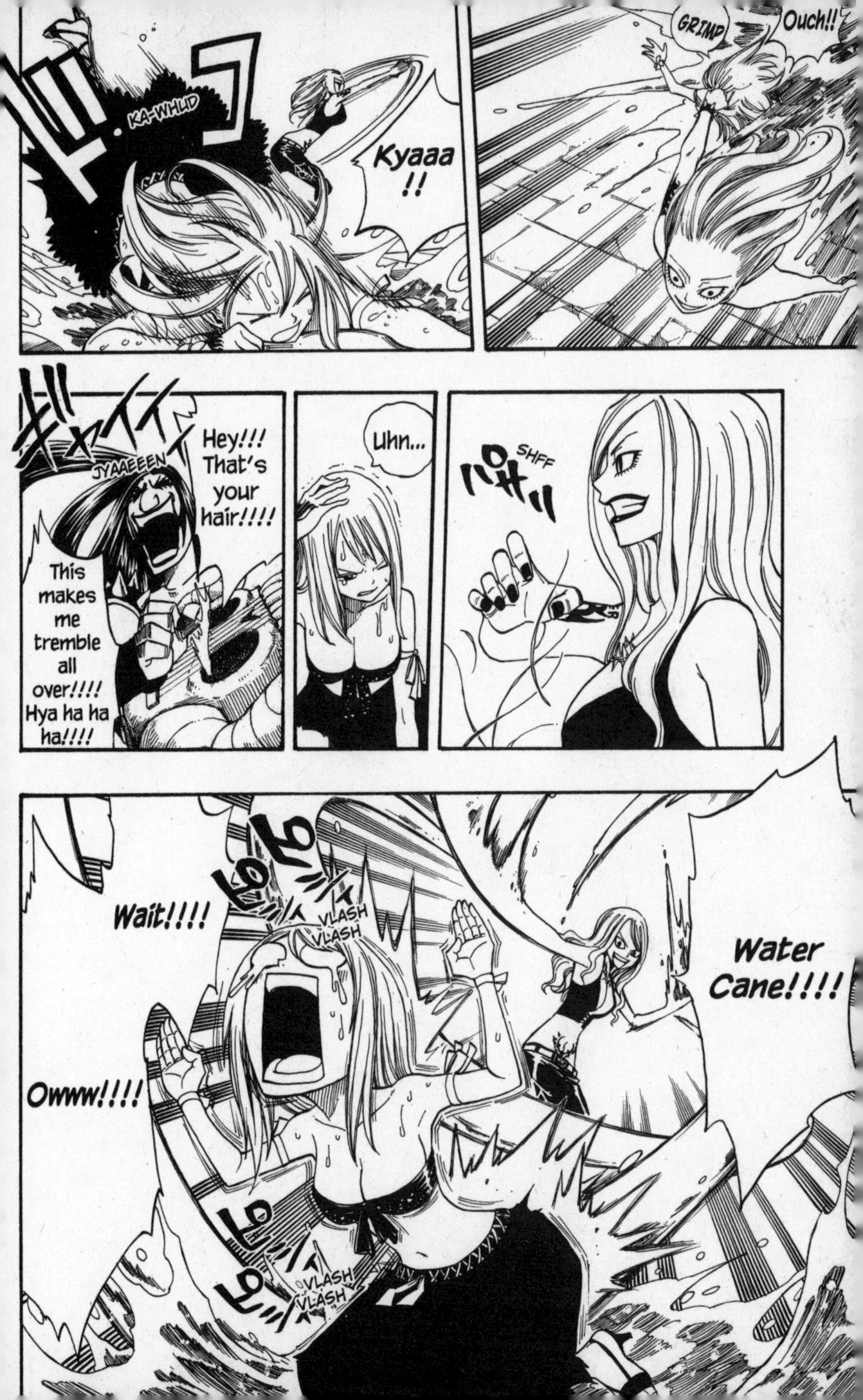
GRIMP
Ouch!!
KA-WHUD
Kyaaa!!
SHFF
Uhn...
JYAAEEEN
Hey!!! That's your hair!!!!
This makes me tremble all over!!!! Hya ha ha ha!!!!
Water Cane!!!!
VLASH VLASH
Wait!!!!
Owww!!!!
VLASH VLASH

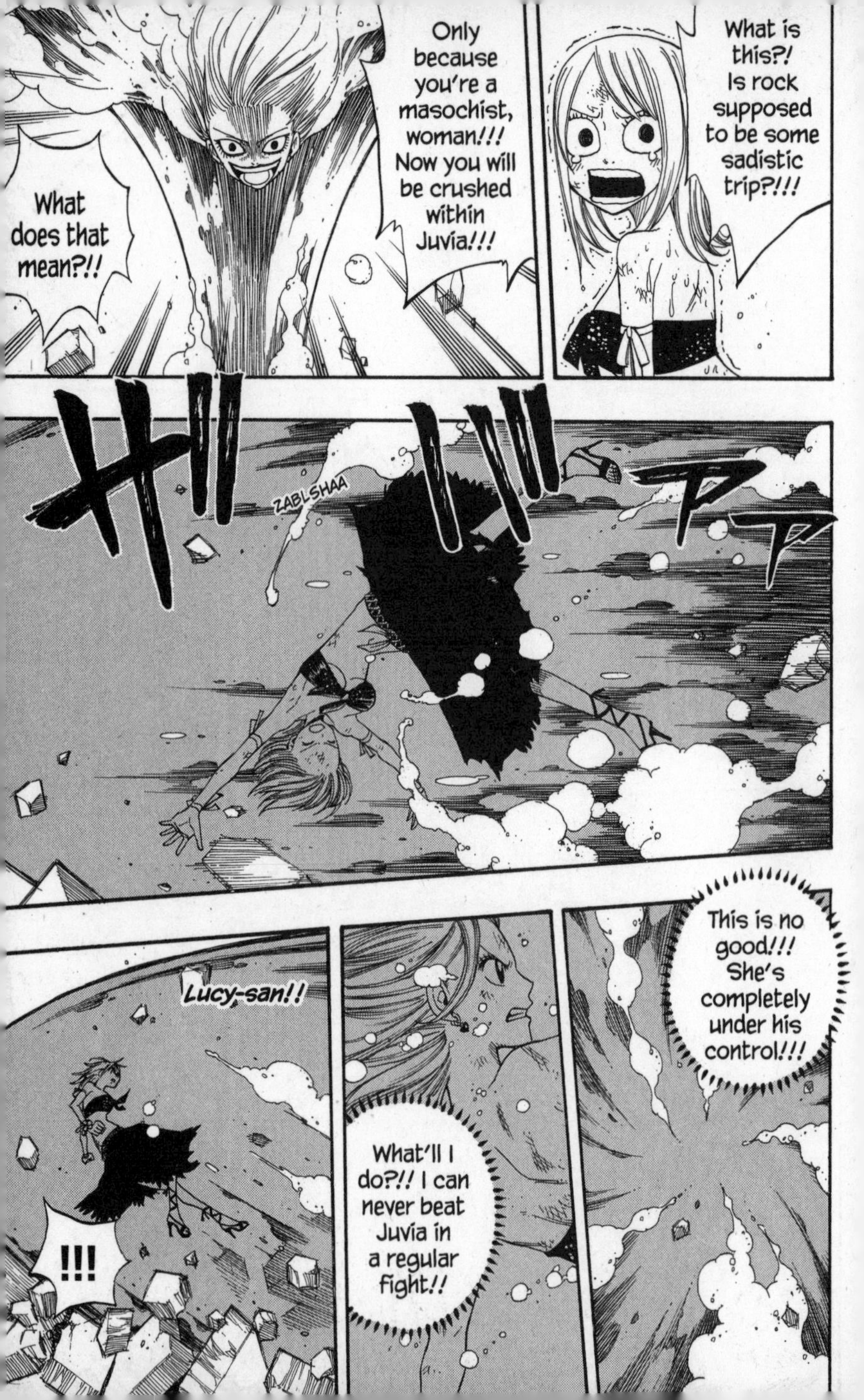
What is this?! Is rock supposed to be some sadistic trip?!!!
Only because you're a masochist, woman!!! Now you will be crushed within Juvia!!!
What does that mean?!!
ZABLSHAA
This is no good!!! She's completely under his control!!!
What'll I do?!! I can never beat Juvia in a regular fight!!
Lucy-san!!
!!!

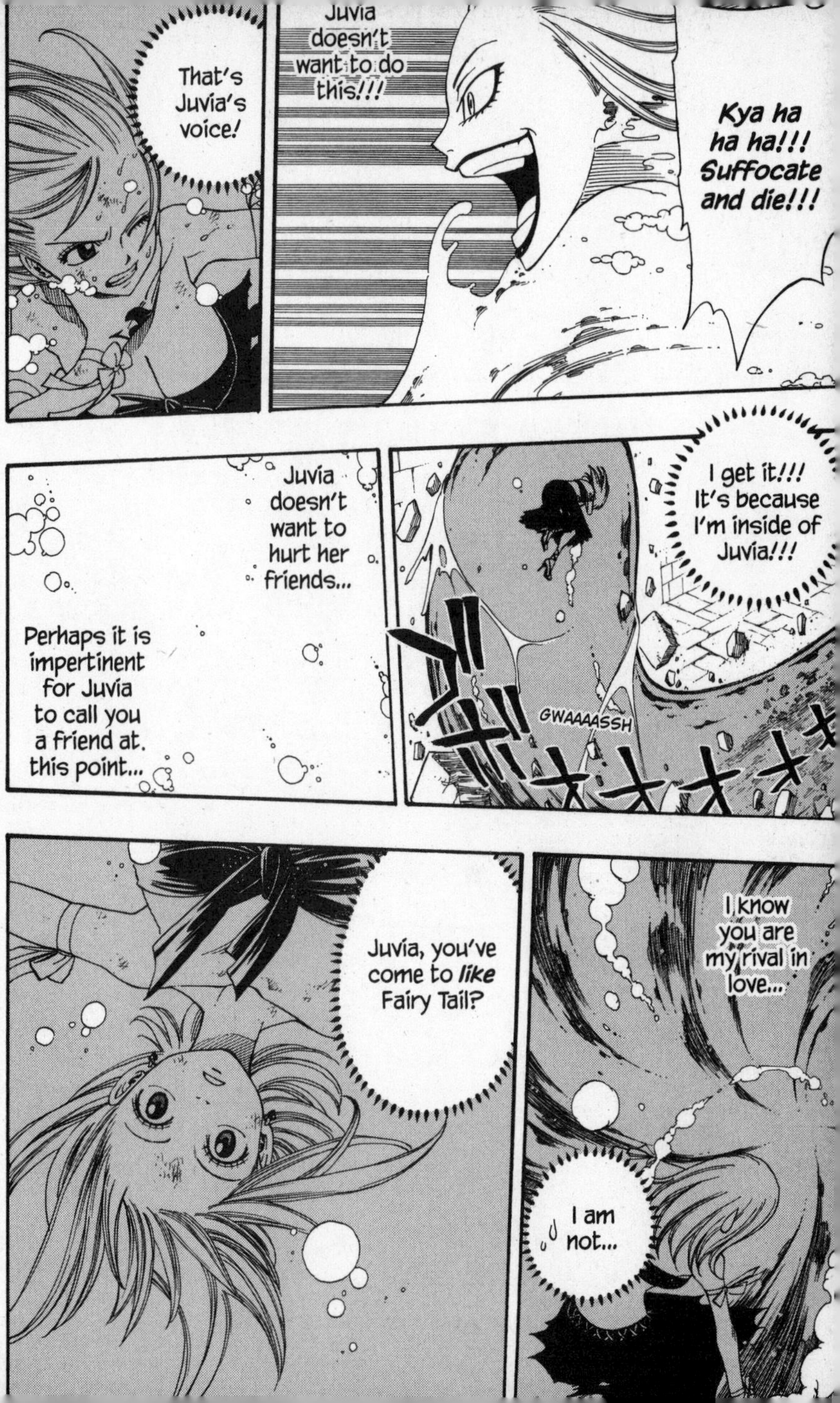

Kya ha ha ha!!! Suffocate and die!!!
Juvia doesn't want to do this!!!
That's Juvia's voice!
I get it!!! It's because I'm inside of Juvia!!!
GWAAAASSH
Juvia doesn't want to hurt her friends...
Perhaps it is impertinent for Juvia to call you a friend at this point...
I know you are my rival in love...
I am not...
Juvia, you've come to *like* Fairy Tail?

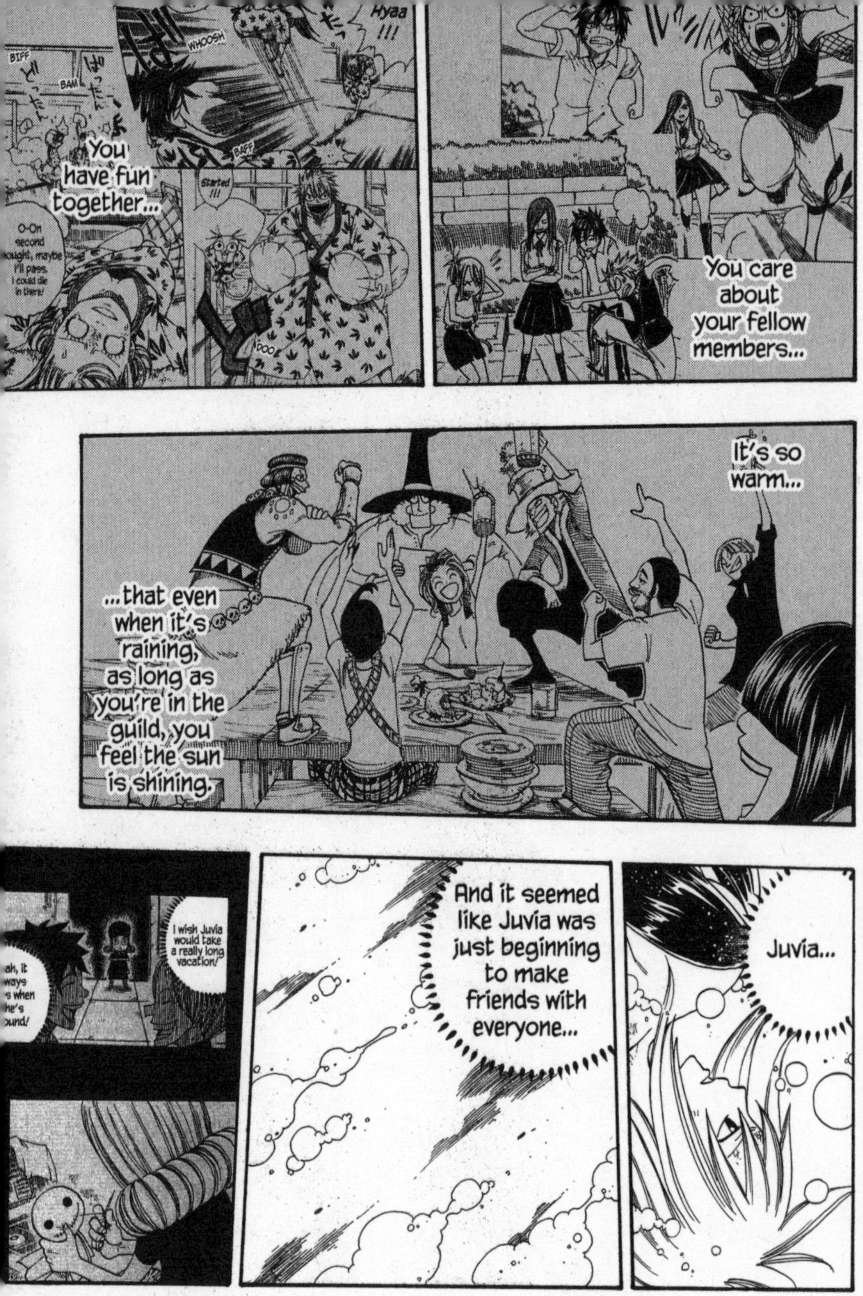
You care about your fellow members...
Hyaa!!!
WHOOSH
BIFF
BAM
BAFF
You have fun together...
Started!!!
O-On second ought, maybe I'll pass. I could die in there!
DOO
It's so warm...
...that even when it's raining, as long as you're in the guild, you feel the sun is shining.
Juvia...
And it seemed like Juvia was just beginning to make friends with everyone...
I wish Juvia would take a really long vacation!

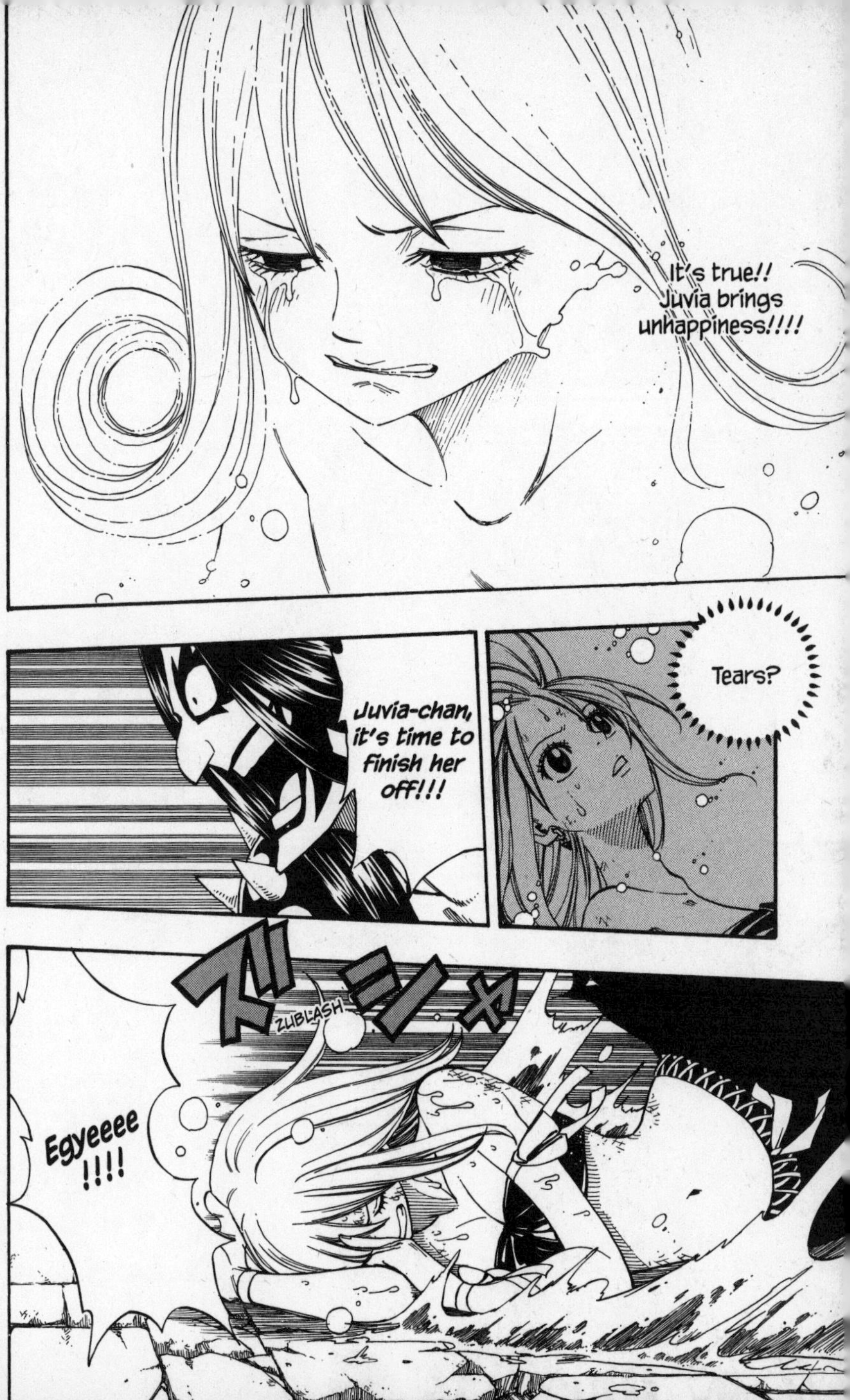
It's true!!
Juvia brings
unhappiness!!!!
Tears?
Juvia-chan, it's time to finish her off!!!
ZUBLASH
Egyeeee !!!!

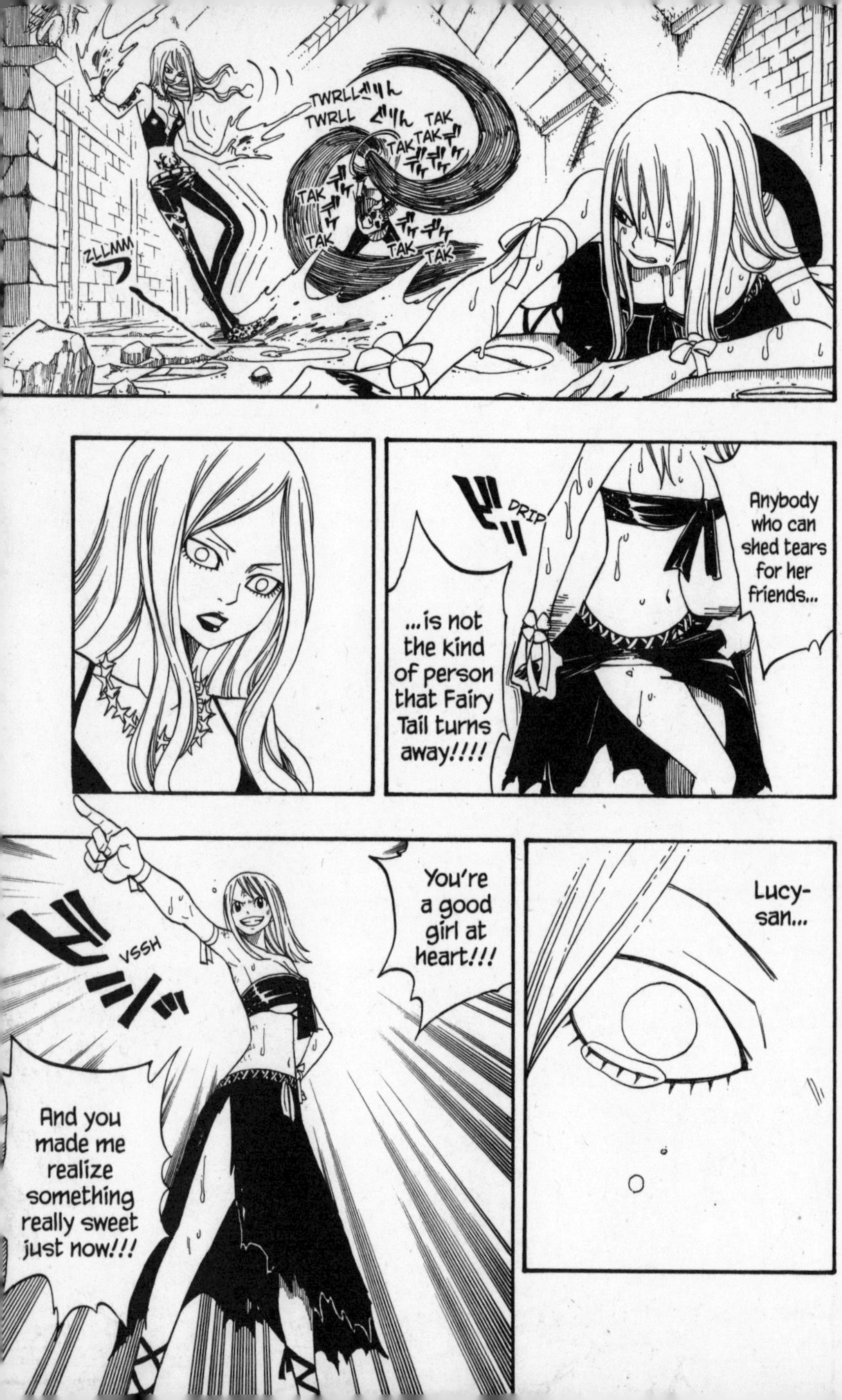
TWRLL
TWRLL
TAK TAK TAK TAK TAK TAK TAK TAK
ZLLMM
DRIP
Anybody who can shed tears for her friends...
...is not the kind of person that Fairy Tail turns away!!!!
Lucy-san...
You're a good girl at heart!!!
VSSH
And you made me realize something really sweet just now!!!

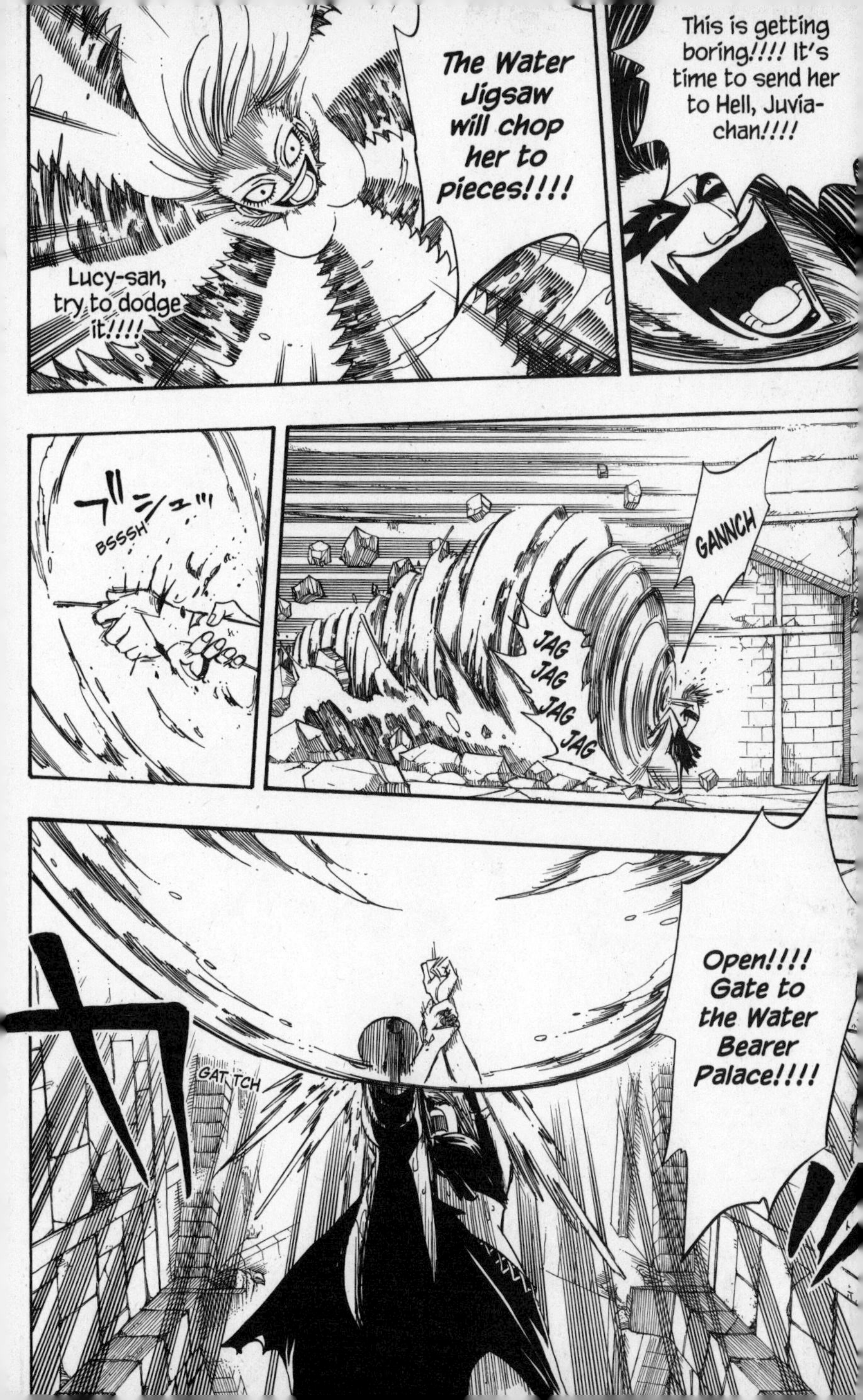
This is getting boring!!!! It's time to send her to Hell, Juvia-chan!!!!
The Water Jigsaw will chop her to pieces!!!!
Lucy-san, try to dodge it!!!!
GANNCH
JAG JAG JAG JAG
ブシュッ
BSSSH
Open!!!! Gate to the Water Bearer Palace!!!!
GAT TCH

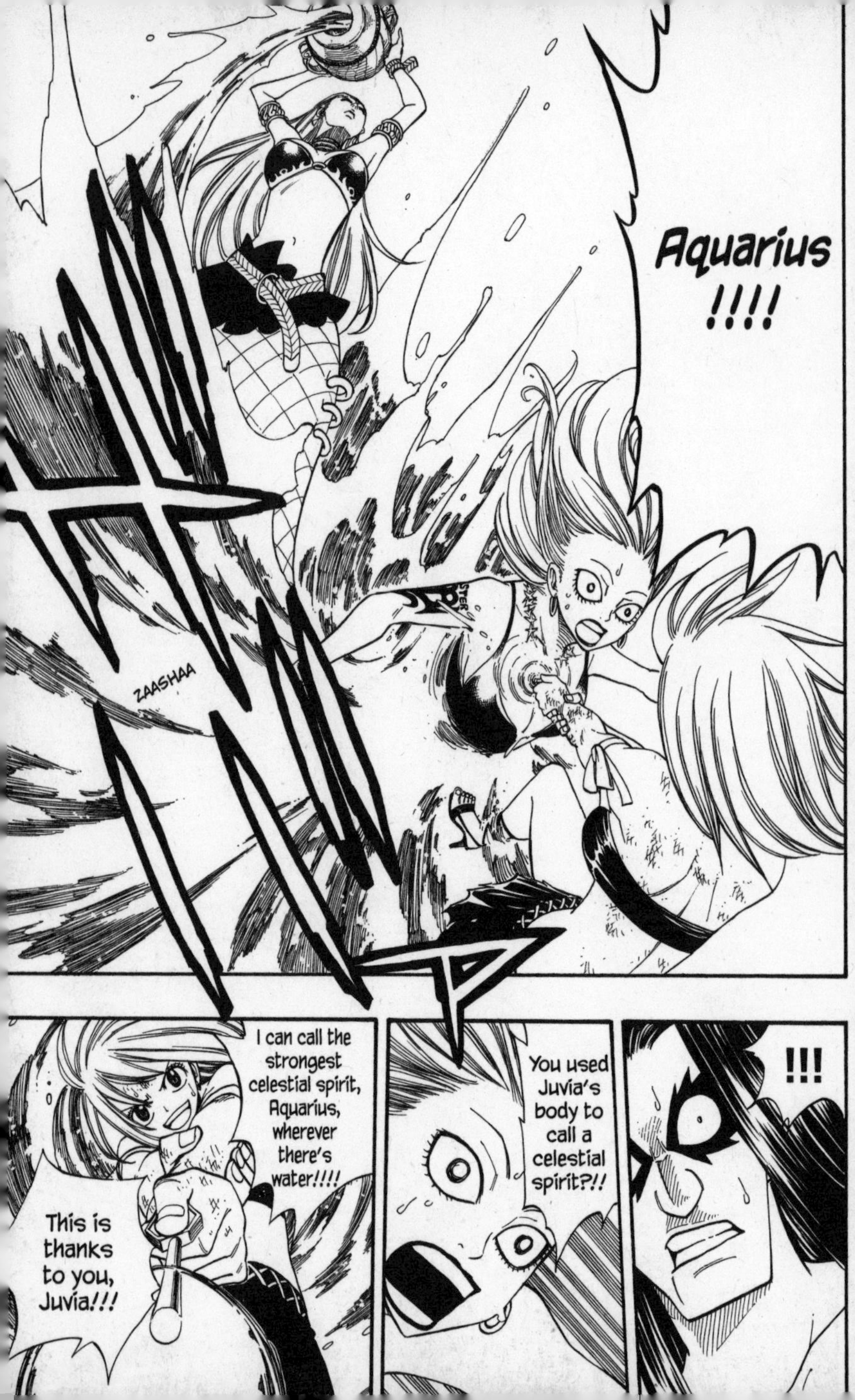
Aquarius !!!!
ZAASHAA
!!!
You used Juvia's body to call a celestial spirit?!!
I can call the strongest celestial spirit, Aquarius, wherever there's water!!!!
This is thanks to you, Juvia!!!

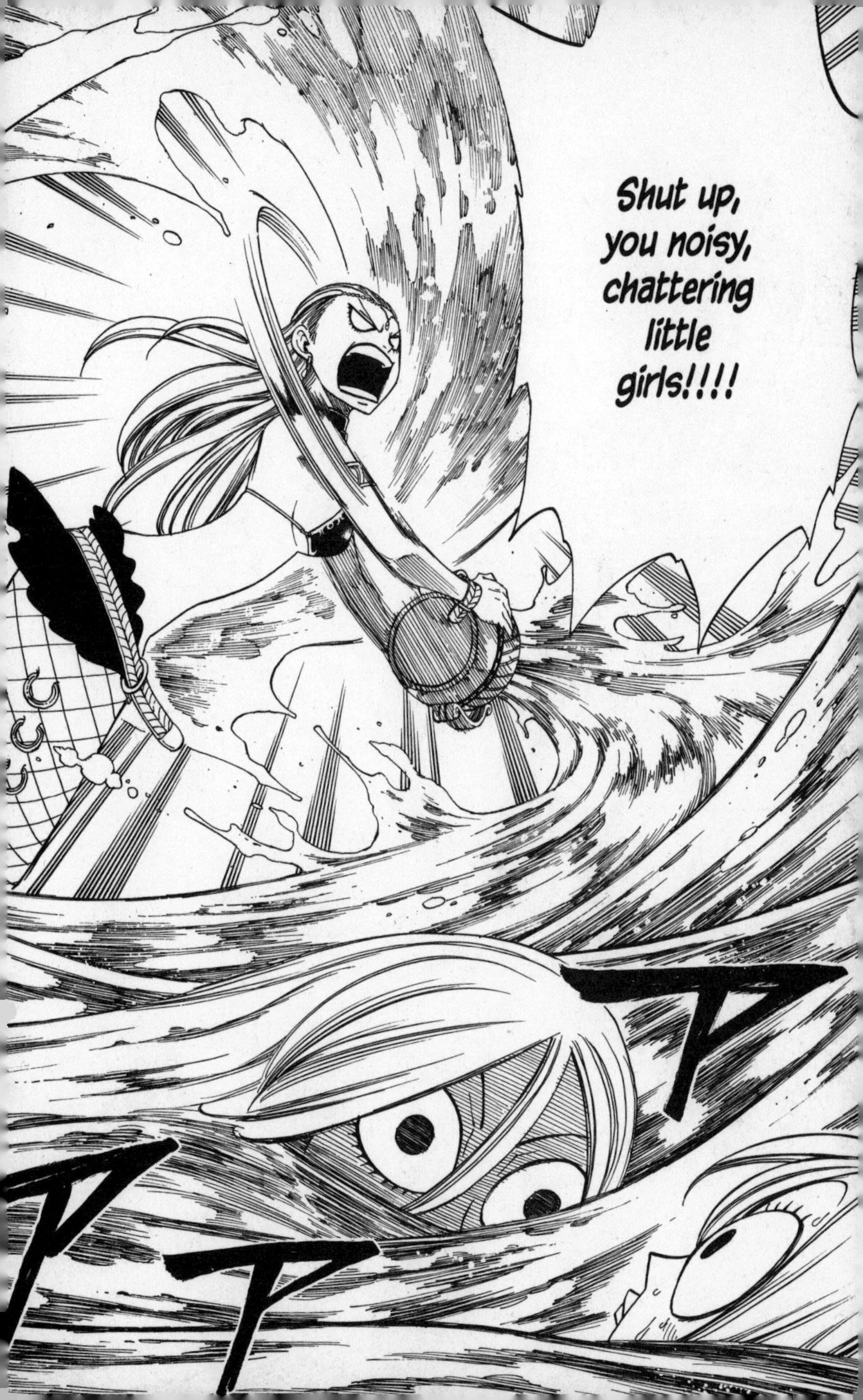
Shut up, you noisy, chattering little girls!!!!

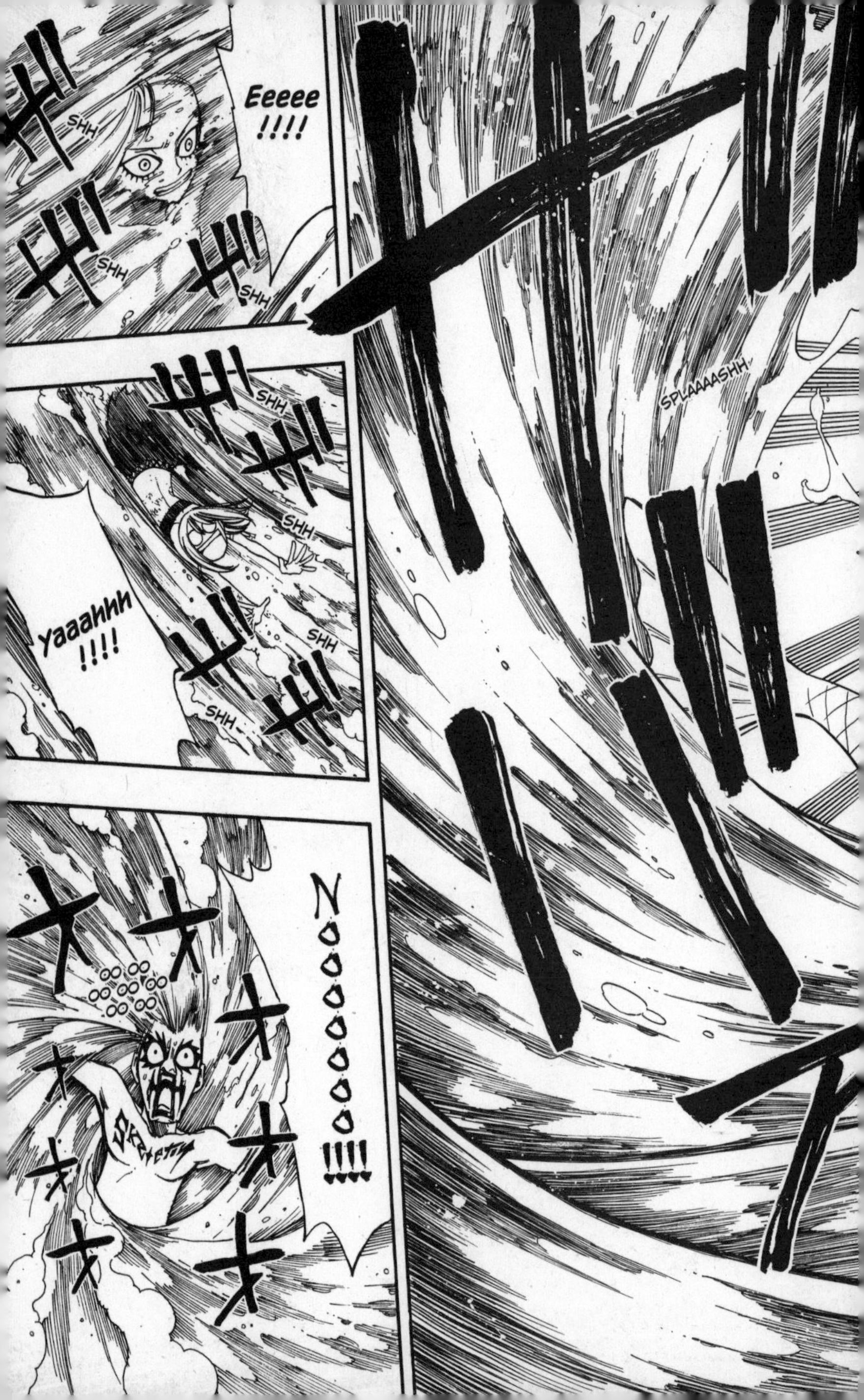
SPLAAAASHH
Eeeee !!!!
SHH
SHH
SHH
SHH
SHH
Yaaahhh !!!!
SHH
SHH
NOOOOOOO!!!!

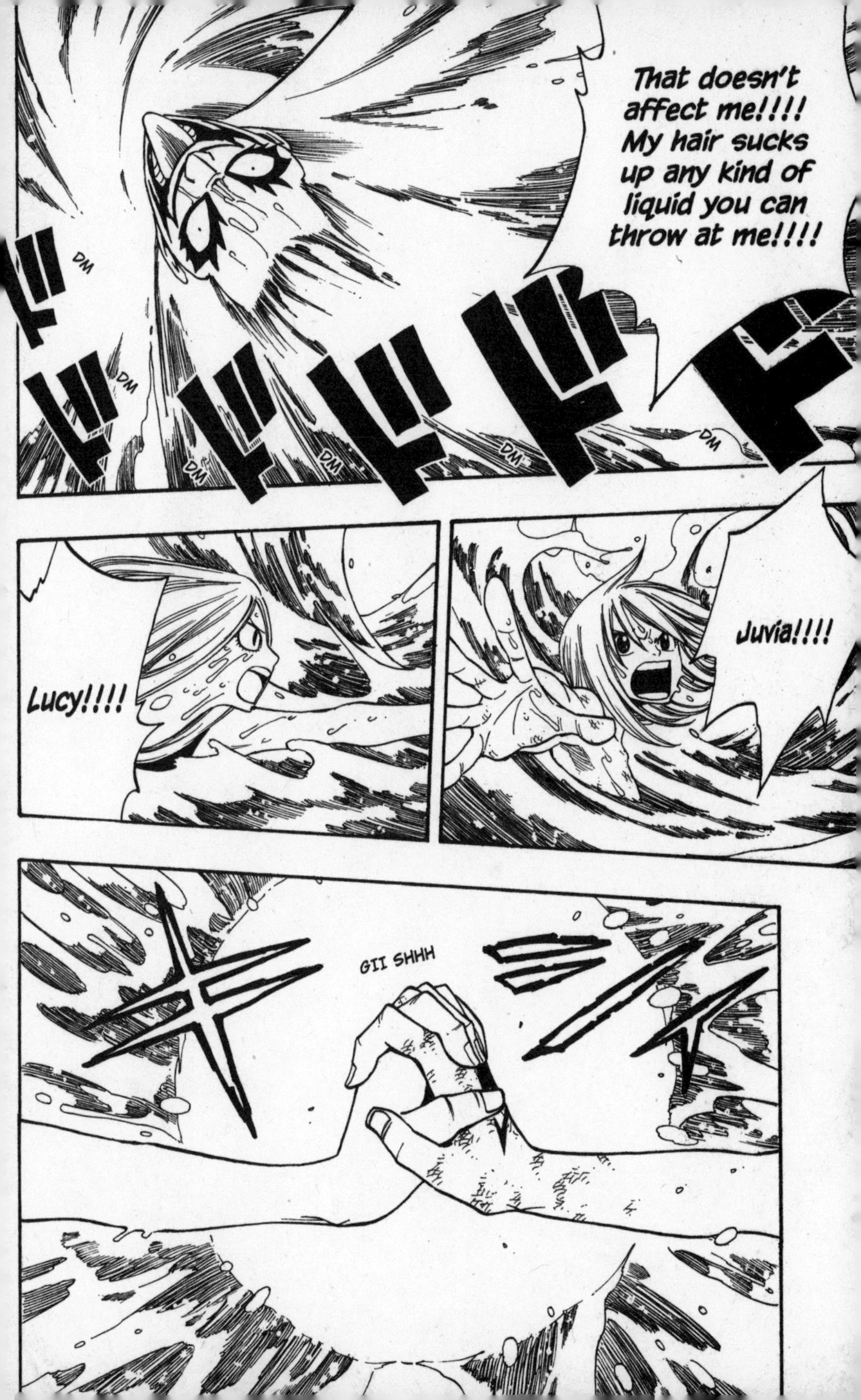
That doesn't affect me!!!! My hair sucks up any kind of liquid you can throw at me!!!!
DM
DM
DM
DM
DM
DM
Juvia!!!!
Lucy!!!!
GII SHHH

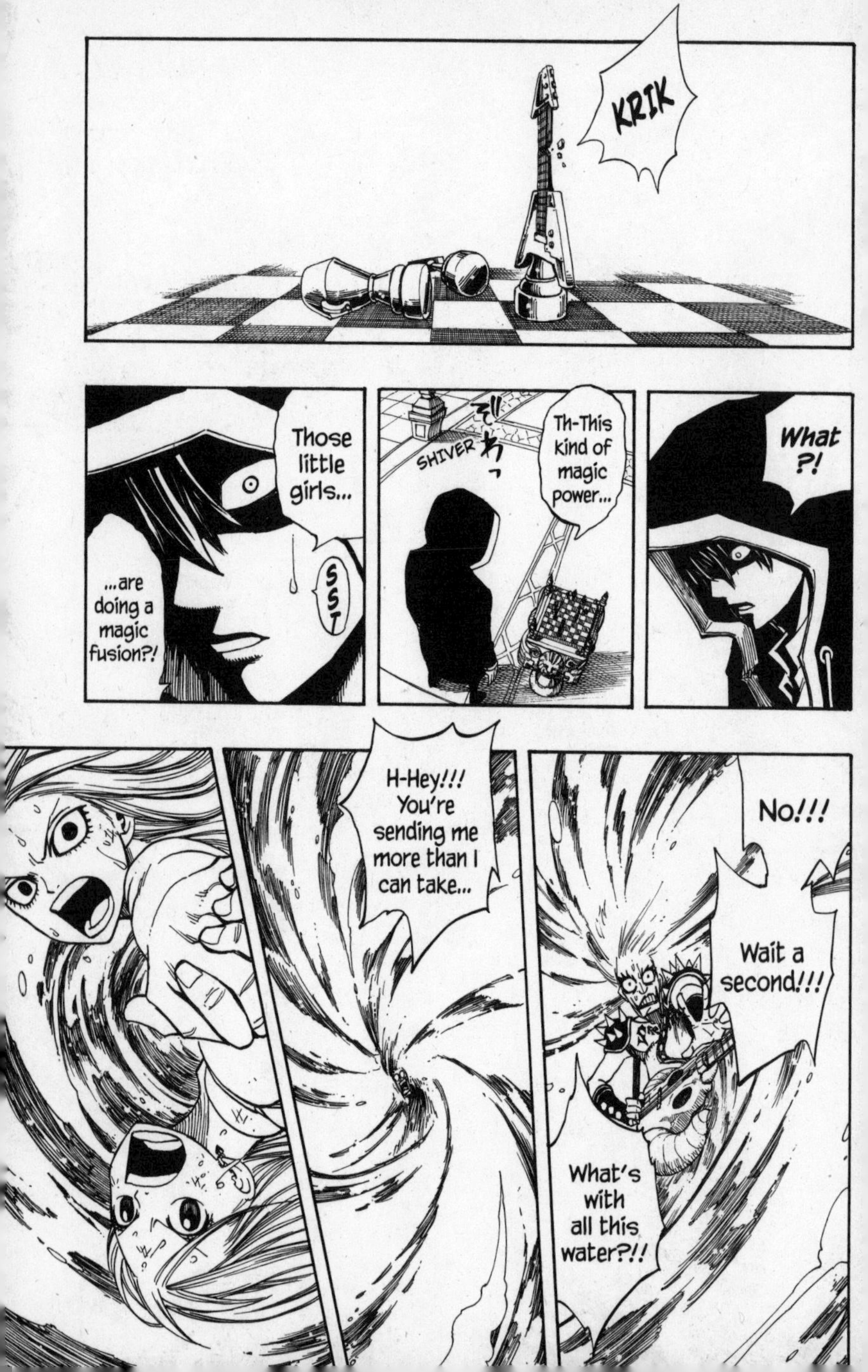
KRIK
What ?!
Th-This kind of magic power...
SHIVER
Those little girls...
SST
...are doing a magic fusion?!
No!!!
Wait a second!!!
What's with all this water?!!
H-Hey!!! You're sending me more than I can take...

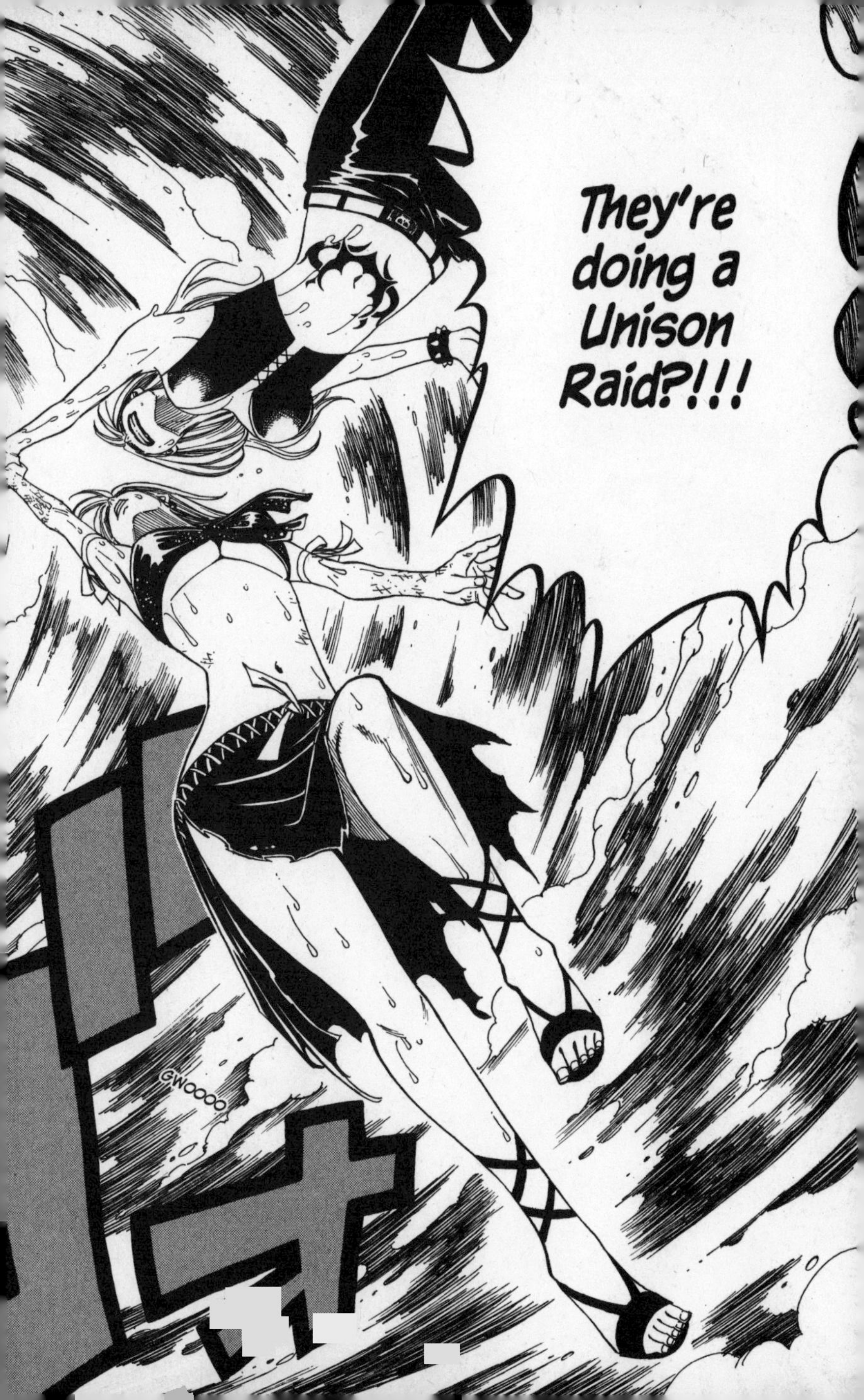
They're doing a Unison Raid?!!!
GWOOOO

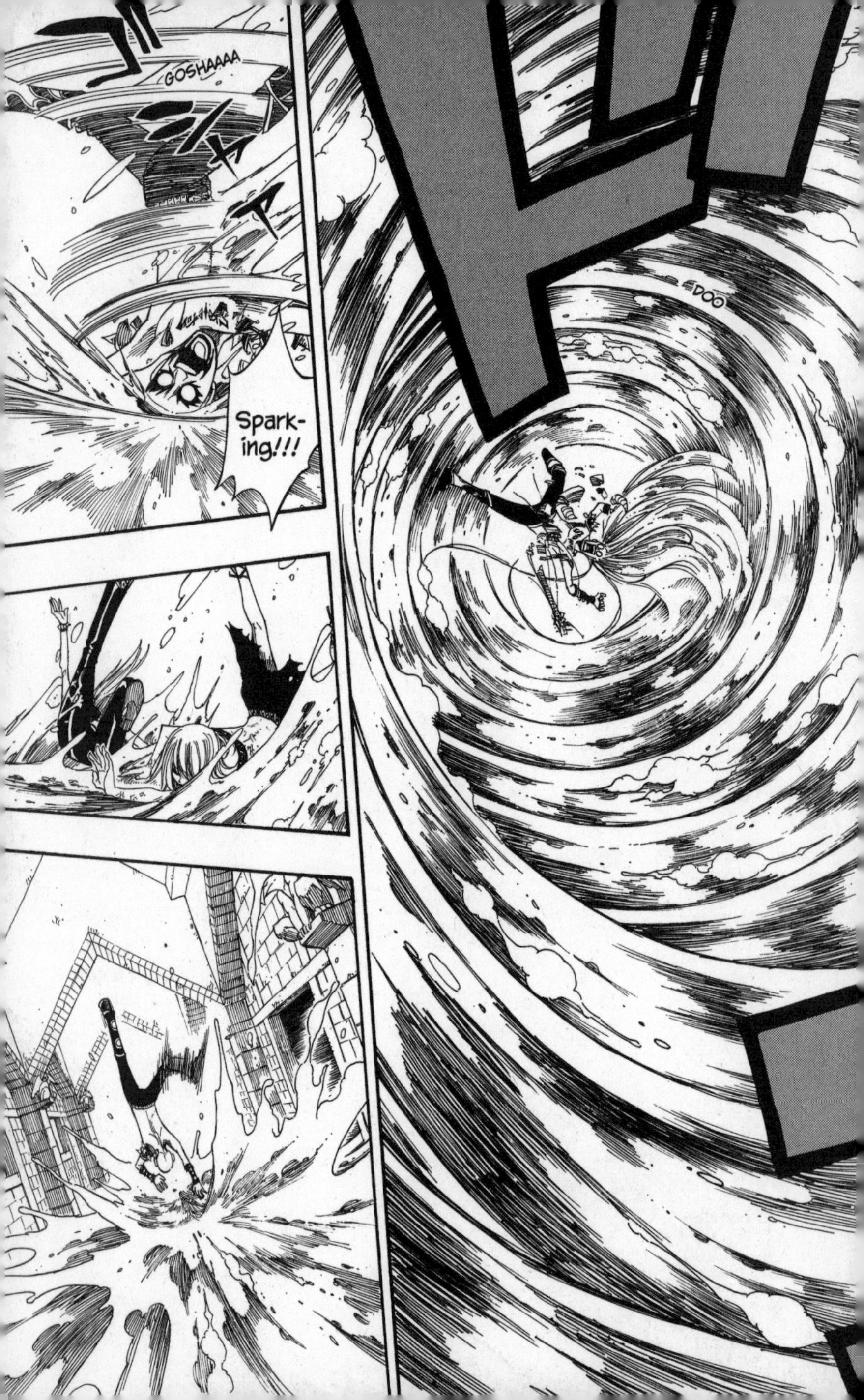
DOO
GOSHAAAA
Spark-ing!!!

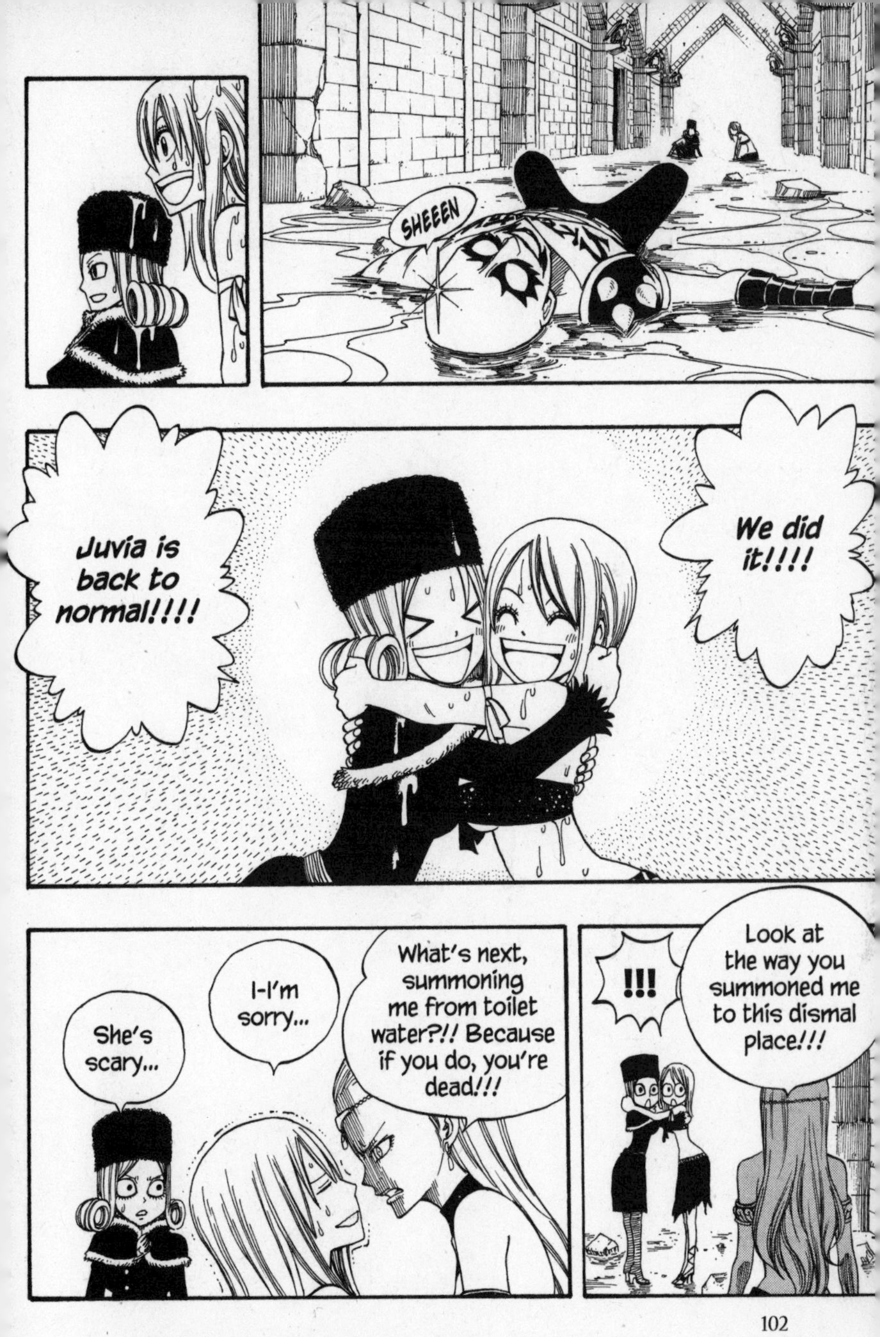
SHEEEN
We did it!!!!
Juvia is back to normal!!!!
Look at the way you summoned me to this dismal place!!!
!!!
What's next, summoning me from toilet water?!! Because if you do, you're dead!!!
I-I'm sorry...
She's scary...

FAIRY TAIL

Chapter 88: Natsu Becomes a Meal

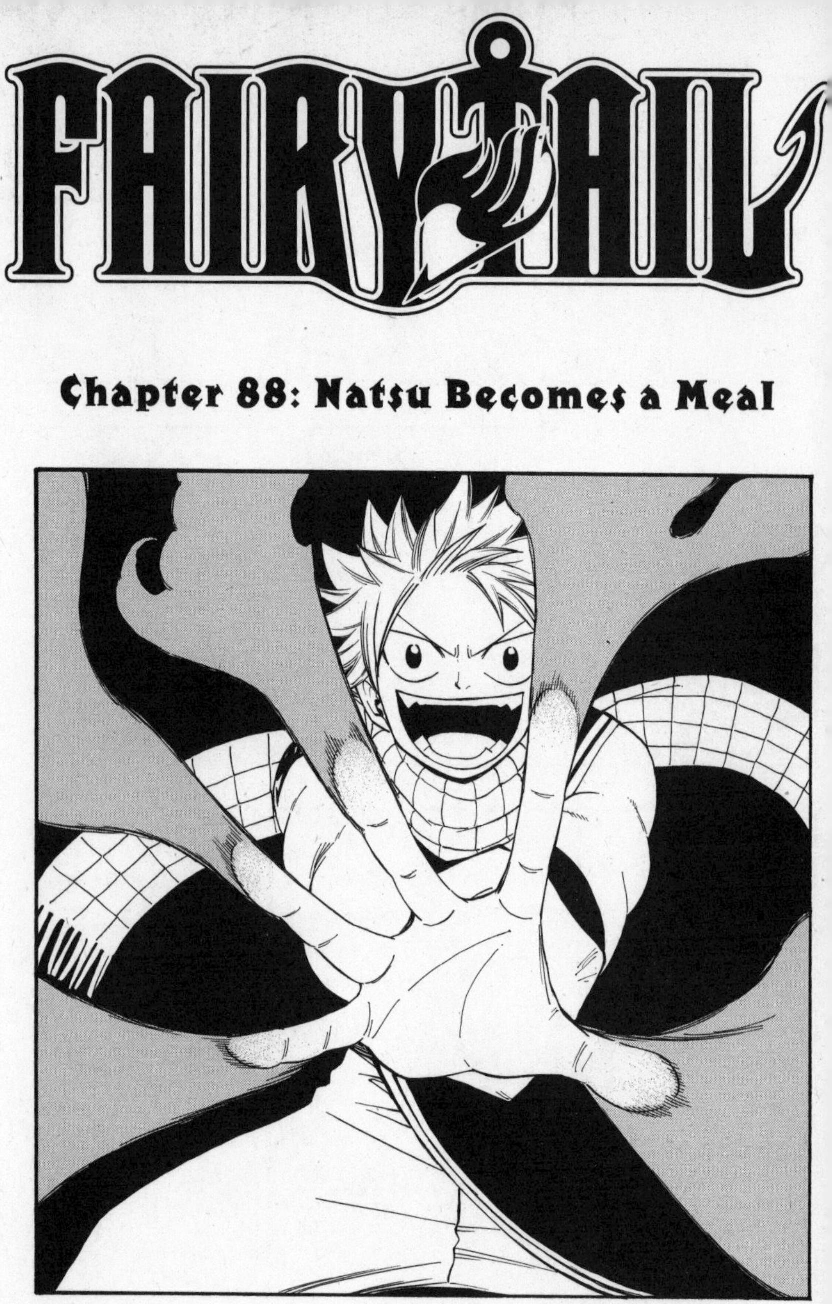

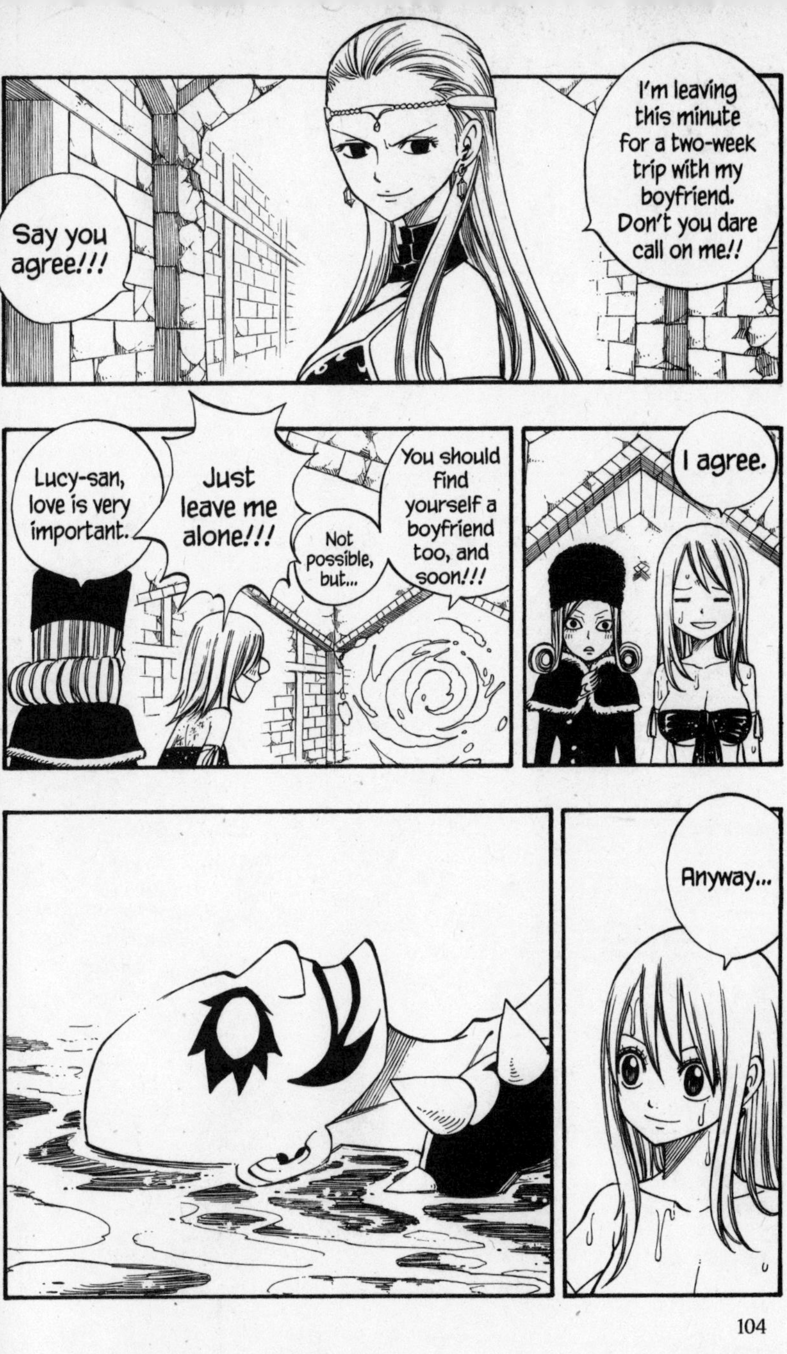
I'm leaving this minute for a two-week trip with my boyfriend. Don't you dare call on me!!
Say you agree!!!
I agree.
You should find yourself a boyfriend too, and soon!!!
Not possible, but...
Just leave me alone!!!
Lucy-san, love is very important.
Anyway...

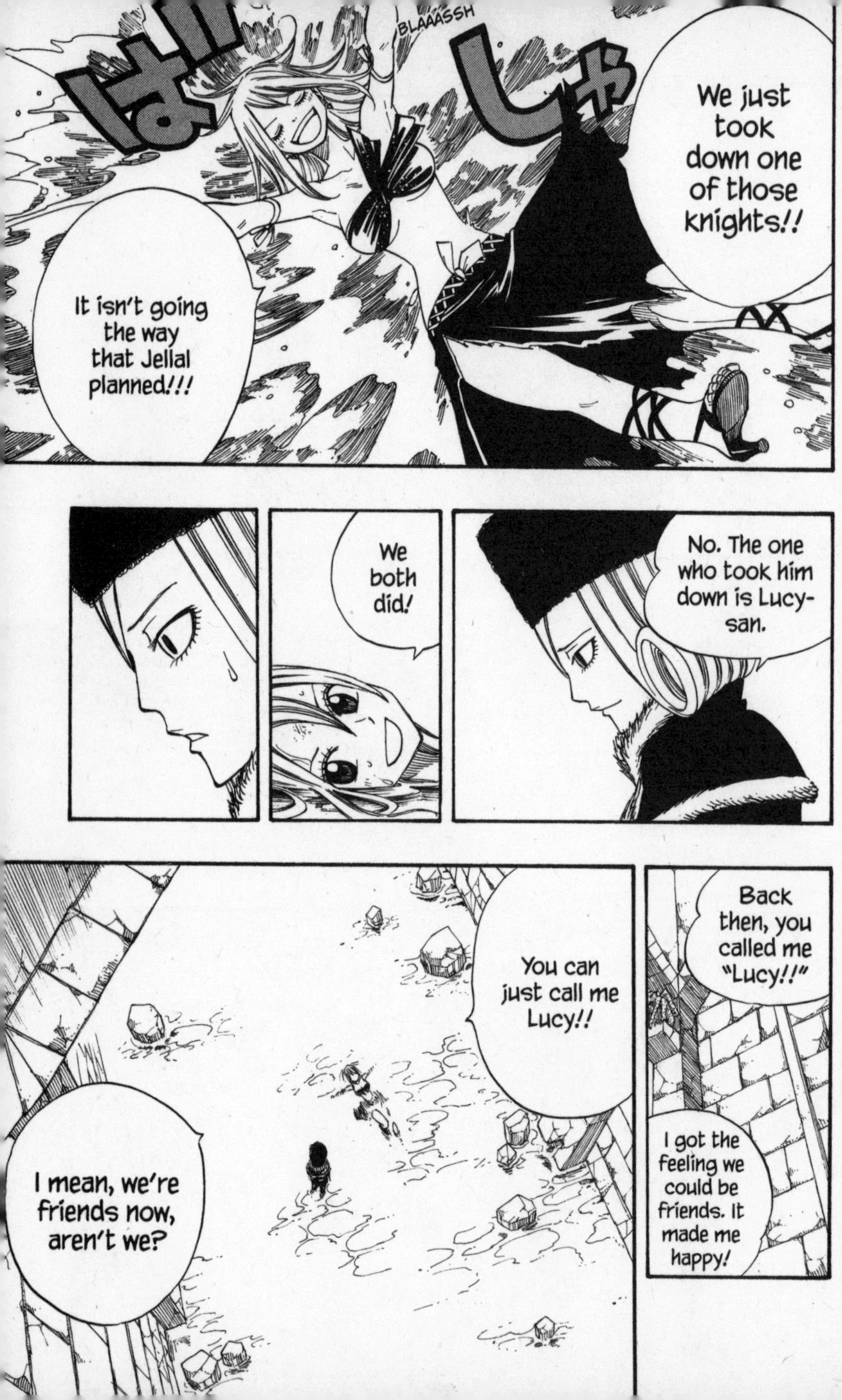
BLAAASSH
ばしゃ
We just took down one of those knights!!
It isn't going the way that Jellal planned!!!
No. The one who took him down is Lucy-san.
We both did!
Back then, you called me "Lucy!!"
I got the feeling we could be friends. It made me happy!
You can just call me Lucy!!
I mean, we're friends now, aren't we?

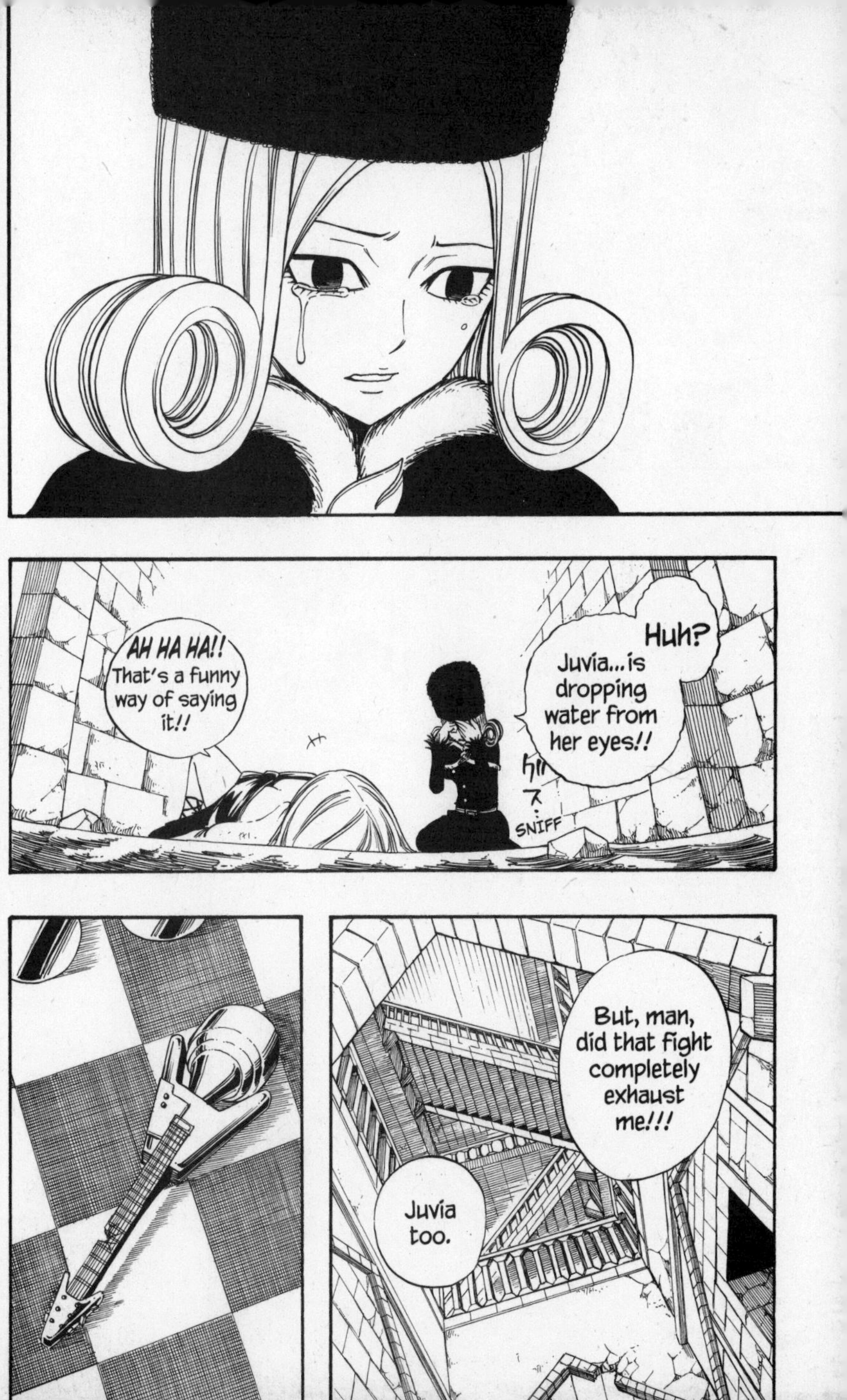
Huh? Juvia...is dropping water from her eyes!!
SNIFF
AH HA HA!! That's a funny way of saying it!!
But, man, did that fight completely exhaust me!!!
Juvia too.

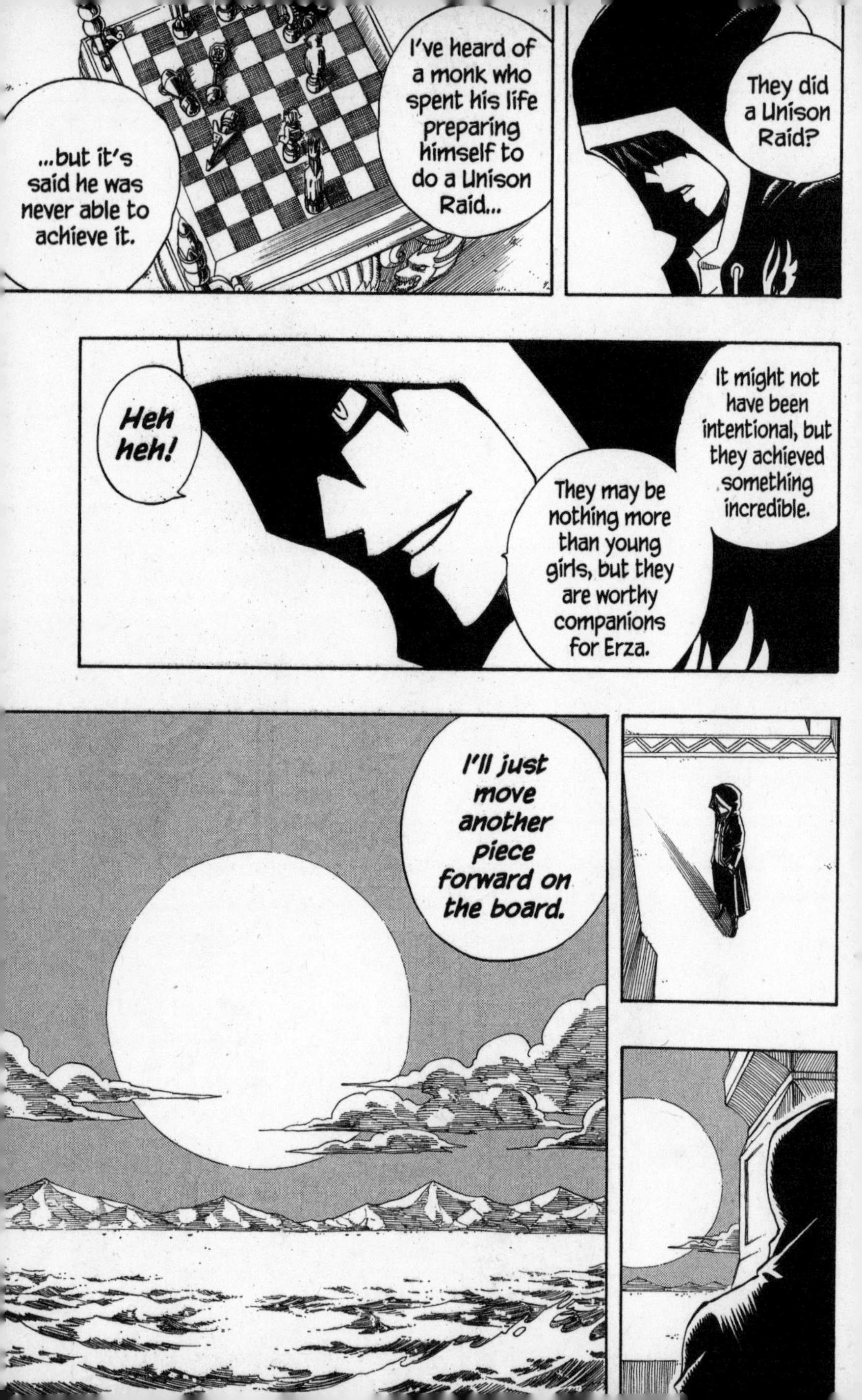
They did a Unison Raid?
I've heard of a monk who spent his life preparing himself to do a Unison Raid...
...but it's said he was never able to achieve it.
It might not have been intentional, but they achieved something incredible.
They may be nothing more than young girls, but they are worthy companions for Erza.
Heh heh!
I'll just move another piece forward on the board.

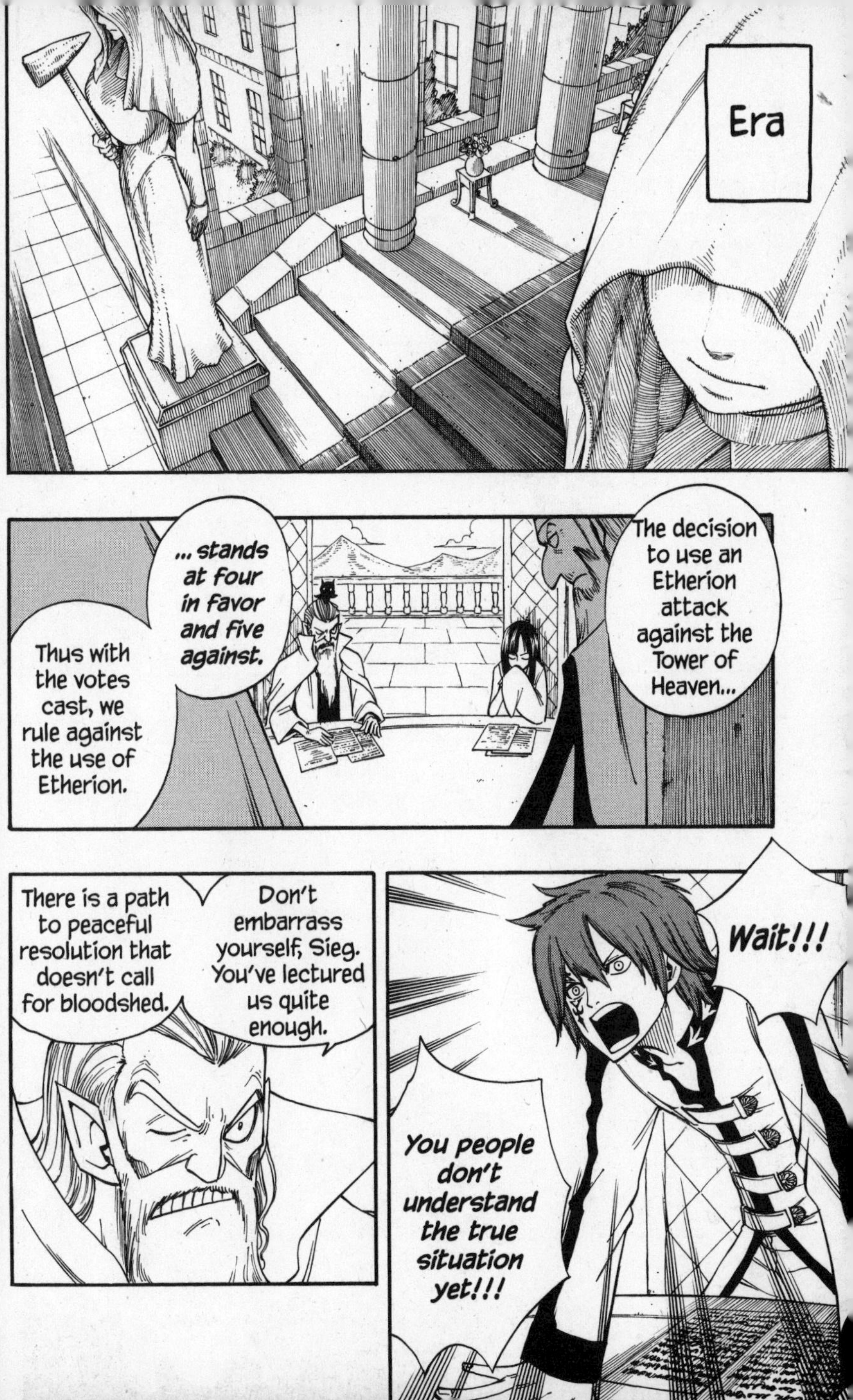
Era
The decision to use an Etherion attack against the Tower of Heaven...
... stands at four in favor and five against.
Thus with the votes cast, we rule against the use of Etherion.
Wait!!!
You people don't understand the true situation yet!!!
Don't embarrass yourself, Sieg. You've lectured us quite enough.
There is a path to peaceful resolution that doesn't call for bloodshed.

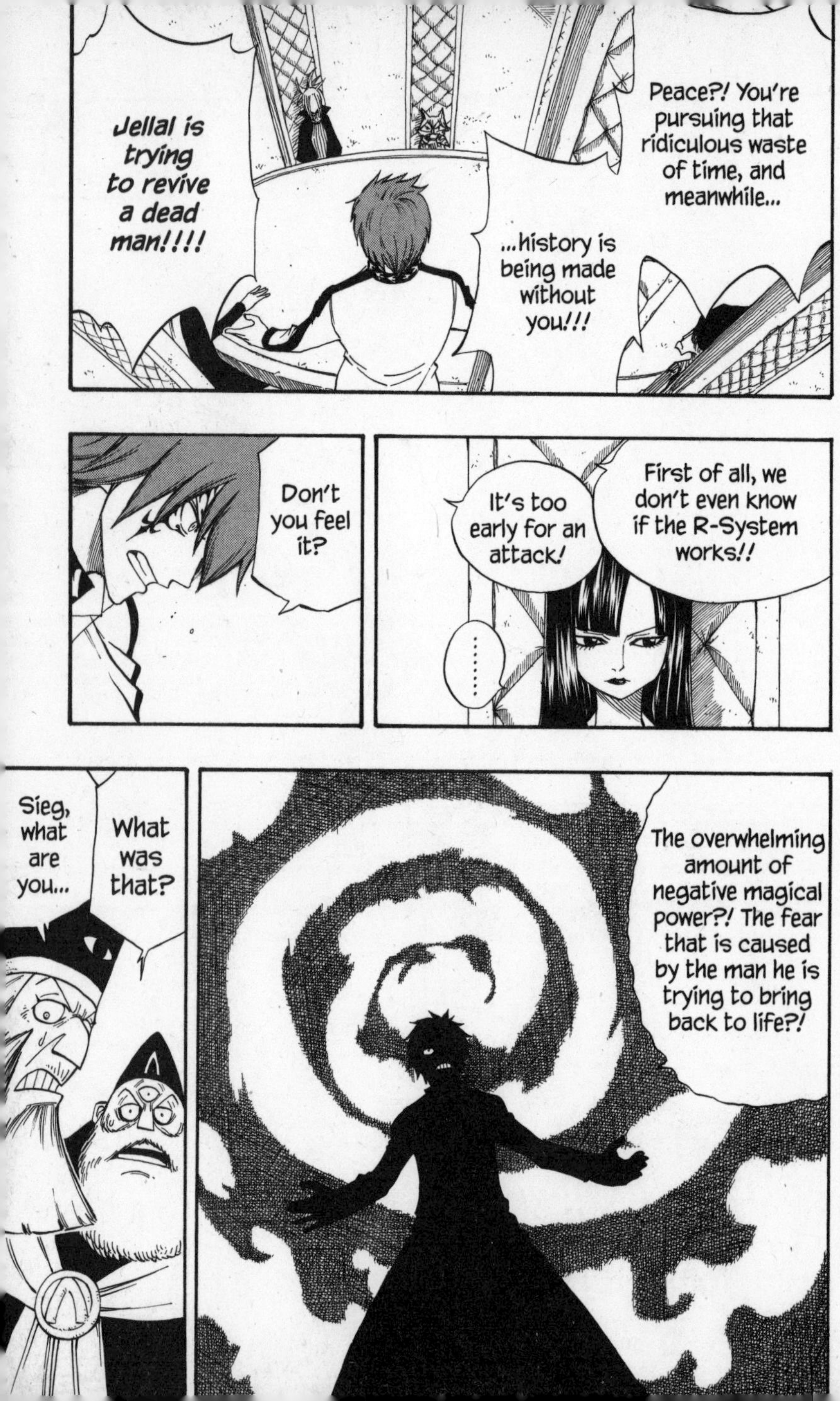
Peace?! You're pursuing that ridiculous waste of time, and meanwhile...
...history is being made without you!!!
Jellal is trying to revive a dead man!!!!
First of all, we don't even know if the R-System works!!
It's too early for an attack!
......
Don't you feel it?
The overwhelming amount of negative magical power?! The fear that is caused by the man he is trying to bring back to life?!
What was that?
Sieg, what are you...

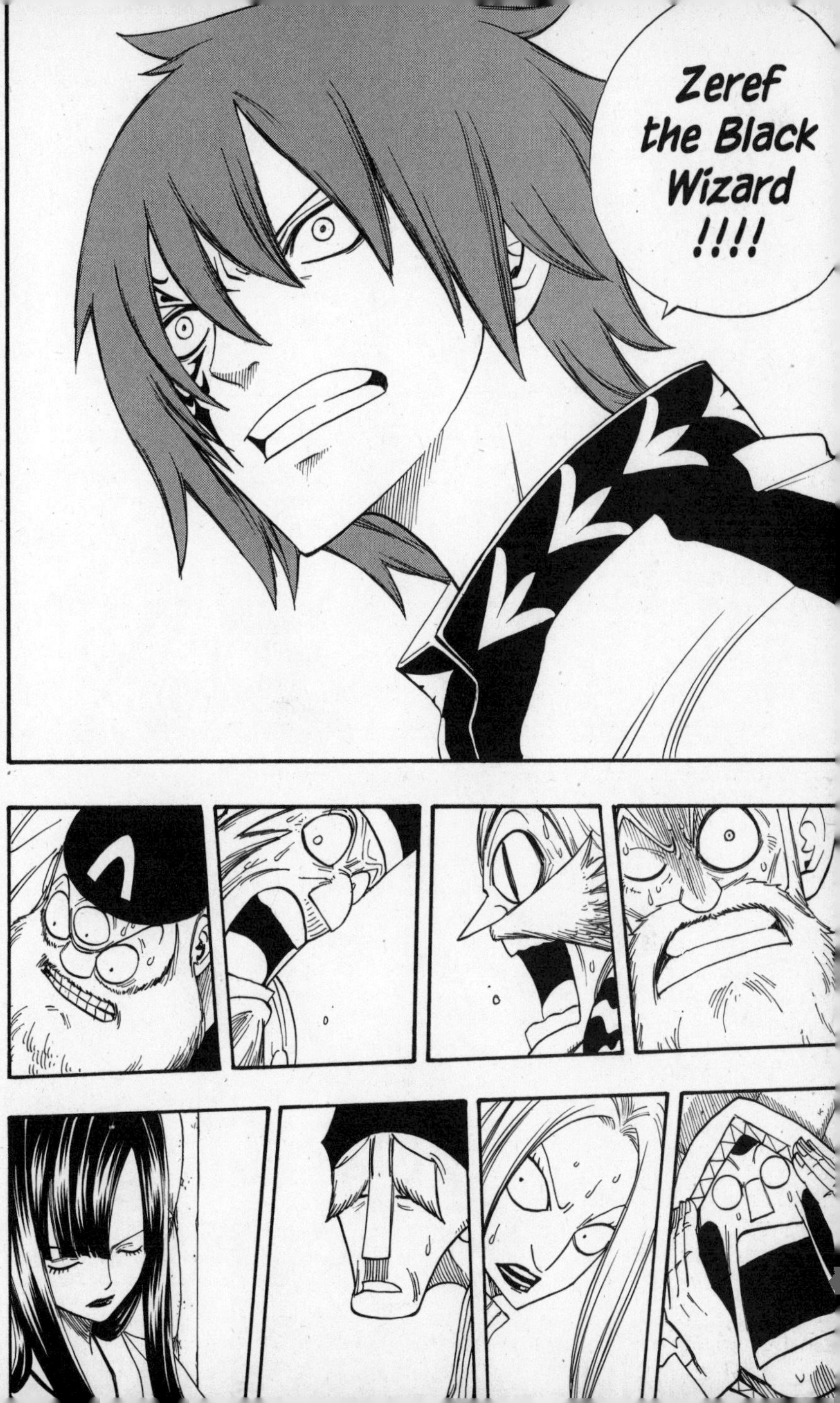
Zeref the Black Wizard !!!!

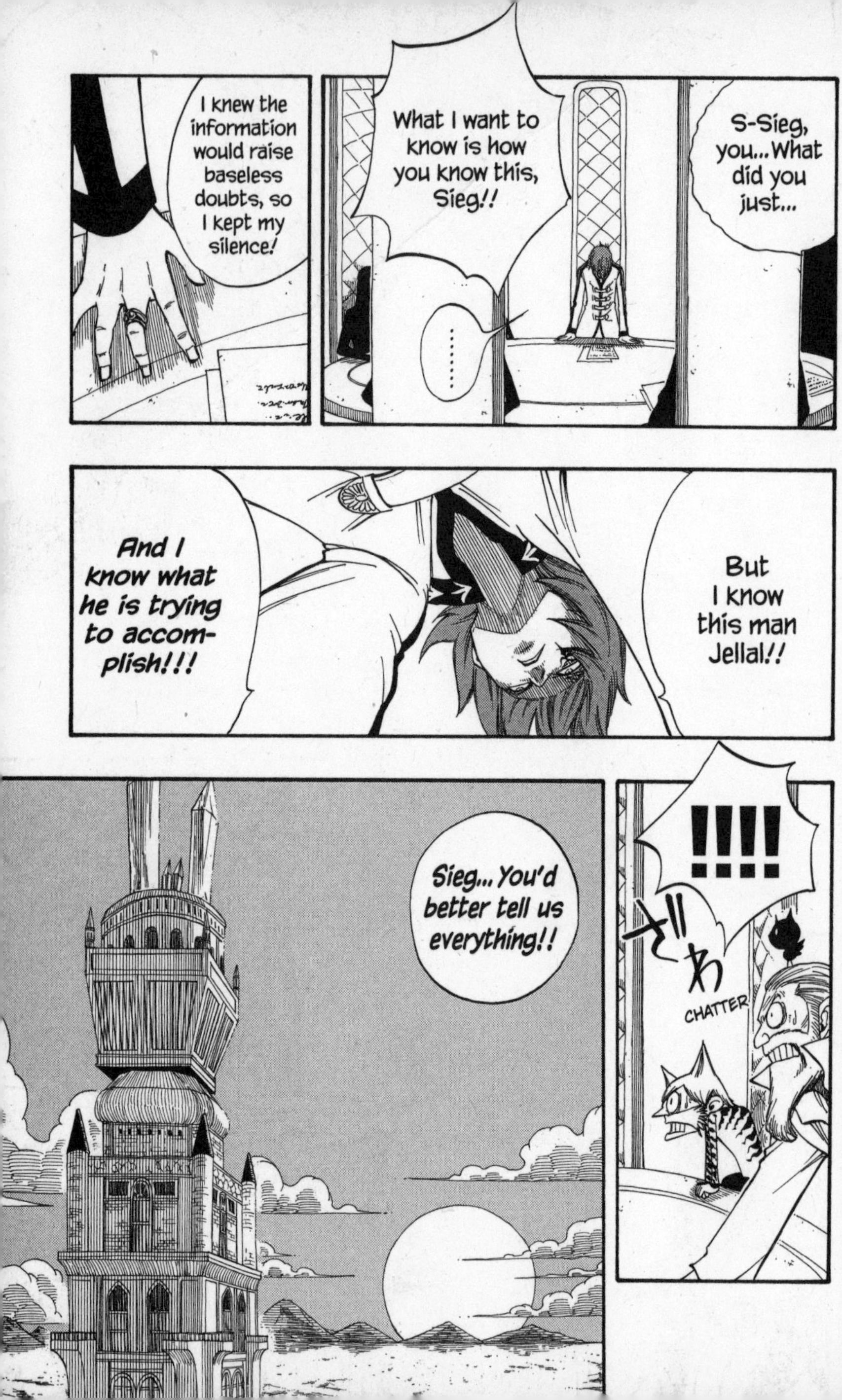
S-Sieg, you...What did you just...
What I want to know is how you know this, Sieg!!
......
I knew the information would raise baseless doubts, so I kept my silence!
But I know this man Jellal!!
And I know what he is trying to accomplish!!!
!!!!
ざわ
CHATTER
Sieg... You'd better tell us everything!!

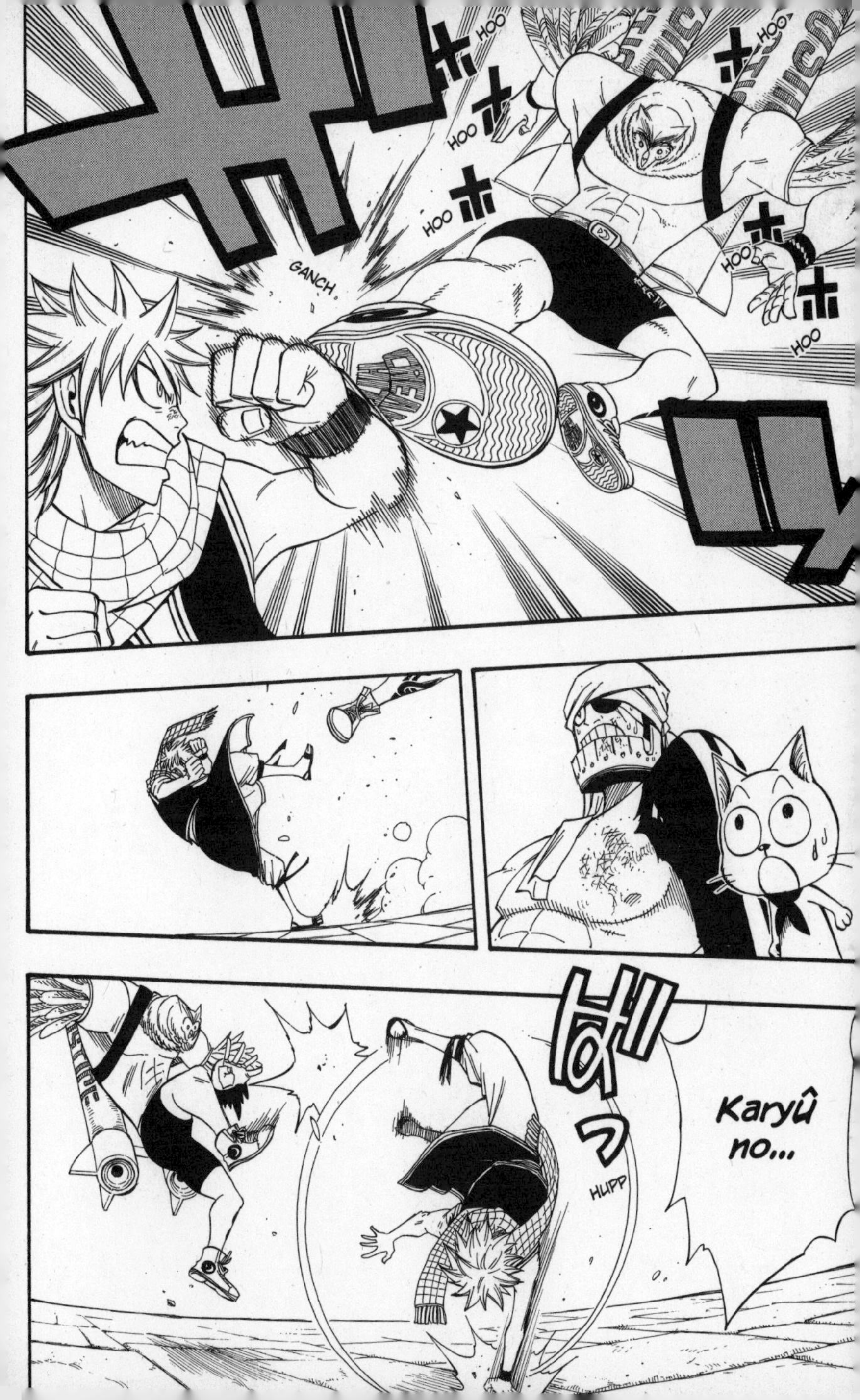
HOO
HOO
HOO
HOO
HOO
HOO
GANCH
Karyû no...
HUPP

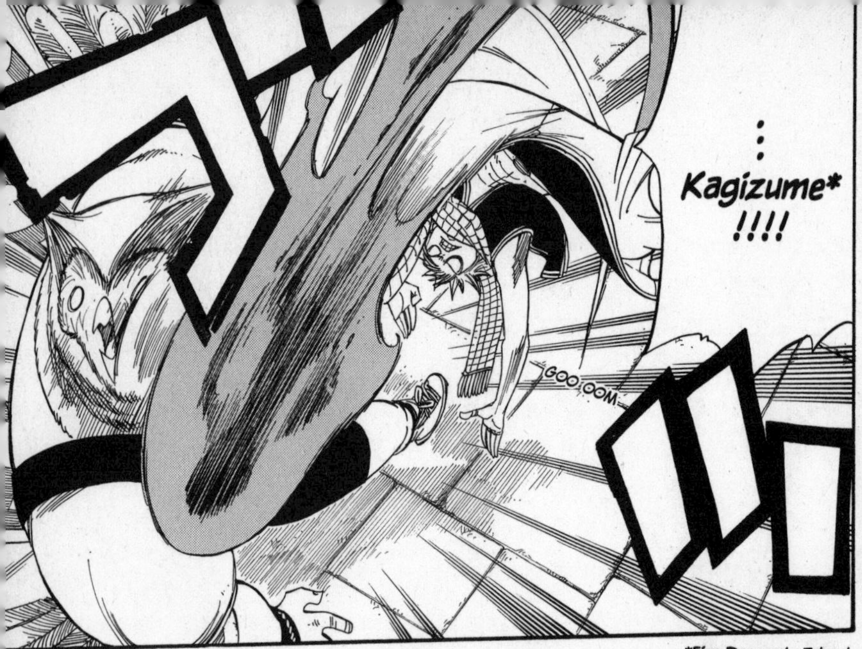

: Kagizume* !!!!
GOO OOM

*Fire Dragon's Talon!

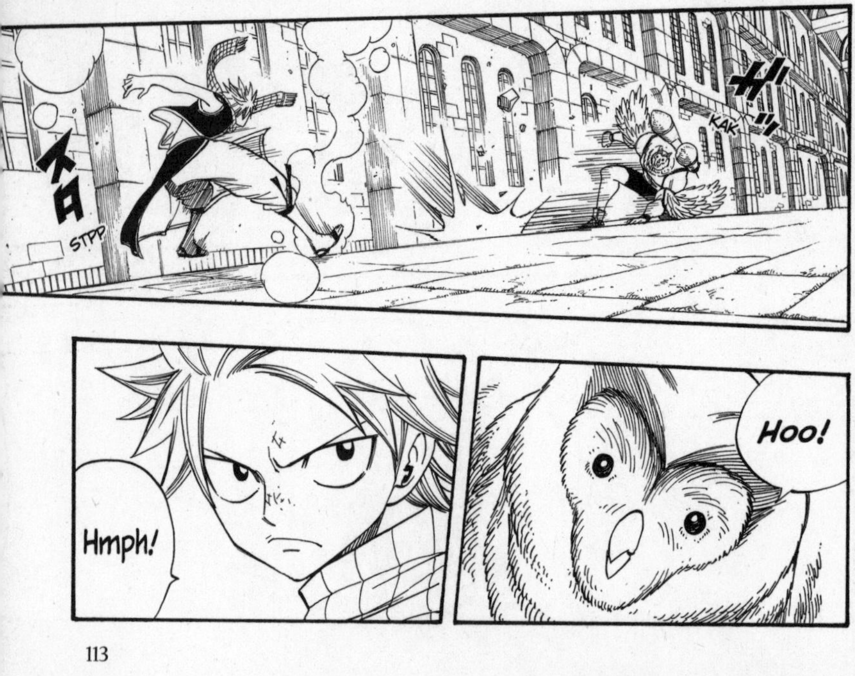

KAK
STPP
Hoo!
Hmph!

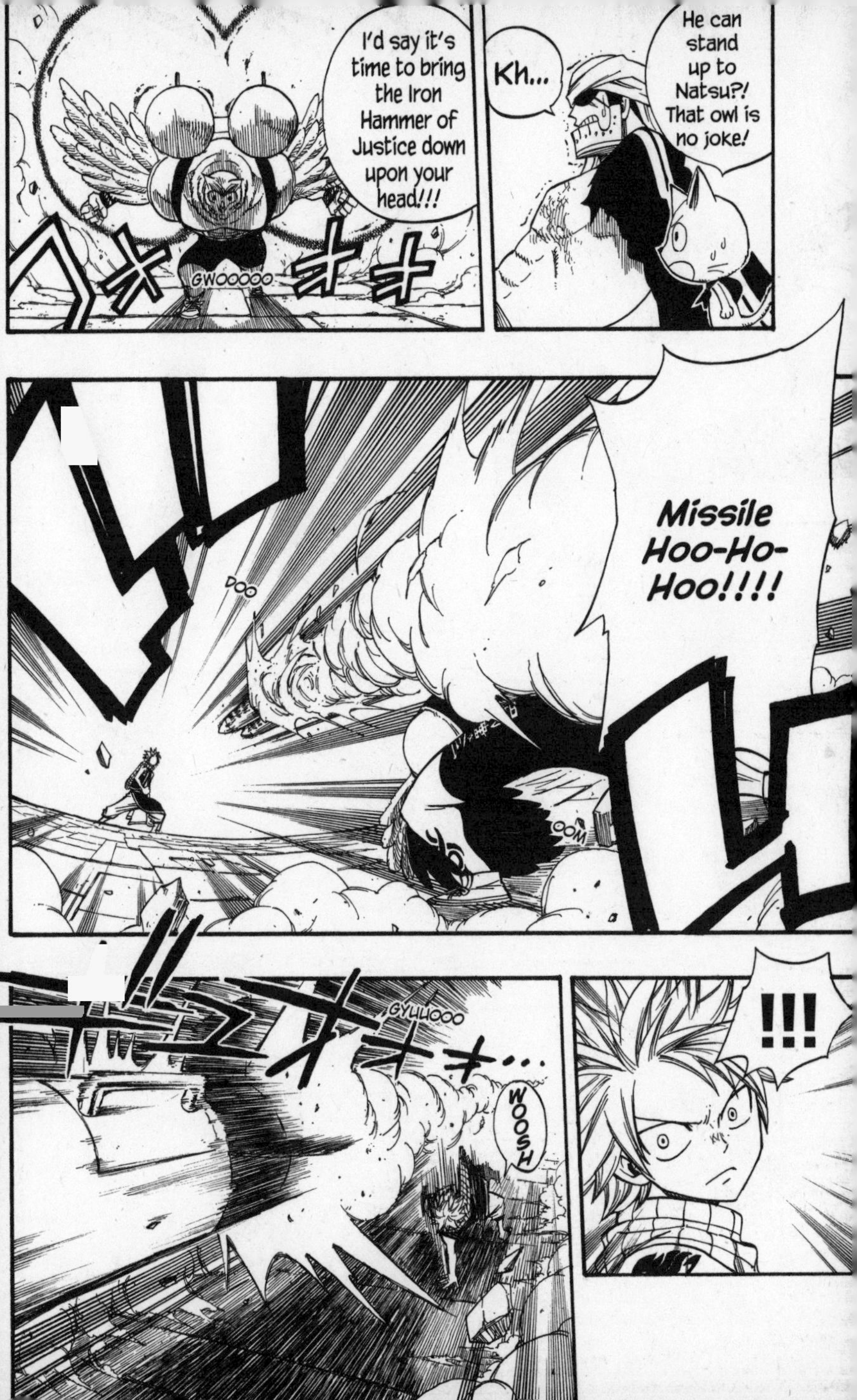
He can stand up to Natsu?! That owl is no joke!
Kh...
I'd say it's time to bring the Iron Hammer of Justice down upon your head!!!
GWOOOOO
Missile Hoo-Ho-Hoo!!!!
DOO
OOM
!!!
GYUUOOO
WOOSH

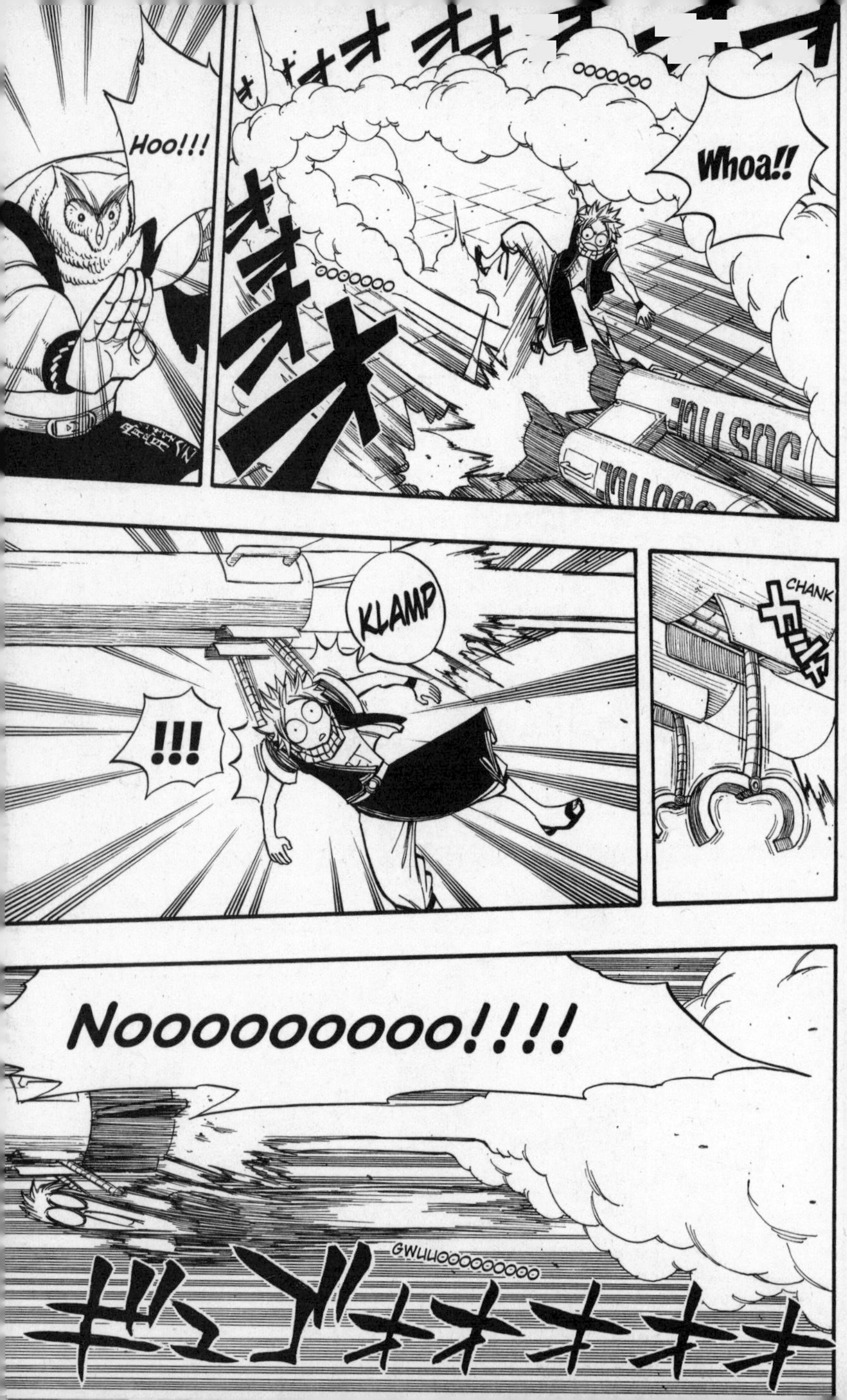
OOOOOOO
Whoa!!
OOOOOOO
JUSTICE
JUSTICE
Hoo!!!
CHANK
KLAMP
!!!
Noooooooooo!!!!
GWUUOOOOOOOOOO

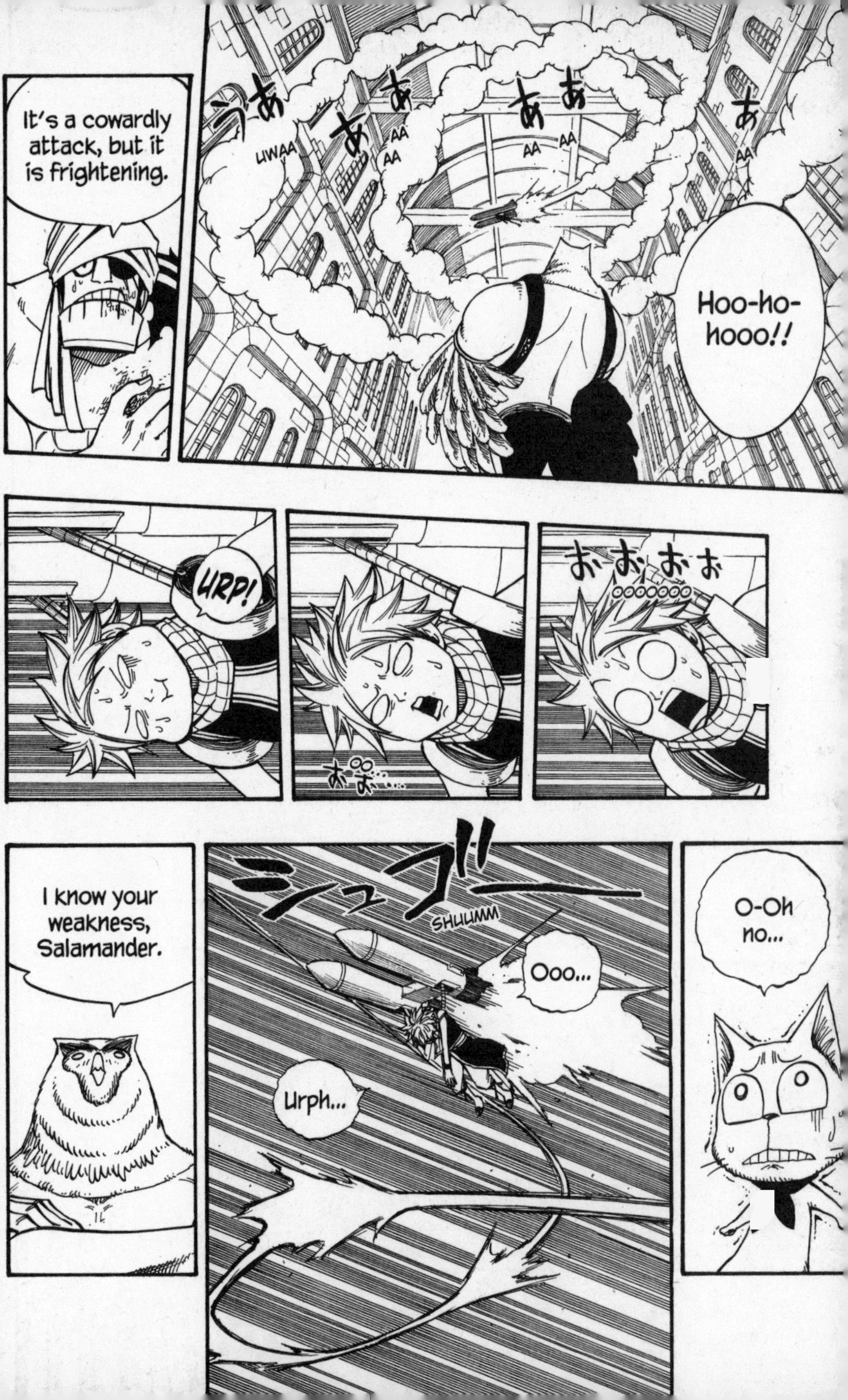
UWAA
AA
AA
AA
AA
AA
Hoo-ho-hooo!!
It's a cowardly attack, but it is frightening.
OOOOOOO
URP!
O-Oh no...
SHUUMM
Ooo...
Urph...
I know your weakness, Salamander.

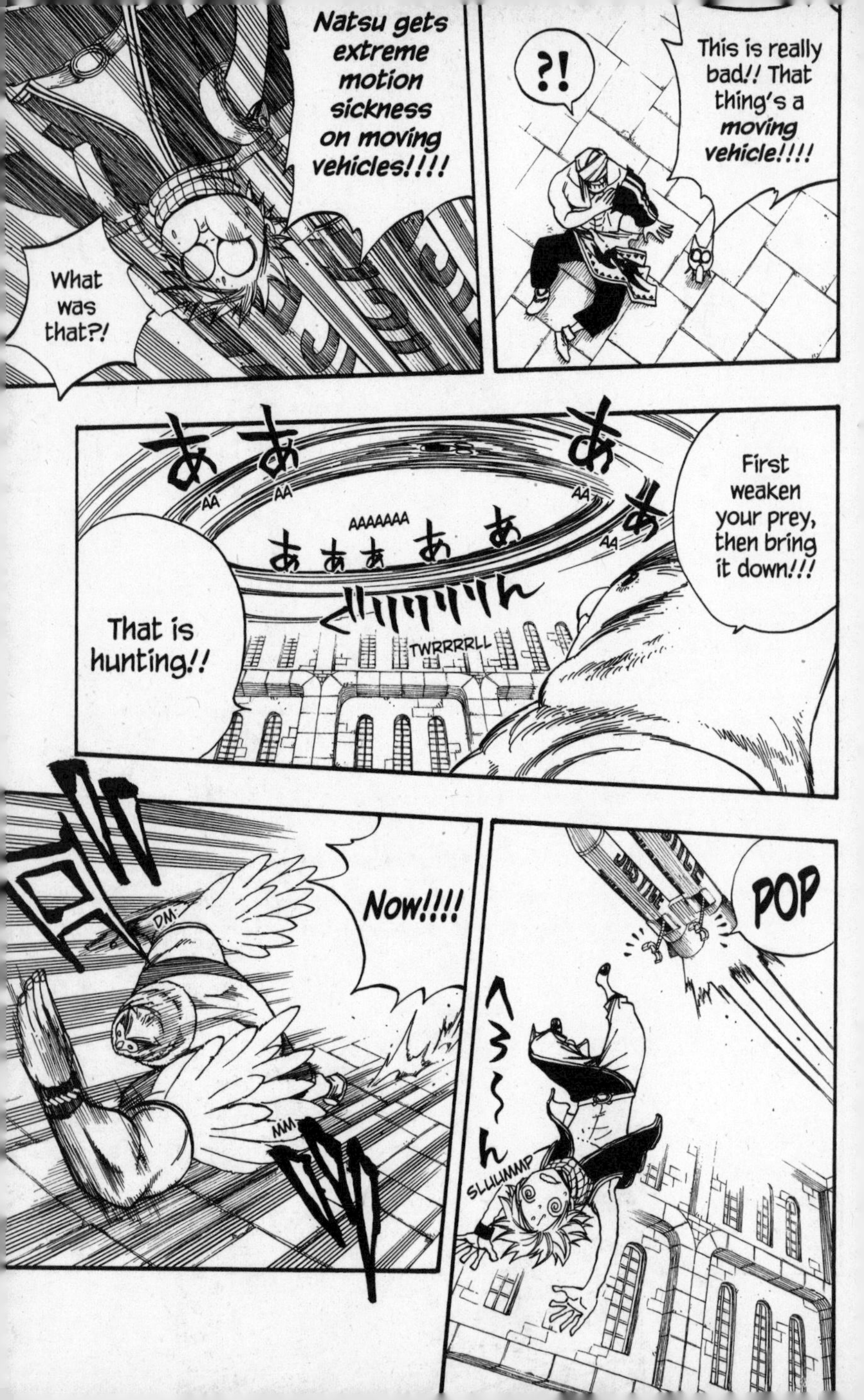
?!
This is really bad!! That thing's a moving vehicle!!!!
Natsu gets extreme motion sickness on moving vehicles!!!!
What was that?!
First weaken your prey, then bring it down!!!
AA
AA
AA
AA
AAAAAAA
TWRRRRLL
That is hunting!!
POP
SLUUMMP
Now!!!!
DM
MM

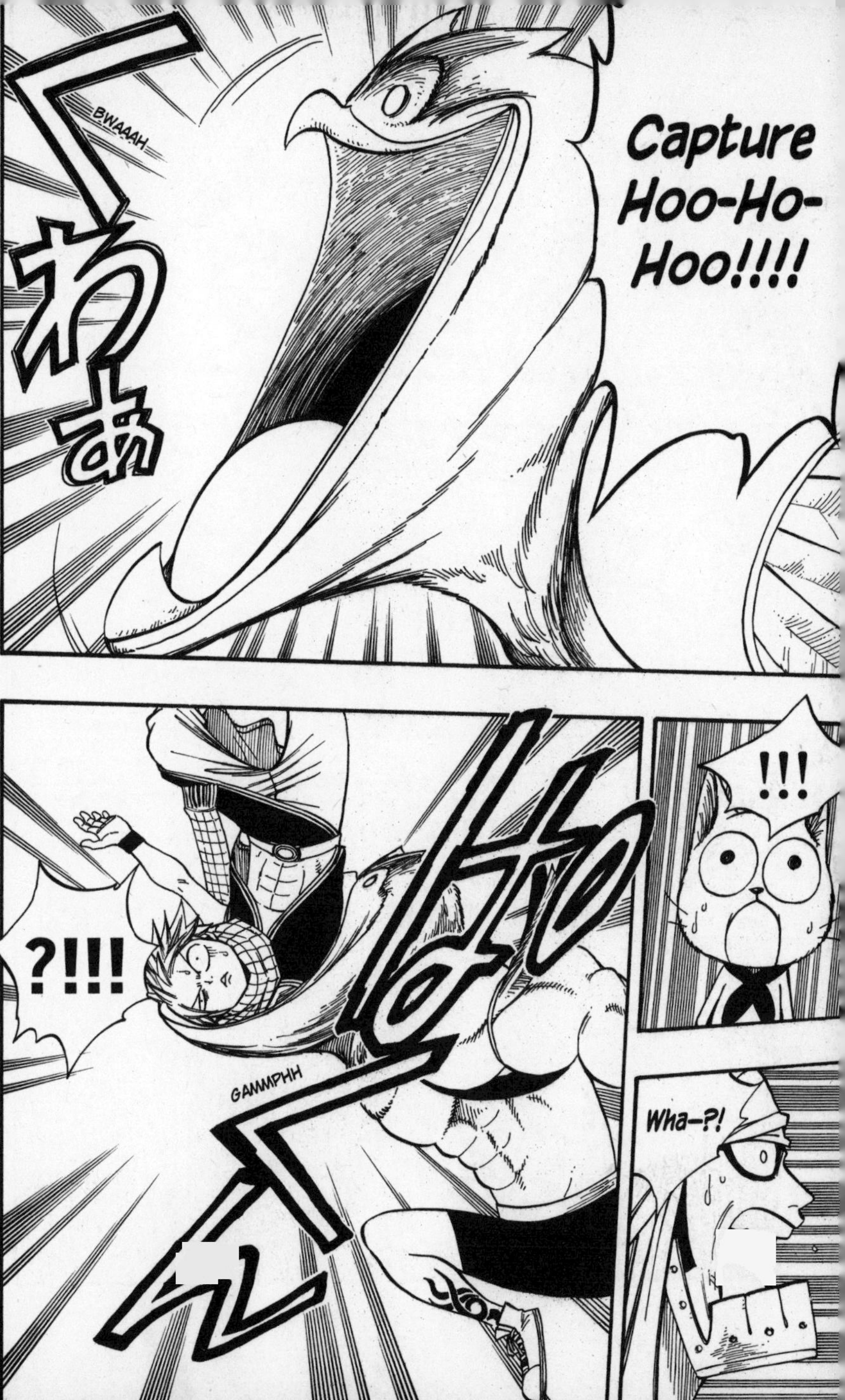
Capture Hoo-Ho-Hoo!!!!
わあ
BWAAAH
!!!
Wha–?!
?!!!
GAMMPHH

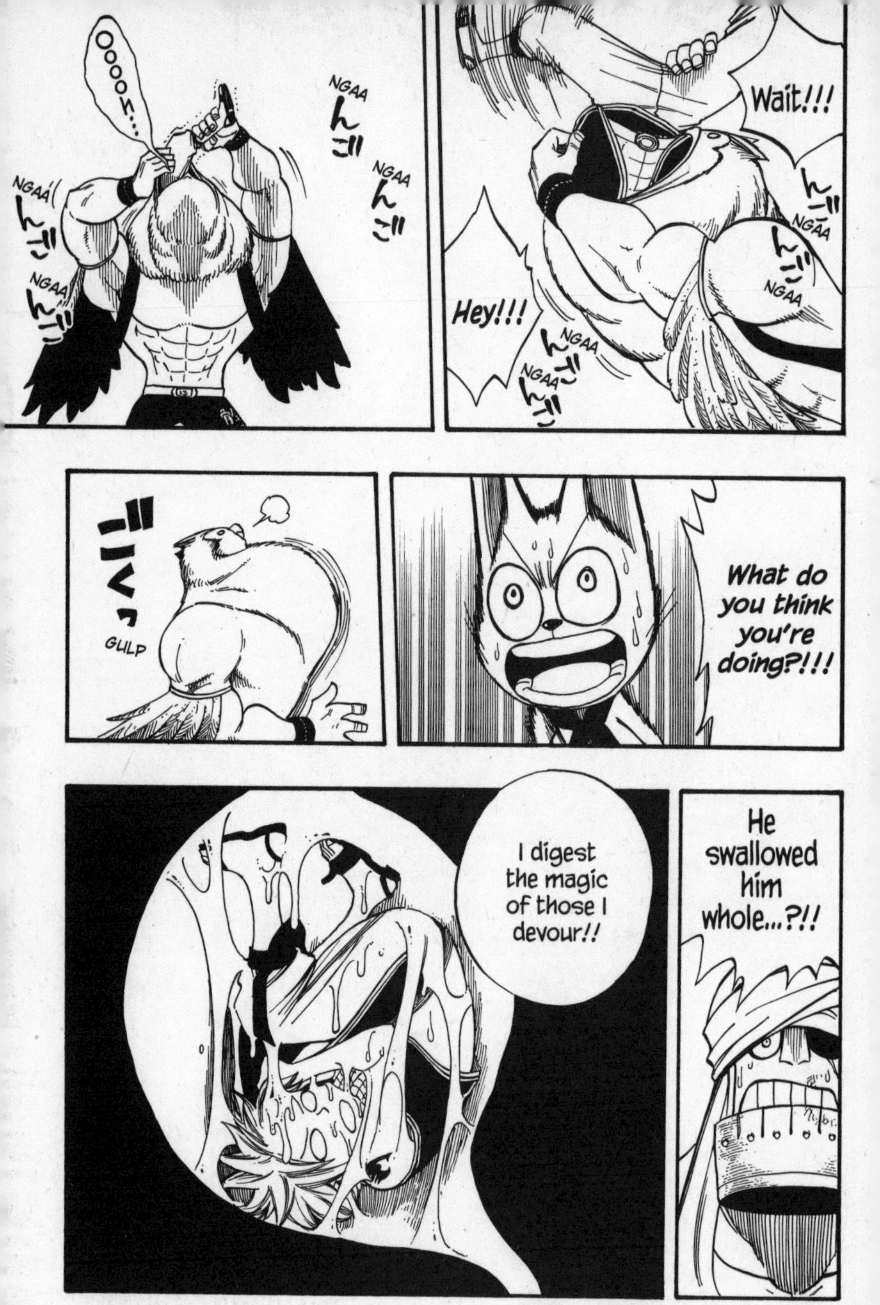

Wait!!!
んごNGAA
んごNGAA
Hey!!!
NGAA んご
NGAA んご
Ooooh...
NGAA んご
NGAA んご
NGAA んご
NGAA んご
What do you think you're doing?!!!
ゴクッ
GULP
He swallowed him whole...?!!
I digest the magic of those I devour!!

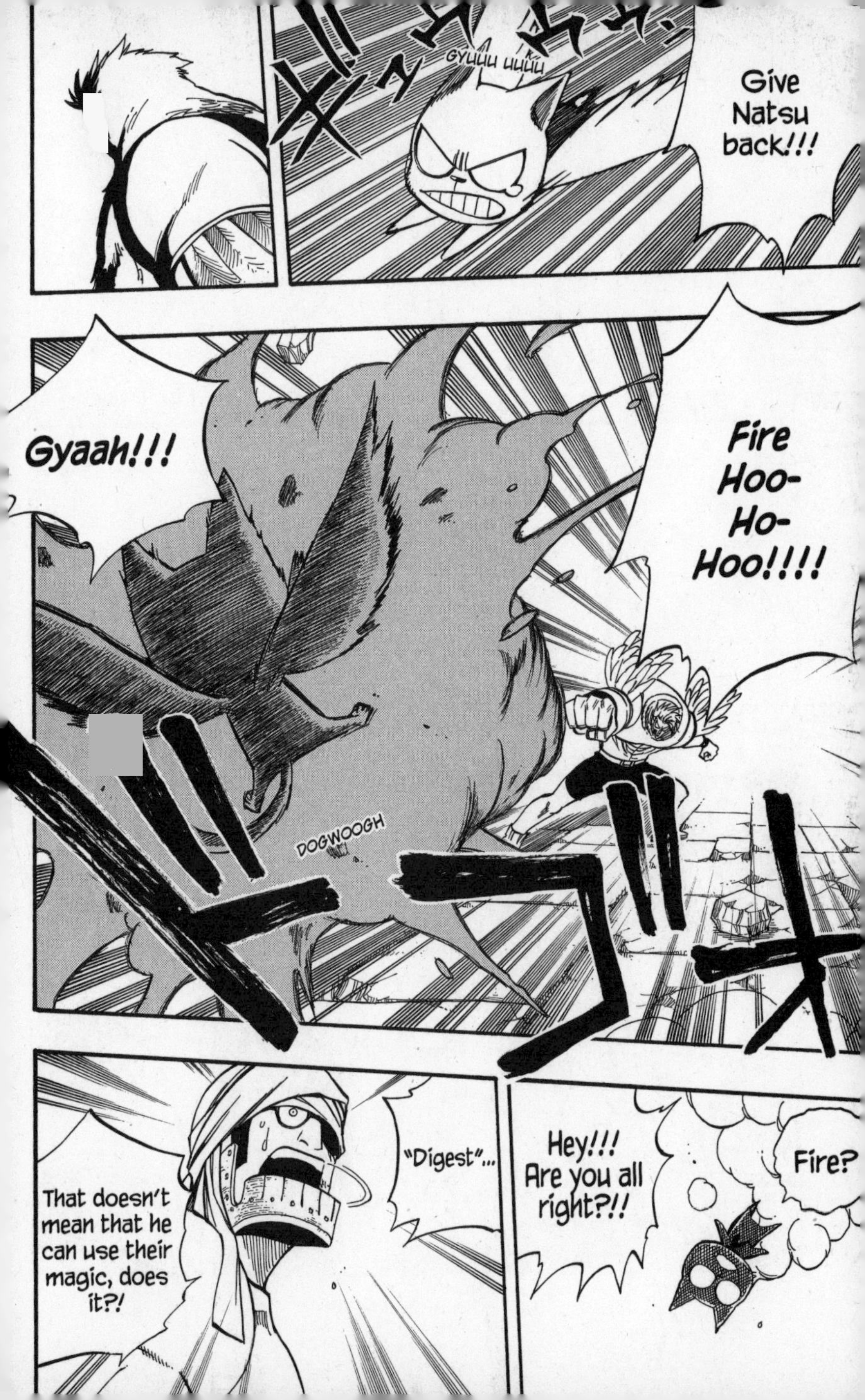
GYUUU UUUU
Give Natsu back!!!
Fire Hoo-Ho-Hoo!!!!
Gyaah!!!
DOGWOOGH
Fire?
Hey!!! Are you all right?!!
"Digest"...
That doesn't mean that he can use their magic, does it?!

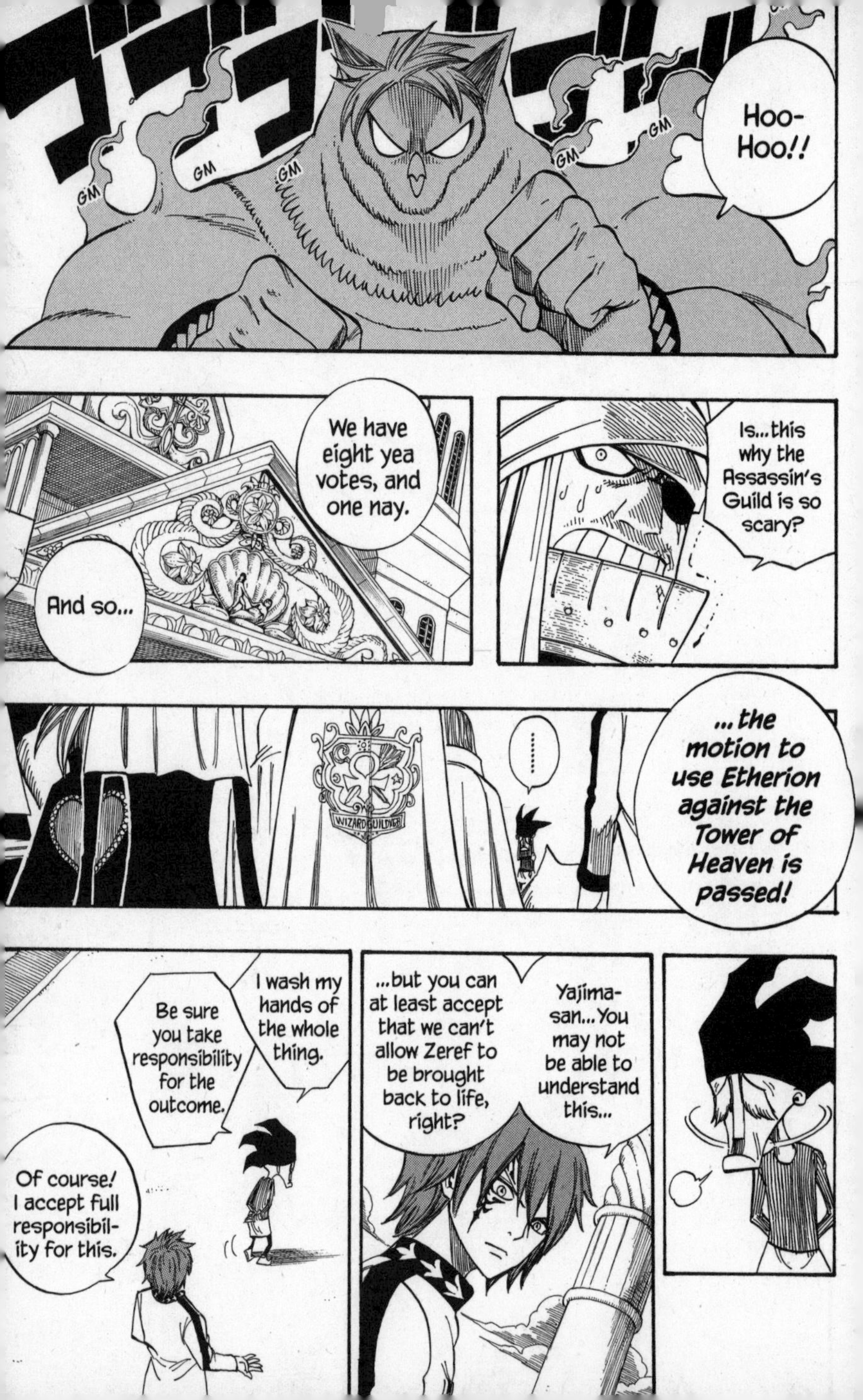
Hoo-Hoo!!
GM GM GM GM GM
Is...this why the Assassin's Guild is so scary?
We have eight yea votes, and one nay.
And so...
...the motion to use Etherion against the Tower of Heaven is passed!
......
Yajima-san...You may not be able to understand this...
...but you can at least accept that we can't allow Zeref to be brought back to life, right?
I wash my hands of the whole thing.
Be sure you take responsibility for the outcome.
Of course! I accept full responsibility for this.

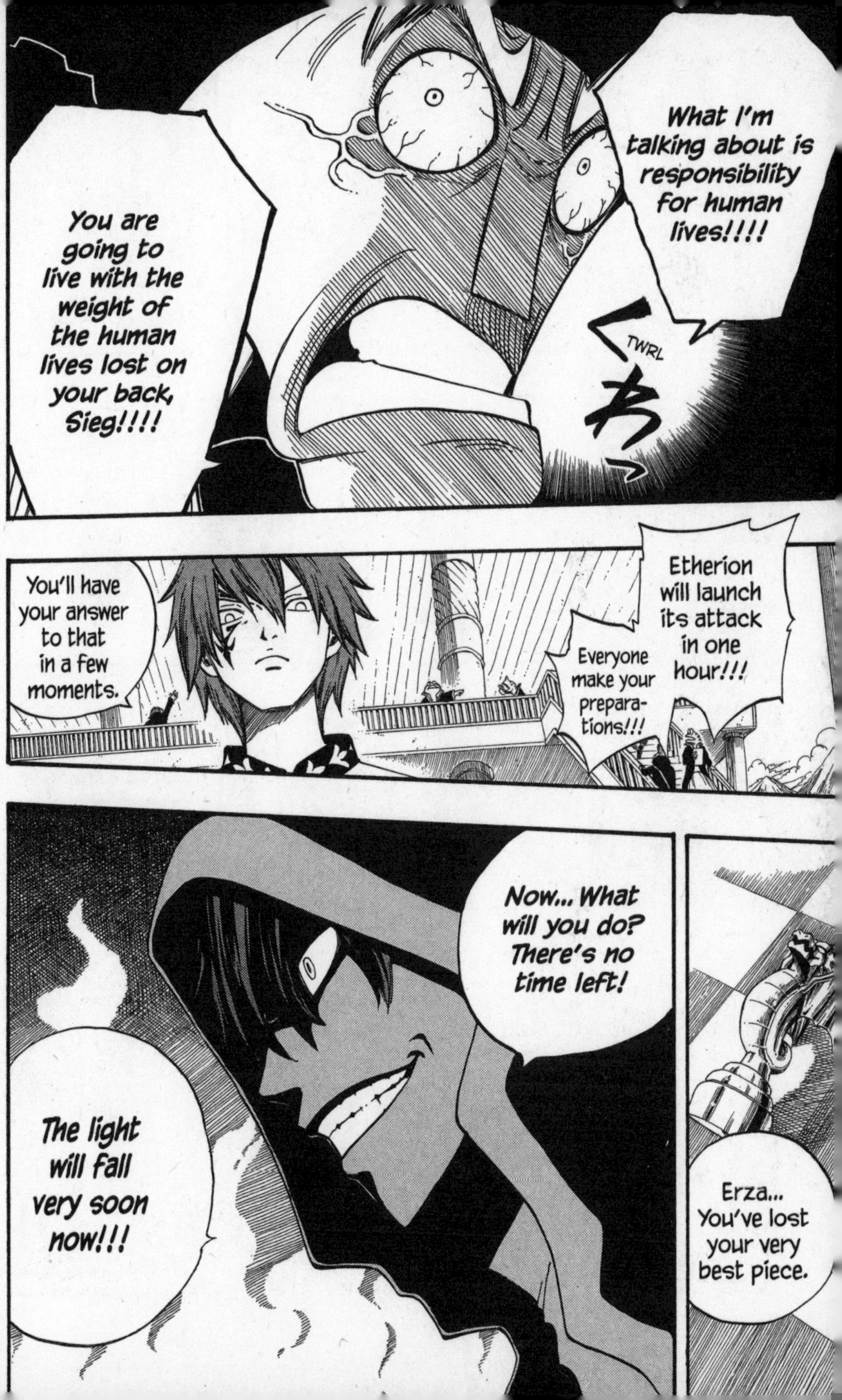
What I'm talking about is responsibility for human lives!!!!
TWRL
You are going to live with the weight of the human lives lost on your back, Sieg!!!!
Etherion will launch its attack in one hour!!!
Everyone make your preparations!!!
You'll have your answer to that in a few moments.
Erza... You've lost your very best piece.
Now... What will you do? There's no time left!
The light will fall very soon now!!!

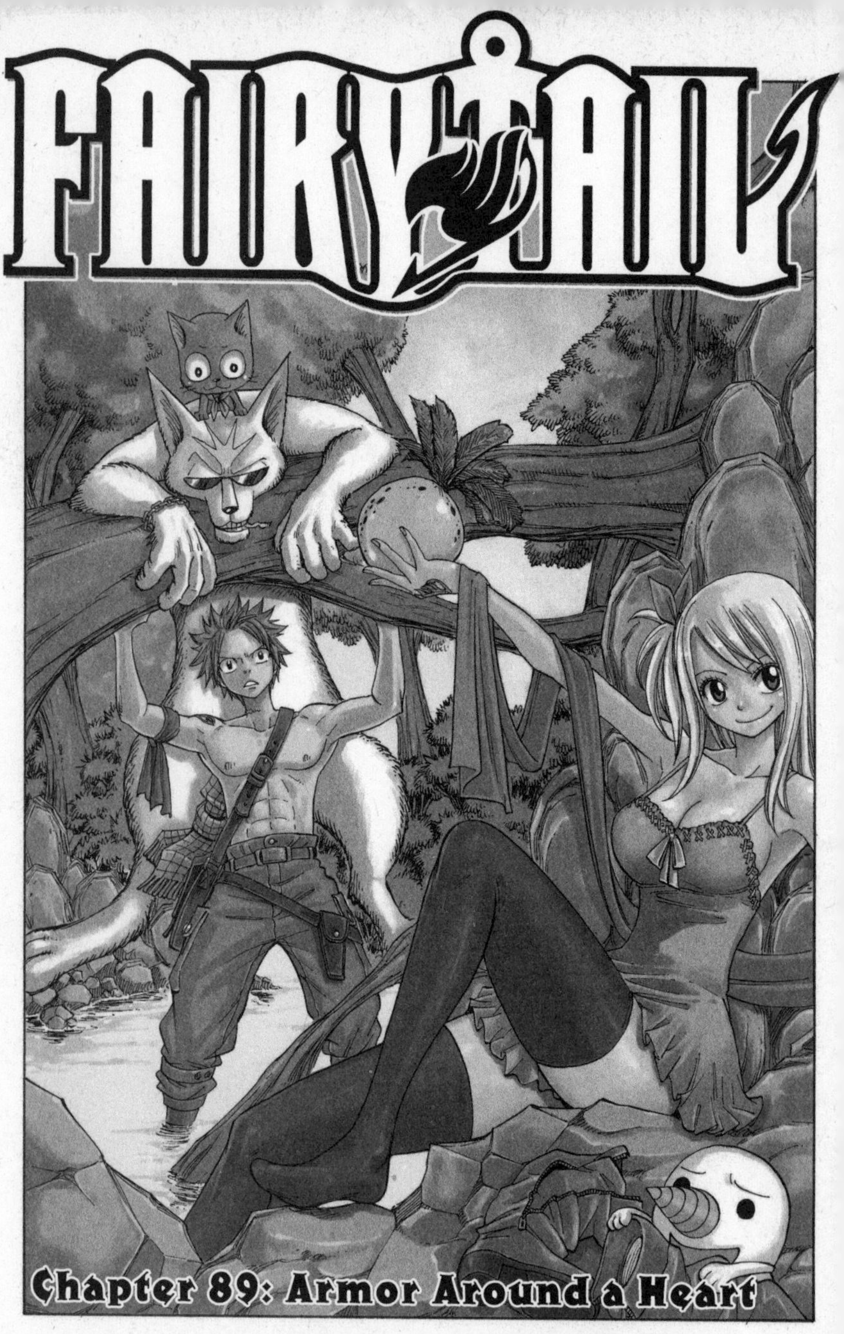
FAIRY TAIL
Chapter 89: Armor Around a Heart

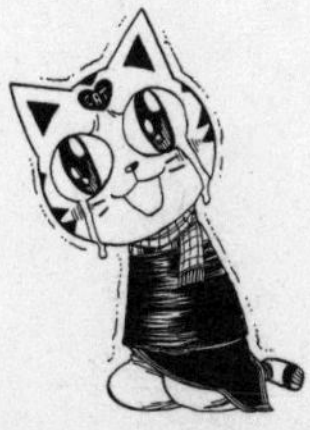

FAIRY TAIL

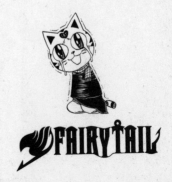

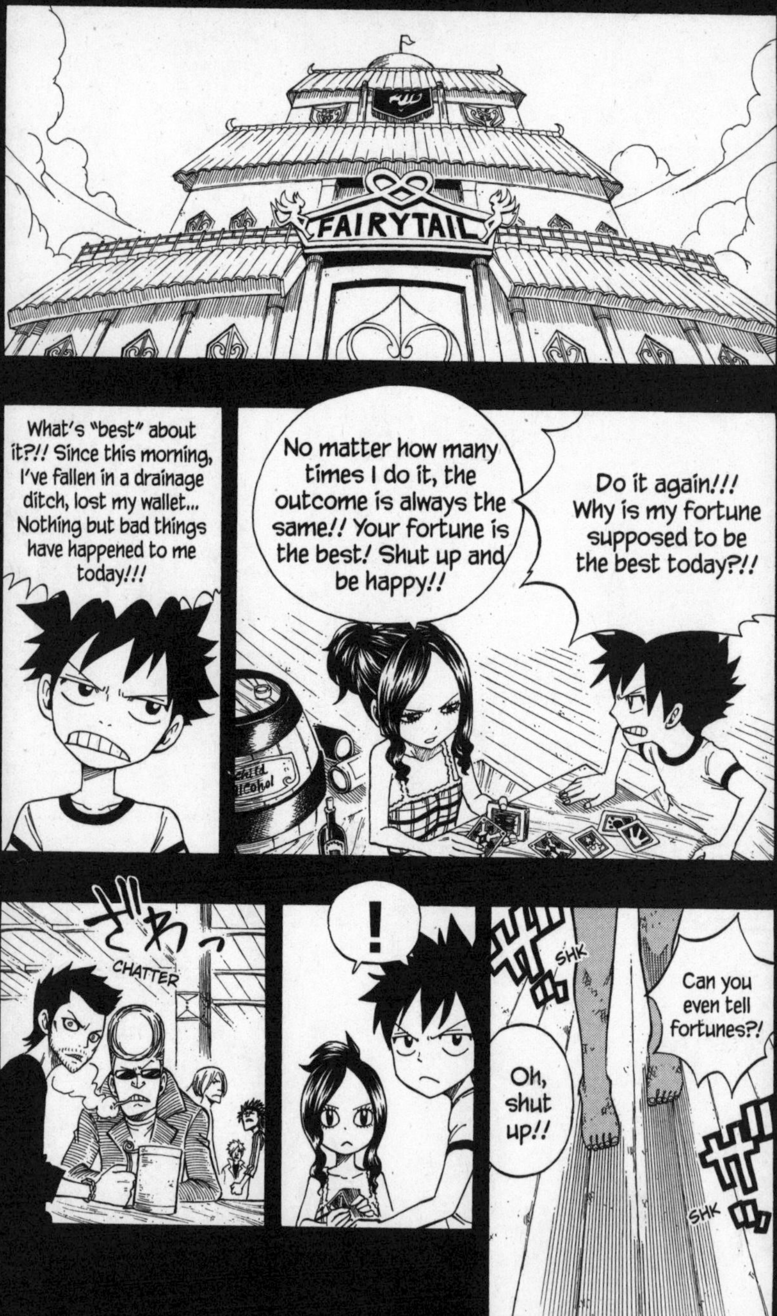
FAIRYTAIL
Do it again!!! Why is my fortune supposed to be the best today?!!
No matter how many times I do it, the outcome is always the same!! Your fortune is the best! Shut up and be happy!!
What's "best" about it?!! Since this morning, I've fallen in a drainage ditch, lost my wallet... Nothing but bad things have happened to me today!!!
Can you even tell fortunes?!
SHK
Oh, shut up!!
SHK
!
ざわっ
CHATTER

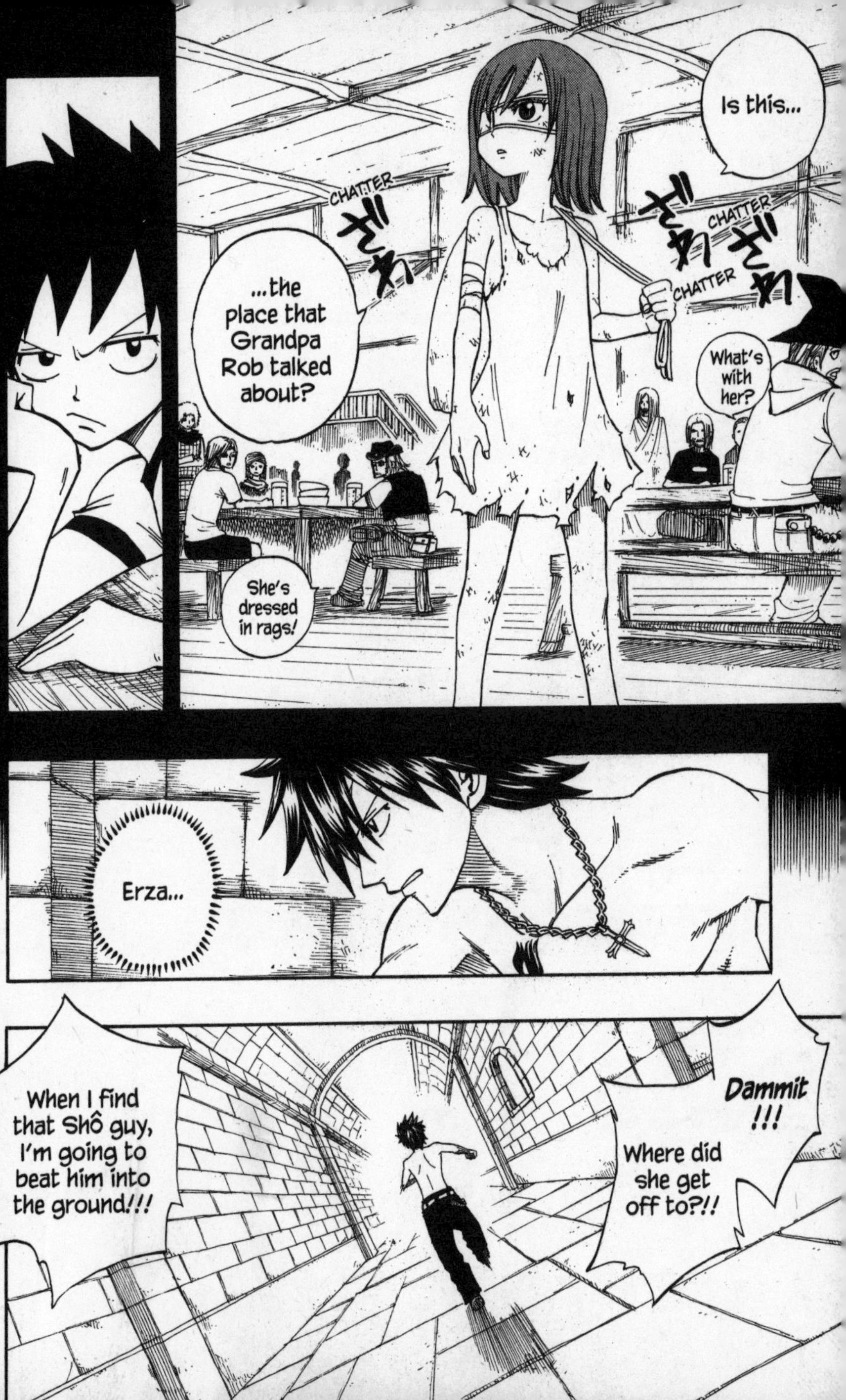

Is this...
CHATTER ざわ
CHATTER ざわ
CHATTER ざわ
...the place that Grandpa Rob talked about?
What's with her?
She's dressed in rags!
Erza...
Dammit!!!
Where did she get off to?!!
When I find that Shô guy, I'm going to beat him into the ground!!!

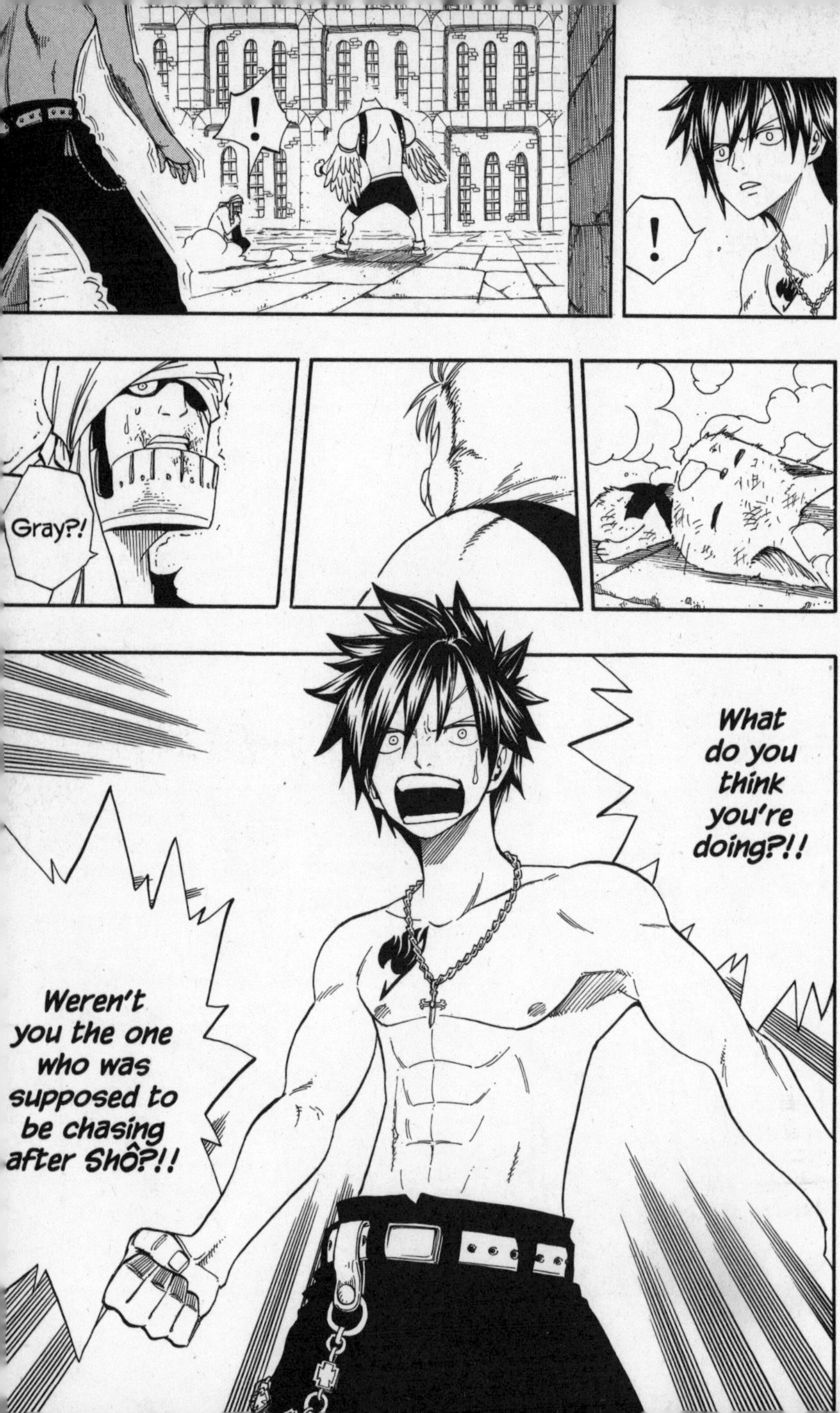
!
!
Gray?!
What do you think you're doing?!!
Weren't you the one who was supposed to be chasing after Shô?!!

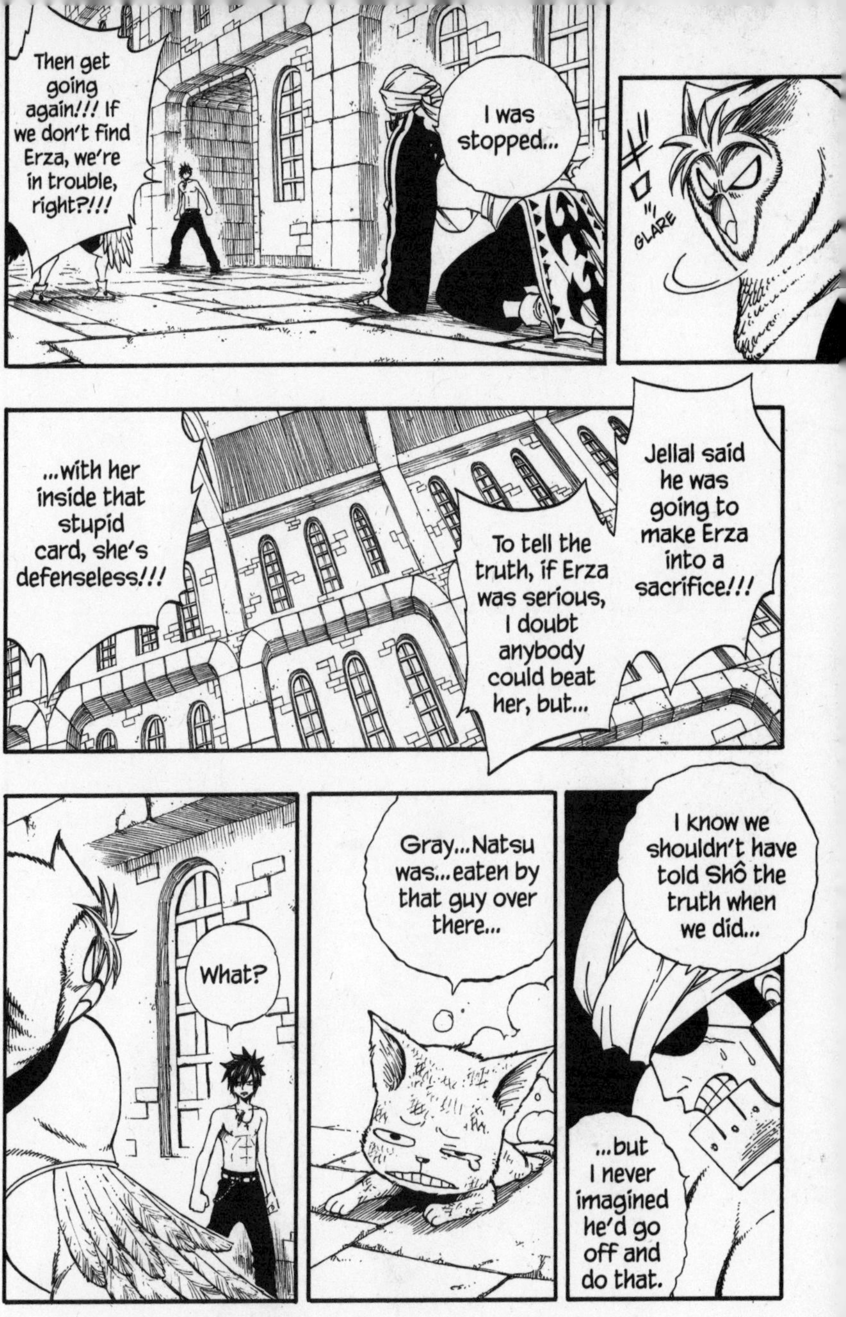
GLARE
I was stopped...
Then get going again!!! If we don't find Erza, we're in trouble, right?!!!
Jellal said he was going to make Erza into a sacrifice!!!
To tell the truth, if Erza was serious, I doubt anybody could beat her, but...
...with her inside that stupid card, she's defenseless!!!
I know we shouldn't have told Shô the truth when we did...
...but I never imagined he'd go off and do that.
Gray...Natsu was...eaten by that guy over there...
What?

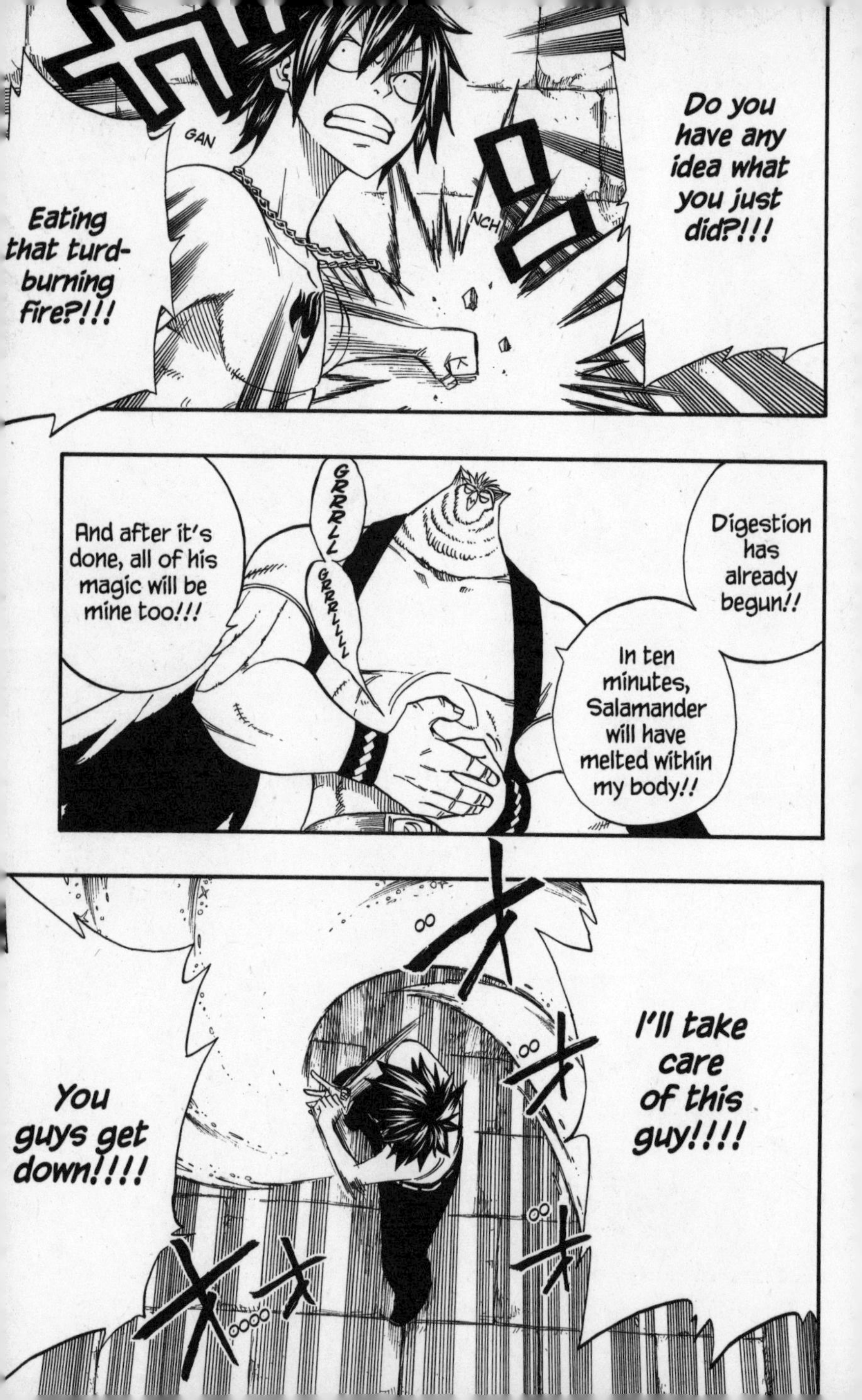
GAN
NCH
Do you have any idea what you just did?!!!
Eating that turd-burning fire?!!!
Digestion has already begun!!
In ten minutes, Salamander will have melted within my body!!
GRRRLL
GRRRLLLL
And after it's done, all of his magic will be mine too!!!
I'll take care of this guy!!!!
You guys get down!!!!

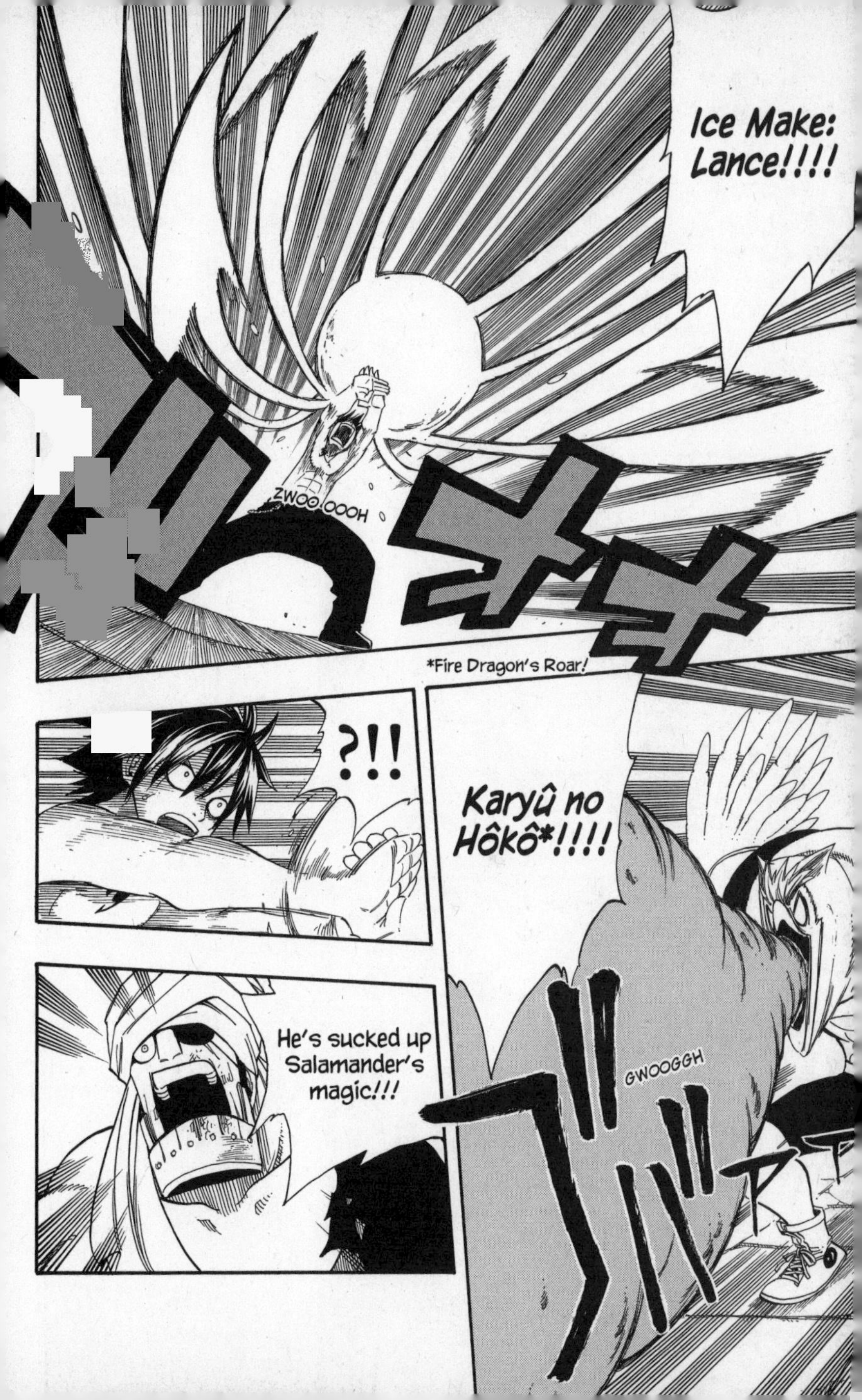
Ice Make: Lance!!!!
ZWOO OOOH
Karyû no Hôkô*!!!!
GWOOGGH
*Fire Dragon's Roar!
?!!
He's sucked up Salamander's magic!!!

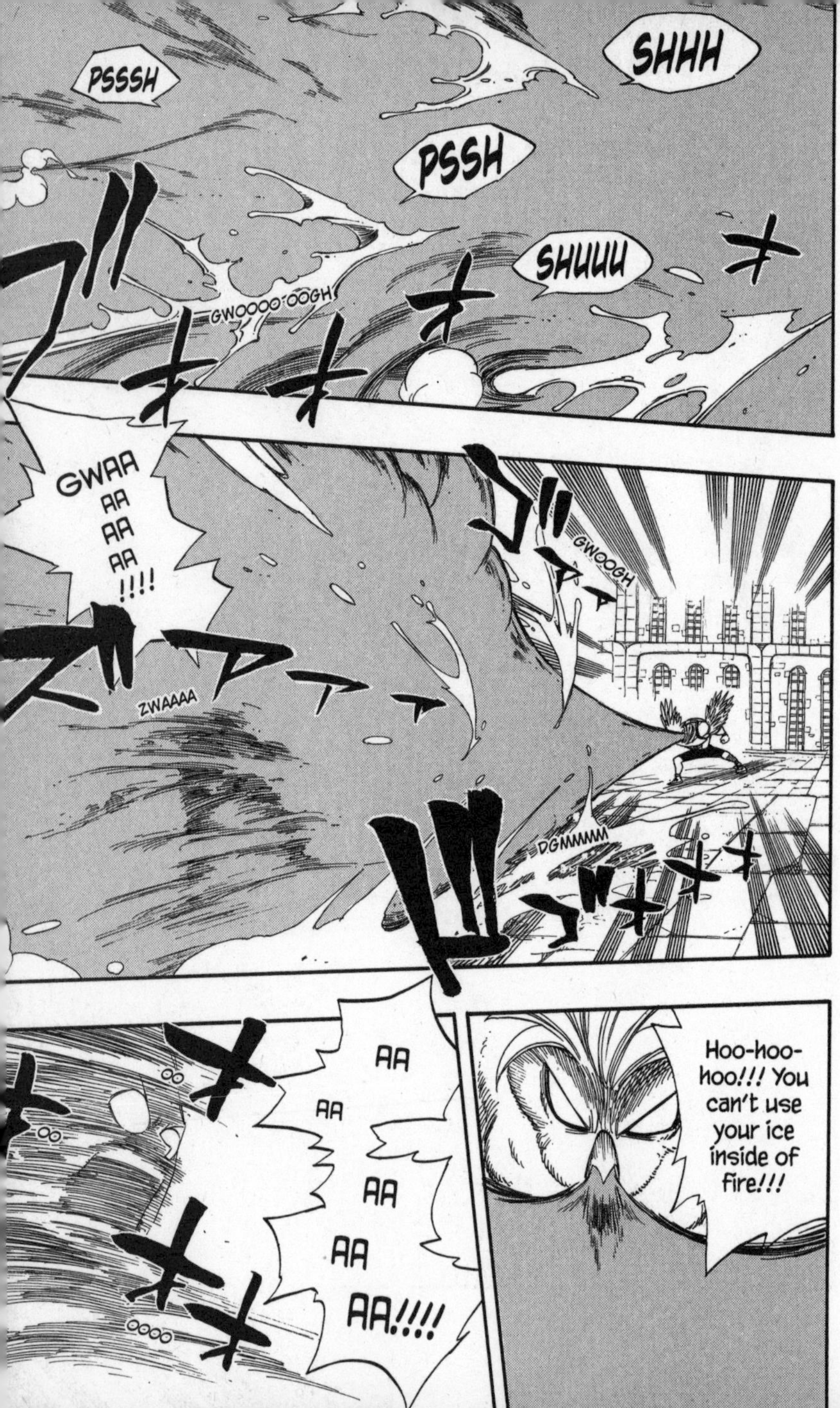
SHHH
SHUUU
PSSH
PSSSH
GWOOOO OOGH
GWOOOGH
D.GMMMMM
GWAA AA AA AA !!!!
ZWAAAA
Hoo-hoo-hoo!!! You can't use your ice inside of fire!!!
AA AA AA AA AA!!!!
OO
OO
OOOO

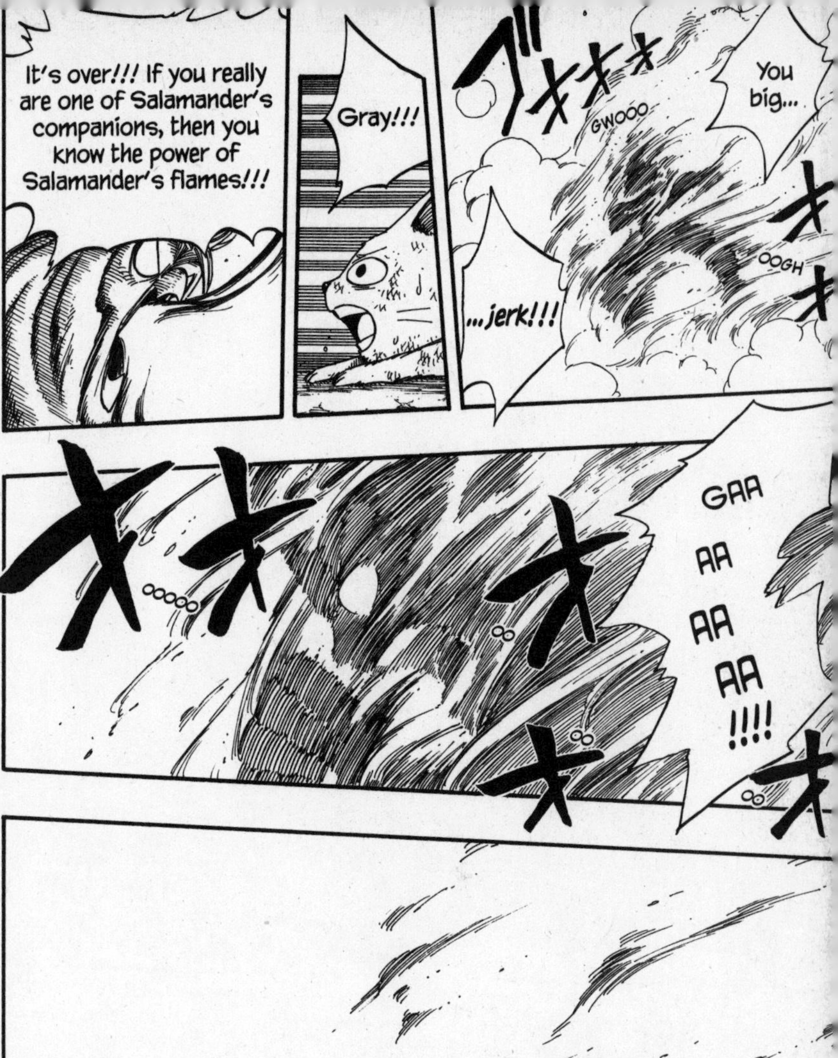
You big...
GWOOO
OOGH
...jerk!!!
Gray!!!
It's over!!! If you really are one of Salamander's companions, then you know the power of Salamander's flames!!!
GAA AA AA AA !!!!
OOOOO

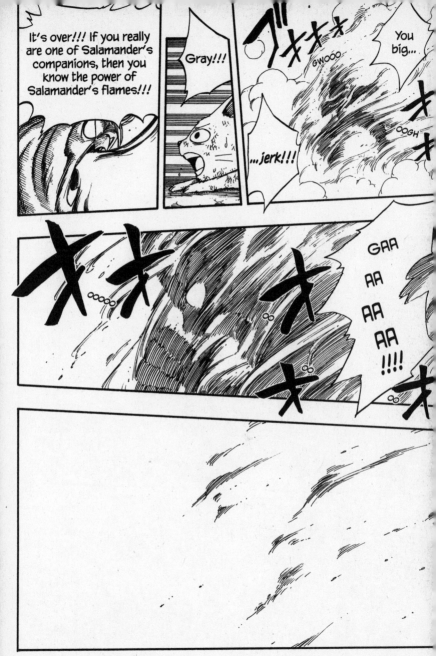

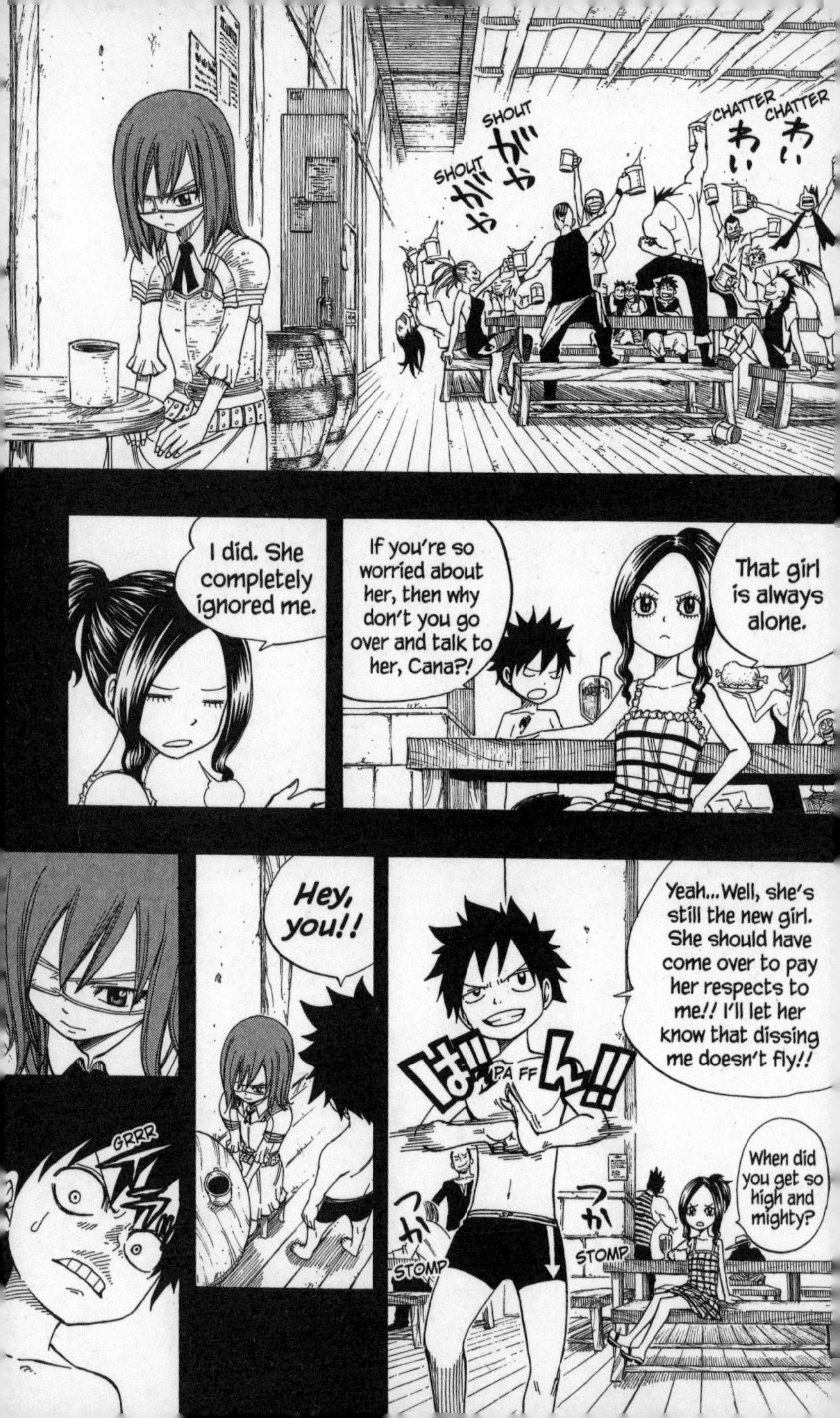
CHATTER
わい
CHATTER
わい
SHOUT
がや
SHOUT
がや
That girl is always alone.
If you're so worried about her, then why don't you go over and talk to her, Cana?!
I did. She completely ignored me.
Yeah...Well, she's still the new girl. She should have come over to pay her respects to me!! I'll let her know that dissing me doesn't fly!!
はん!!
PAFF
つか
STOMP
つか
STOMP
When did you get so high and mighty?
Hey, you!!
GRRR

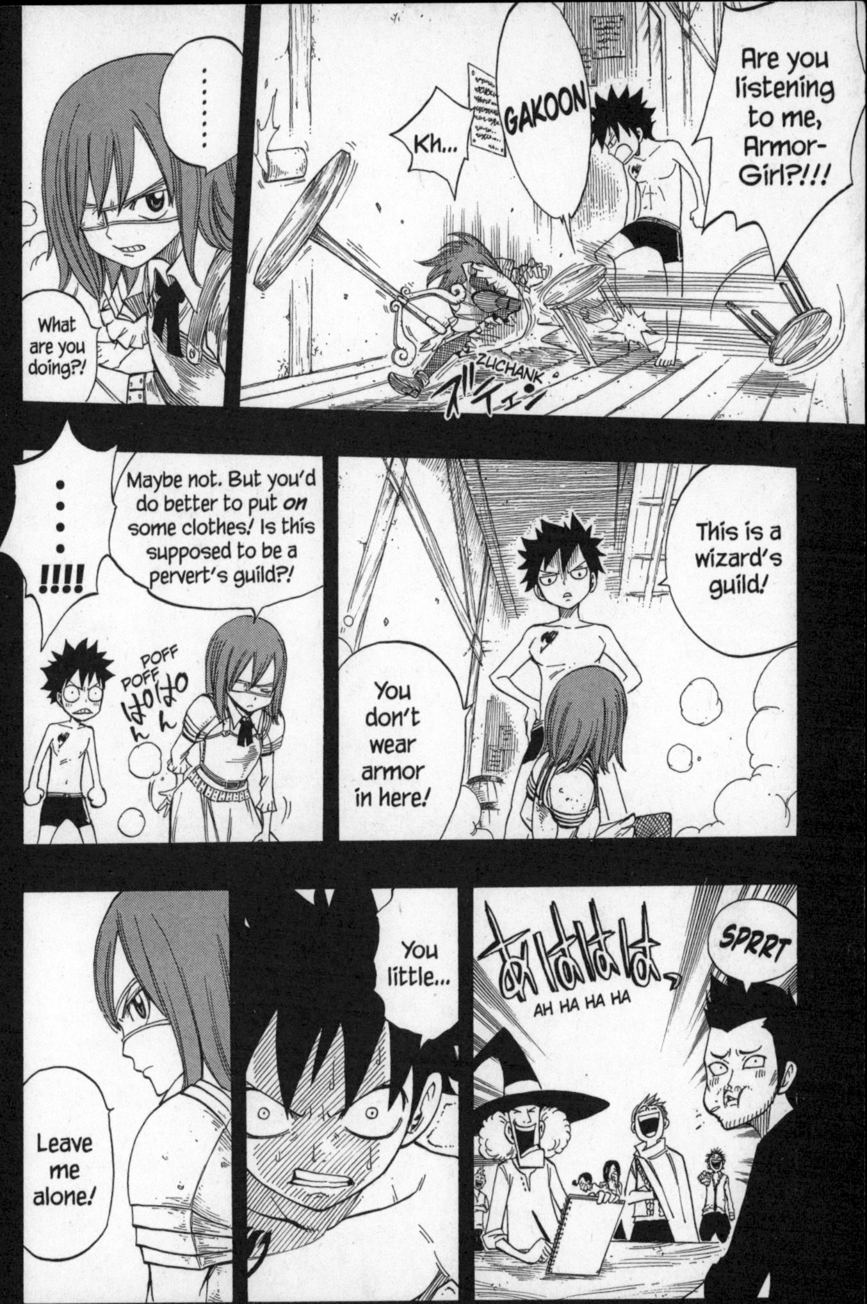
Are you listening to me, Armor-Girl?!!!
GAKOON
Kh...
ZUCHANK
......
What are you doing?!
This is a wizard's guild!
You don't wear armor in here!
Maybe not. But you'd do better to put *on* some clothes! Is this supposed to be a pervert's guild?!
....!!!!
POFF POFF
SPRRT
AH HA HA HA
You little...
Leave me alone!

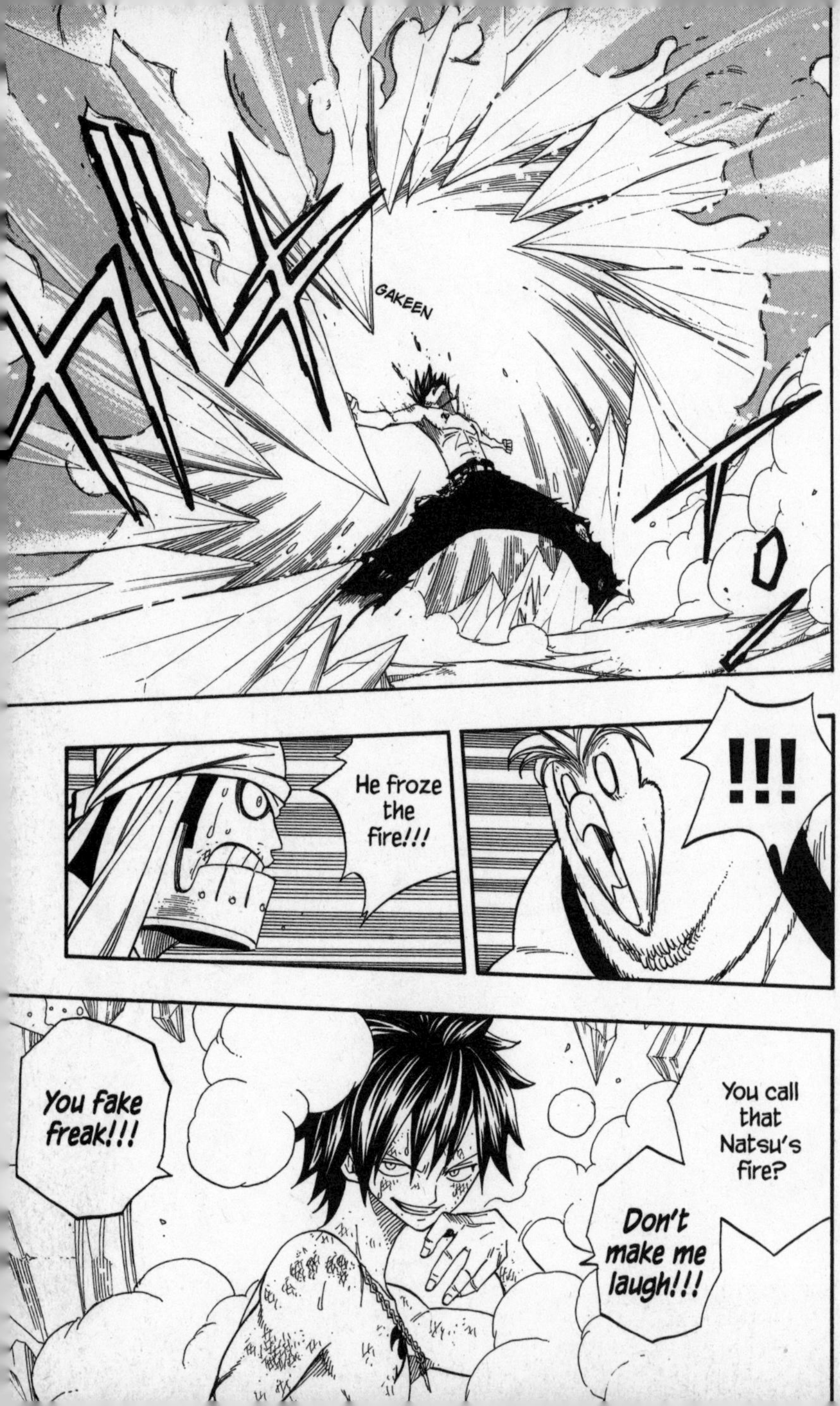
GAKEEN
!!!
He froze the fire!!!
You call that Natsu's fire?
Don't make me laugh!!!
You fake freak!!!

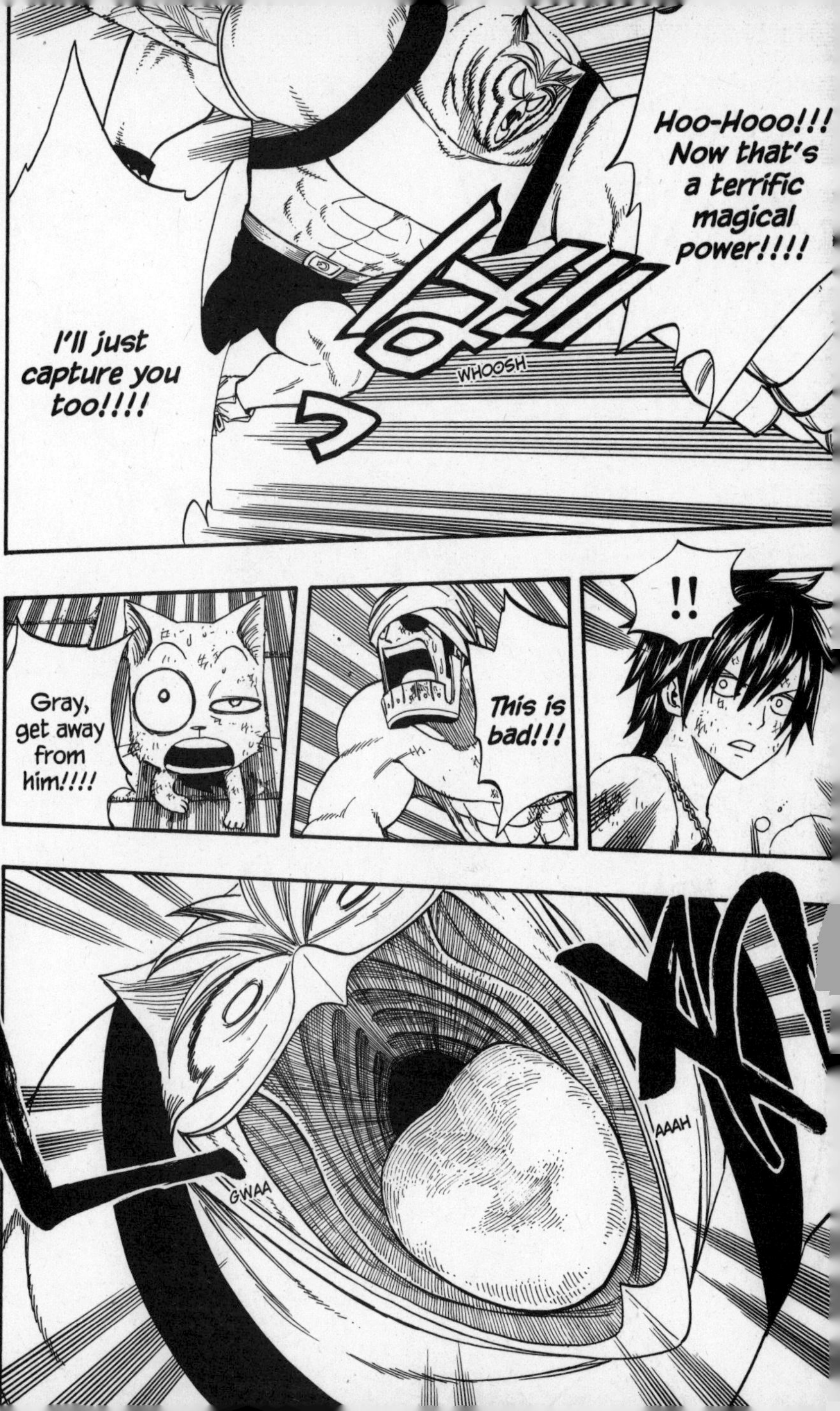
Hoo-Hooo!!! Now that's a terrific magical power!!!!
I'll just capture you too!!!!
WHOOSH
!!
This is bad!!!
Gray, get away from him!!!!
AAAH
GWAA

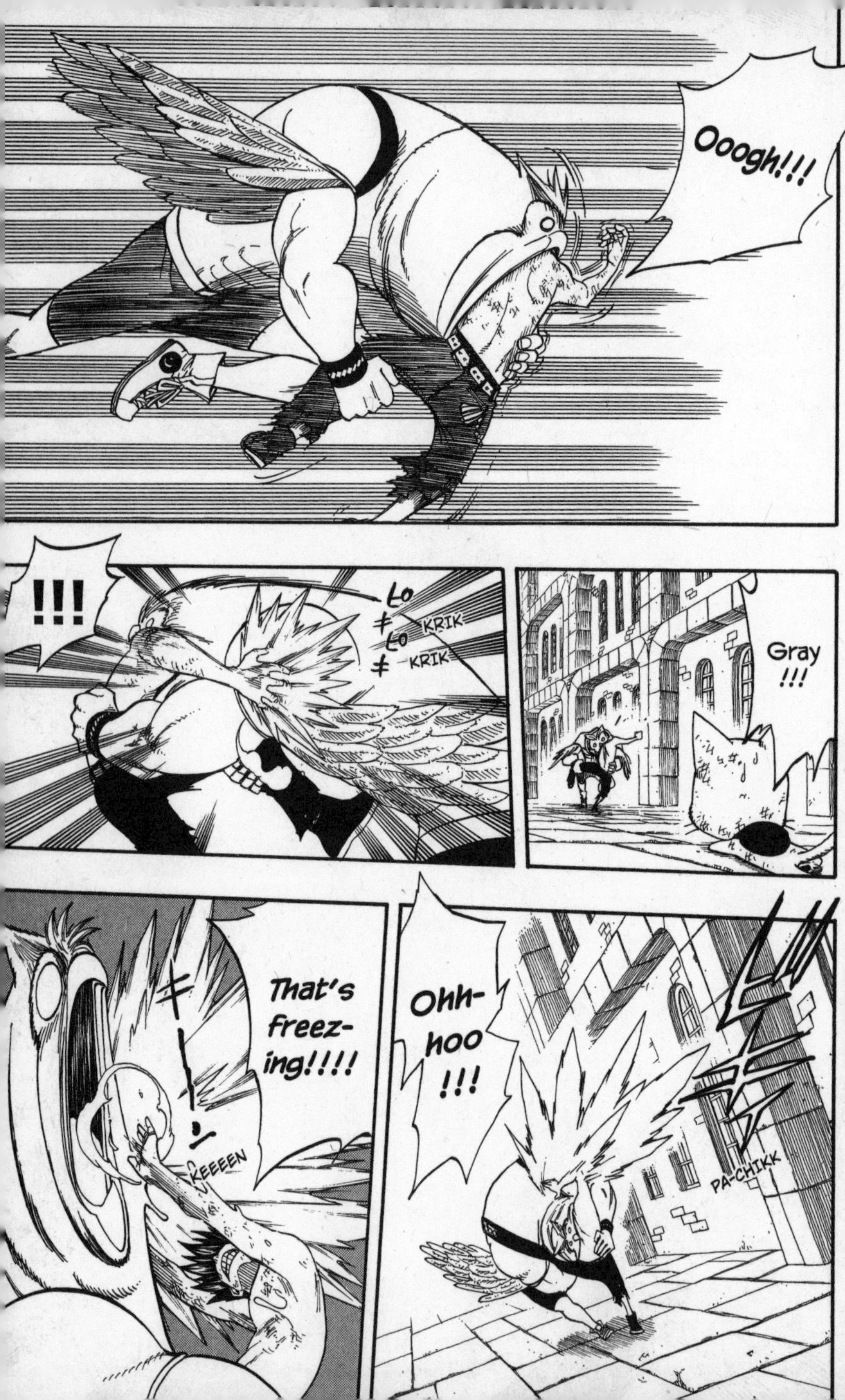

Ooogh!!!
Gray !!!
!!!
KRIK
KRIK
Ohh-hoo !!!
PA-CHIKK
That's freez-ing!!!!
KEEEEN

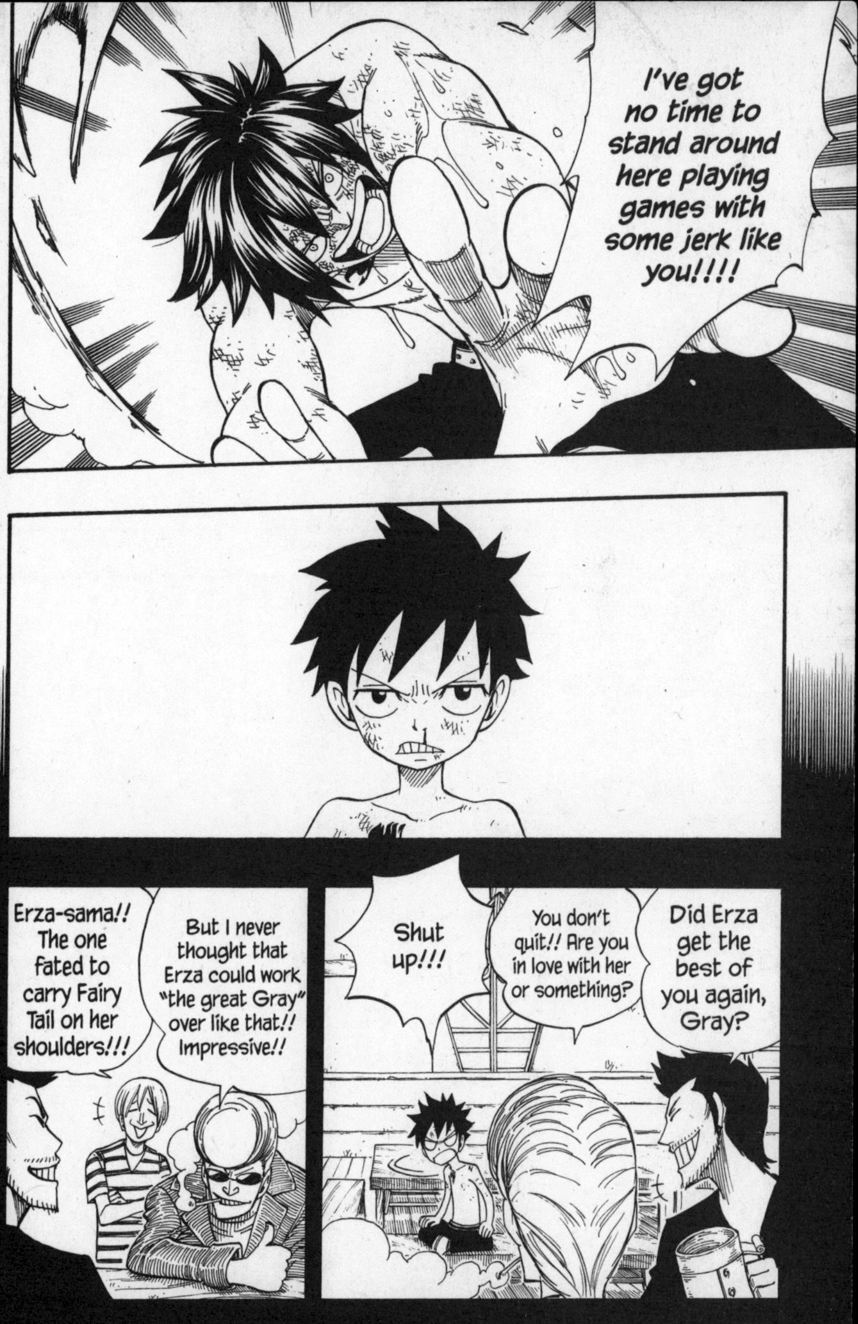
I've got no time to stand around here playing games with some jerk like you!!!!
Did Erza get the best of you again, Gray?
You don't quit!! Are you in love with her or something?
Shut up!!!
But I never thought that Erza could work "the great Gray" over like that!! Impressive!!
Erza-sama!! The one fated to carry Fairy Tail on her shoulders!!!

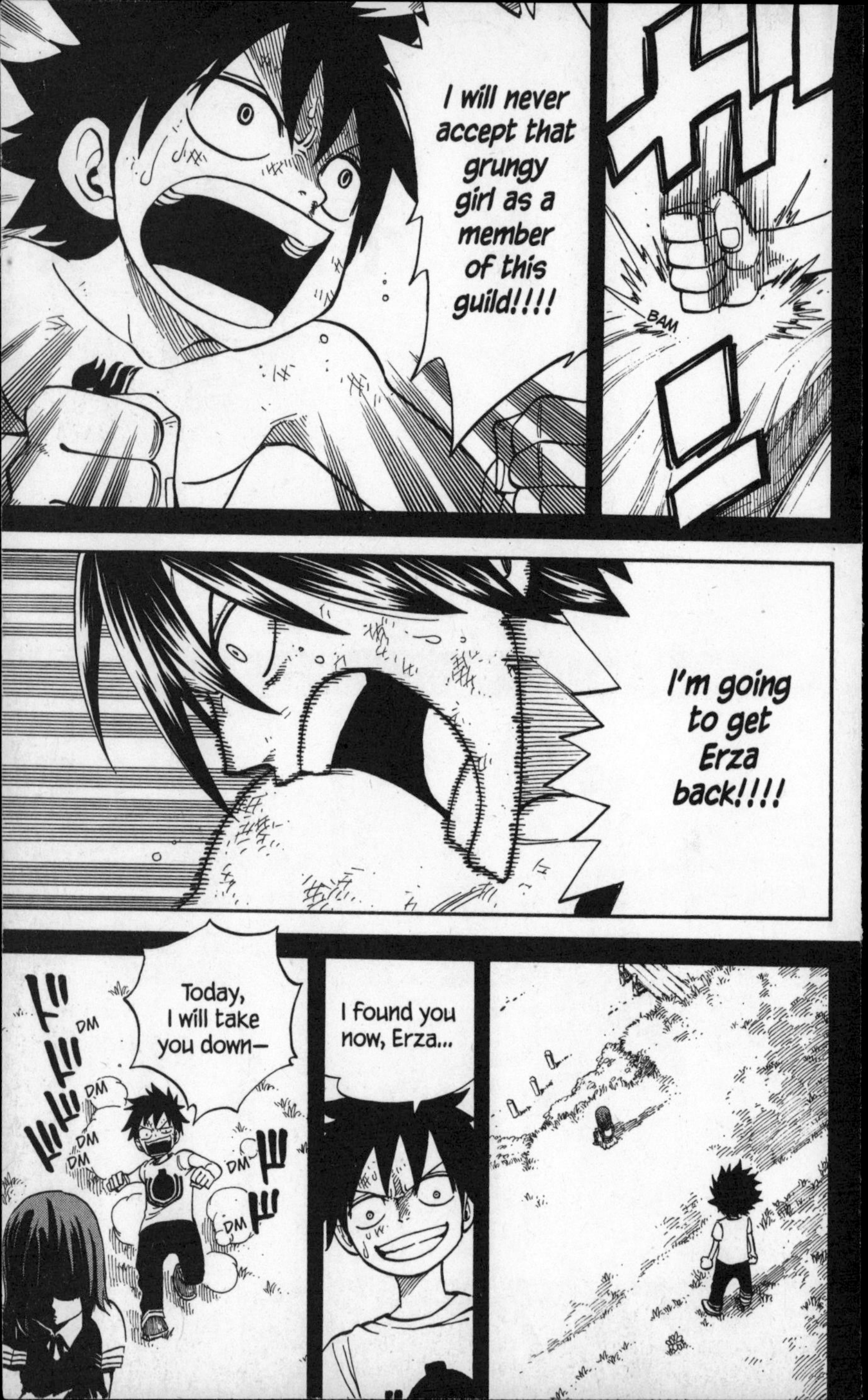
BAM
I will never accept that grungy girl as a member of this guild!!!!
I'm going to get Erza back!!!!
I found you now, Erza...
Today, I will take you down—
DM
DM
DM
DM
DM
DM

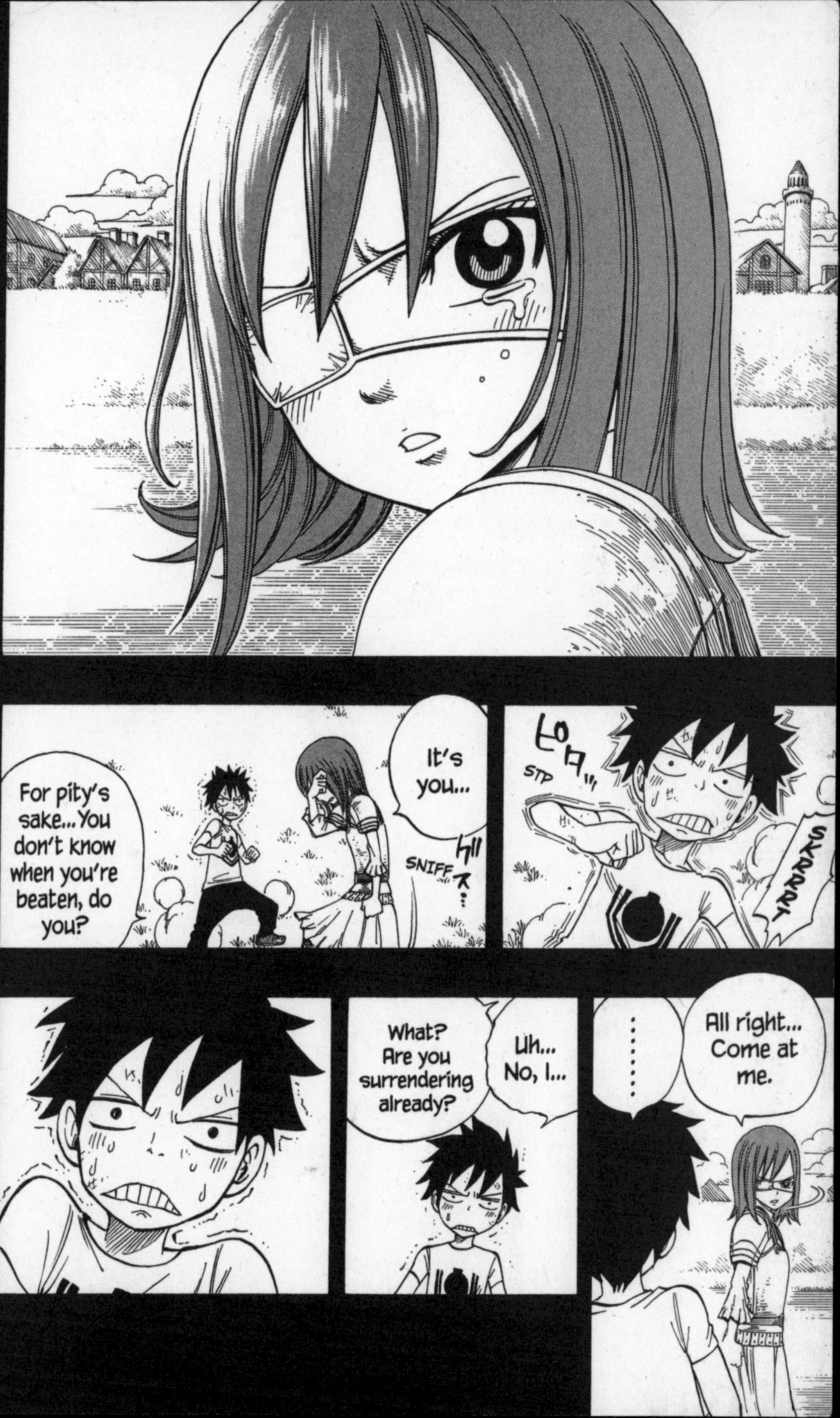
STP
SKRRRT
It's you...
SNIFF
For pity's sake...You don't know when you're beaten, do you?
All right... Come at me.
......
Uh... No, I...
What? Are you surrendering already?

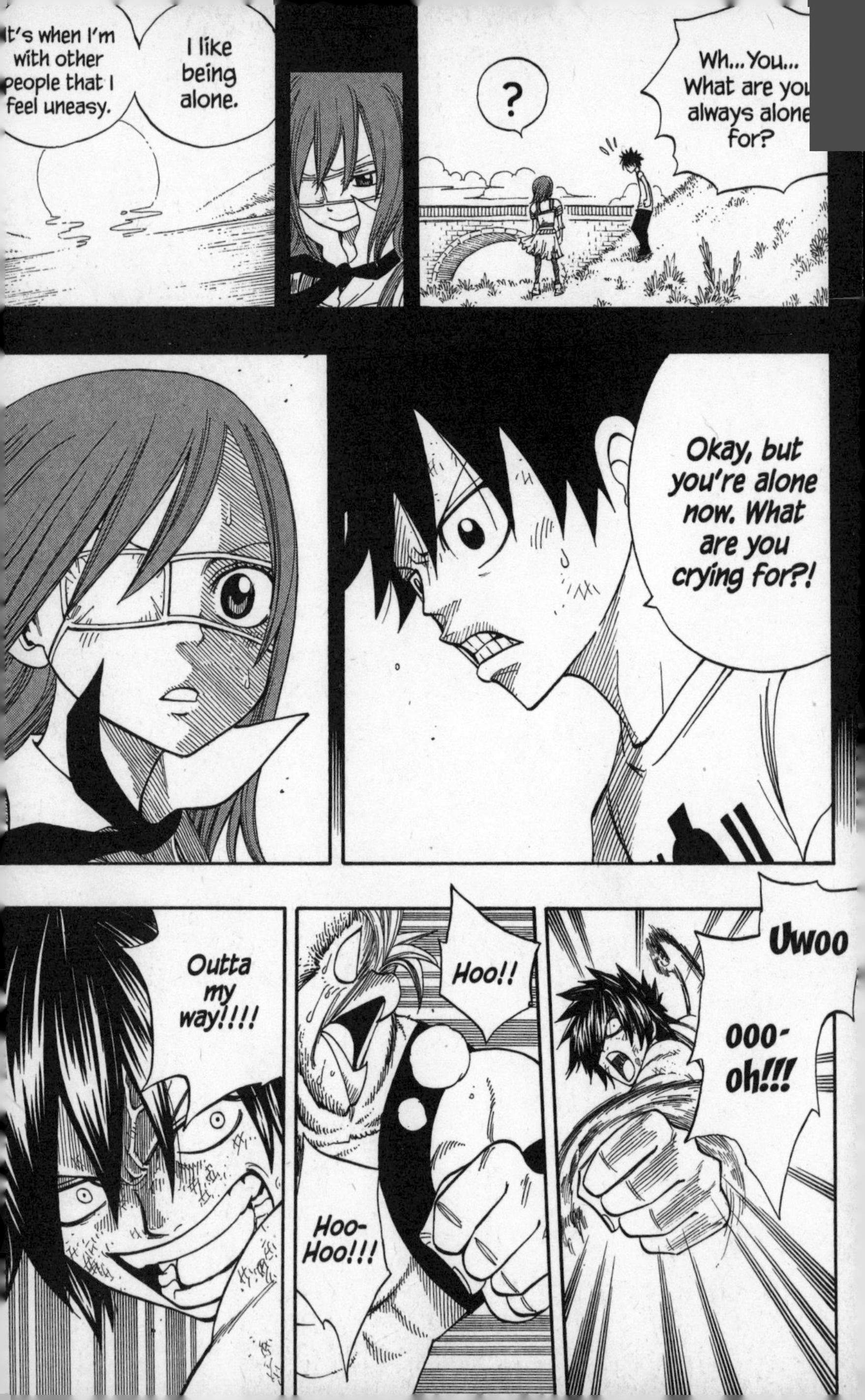
Wh...You... What are you always alone for?
?
I like being alone.
t's when I'm with other people that I feel uneasy.
Okay, but you're alone now. What are you crying for?!
Uwoo ooo- oh!!!
Hoo!!
Hoo- Hoo!!!
Outta my way!!!!

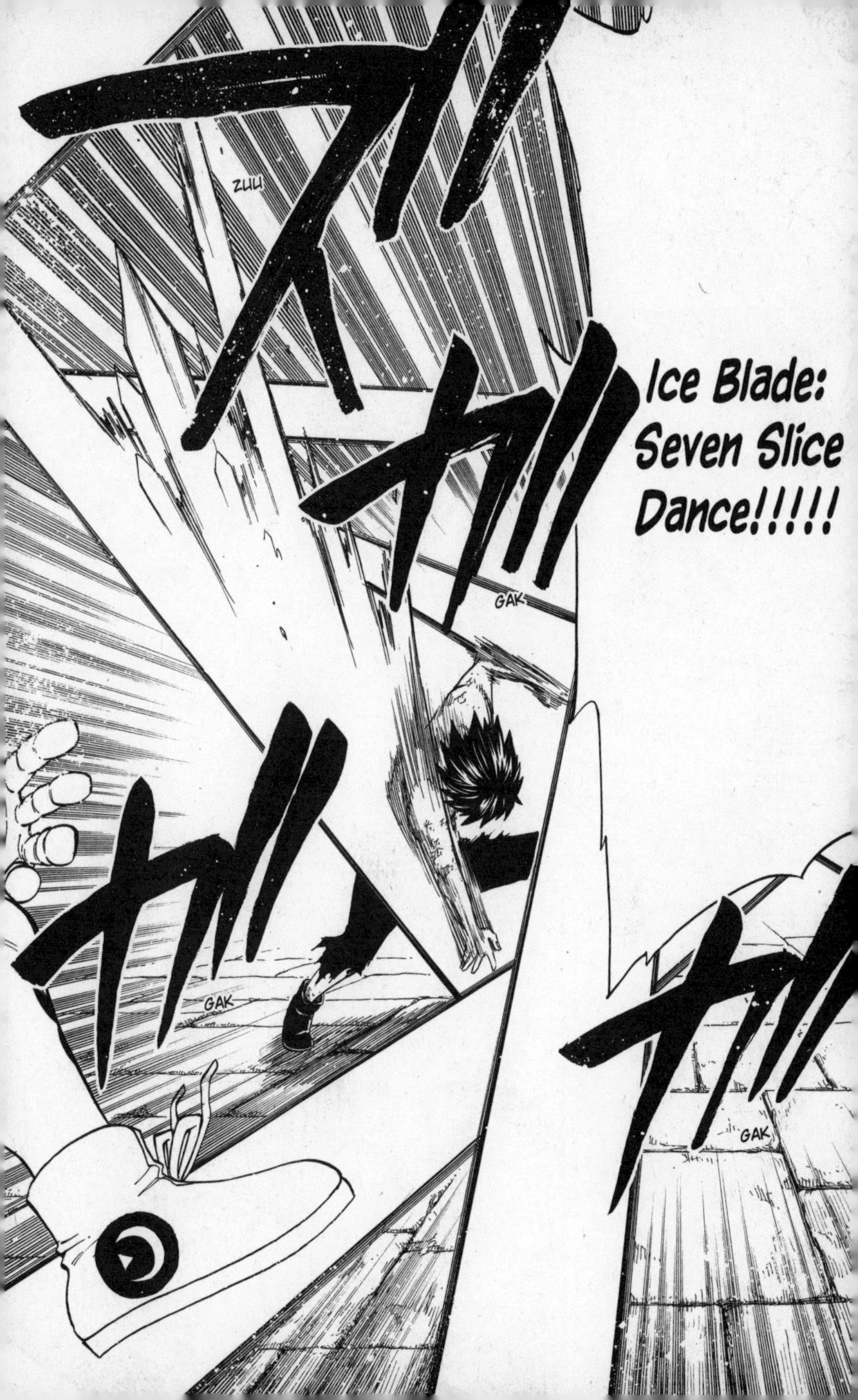
Ice Blade: Seven Slice Dance!!!!!
ZUU
GAK
GAK
GAK

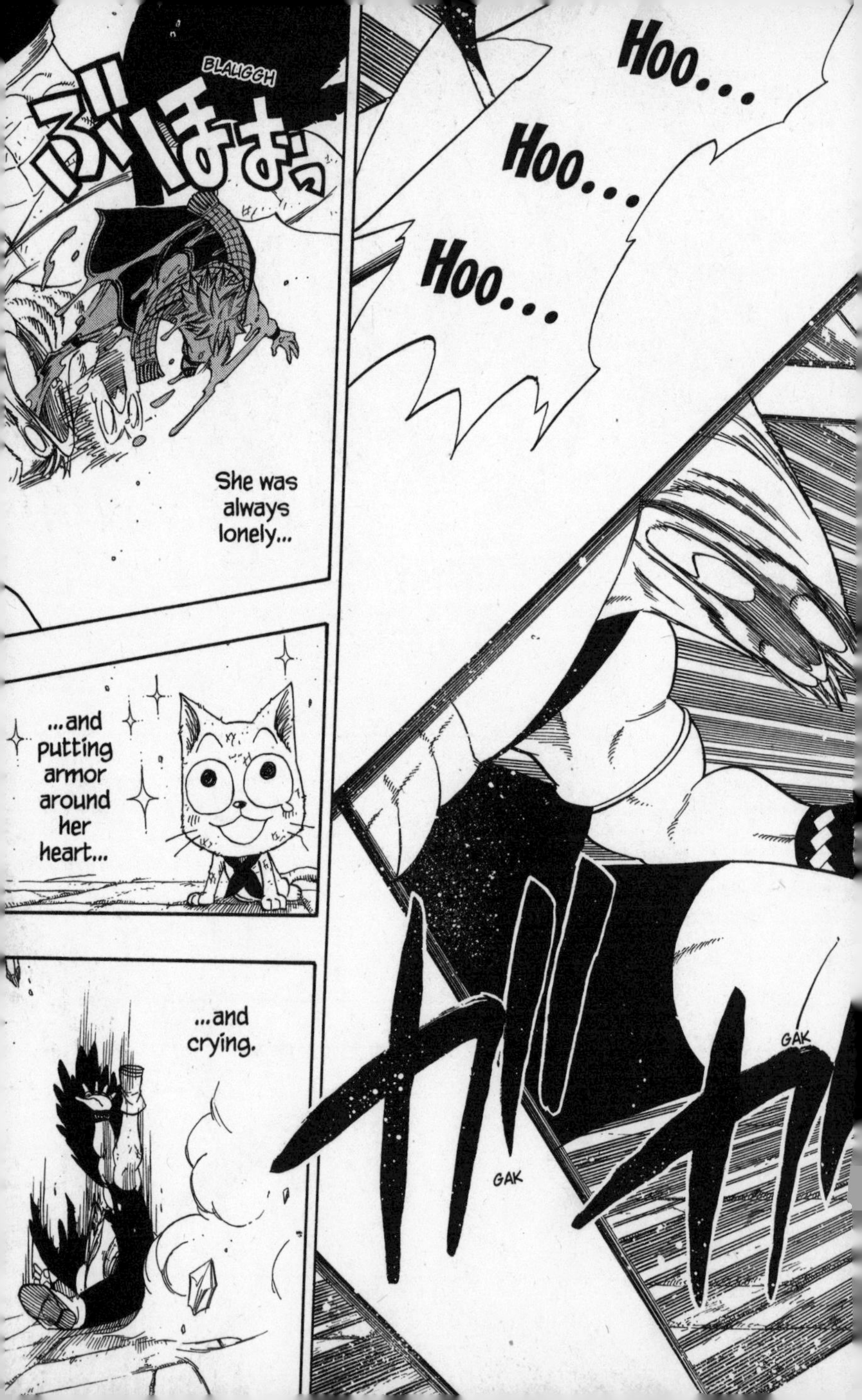
Hoo...
Hoo...
Hoo...
GAK
GAK
BLAUGGH
She was always lonely...
...and putting armor around her heart...
...and crying.

Erza has to be in Fairy Tail!!!

So that she doesn't have to cry again!!!!

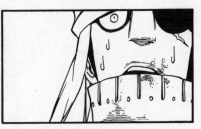

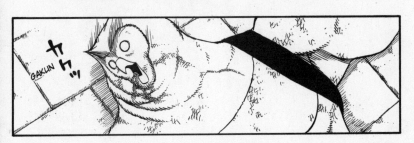

GAKLIN

144

FAIRY TAIL

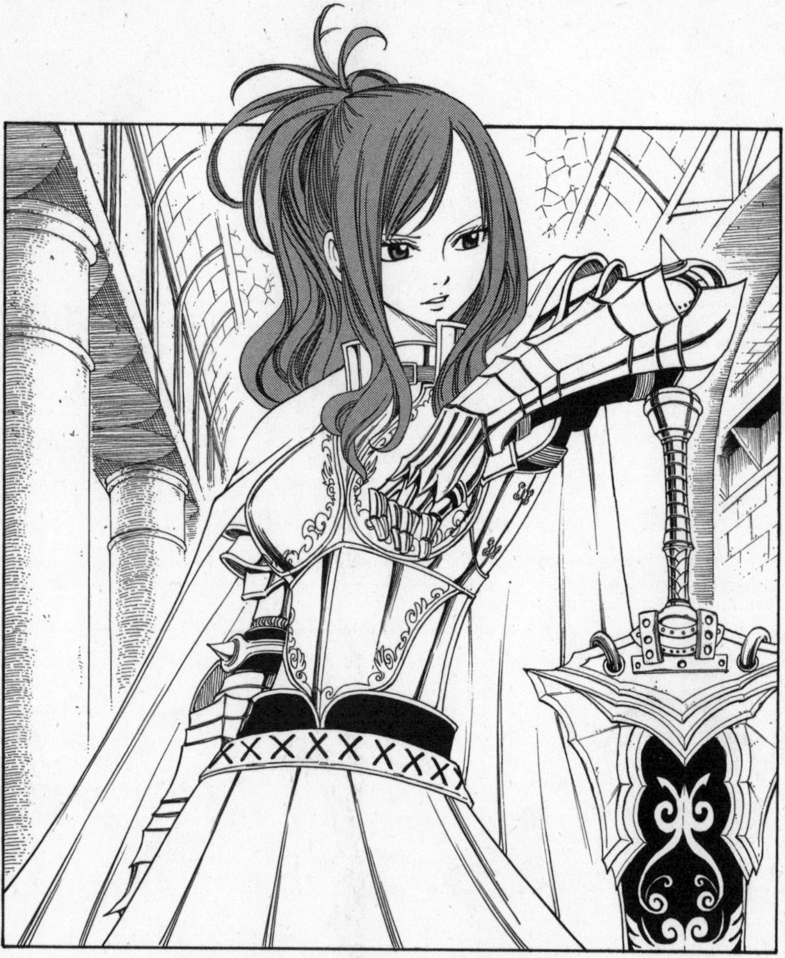

Chapter 90: Ikaruga

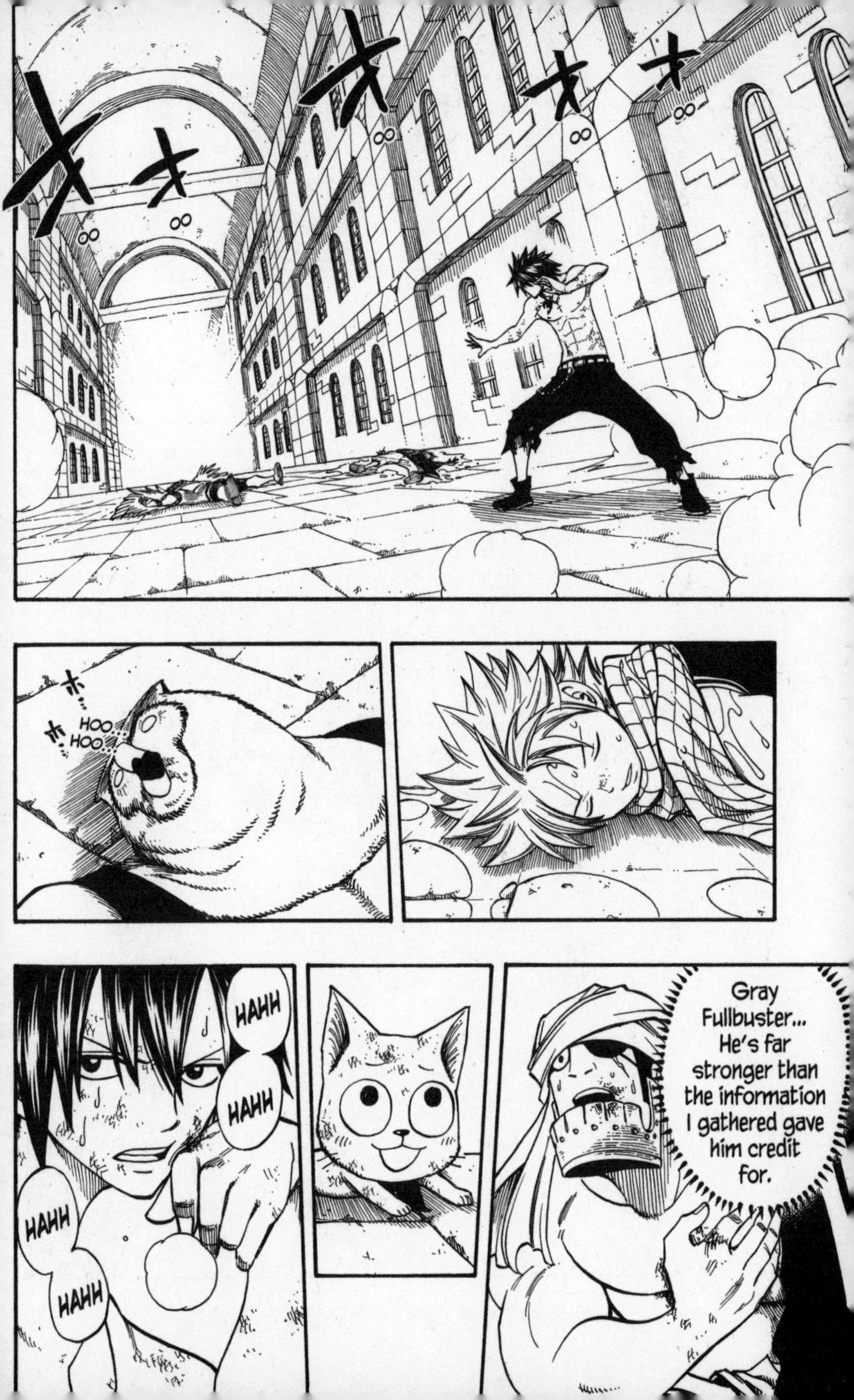
HOO HOO
Gray Fullbuster... He's far stronger than the information I gathered gave him credit for.
HAHH
HAHH
HAHH
HAHH

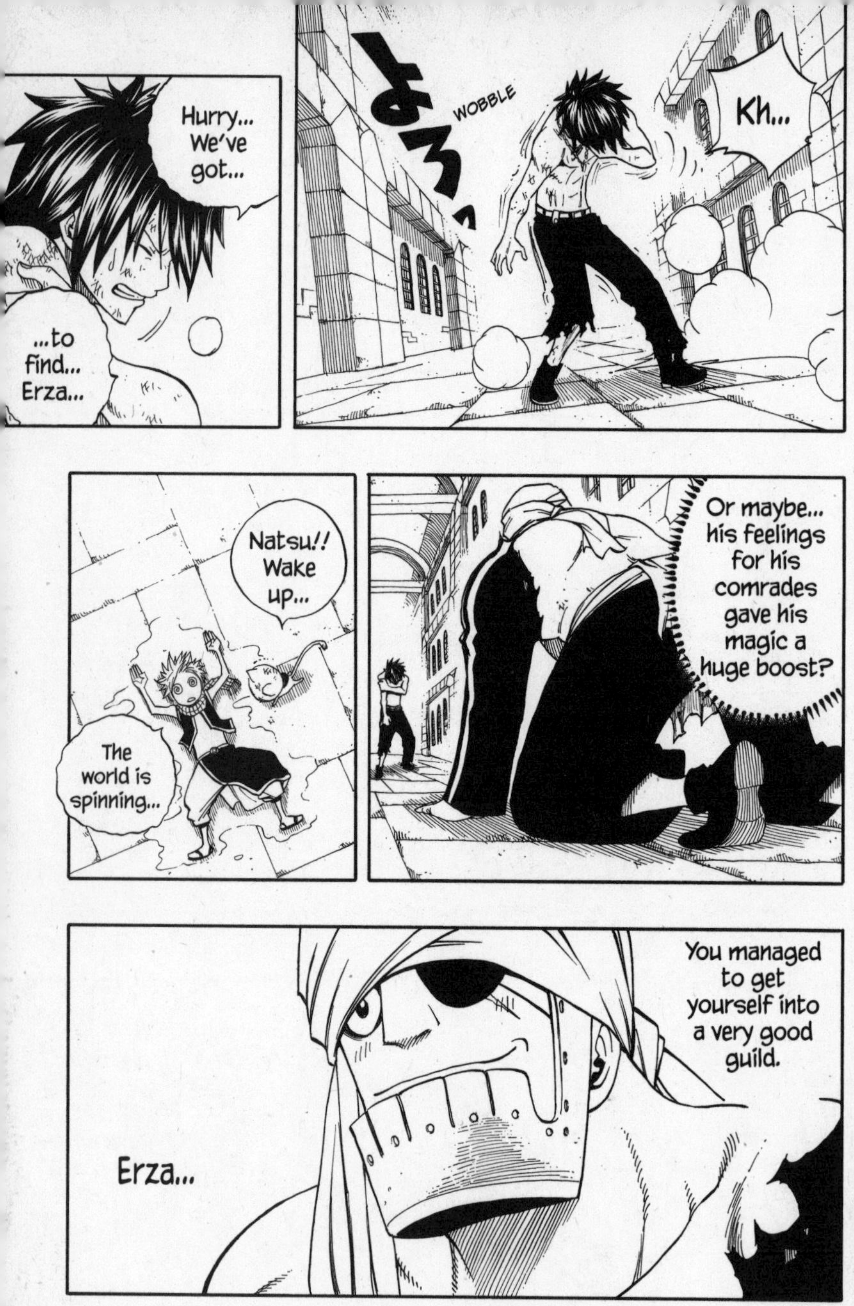
WOBBLE
Kh...
Hurry... We've got...
...to find... Erza...
Or maybe... his feelings for his comrades gave his magic a huge boost?
Natsu!! Wake up...
The world is spinning...
You managed to get yourself into a very good guild.
Erza...

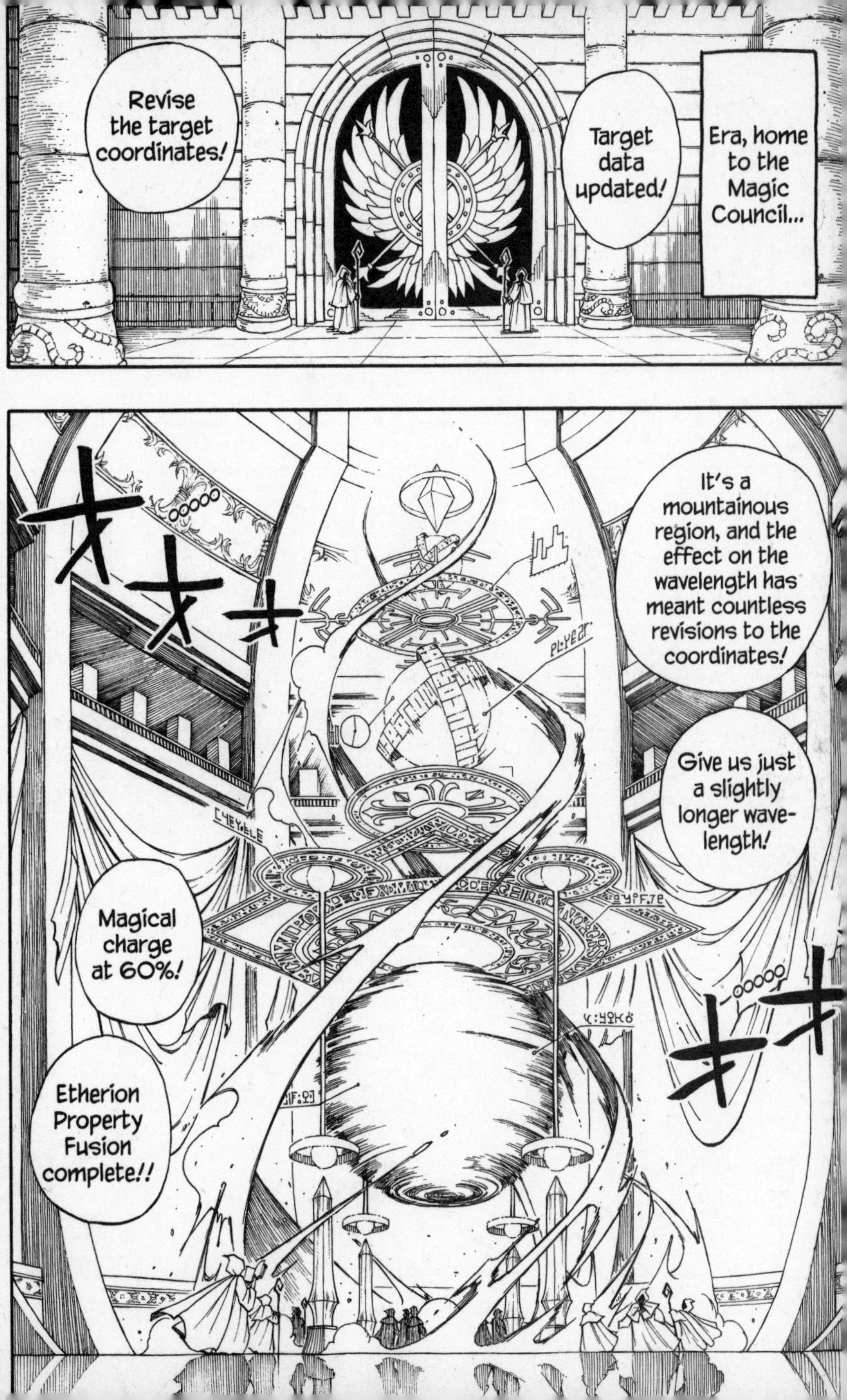

Era, home to the Magic Council...
Target data updated!
Revise the target coordinates!
It's a mountainous region, and the effect on the wavelength has meant countless revisions to the coordinates!
Give us just a slightly longer wave-length!
-ooooo
ooooo
Magical charge at 60%!
Etherion Property Fusion complete!!

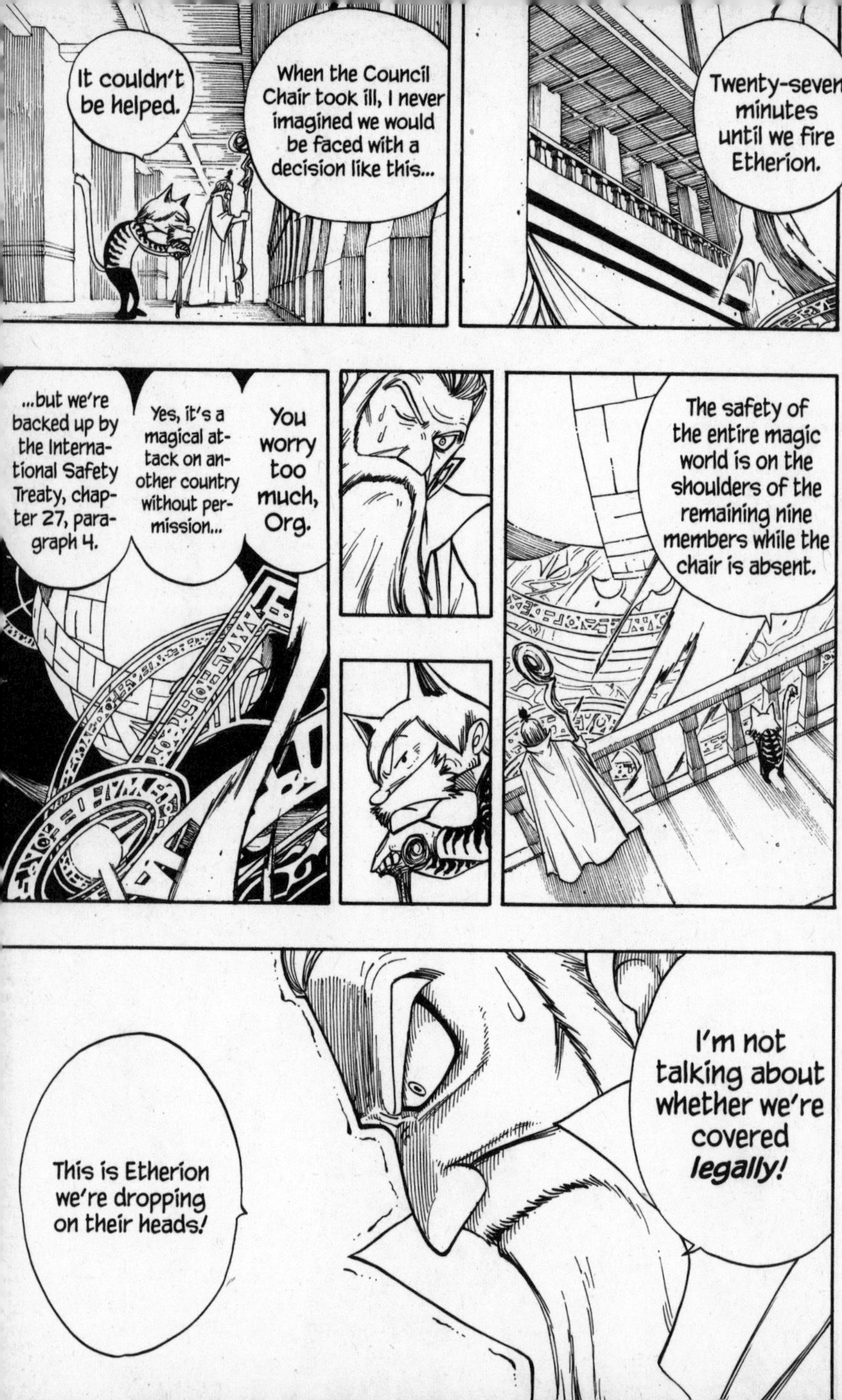
Twenty-seven minutes until we fire Etherion.
When the Council Chair took ill, I never imagined we would be faced with a decision like this...
It couldn't be helped.
The safety of the entire magic world is on the shoulders of the remaining nine members while the chair is absent.
You worry too much, Org.
Yes, it's a magical attack on another country without permission...
...but we're backed up by the International Safety Treaty, chapter 27, paragraph 4.
I'm not talking about whether we're covered *legally!*
This is Etherion we're dropping on their heads!

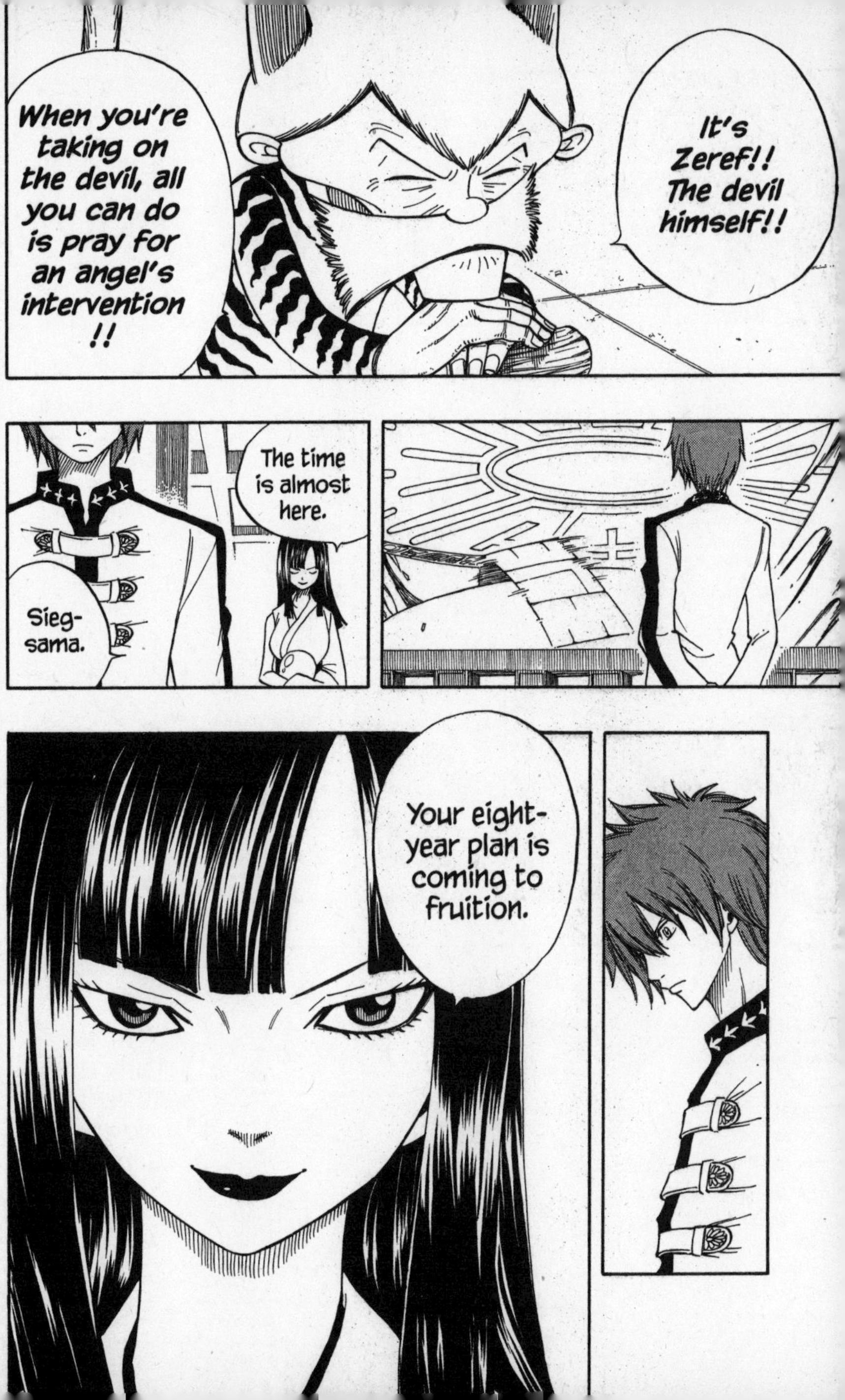
It's Zeref!! The devil himself!!
When you're taking on the devil, all you can do is pray for an angel's intervention!!
The time is almost here.
Sieg-sama.
Your eight-year plan is coming to fruition.

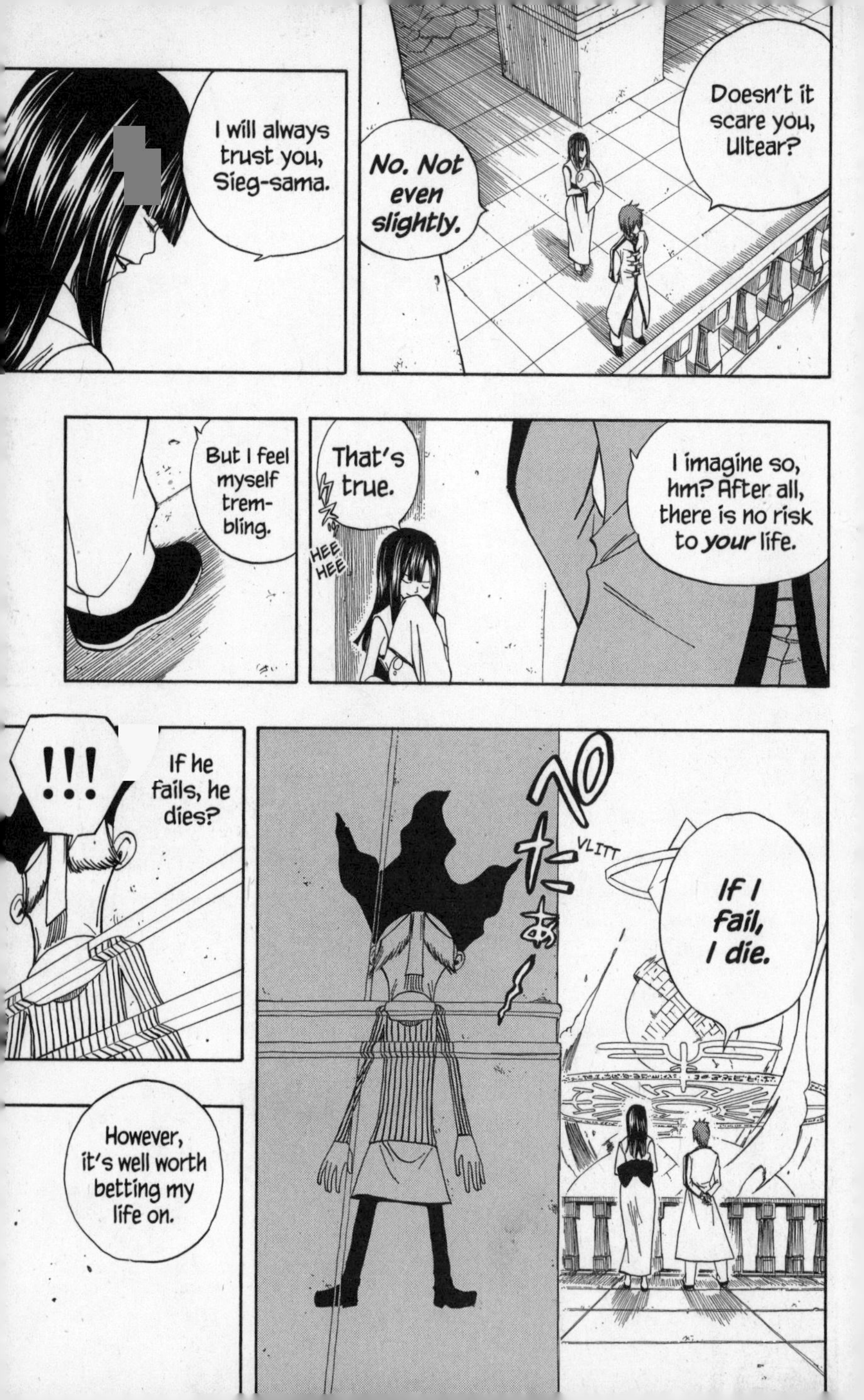
Doesn't it scare you, Ultear?
No. Not even slightly.
I will always trust you, Sieg-sama.
I imagine so, hm? After all, there is no risk to your life.
That's true.
HEE HEE
But I feel myself trem-bling.
If I fail, I die.
VLITT
!!!
If he fails, he dies?
However, it's well worth betting my life on.

For the sake of my ideal!!

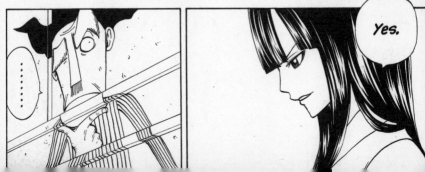

Yes.

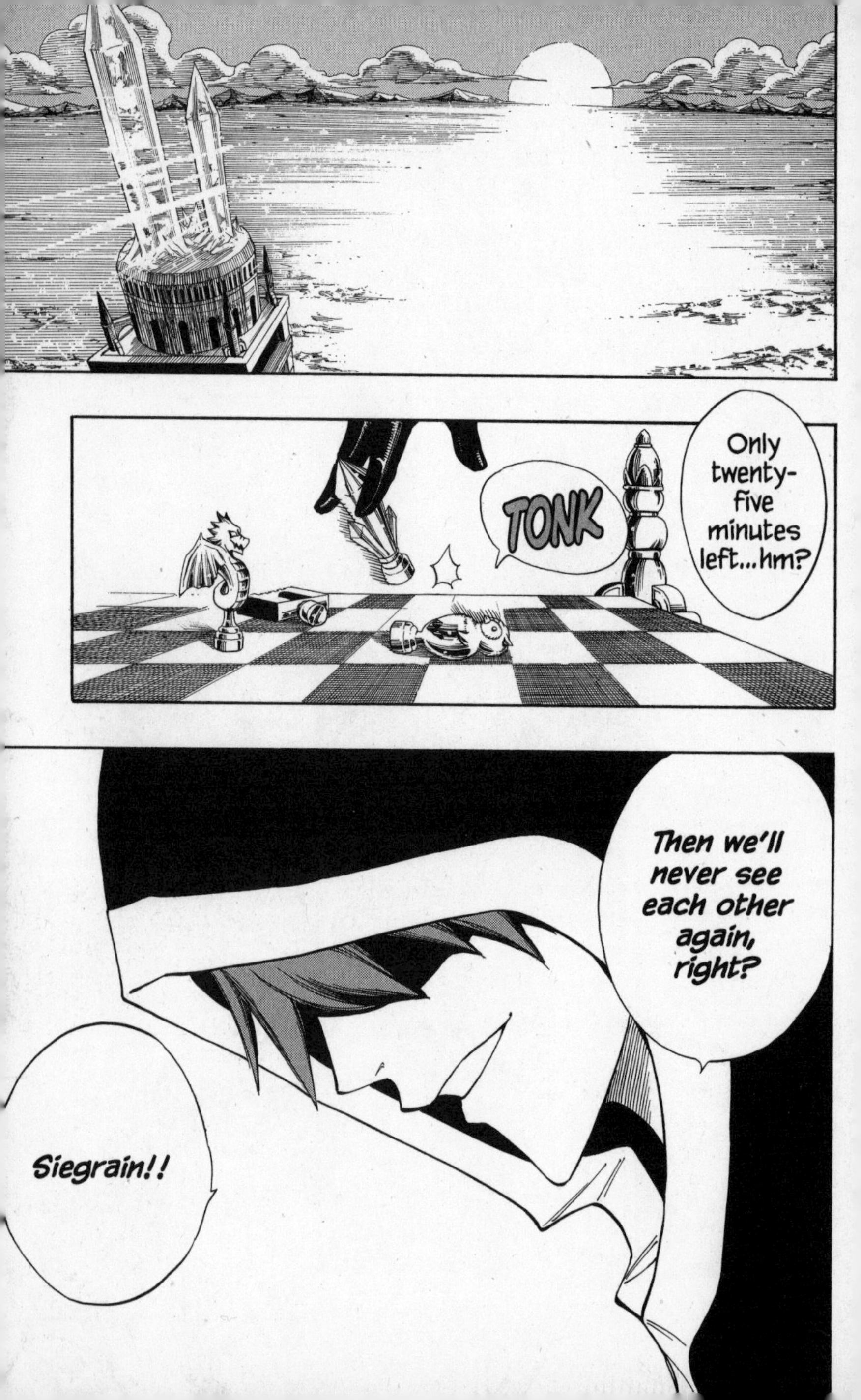
Only twenty-five minutes left...hm?
TONK
Then we'll never see each other again, right?
Siegrain!!

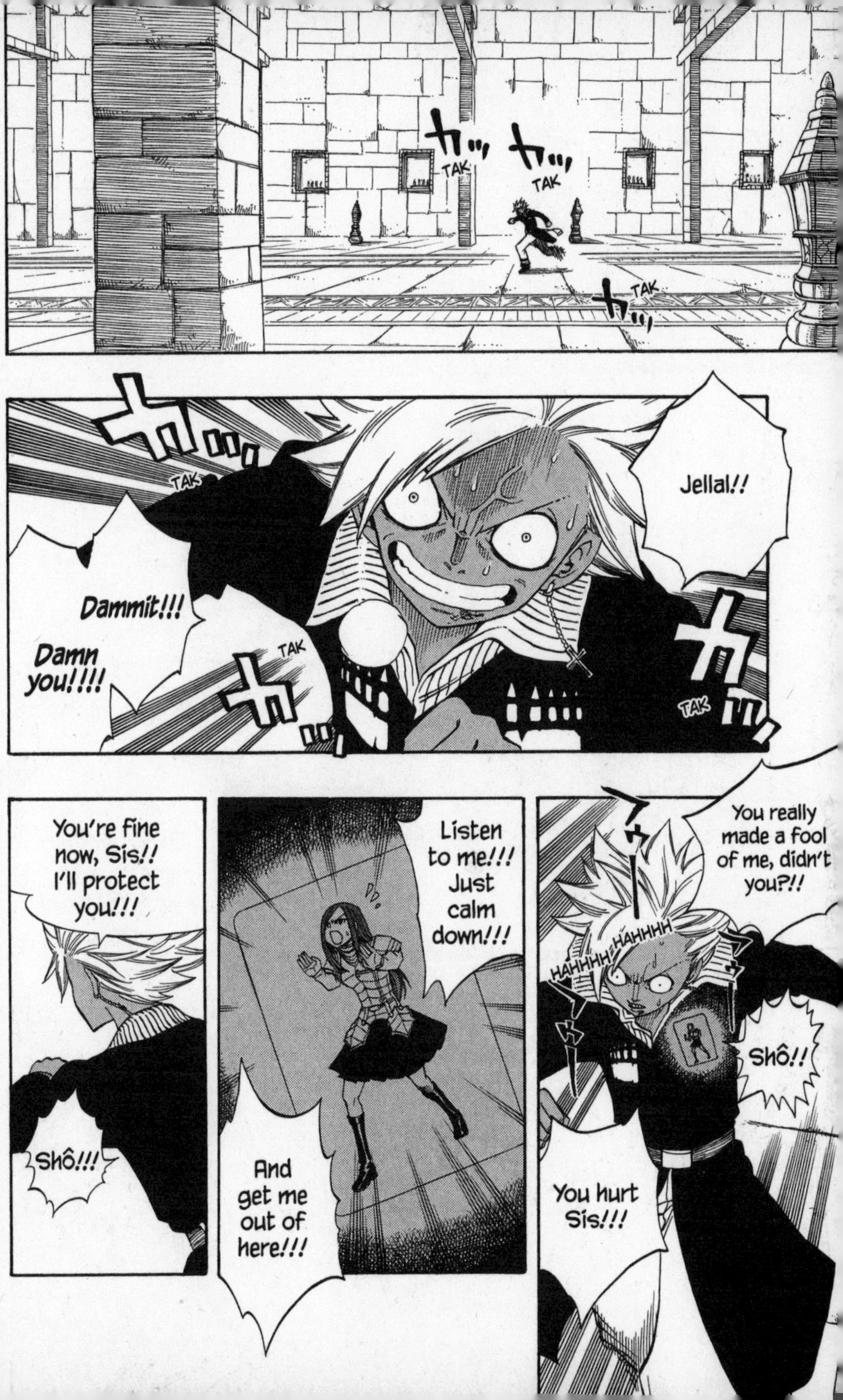
TAK
TAK
TAK
Jellal!!
TAK
TAK
TAK
Dammit!!!
Damn you!!!!
You really made a fool of me, didn't you?!!
HAHHHH HAHHHH
Shô!!
You hurt Sis!!!
Listen to me!!! Just calm down!!!
And get me out of here!!!
You're fine now, Sis!! I'll protect you!!!
Shô!!!

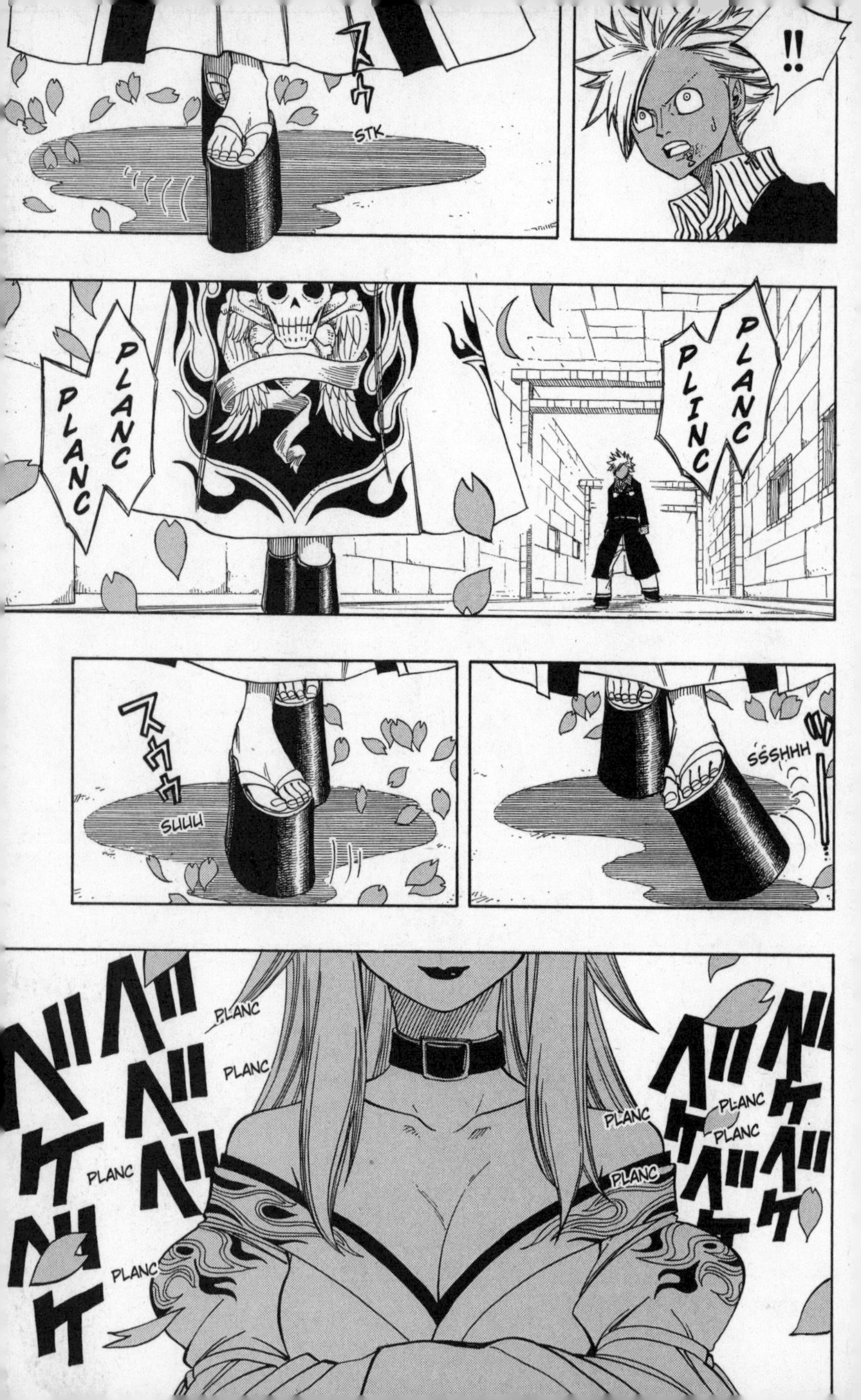
!!
STK
PLANC
PLINC
PLANC
PLANC
SSSHHH
SUUU
PLANC
PLANC
PLANC
PLANC
PLANC
PLANC
PLANC
PLANC

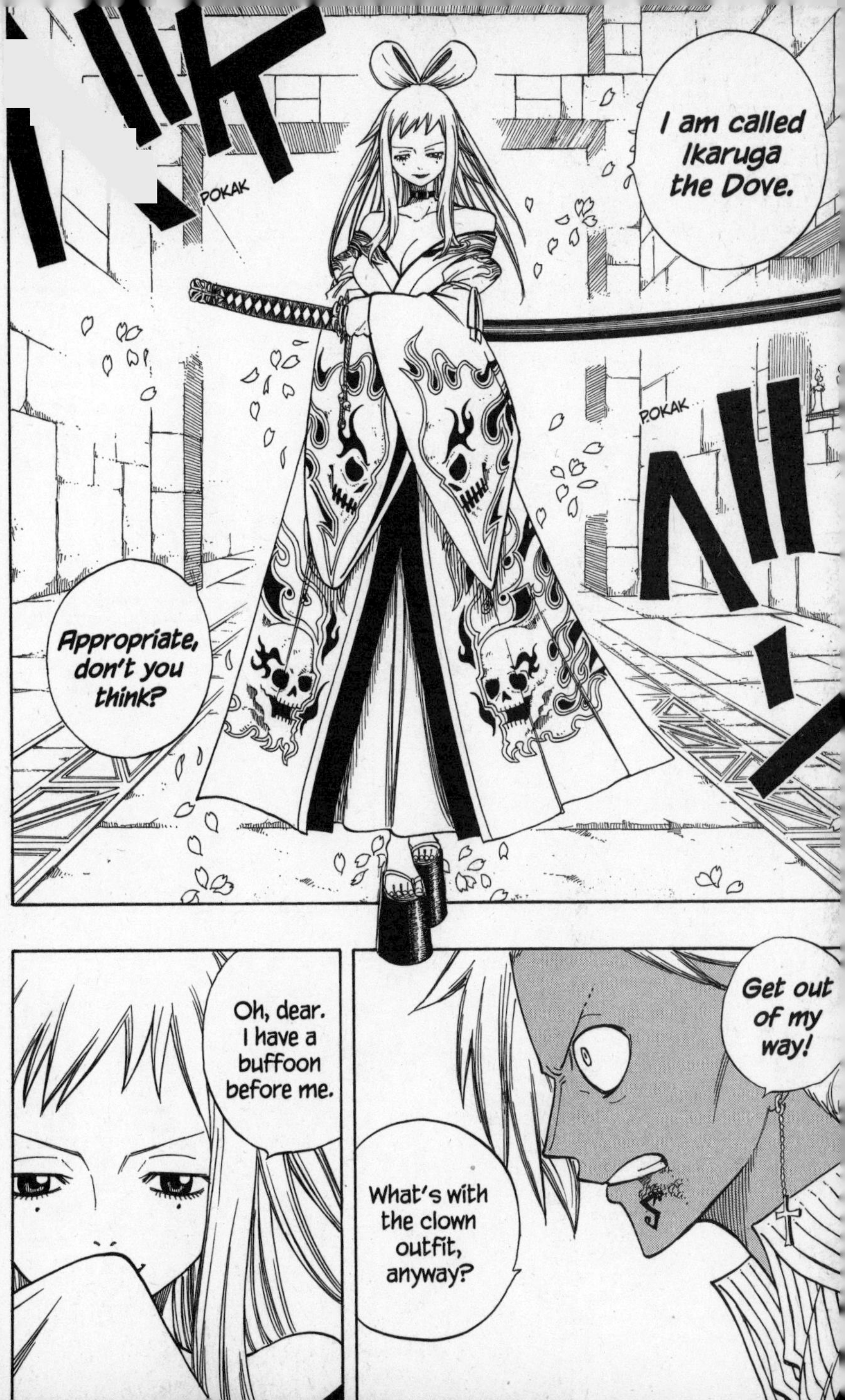
I am called Ikaruga the Dove.
POKAK
POKAK
Appropriate, don't you think?
Get out of my way!
What's with the clown outfit, anyway?
Oh, dear. I have a buffoon before me.

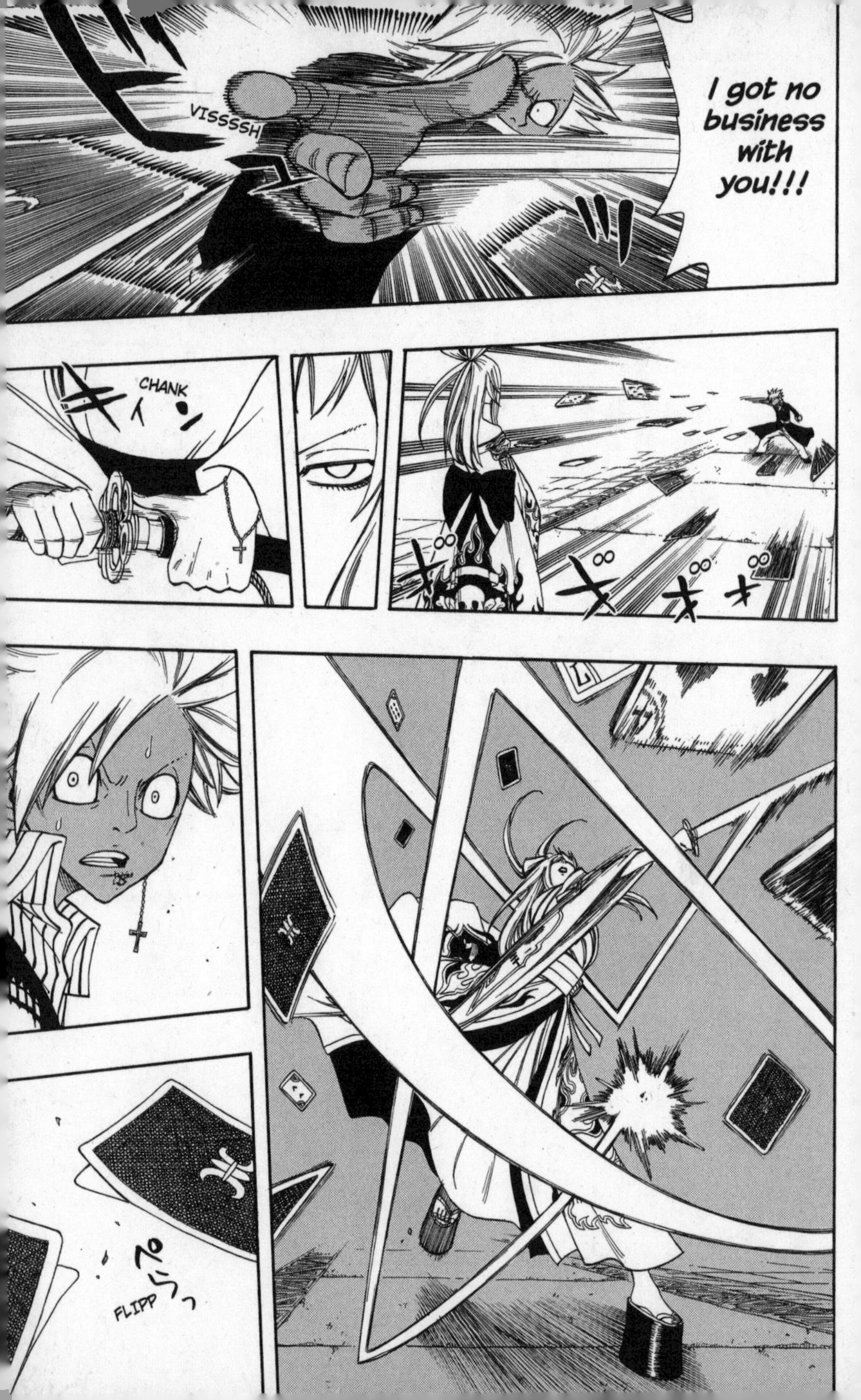
I got no business with you!!!
VISSSSH
CHANK
FLIPP

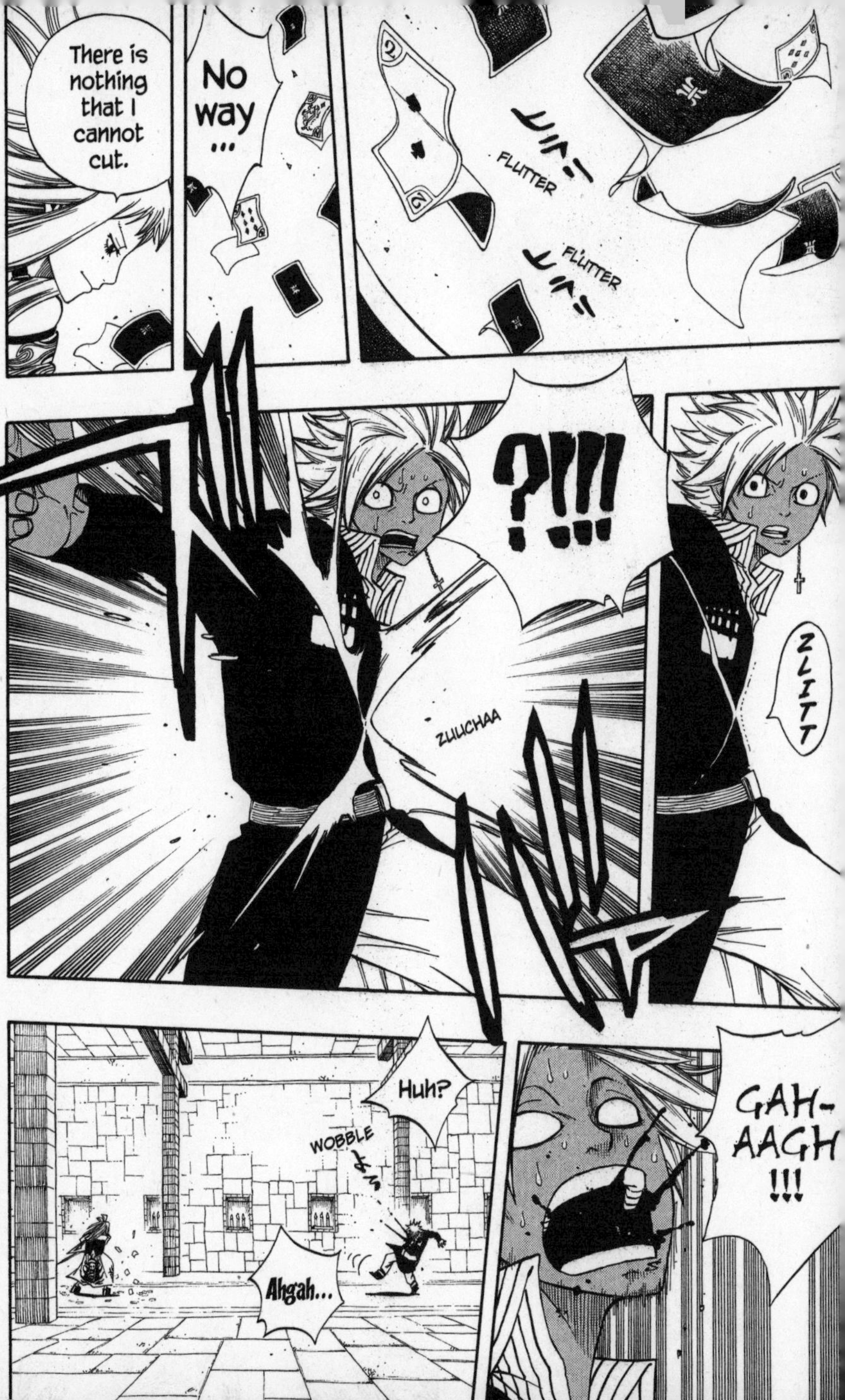
FLUTTER
FLUTTER
No way ...
There is nothing that I cannot cut.
?!!!
ZLITT
ZUUCHAA
GAH-AAGH !!!
Huh?
WOBBLE
Ahgah...

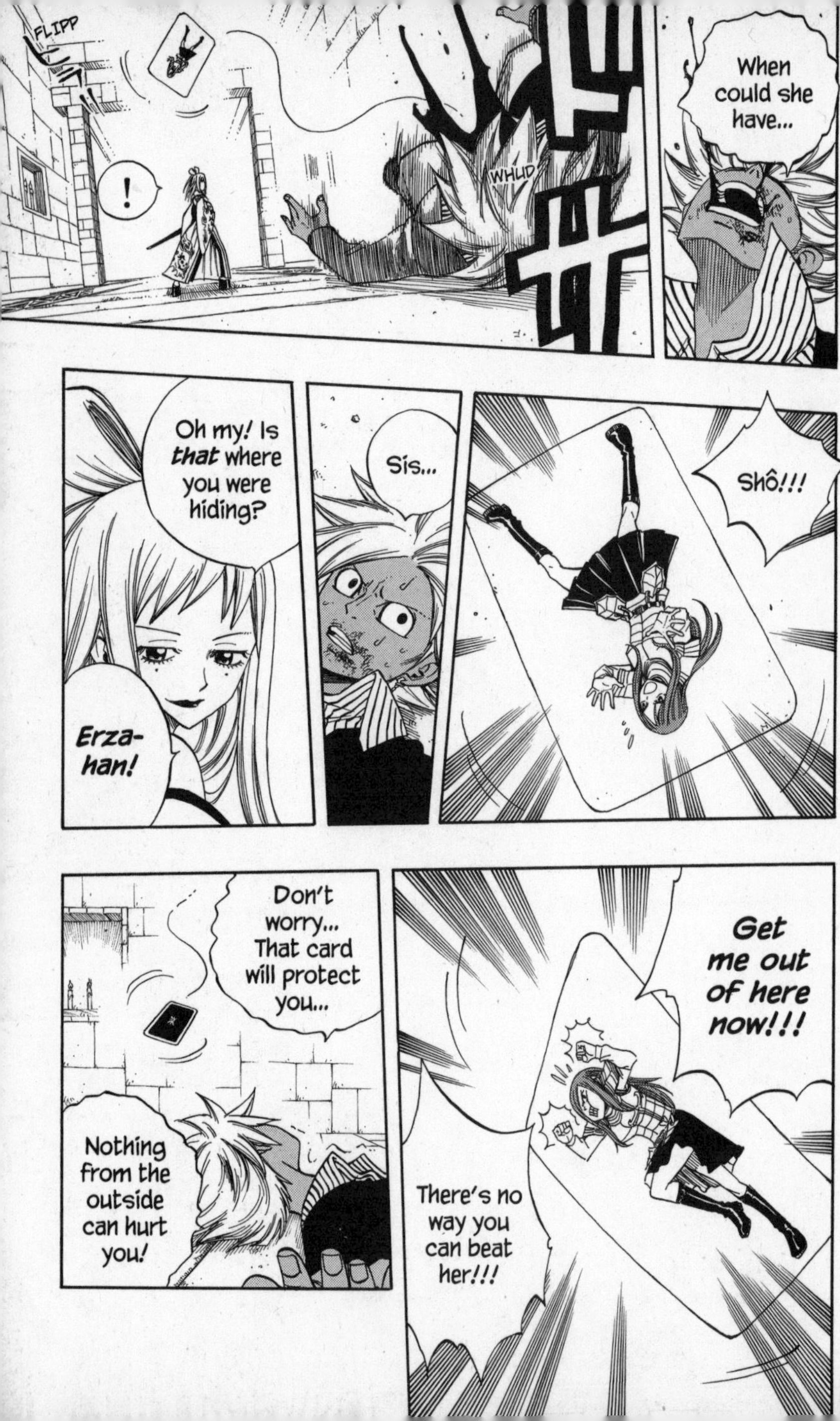
When could she have...
FLIPP
WHUD
!
Shô!!!
Sis...
Oh my! Is *that* where you were hiding?
Erza-han!
Get me out of here now!!!
There's no way you can beat her!!!
Don't worry... That card will protect you...
Nothing from the outside can hurt you!

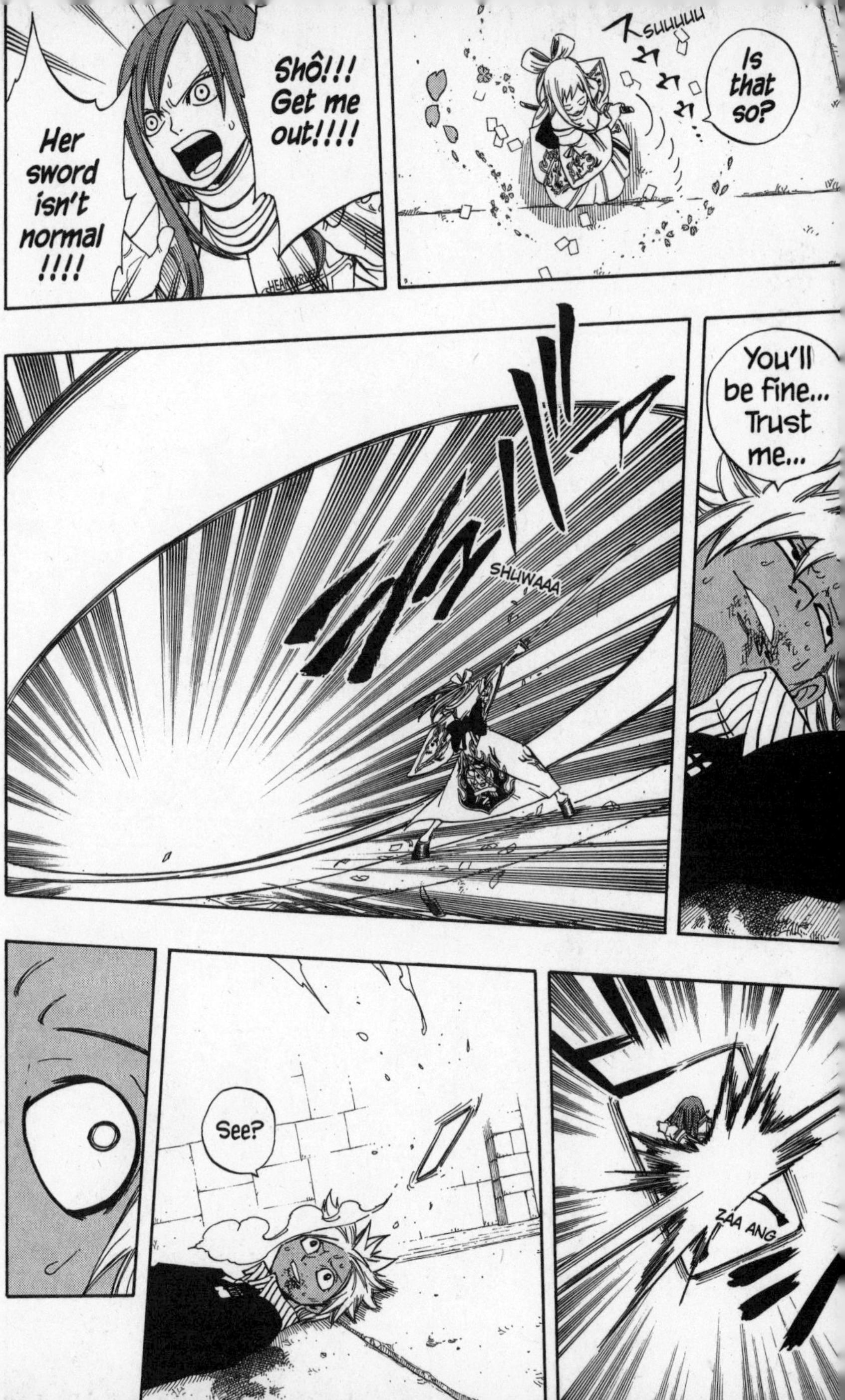
SUUUUUU
Is that so?
Shô!!! Get me out!!!!
Her sword isn't normal!!!!
You'll be fine... Trust me...
SHUWAAA
ZAA ANG
See?

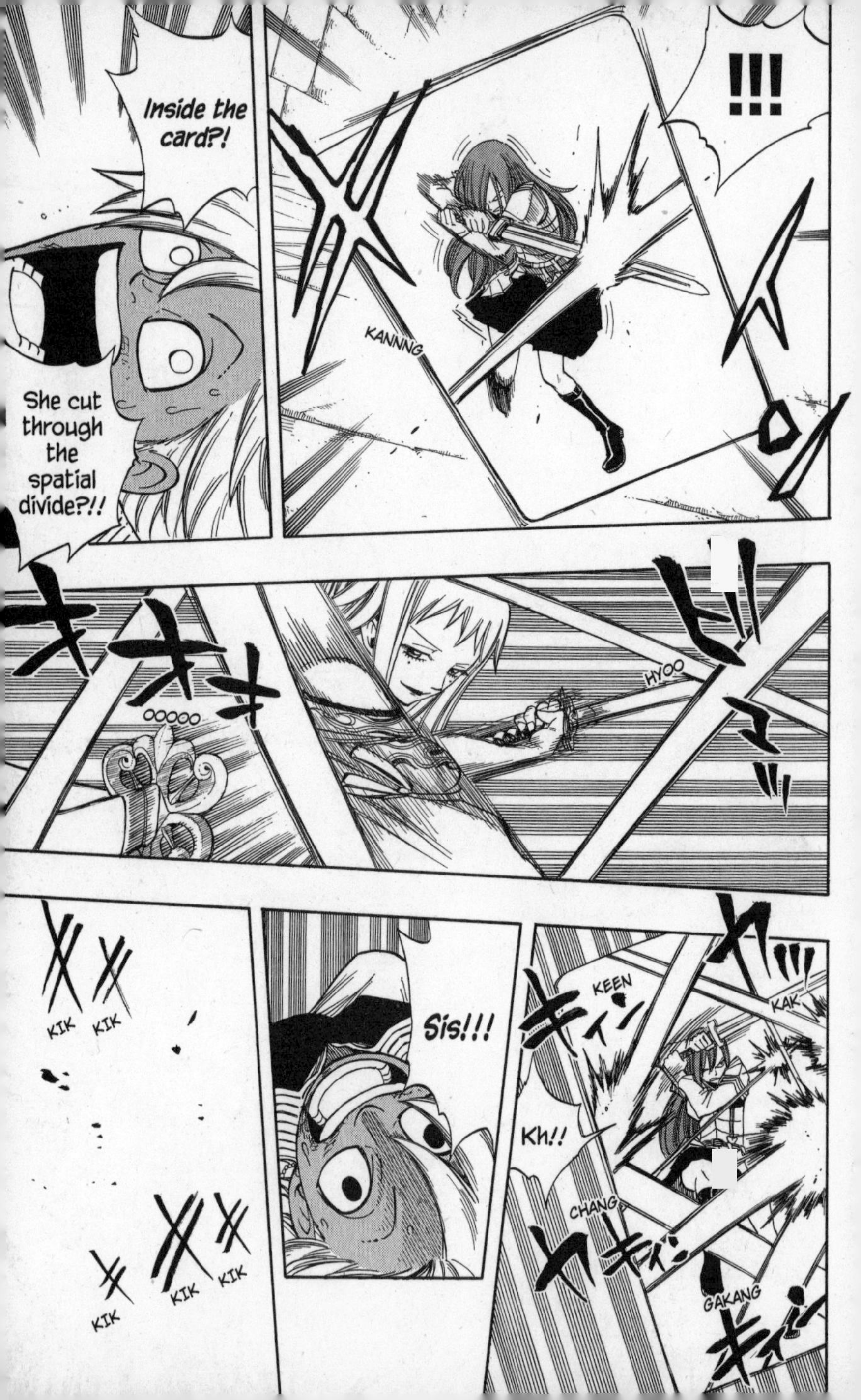
!!!
KANNNG
Inside the card?!
She cut through the spatial divide?!!
HYOO
ooooo
KAK
KEEN
Kh!!
CHANG
GAKANG
Sis!!!
KIK
KIK
KIK
KIK
KIK

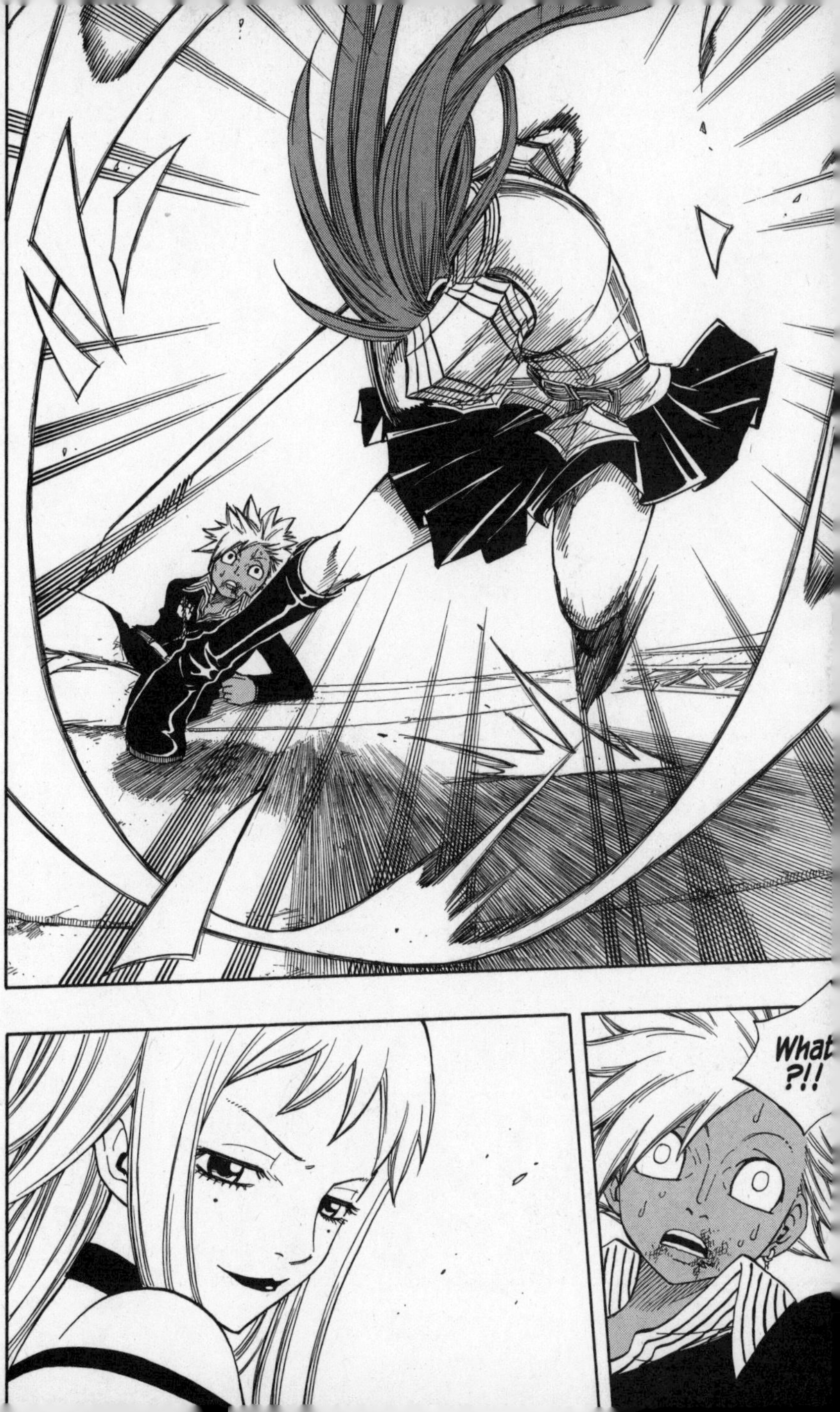
What ?!!

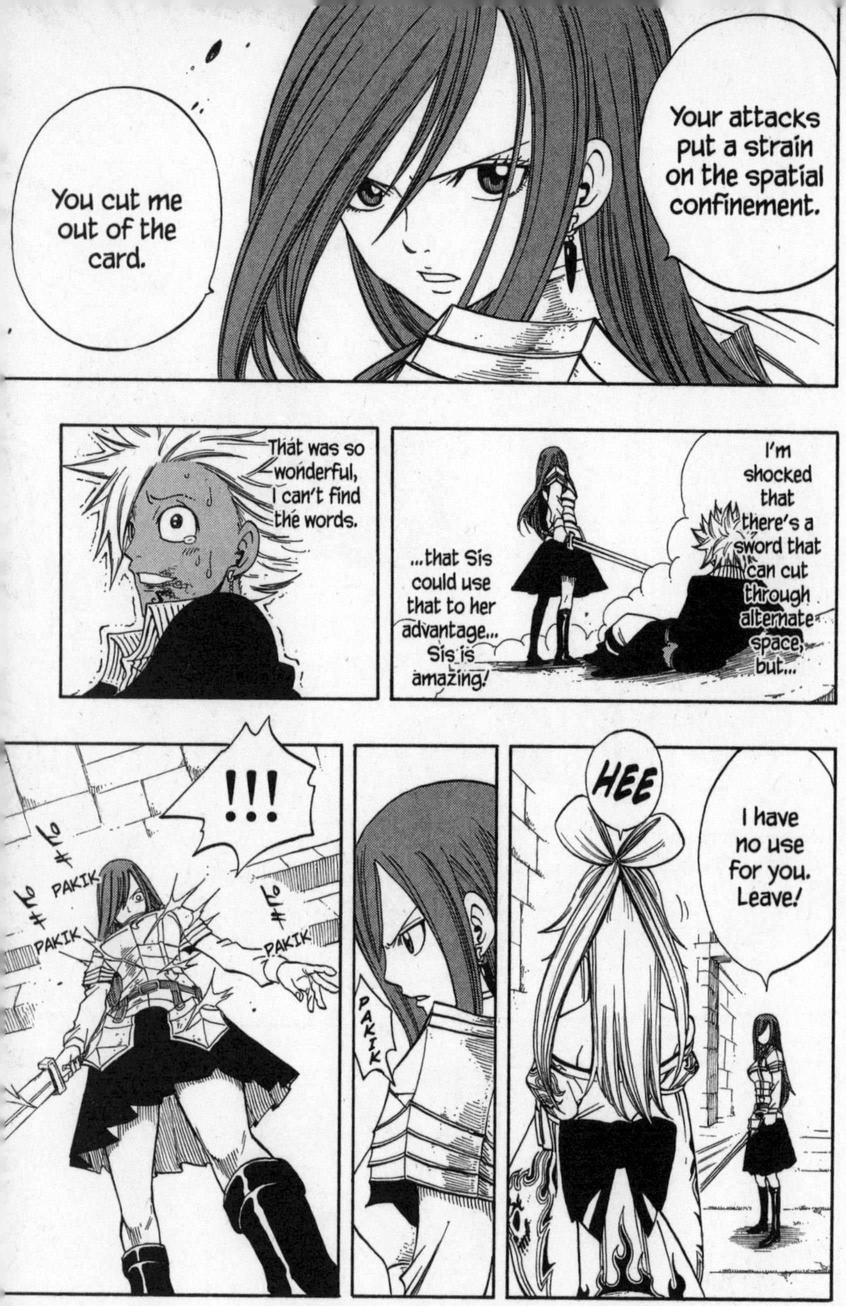
Your attacks put a strain on the spatial confinement.
You cut me out of the card.
I'm shocked that there's a sword that can cut through alternate space, but...
...that Sis could use that to her advantage... Sis is amazing!
That was so wonderful, I can't find the words.
HEE
I have no use for you. Leave!
PAKIK
!!!
PAKIK
PAKIK
PAKIK

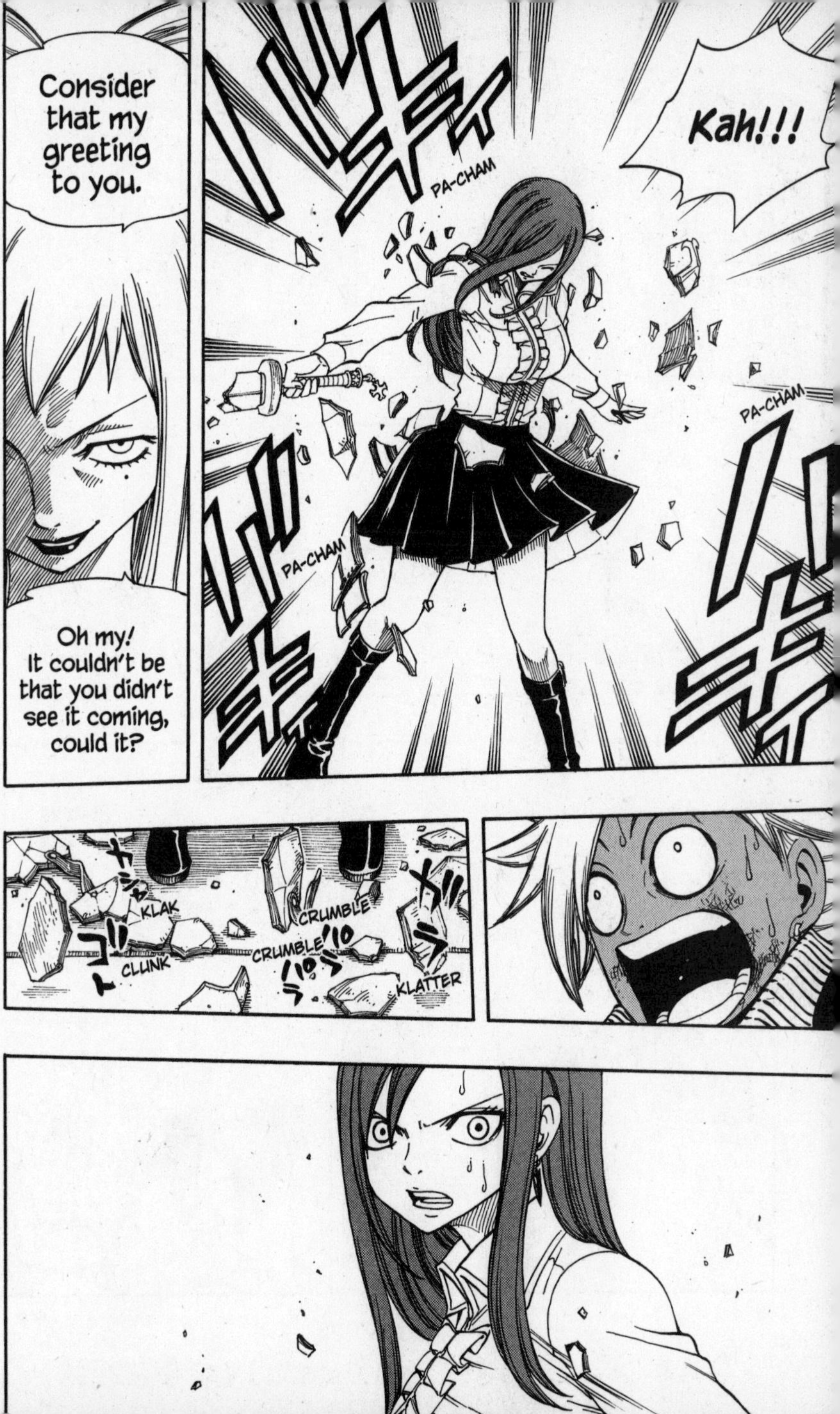
Kah!!!
PA-CHAM
PA-CHAM
PA-CHAM
Consider that my greeting to you.
Oh my! It couldn't be that you didn't see it coming, could it?
CRUMBLE
CRUMBLE
KLATTER
KLAK
CLUNK

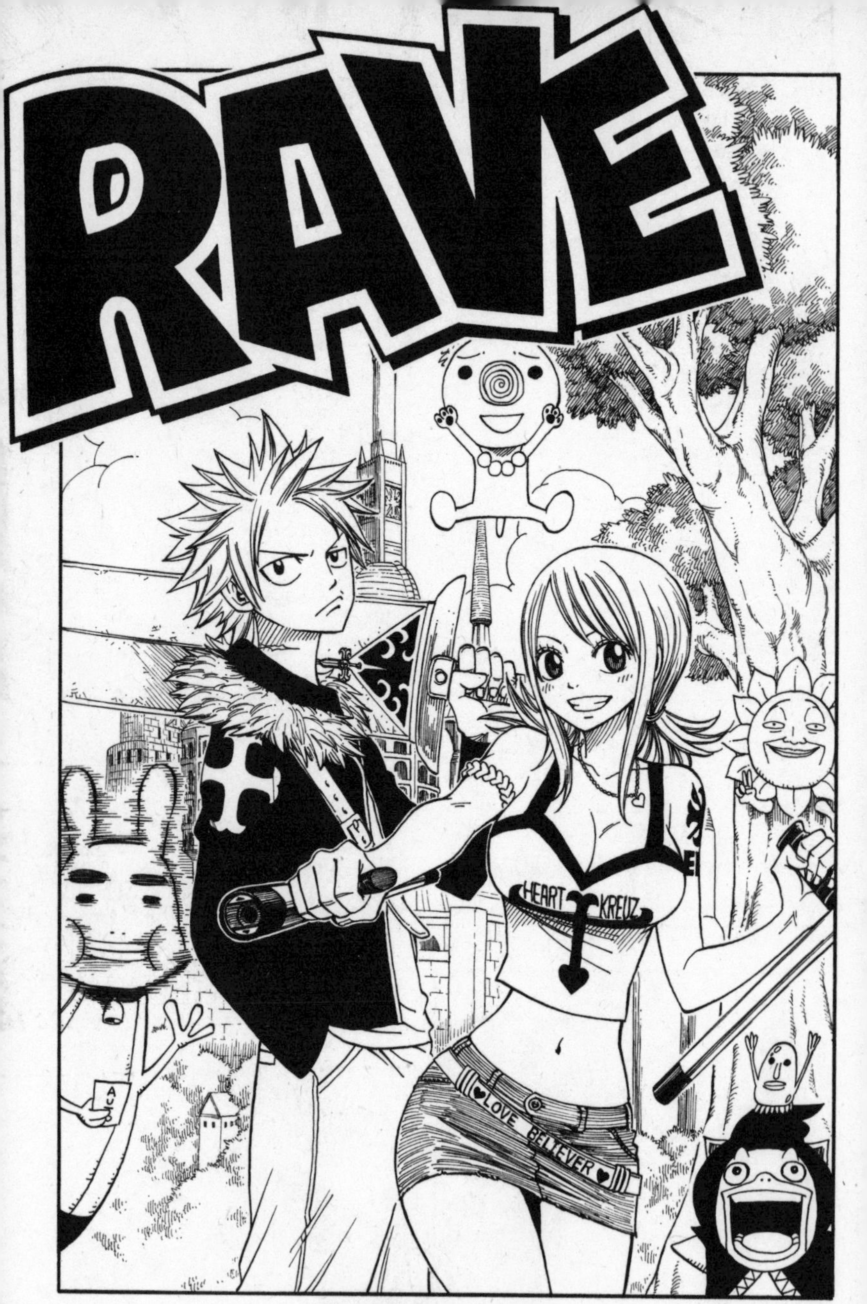
RAVE
HEART
KREUZ
LOVE BELIEVER

Chapter 91:
One Woman! The Decisive Outfit

KRAK

GUNCH

CRASH

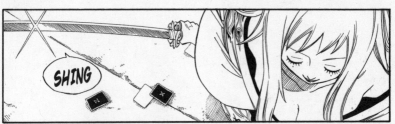

SHING

Wh-What kind of speed with her sword does that woman have?!

Was Sis not able to see it either?

166

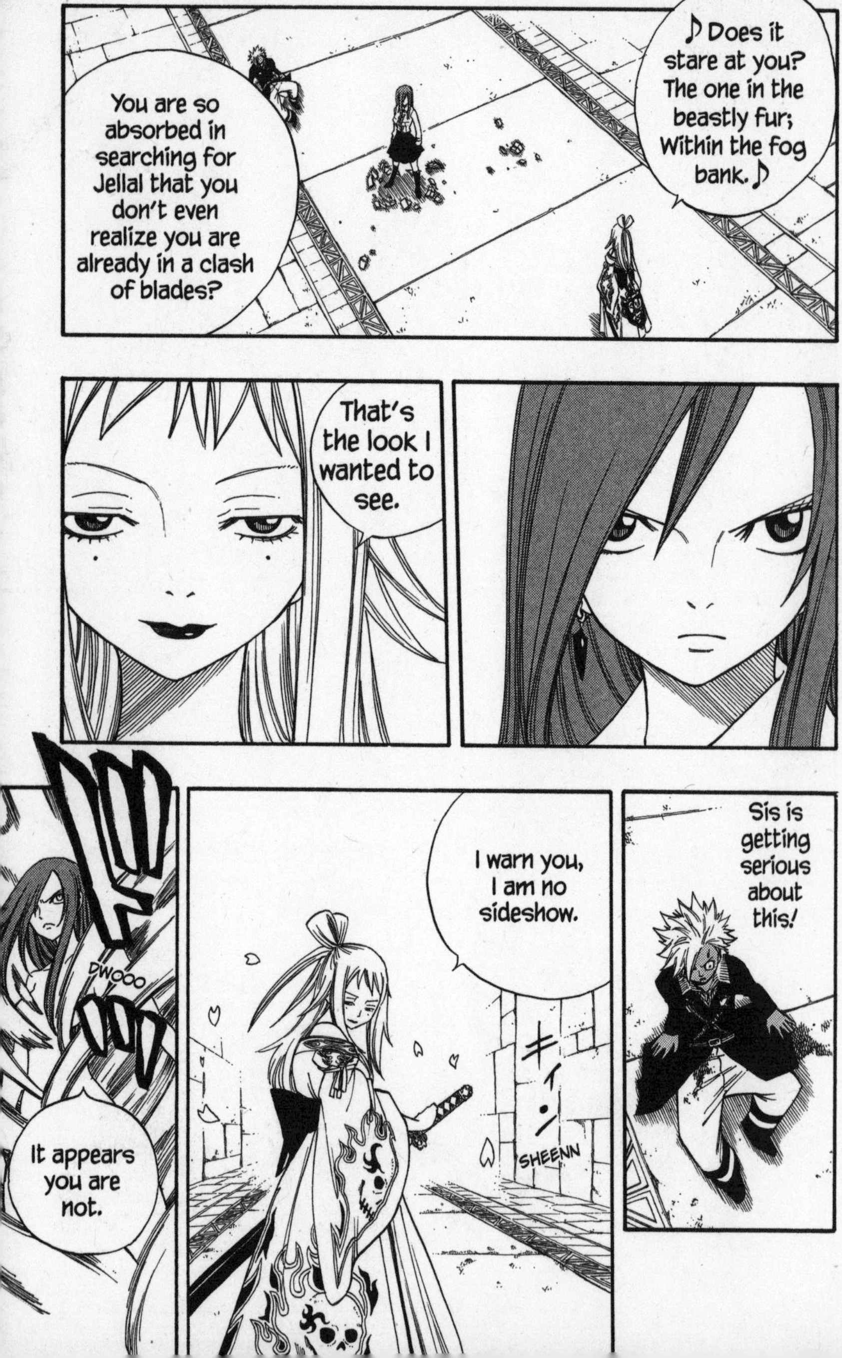
♪Does it stare at you? The one in the beastly fur; Within the fog bank.♪
You are so absorbed in searching for Jellal that you don't even realize you are already in a clash of blades?
That's the look I wanted to see.
Sis is getting serious about this!
I warn you, I am no sideshow.
SHEENN
DWOOO
It appears you are not.

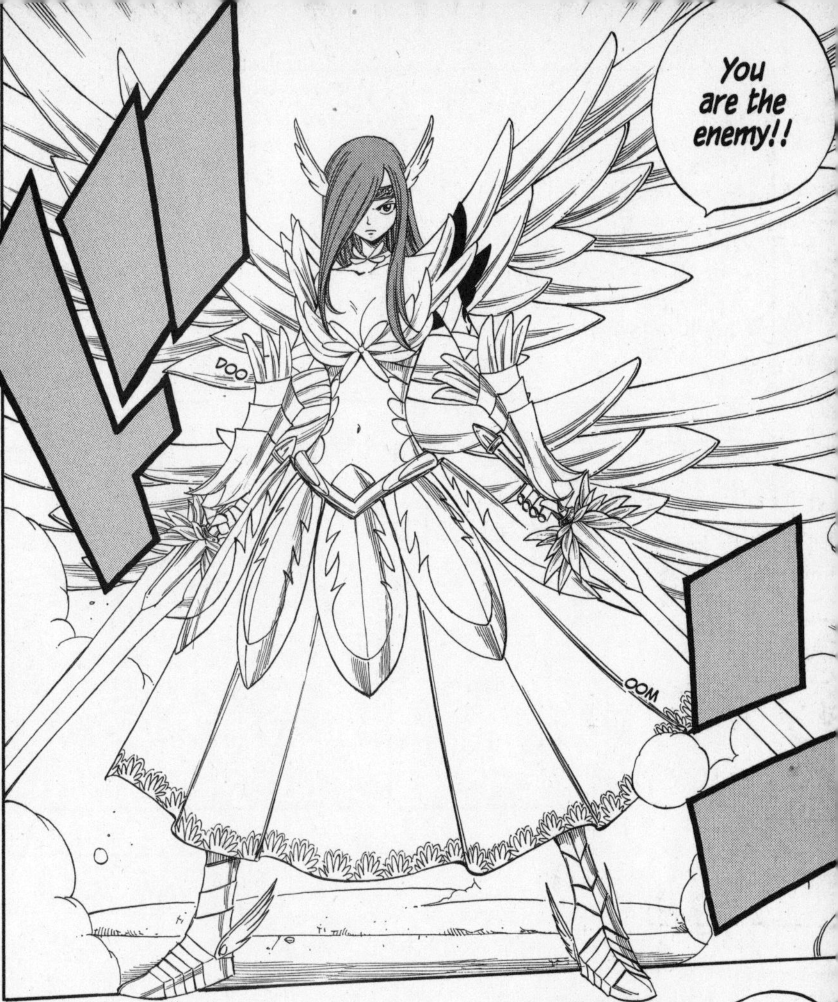
You are the enemy!!
DOO
OOM
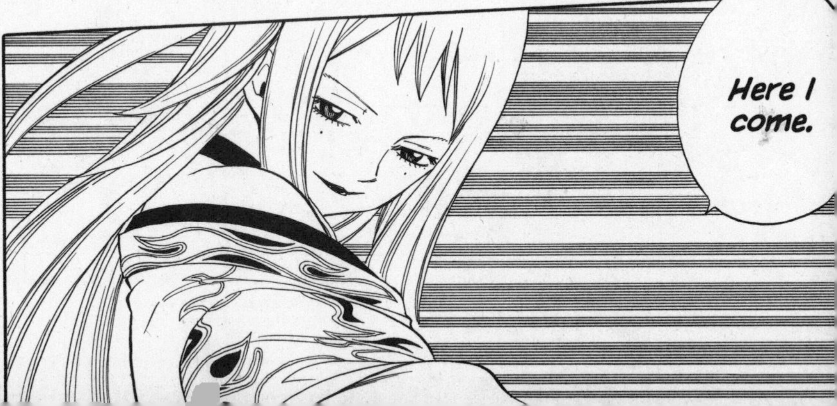
Here I come.

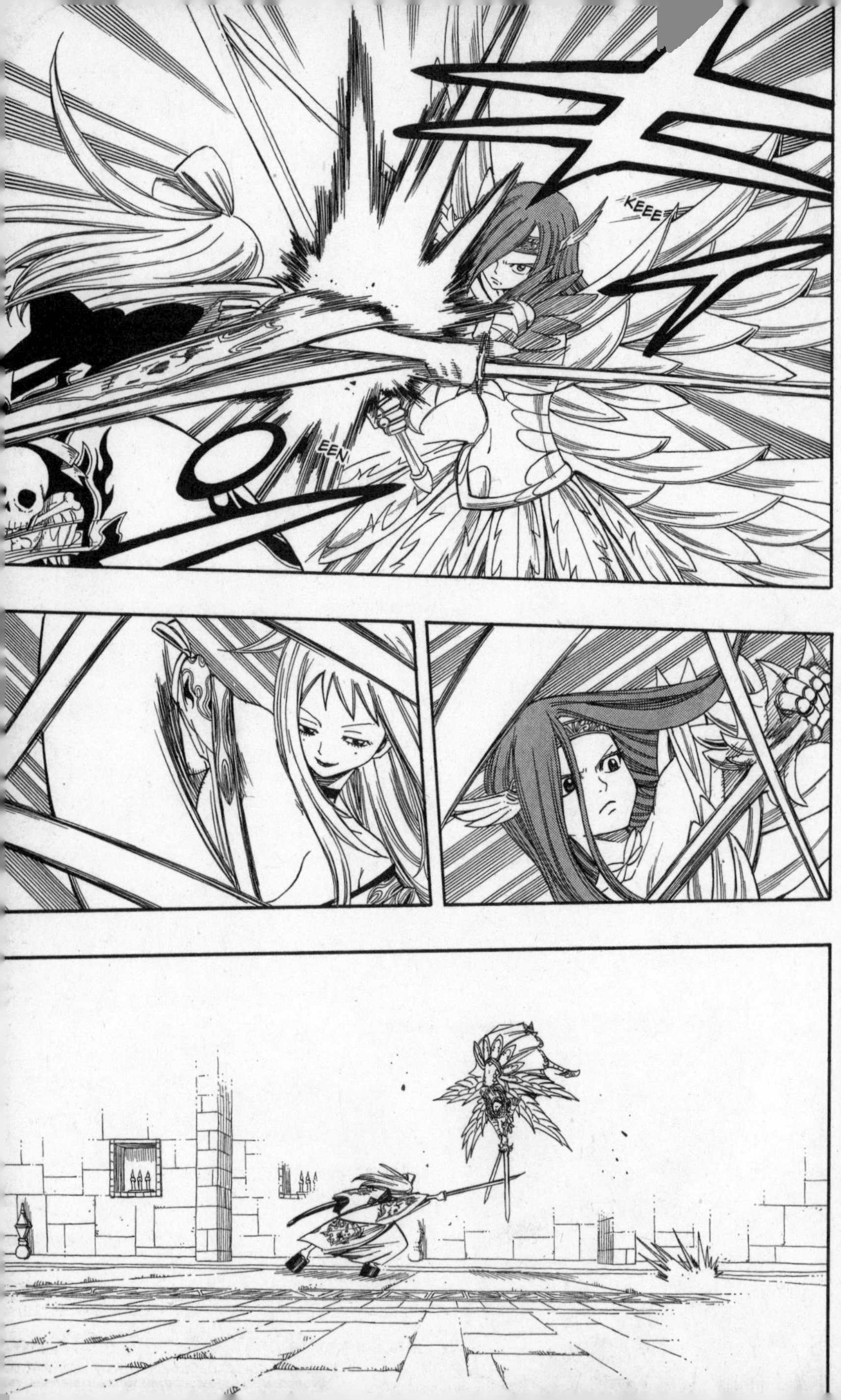
KEEE
EEN

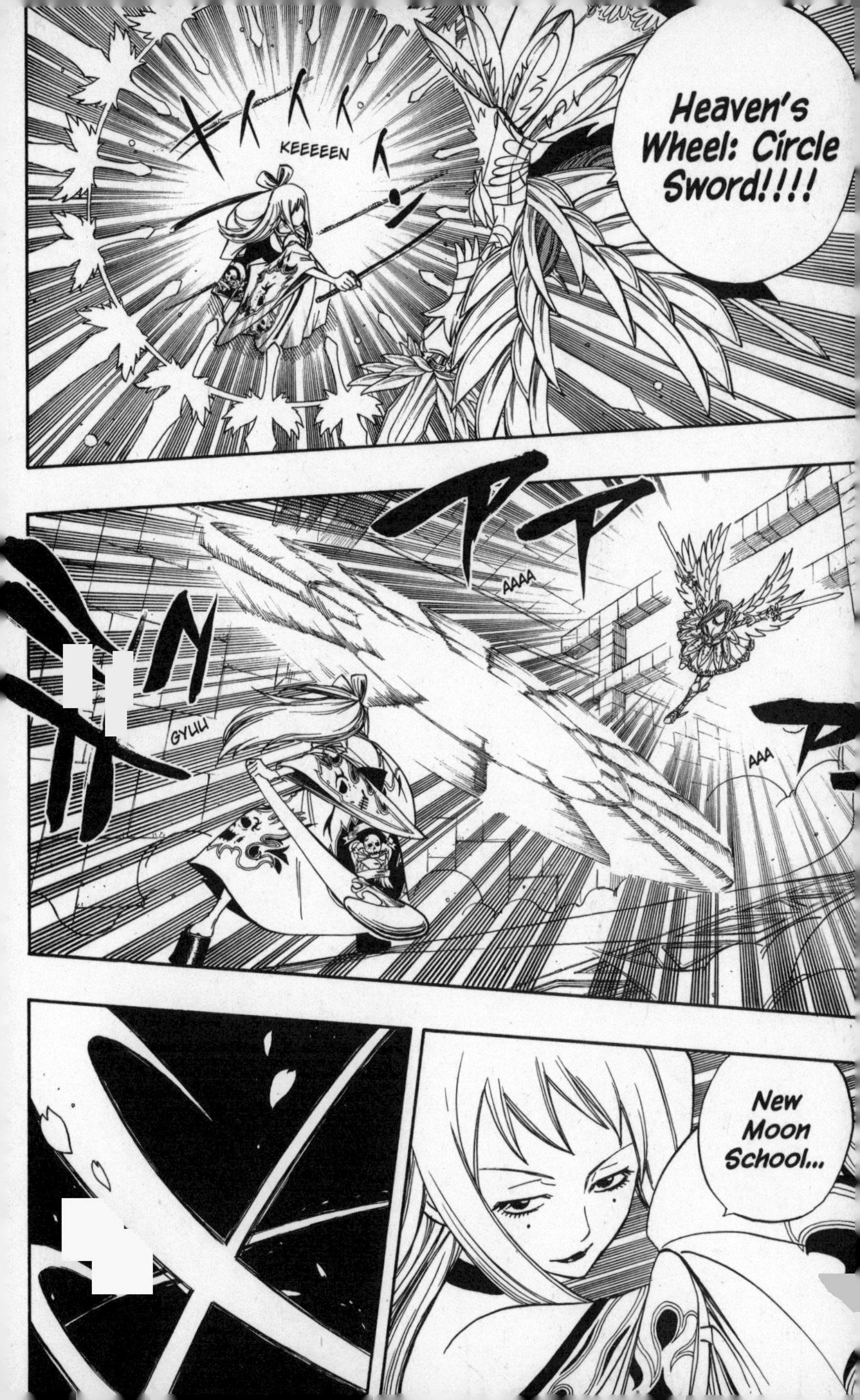
Heaven's Wheel: Circle Sword!!!!
KEEEEEN
AAAA
AAA
GYUU
New Moon School...

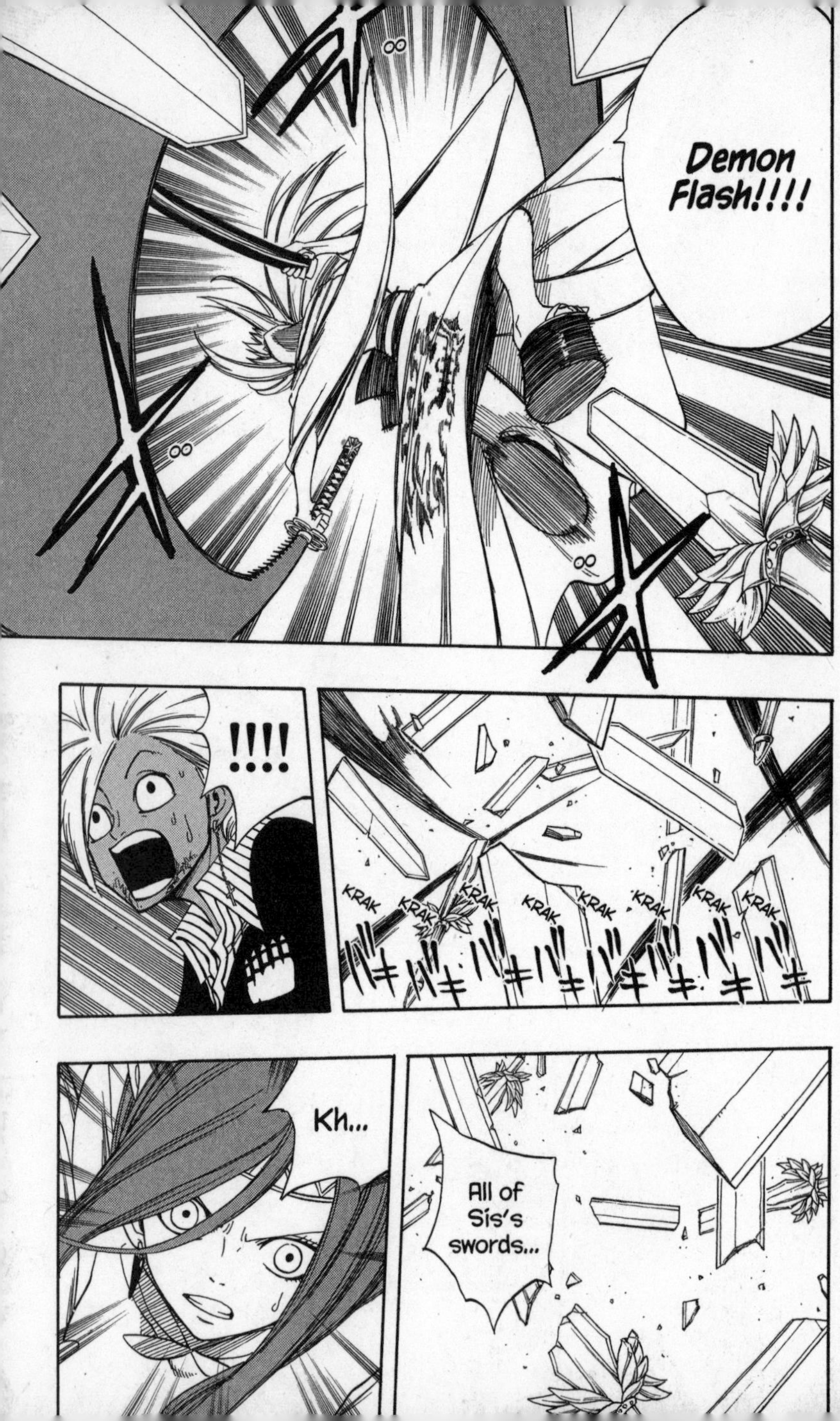
Demon Flash!!!!
KRAK KRAK KRAK KRAK KRAK KRAK KRAK KRAK
バキバキバキバキバキバキバキバキ
!!!!
All of Sis's swords...
Kh...

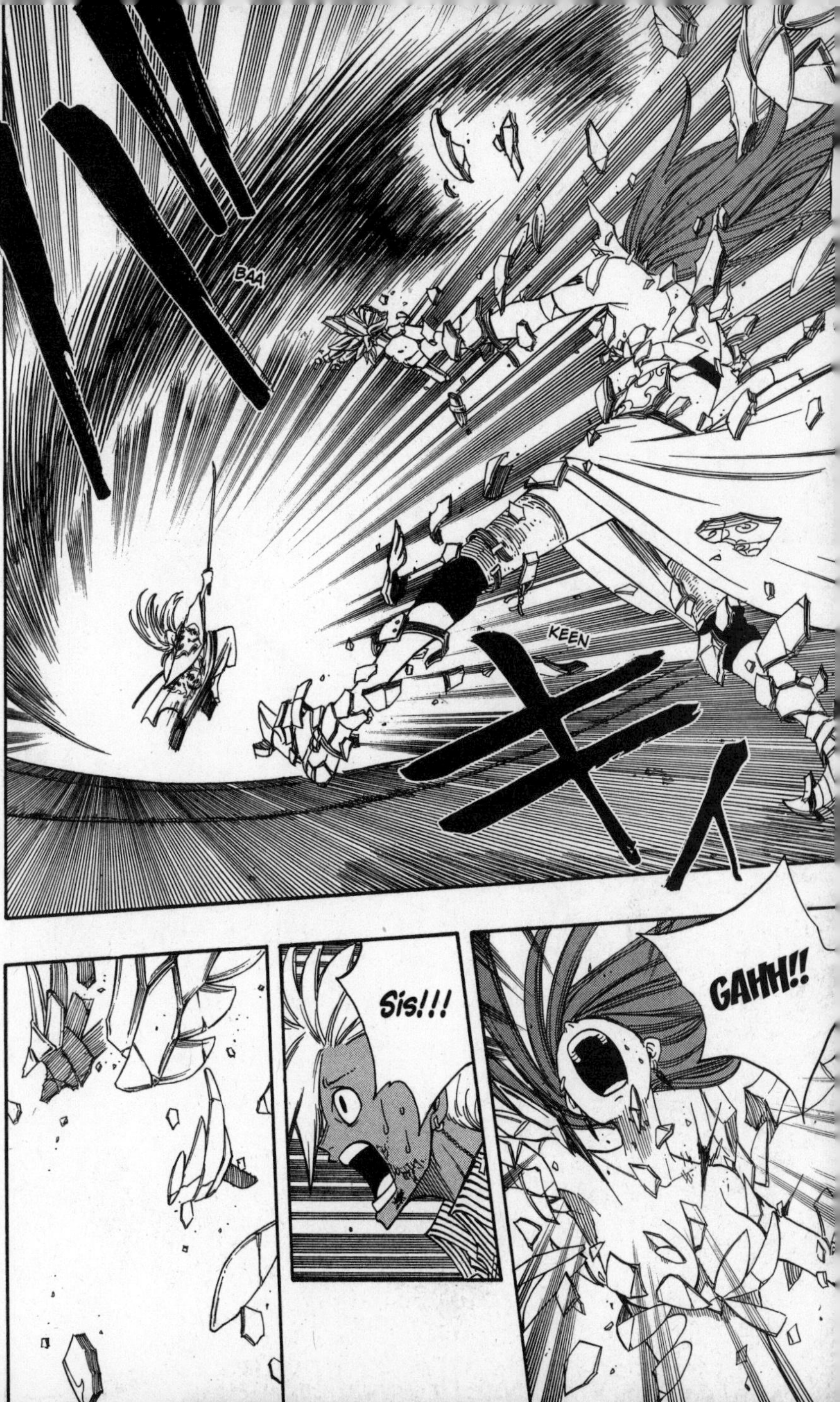
BAA
KEEN
GAHH!!
Sis!!!

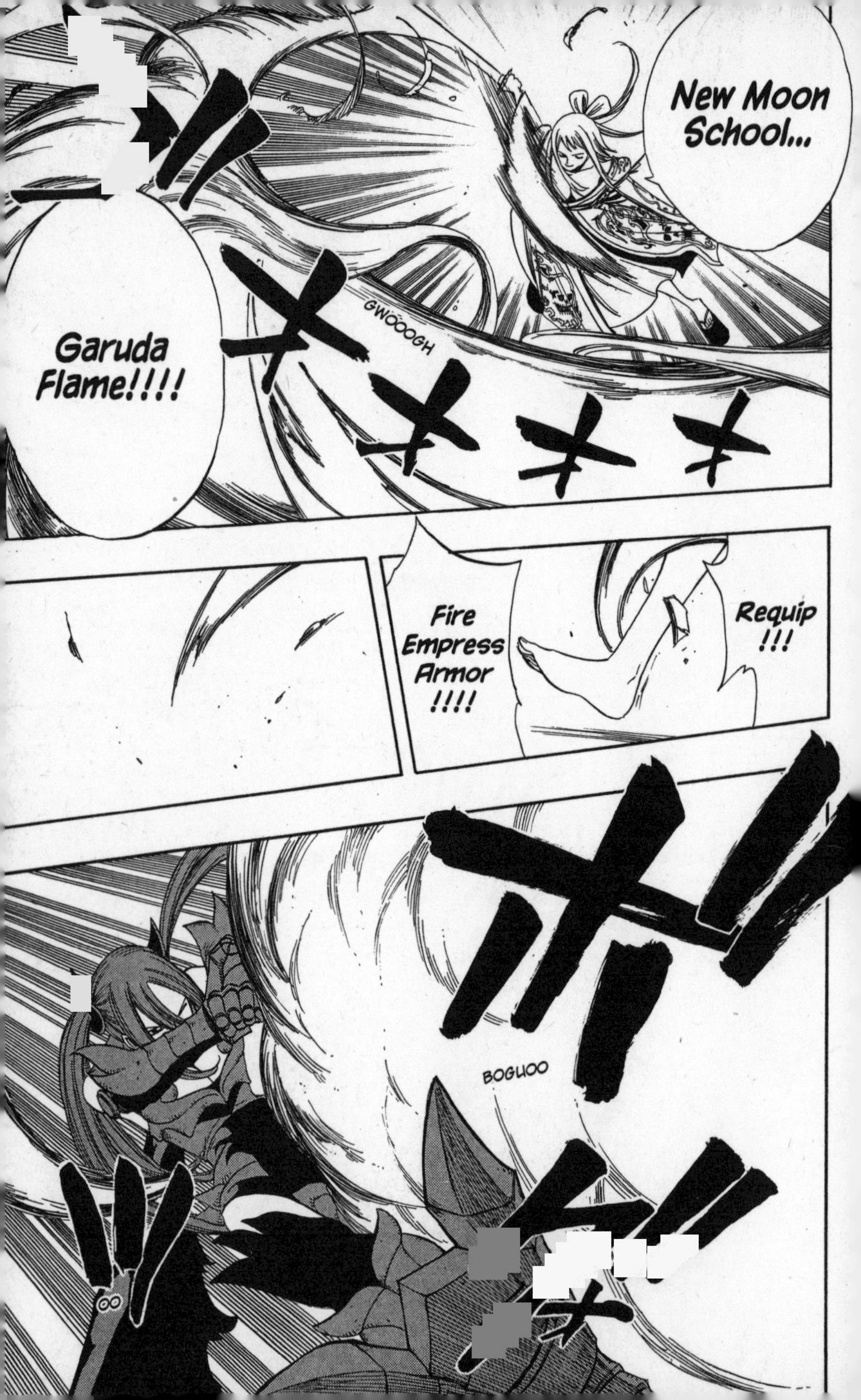
New Moon School...
Garuda Flame!!!!
GWOOOGH
Requip!!!
Fire Empress Armor!!!!
BOGUOO

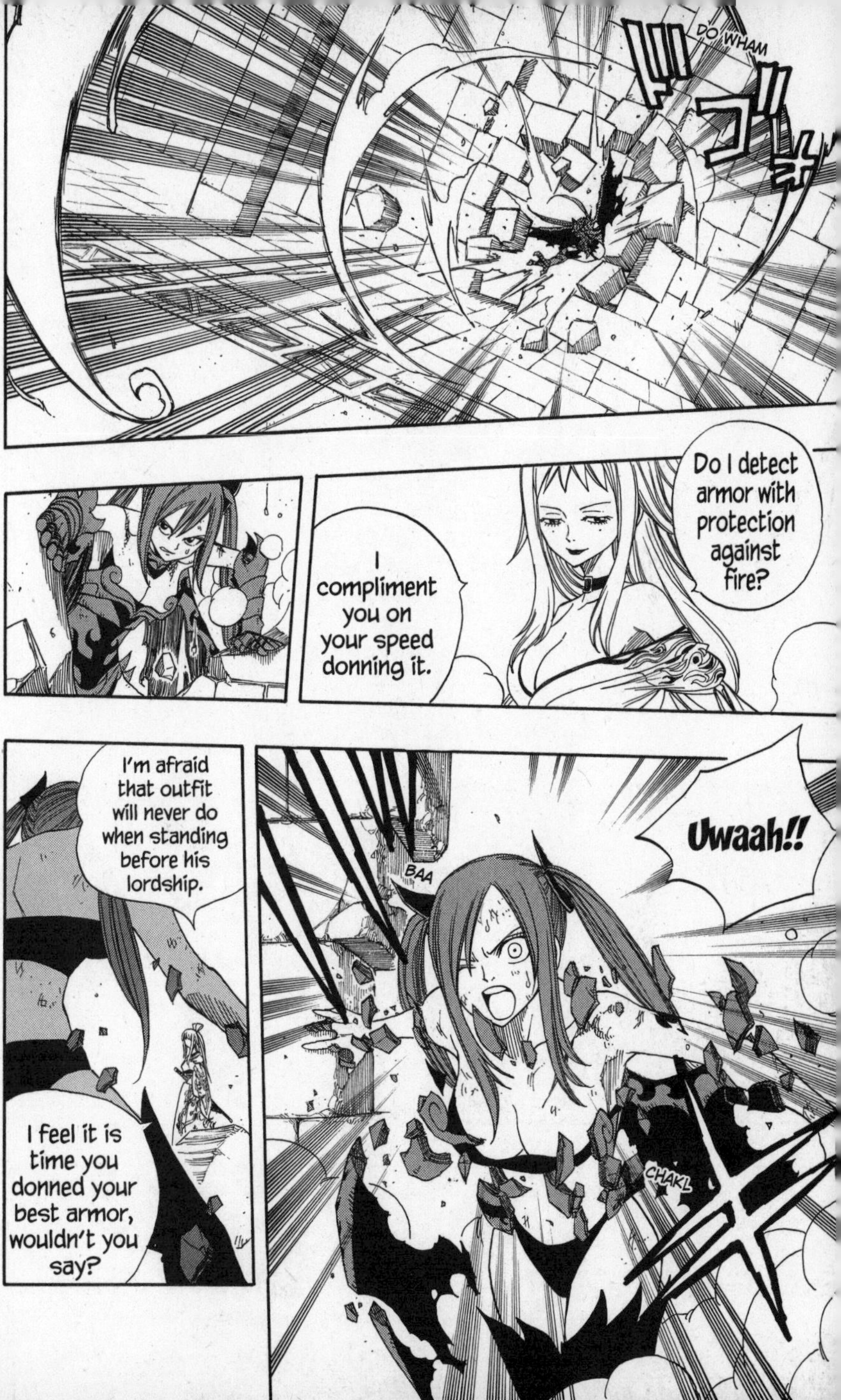
DO WHAM
Do I detect armor with protection against fire?
I compliment you on your speed donning it.
Uwaah!!
BAA
CHAKL
I'm afraid that outfit will never do when standing before his lordship.
I feel it is time you donned your best armor, wouldn't you say?

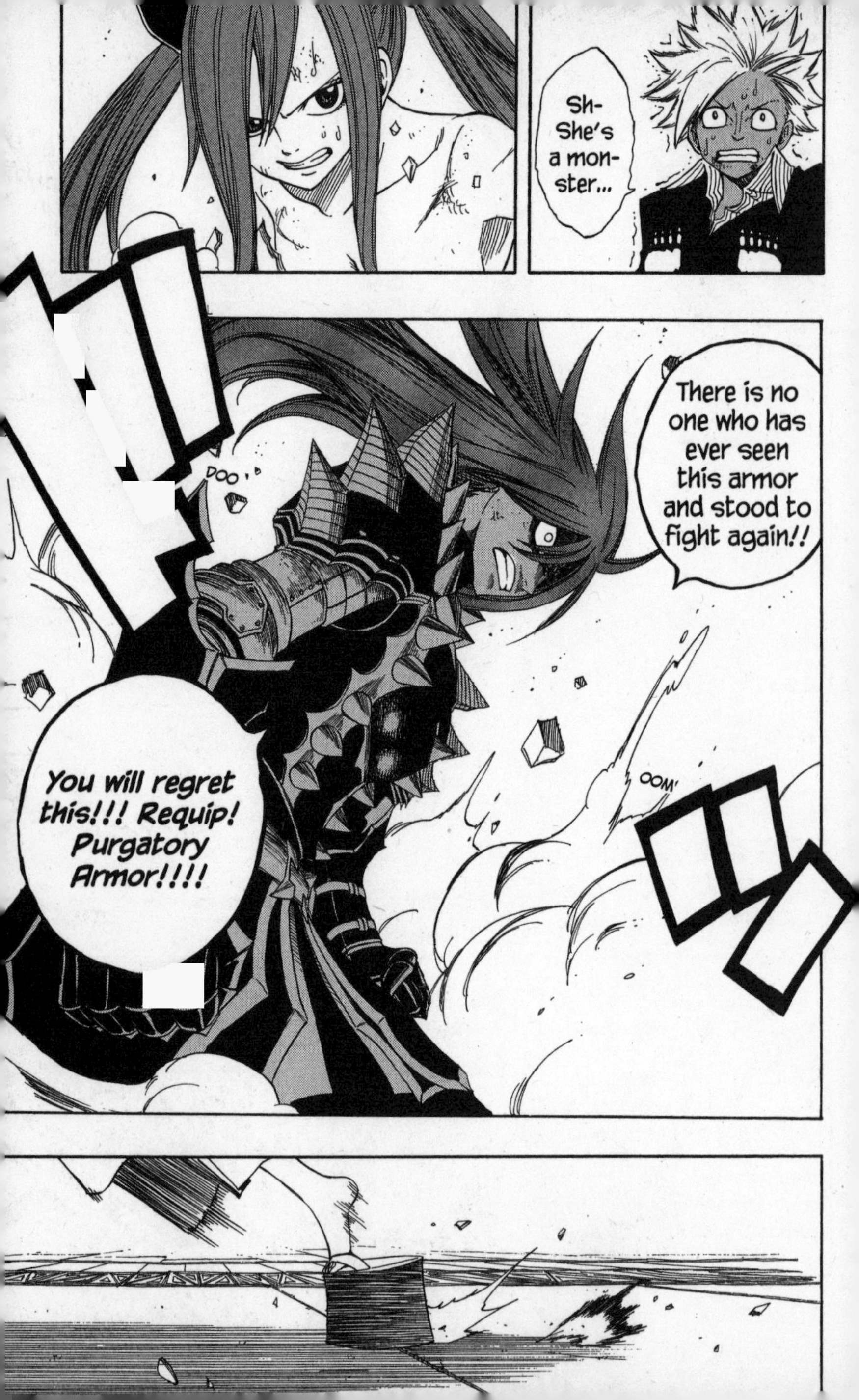
Sh- She's a monster...
There is no one who has ever seen this armor and stood to fight again!!
DOO
OOM
You will regret this!!! Requip! Purgatory Armor!!!!

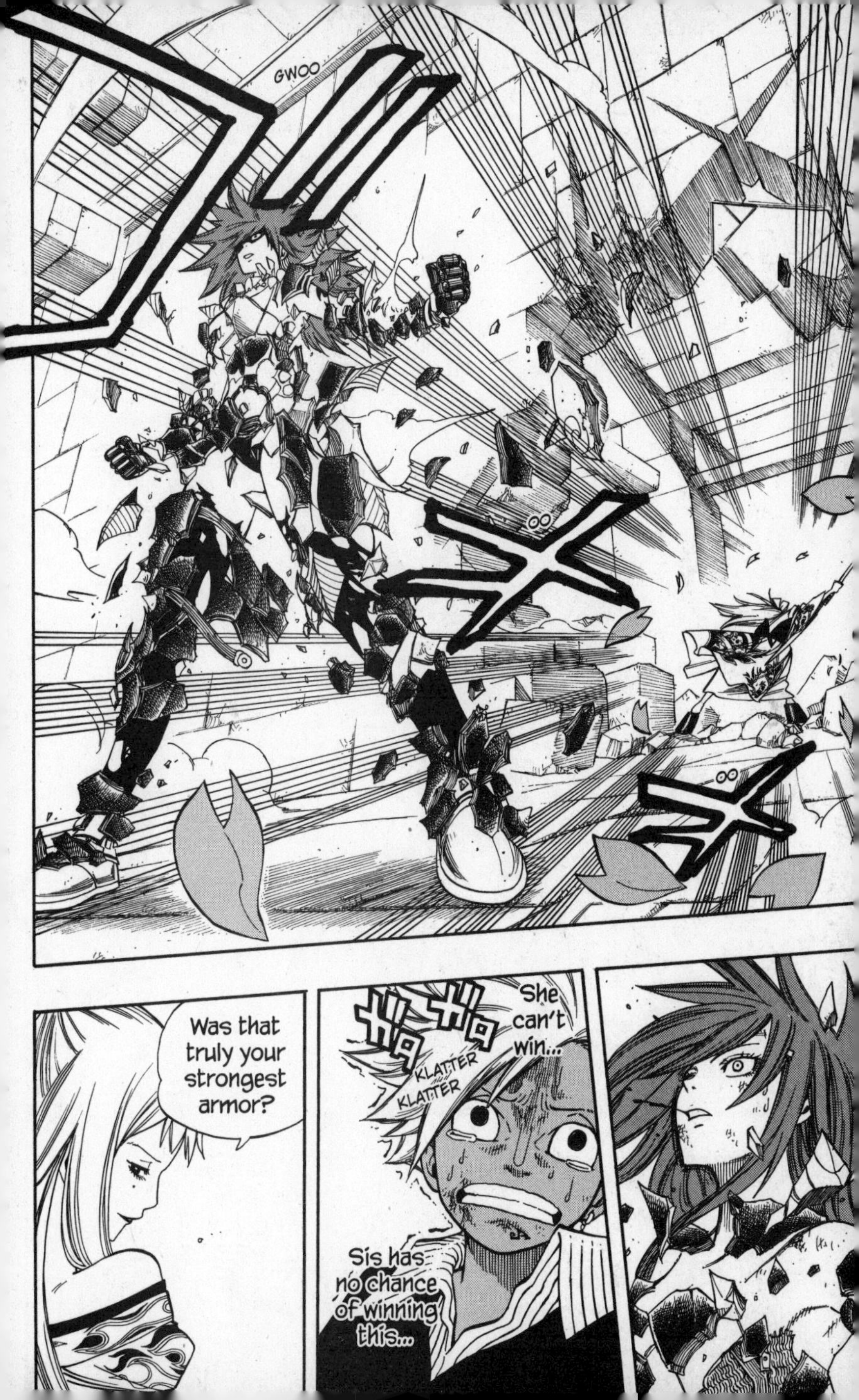
GWOO
She can't win...
KLATTER
KLATTER
Sis has no chance of winning this...
Was that truly your strongest armor?

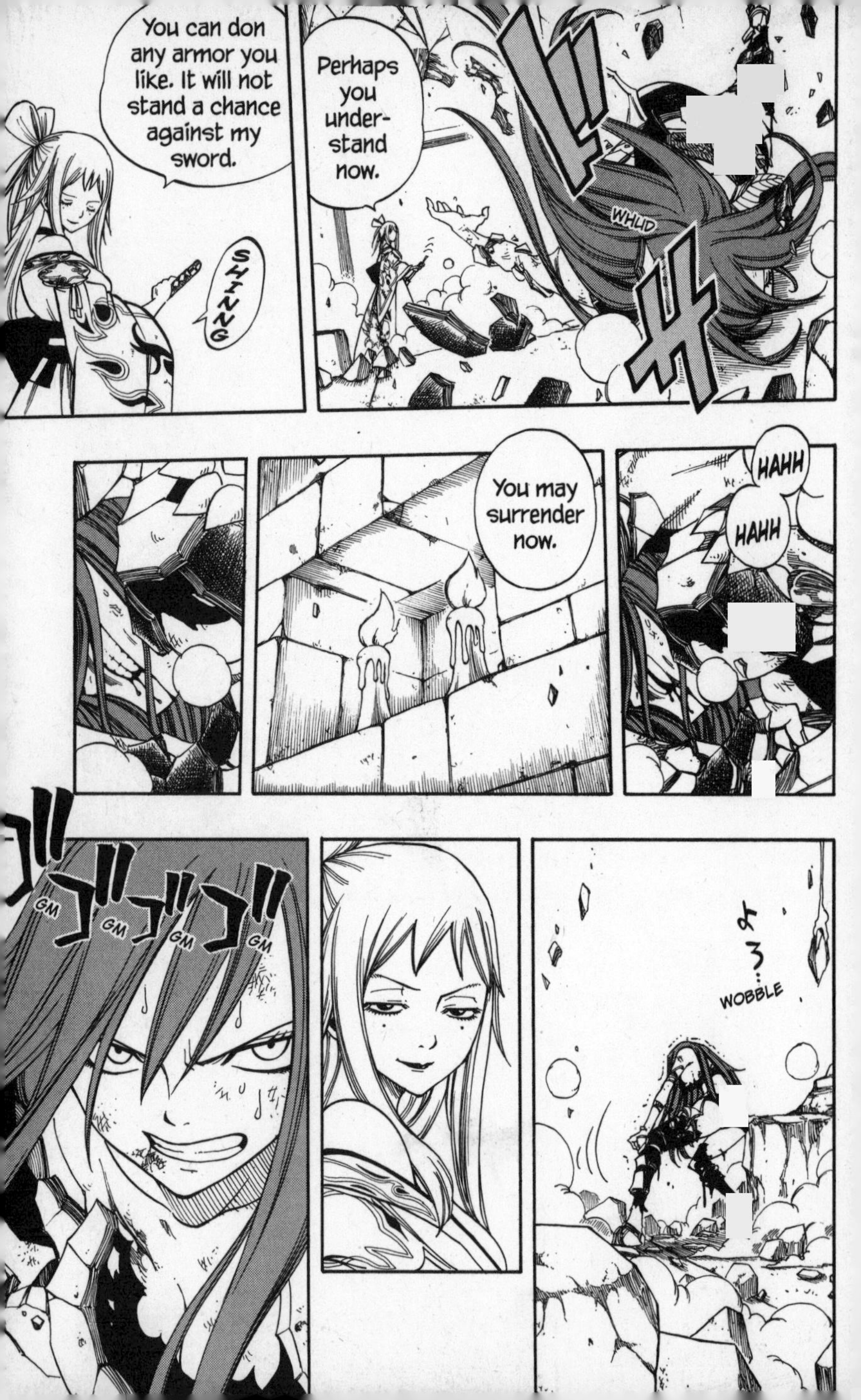
WHUD
Perhaps you under-stand now.
You can don any armor you like. It will not stand a chance against my sword.
SHINNG
HAHH
HAHH
You may surrender now.
よろ…
WOBBLE
GM
GM
GM
GM

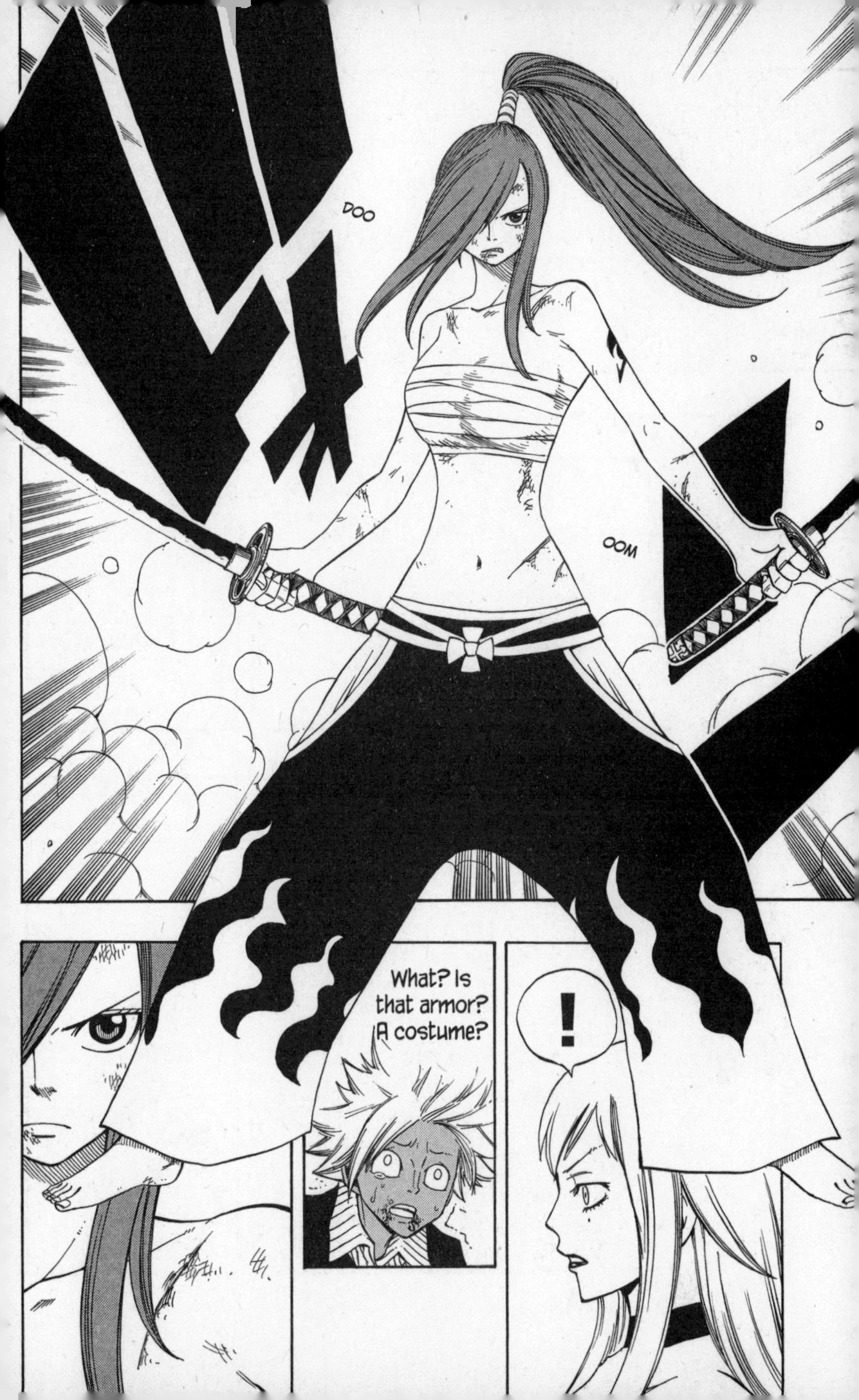
DOO
OOM
!
What? Is that armor? A costume?

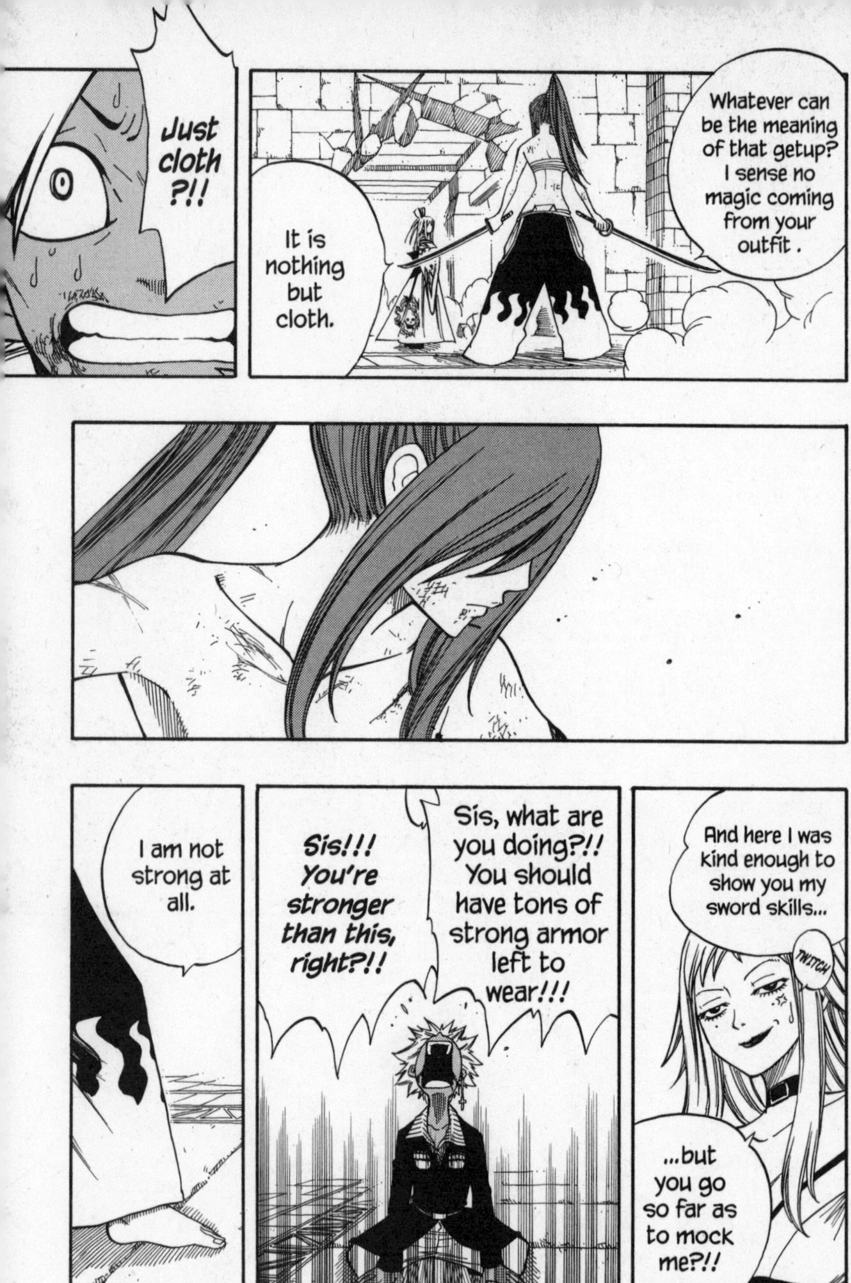
Whatever can be the meaning of that getup? I sense no magic coming from your outfit .
It is nothing but cloth.
Just cloth ?!!
And here I was kind enough to show you my sword skills...
TWITCH
...but you go so far as to mock me?!!
Sis, what are you doing?!! You should have tons of strong armor left to wear!!!
Sis!!! You're stronger than this, right?!!
I am not strong at all.

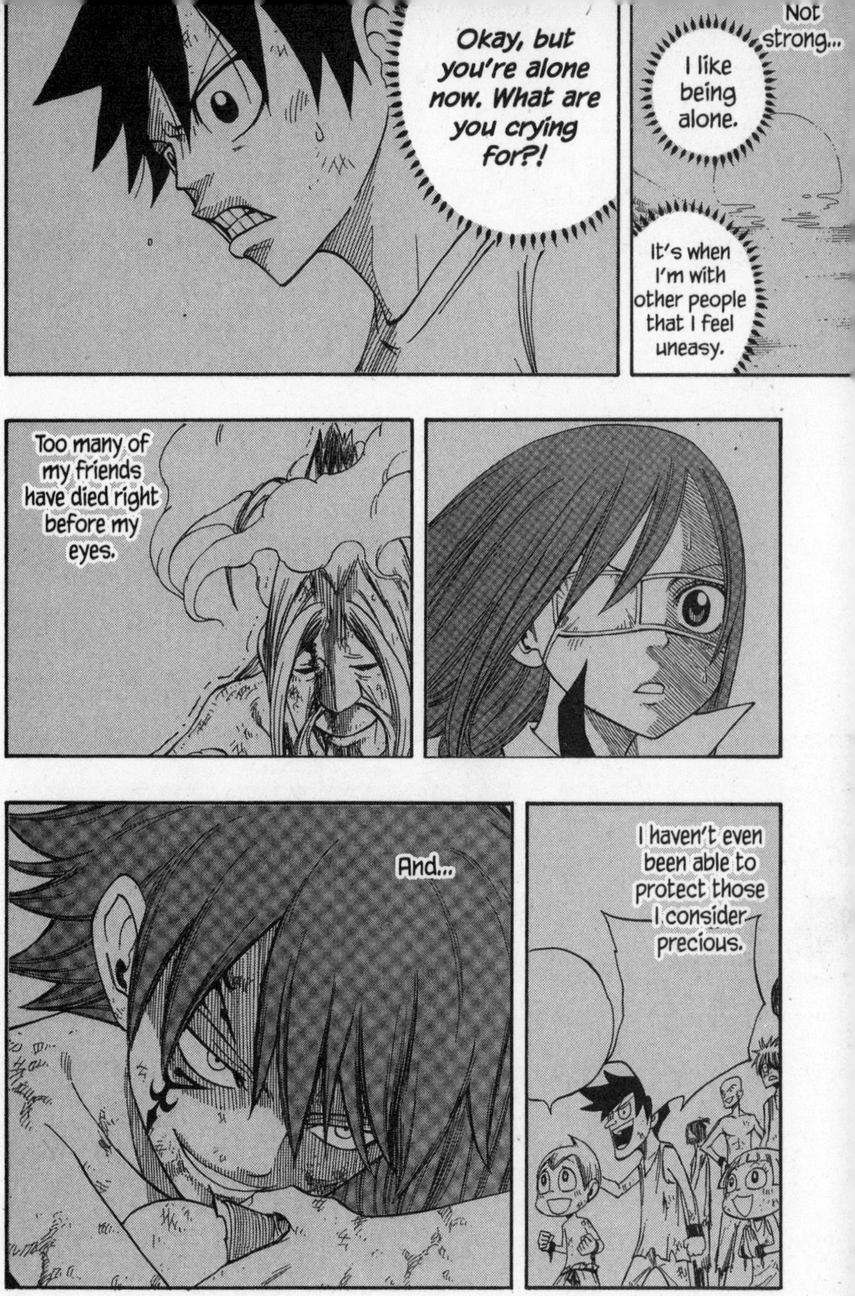
Not strong...
I like being alone.
It's when I'm with other people that I feel uneasy.
Okay, but you're alone now. What are you crying for?!
Too many of my friends have died right before my eyes.
I haven't even been able to protect those I consider precious.
And...

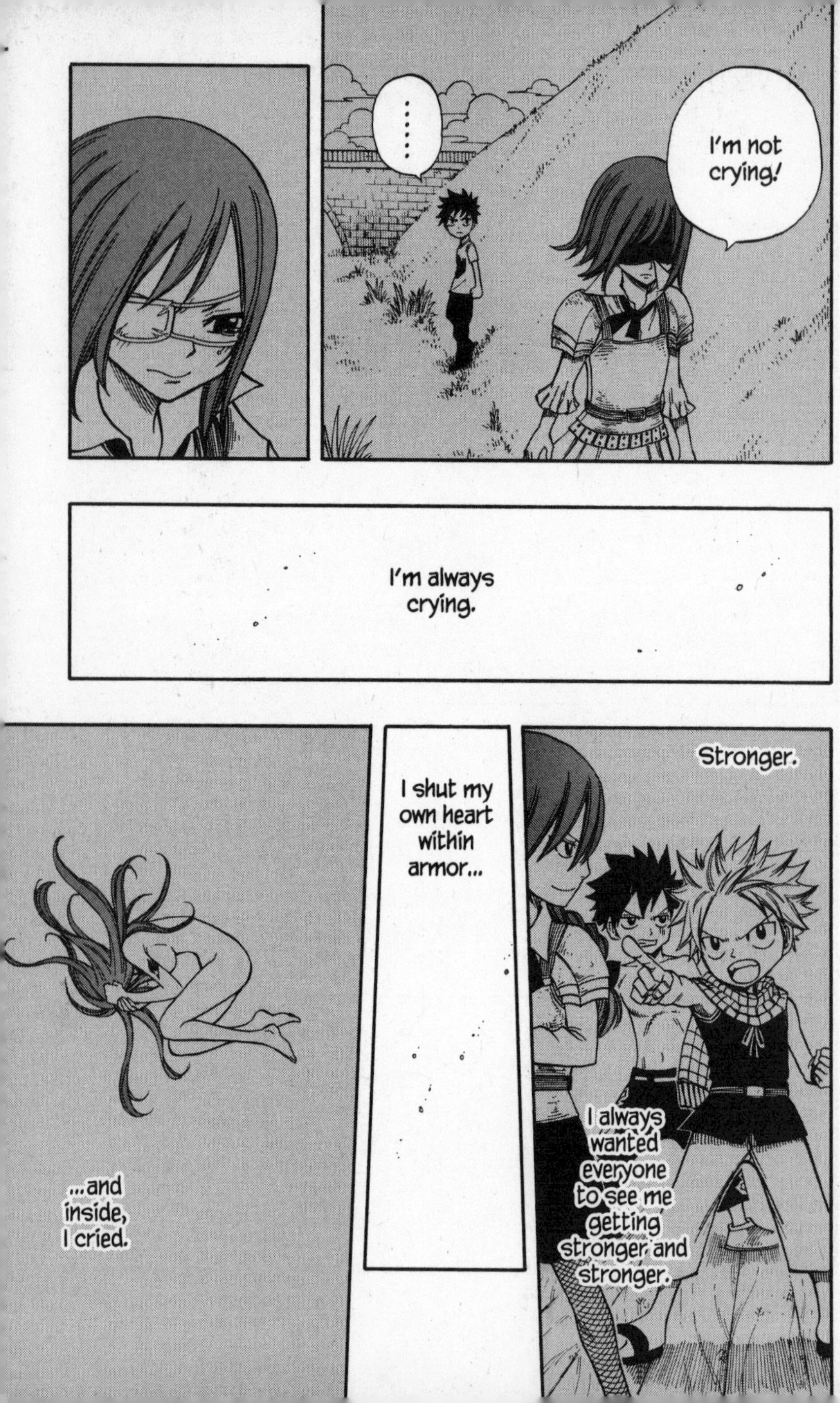
I'm not crying!
......
I'm always crying.
Stronger.
I always wanted everyone to see me getting stronger and stronger.
I shut my own heart within armor...
...and inside, I cried.

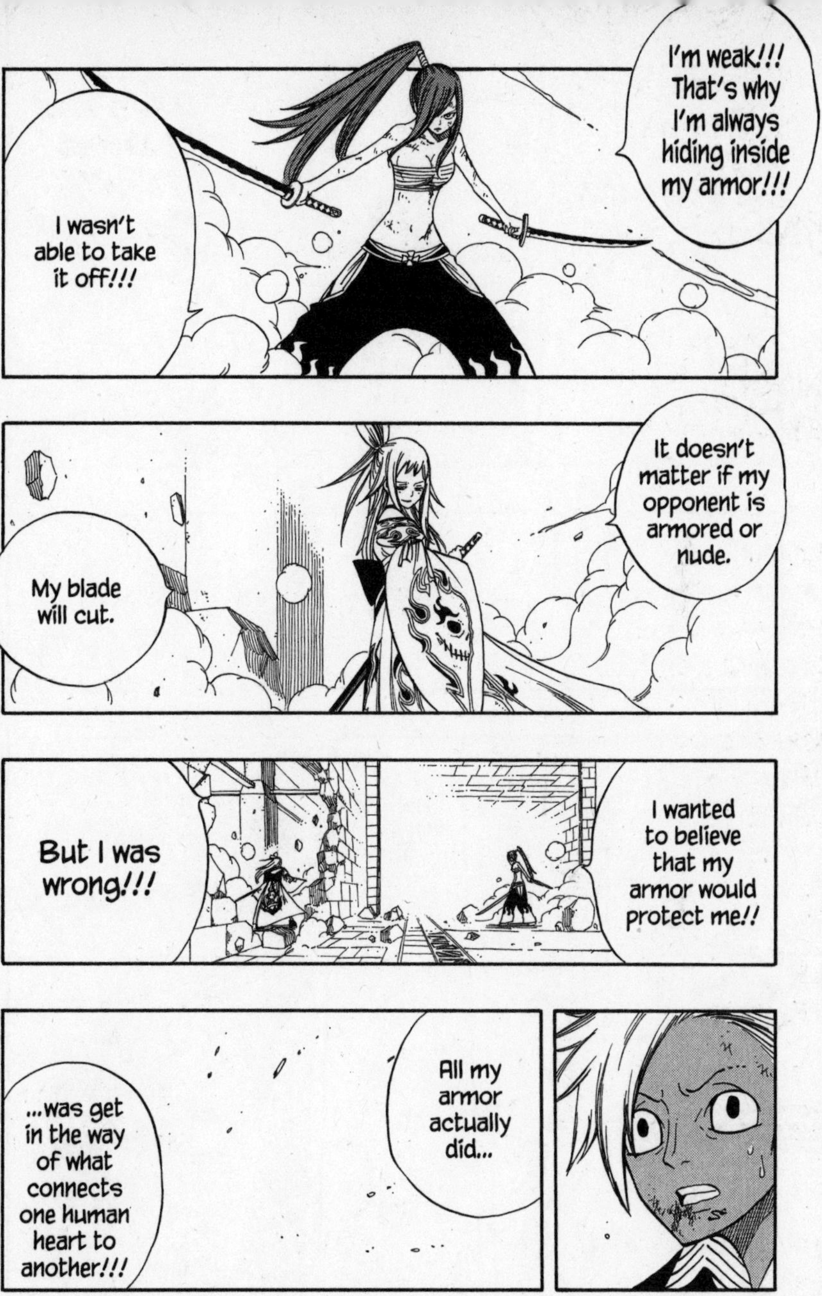
I'm weak!!! That's why I'm always hiding inside my armor!!!
I wasn't able to take it off!!!
It doesn't matter if my opponent is armored or nude.
My blade will cut.
I wanted to believe that my armor would protect me!!
But I was wrong!!!
All my armor actually did...
...was get in the way of what connects one human heart to another!!!

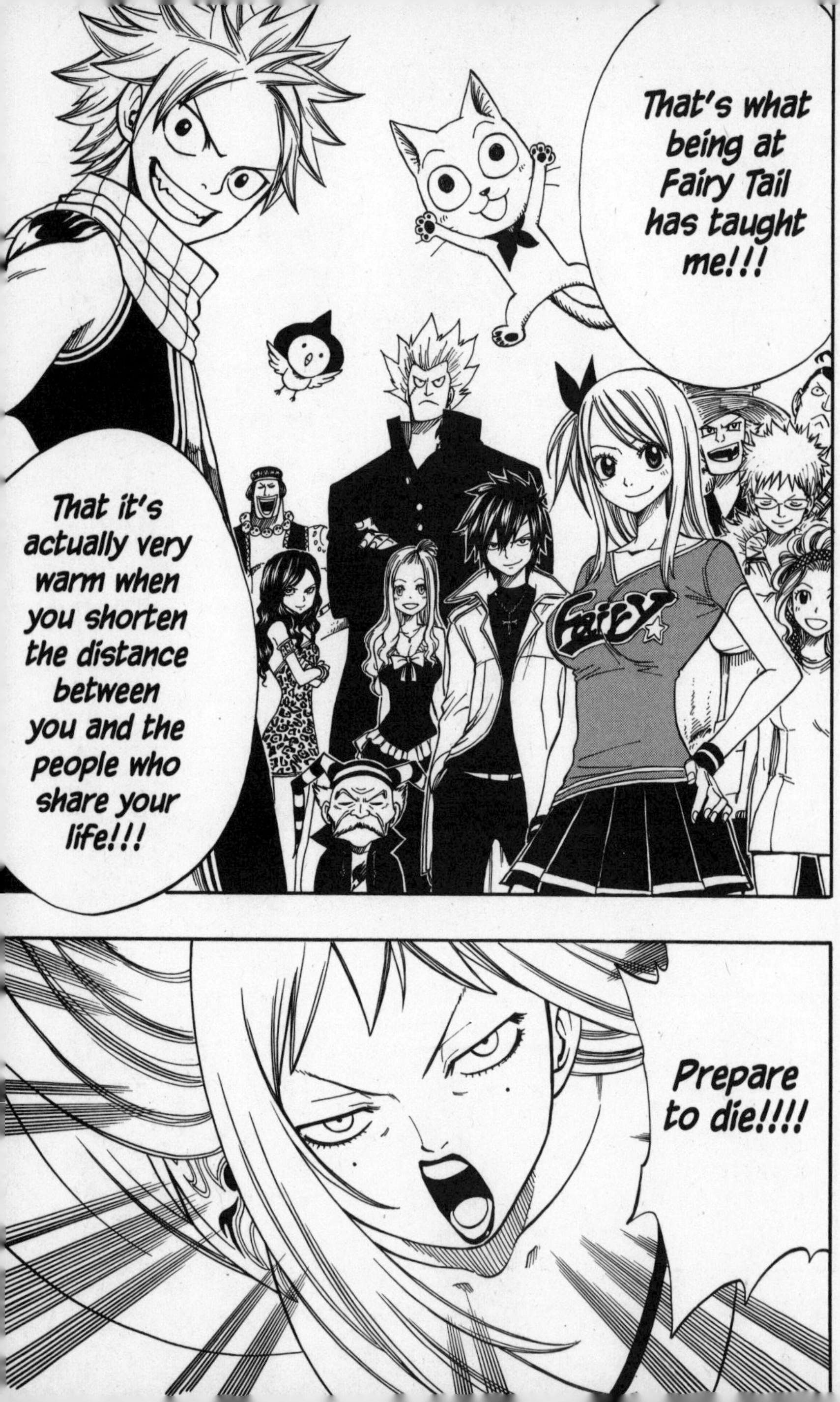
That's what being at Fairy Tail has taught me!!!
That it's actually very warm when you shorten the distance between you and the people who share your life!!!
Prepare to die!!!!

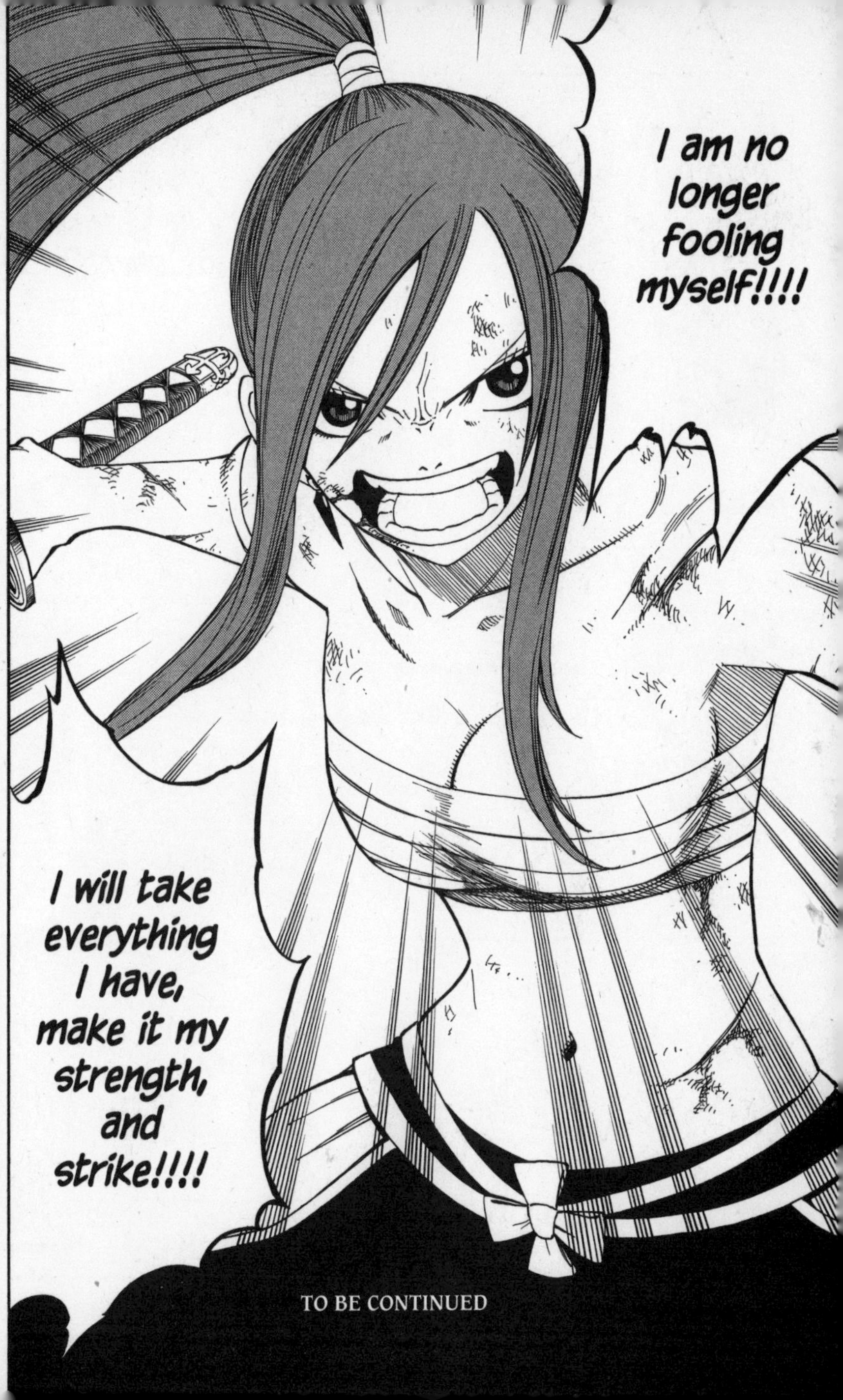
I am no longer fooling myself!!!!
I will take everything I have, make it my strength, and strike!!!!
TO BE CONTINUED

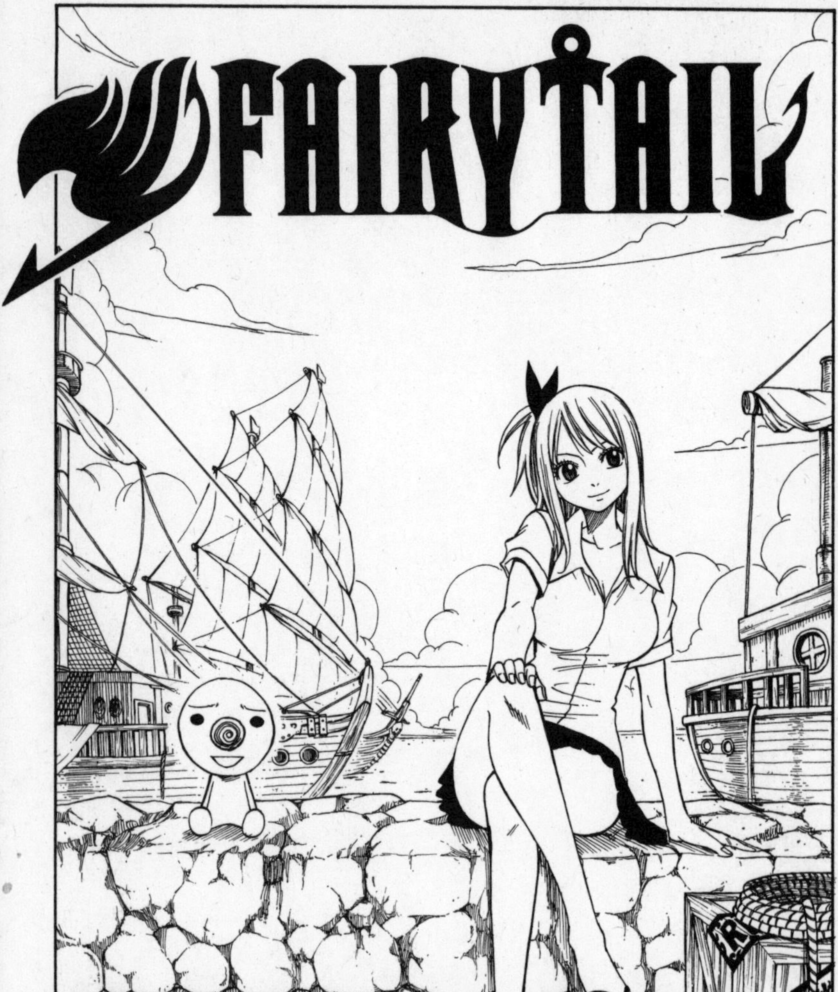
FAIRY TAIL

TAIL d'ART

The *Fairy Tail* Guild d'Art is an explosion of fan art! Please send in your black-and-white art on large postcard stock!! Those chosen to be published will get a signed mini poster! ♪ Make sure you write your real name and address on the back of your postcard!

▼Now, how is it going to turn out between these two...?

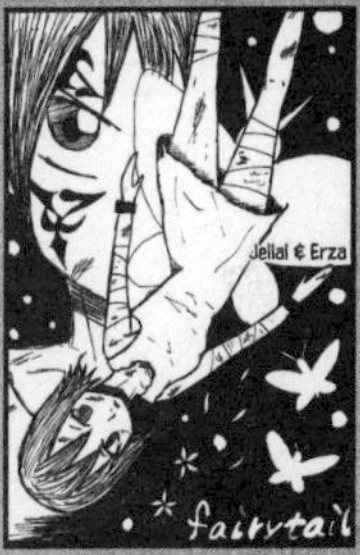
Jellal & Erza
fairytail

Kanagawa Prefecture, Kirin

▼Thank you!! And I love anybody who can draw such a cute Lucy!♥

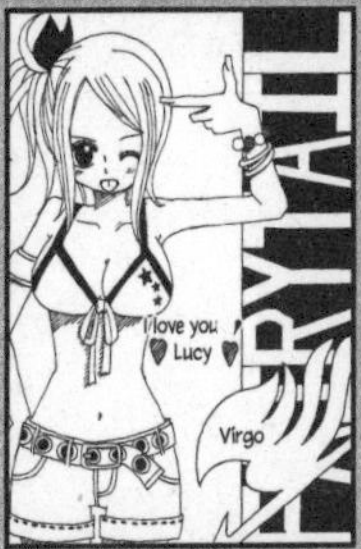
FAIRYTAIL
I love you Lucy
Virgo

Nagasaki Prefecture, Yû

▼Ohh!! There's a dragon coming out of that fire!! Now that's hot!

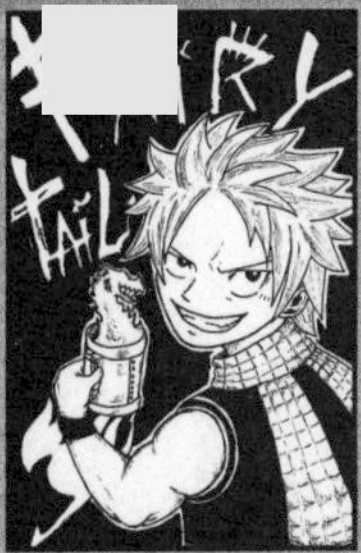

Fukuoka Prefecture, Keel

▼Now that's an amazingly girlish picture of Erza!! That doesn't happen very often!

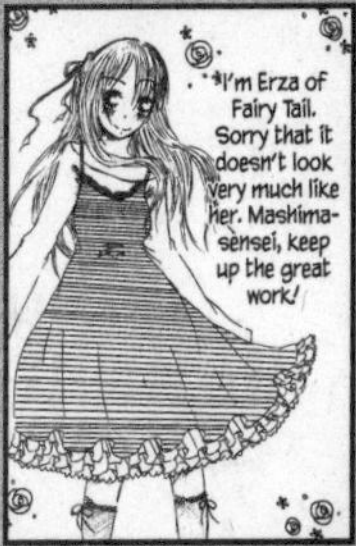
I'm Erza of Fairy Tail. Sorry that it doesn't look very much like her. Mashima-sensei, keep up the great work!

Saitama Prefecture, Haruka

▼This is a very rare pairing... I like the face Cancer is making!

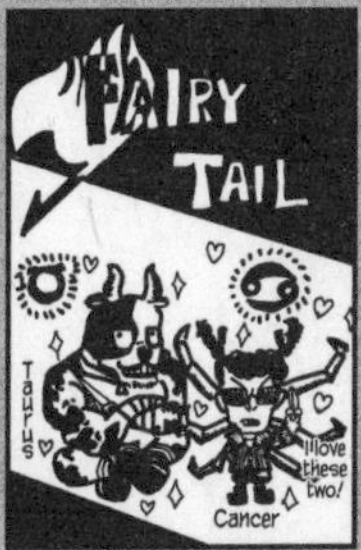
FAIRY TAIL
Taurus
I love these two!
Cancer

Hyogo Prefecture, Mitsunari Kawabata

▼Loke will show up again! Message to his fans, look for him!

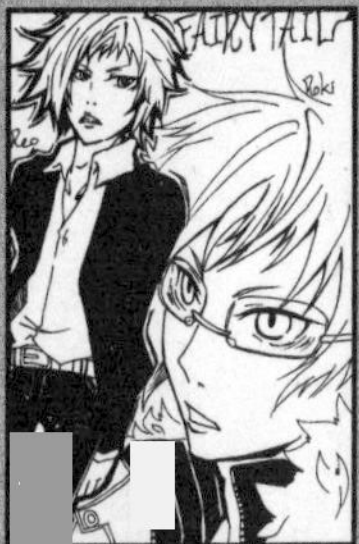
FAIRY TAIL

Iwate Prefecture, Yurie Abe

▼Yes, who is the heroine? That is the question?! I vote for Tomeko! Heh heh...

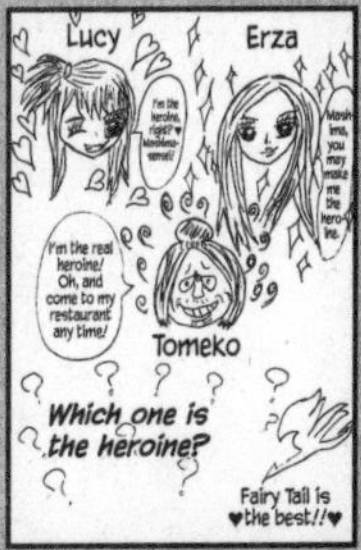
Lucy
Erza
I'm the real heroine! Oh, and come to my restaurant any time!
Tomeko
Which one is the heroine?
Fairy Tail is ♥the best!!♥

Kanagawa Prefecture, M.I.

▼A very sexy Mira-chan! She hasn't had much of a part recently...

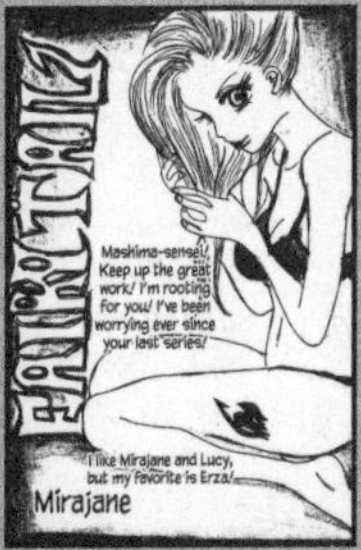
Maskima-sensei, Keep up the great work! I'm rooting for you! I've been worrying ever since your last series!
I like Mirajane and Lucy, but my favorite is Erza!
Mirajane

Gunma Prefecture, Umi

▼Kittymander...Breathes fire... Is this really how Kittymander should be drawn?!

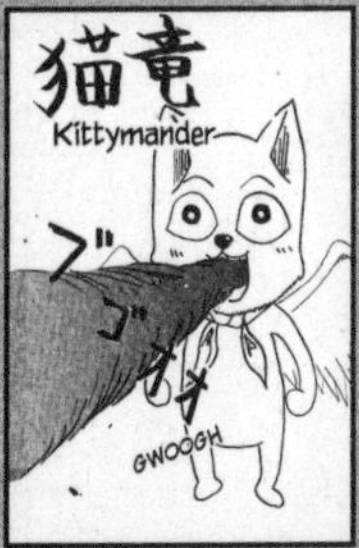
猫竜
Kittymander
GWOOGH

Hiroshima Prefecture, Momiji

FAIRY GUILD

▼ I get postcard after postcard from fans who are rooting for Laxus!!

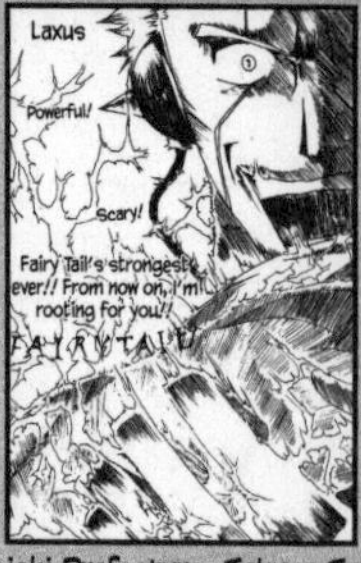
Laxus
Powerful!
Scary!
Fairy Tail's strongest ever!! From now on, I'm rooting for you!!
FAIRY TAIL

Aichi Prefecture, Takuya Takigawa

▼ Wakaba!! You're always looking weathered. Charge!! Down the path to middle-agedness!

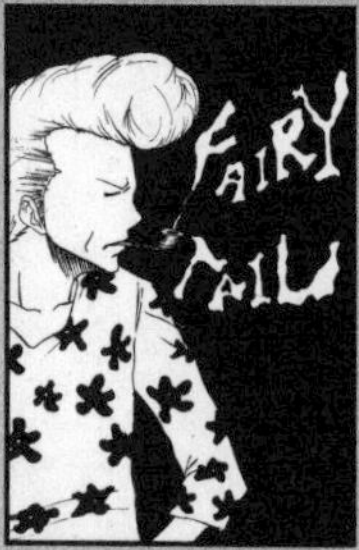
FAIRY TAIL

Saga Prefecture, Shûichiro Iwasaki

Okinawa Prefecture, Akemi Teruya

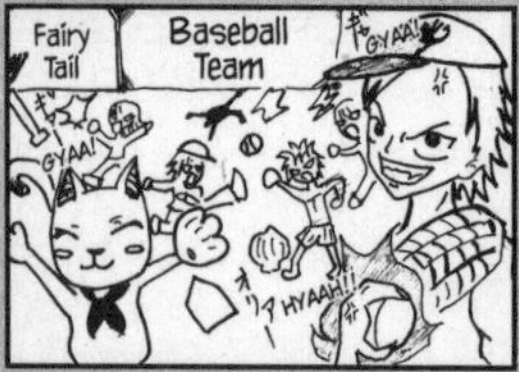
Fairy Tail
Baseball Team
GYAA!
GYAA!
HYAAH!!

▲ This is pretty messed up, huh? There are people kicking things out there! (laughs)

▼ You know, I think this is cuter and more erotic than the way I draw it!

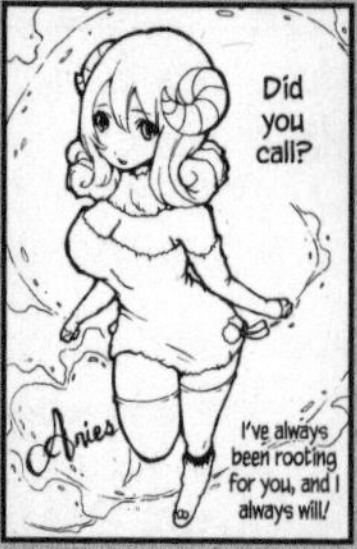
Did you call?
Aries
I've always been rooting for you, and I always will!

Aichi Prefecture, Anzu

● Any letters and postcards you send means that your personal information, such as your name, address, postal code, and other information, you include will be handed over, as is, to the author. When you send mail, please keep that in mind.

Rejection Corner

▼ That's a pretty good dandy! Hang in there, Wally!

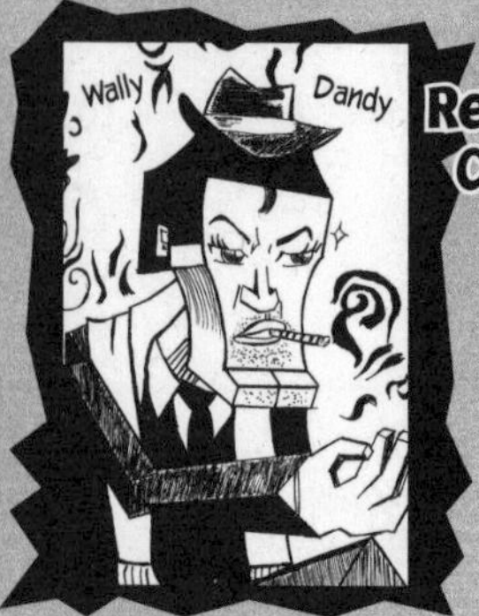
Wally
Dandy

Hyogo Prefecture, Misaki

▼ This is very well drawn! I'm a pro, and I throw up my hands in surrender!

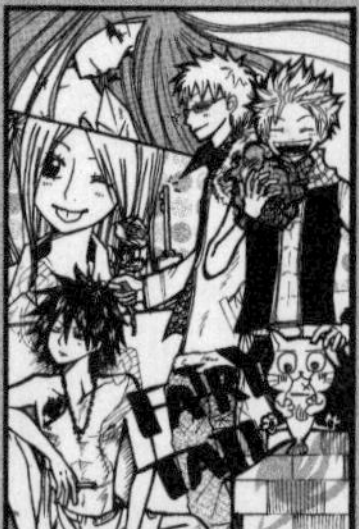
FAIRY TAIL

Kagoshima Prefecture, Mugen

Send to Kodansha Comics
Hiro Mashima
451 Park Ave. South
7th Floor
New York, NY 10016

Continued from the left-hand page ⬇

Mira: Let's continue with the next question.

Could you let me know the order from strongest to weakest of Lucy's Twelve Golden Gate Celestial Spirits?

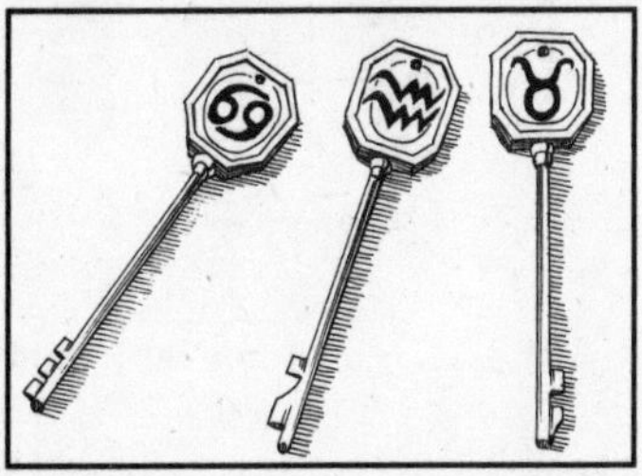

Lucy: Ehh? That's a hard question! Celestial spirits have all sorts of different strengths and weaknesses. Hm...
Mira: Okay, after reading all the volumes so far, I'll give you my impressions.

#1. Plue (Seems to be unrivaled)
#2. Aquarius (Strong!)
#3. Loke (Sort of strong)
#4. The cow and the crab, and the others.

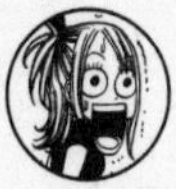
: That's awful!!! Plue's not even a celestial spirit of the Twelve Golden Gates!!

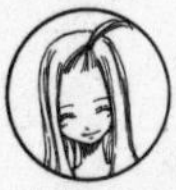
: Huh? I thought my assessment was pretty accurate.

Lucy: Not only that, but actually Taurus (Bull) and Cancer (Crab) are both pretty strong!
Mira: What about the maid and the horse guy?

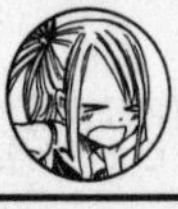
: They're really strong too!! Anyway, I can't decide an order!!

Mira: Then we'll just go on to the final question.

Why did Wally turn into that boxy guy?

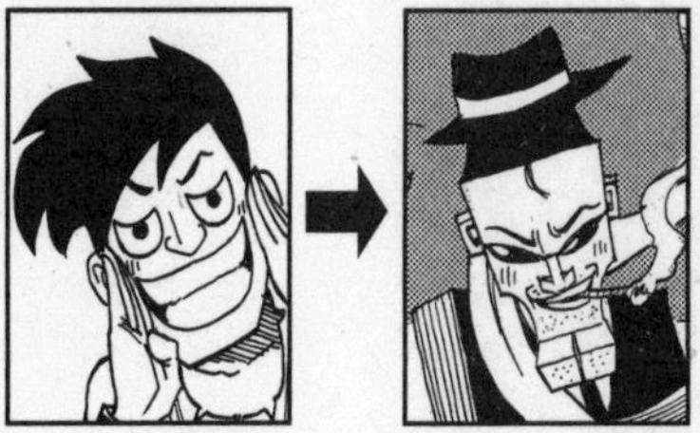

Lucy: Hmm...
Mira: I wonder...
Lucy: Maybe he was pursuing being the perfect dandy, and he just turned out that way.
Mira: I've known it to happen.
Lucy: Or maybe he was going down a boxy-like passageway and by the end, he was boxy too.
Mira: Happens all the time.
Lucy: Or maybe one day, a goddess appeared before his eyes. And she ordered him to be boxy from that moment on.
Mira: Nope. That would never happen.

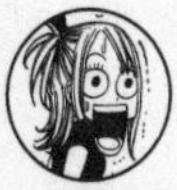
: What's with the sudden rejection?

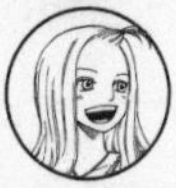
: I think it was love.

Lucy: L-Love?

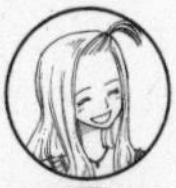
: Isn't that how the old saying goes? "Love makes you boxy"?

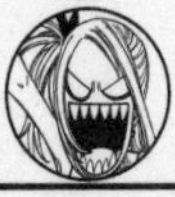
: Nobody has ever said that!!!

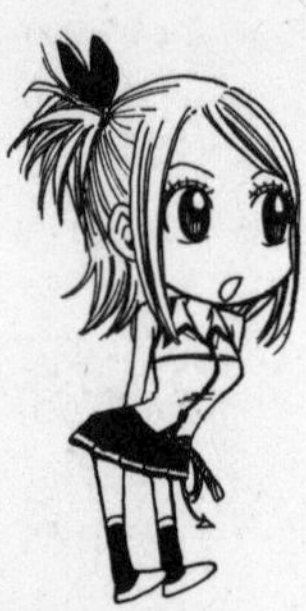

Emergency Request
Explain the Mysteries of...
FAIRY TAIL

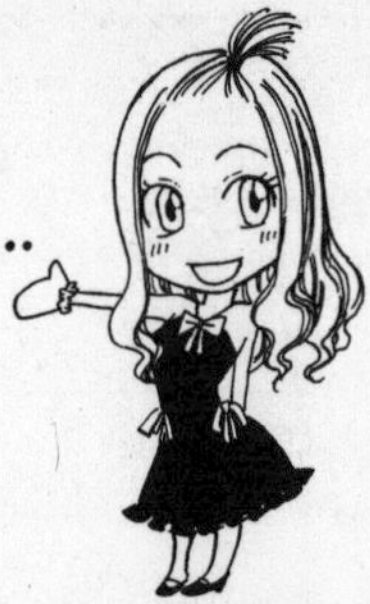

From the Counter at Fairy Tail...

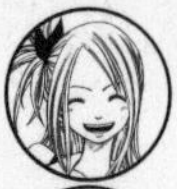

: Hi everybody! Long time, no see!!

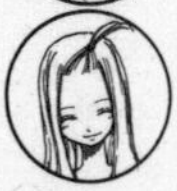

: We were only absent from one volume.

Lucy: Honestly! When this corner was left out of the last volume, I was shocked! I thought it was all over for us!!
Mira: It can't end like that! There's still so much for readers to complain about in this manga!
Lucy: I don't know whether to be happy or sad about that! (sweat, sweat)
Mira: Let's get to the first question.

> ***I think Lucy's hairstyle is cute, and I'd like to do the same with my hair. How do I do it?***

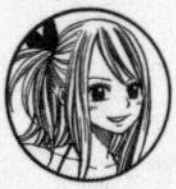

: Well! ♥ What a wonderful question!

Mira: It's from a grade-school-aged girl.
Lucy: Okay, let me teach you a simple way of doing it.

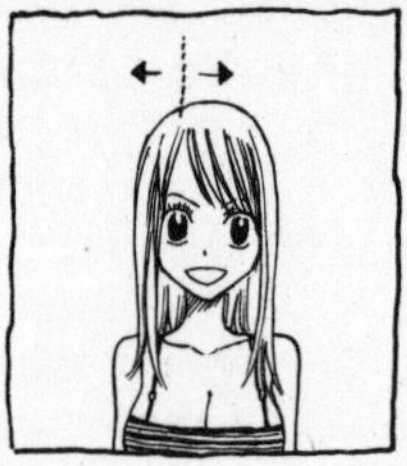

First, I part my hair somewhere about one quarter of the way across the bangs. But you can do it wherever you like, really.

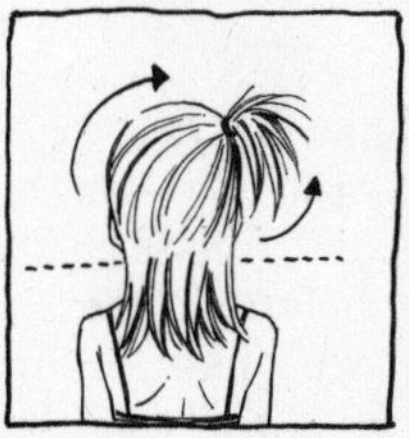

You want to take up some of your hair from a line above the nape of the neck, and be sure to leave some behind. You want to gather it and tie it on the top-right side of your head. Don't worry about it too much. Just do whatever you can with it.

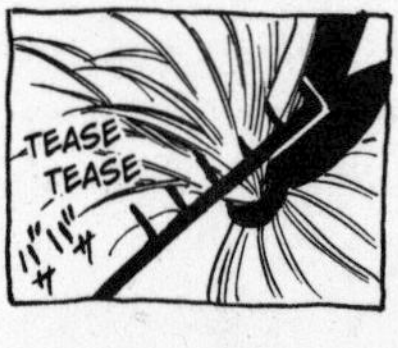
TEASE
TEASE

Tie it off with a hair band and decorate it with a ribbon. Then take a comb and tease the gathered hair until it shifts around easily. Again, there's no need to obsess. Just do what you can.

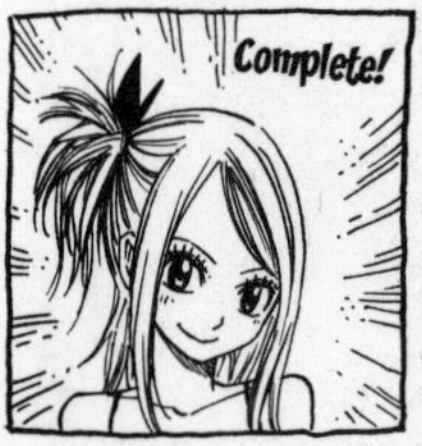
Complete!

If you put a little hairspray on it, it'll look a little better. And you're done!!

Continued on the right-hand page

AFTERWORD

Trinity Raven! I came up with them at the last moment. Originally the ones who were going to stand between our heroes and Jellal were Shô, Simon, and the others. But while I was writing the chapters of Erza's past (the chapters toward the end of the last volume), I started feeling really sorry for them. Even if Natsu and Gray were to defeat them, it wouldn't really solve their conflicts. And so, all very quickly, I set up the Trinity Raven. The scene of the fight between Natsu and Wally and Millianna was done in a very comical way, so it didn't draw the same kind of sympathy that my original idea had.

People who read these Afterword sections might have come to notice already, but tales like this change an awful lot. It happens all the time that a story I've completely thought through will take an unexpected turn. In this particular story arc, there have been a number of changes. The Trinity Raven is just a typical example. And my style is to not think too much about what comes after, so every week I find myself saying, *I wonder what will come next?* (Or, *what'll I do now?!!*) That's the way I am, but here, I actually have given the way this story arc ends a lot of thought. Well, I gave it a bit of vague thought on all the other stories. (sweat, sweat) For the end of the Deliora story arc, I thought, *Gray'll end up winning...right?* For the Phantom arc, *Makarov will prove to be really strong...right?* I sort of muddle through to the end.

But not this time!! I've given the end of this story arc some concrete thought!!! And it looks like it will turn out to be a really good story... At least I hope it turns out good...So expect great things!!

About the Creator

HIRO MASHIMA was born May 3, 1977, in Nagano Prefecture. His series *Rave Master* has made him one of the most popular manga artists in America. *Fairy Tail*, currently being serialized in *Weekly Shônen Magazine*, is his latest creation.

My name is Tama
Gonzaburo!!
I'm going to slide right
down your throat!!
And just think how tasty
your beef bowl would be
with me on top!!
Can you even imagine
breakfast without me?!
Wow-wow!! I'm a
reproductive cell!!...
Sorry.
I'm really tired.

—Hiro Mashima

Translation Notes

Japanese is a tricky language for most Westerners, and translation is often more art than science. For your edification and reading pleasure, here are notes on some of the places where we could have gone in a different direction in our translation of the work, or where a Japanese cultural reference is used.

General Notes:
Wizard

In the original Japanese version of *Fairy Tail*, you'll find panels in which the English word "wizard" is part of the original illustration. So this translation has taken that as its inspiration and translated the word *madôshi* as "wizard." But *madôshi*'s meaning is similar to certain Japanese words that have been borrowed by the English language, such as judo (the soft way) and kendo (the way of the sword). *Madô* is the way of magic, and *madôshi* are those who follow the way of magic. So although the word "wizard" is used in the original dialogue, a Japanese reader would be likely to think not of traditional Western wizards, such as Merlin or Gandalf, but of martial artists.

Names

Hiro Mashima has graciously agreed to provide official English spellings for just about all of the characters in *Fairy Tail*. Because this version of *Fairy Tail* is the first publication of most of these spellings, there will inevitably be differences between these spellings and some of the fan interpretations that may have spread throughout the Web or in other fan circles. Rest assured that the spellings contained in this book are the spellings that Mashima-sensei wanted for *Fairy Tail*.

Tama Gonzaburo, page 191

The Japanese word for "egg" is *tamago*. So Tama Gonzaburo is something of a pun on the word "egg."

Sneezing when someone is gossiping about you, page 27

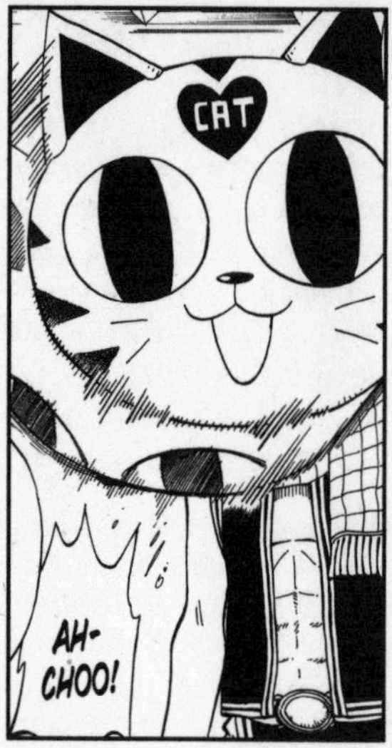
CAT
AH-CHOO!

There is an old saying that when you sneeze, someone is talking about you. This has turned into a shorthand version of a standard joke in Japanese TV dramas, anime, manga, and other media. A group of people are talking about a character, then there is a sudden scene change to that character who sneezes and wonders if he is coming down with a cold. In reality, very few people believe this is true, but the joke still "plays" nonetheless.

In-cat-ceration Tube, page 31

The Japanese word for "incarceration" or "restraint" is *kôsoku*, and the Japanese word for "cat" is *neko*. Millianna's attack in Japanese was, *Ne-kôsoku* Tube (with "tube" being in English). Since there was no way to translate the pun on the manga page, I replaced it with an English pun and elected to explain it here in the notes.

The names of the Trinity Raven, page 42

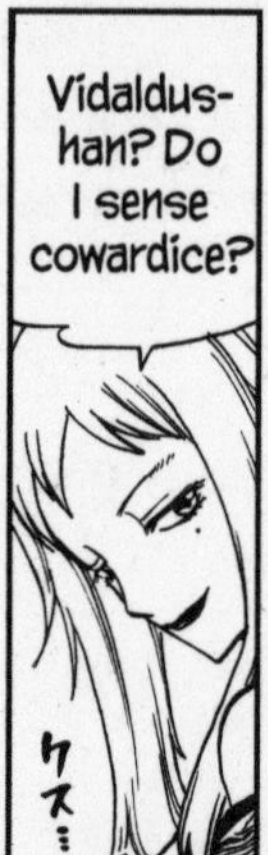
Vidaldus-han? Do I sense cowardice?
クス…
TEEHEE

All of the names of the members of Trinity Raven are Japanese words for birds. As you, the reader, have probably already guessed, *fukuro* is the Japanese word for "owl." Slightly less obvious are *taka,* which means "hawk," and *ikaruga,* which is the word used when referring to a bird known as the Japanese grosbeak. (That's why Ikaruga calls herself "Ikaruga the Dove" later on. We just thought "dove" sounded more elegant than "grosbeak."

Vidaldus-han, page 50

Japanese grosbeak speaks in the Kyoto version of the *Kansai-ben* dialect (accent for the *Kansai* region that mainly consists of Kobe, Osaka, Kyoto, and Nara but also includes the surrounding areas). In many versions of the *Kansai* accent of Japanese, the honorific *-san* is pronounced *-han*.

Faakin' Gals, page 72

Okay, I chickened out a little and transliterated (put the Japanese pronunciation intact in the alphabet) rather than translated Vidaldus's line. But there are reasons for it. The F-bomb has a certain amount of emotional content in English that it doesn't have in Japanese. In Japanese, it's just something that heavy-metal rockers or tough guys in movies say. While at the same time, the Japanese "swear words" being used in *Fairy Tail* are all rather tame—they might be said on TV without anyone batting an eye. Any Japanese equivalent to the F-bomb would be out of place in the Japanese version, and the actual F-bomb would be out of place in the American version.

Lock and rock, page 76

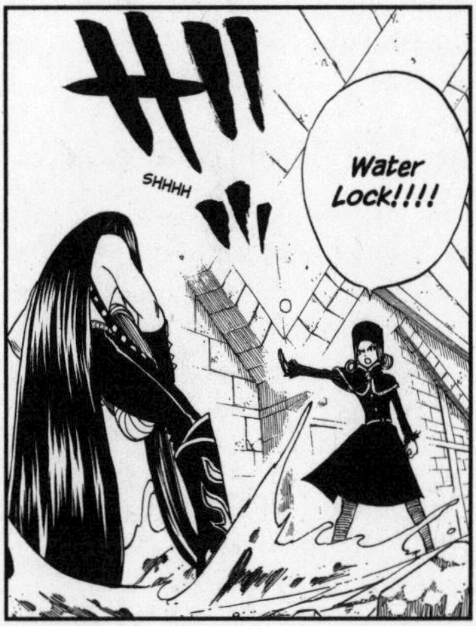
Water Lock!!!!
SHHHH

As any first-year Japanese language course will tell you, the Japanese people (who don't have training in the English language) cannot hear the difference between the *l* and *r* sounds. For example, the words "correction" and "collection" sound exactly the same to a Japanese native speaker. (The same kind of thing goes both ways. Native English speakers, at first, have a tough time distinguishing between the short and long vowels of Japanese words. "Mr. Oka," *Oka-san,* sounds very much like the Japanese word for "mother," *okaa-san.*) To a native Japanese speaker, "lock" and "rock" sound exactly the same and are spelled the same in Japanese.

Shampooing every morning, page 78

There is some research to back up Vidaldus's claim. Reportedly, daily washing strips the scalp of a beneficial oil called sebum, and can damage hair. Apparently the scalp tries to compensate for the washed-off oil by producing more oil, but breaking the daily shampooing habit will, within a little while, cause the scalp to return to its normal oil production, and one's hair will not be as greasy as it will seem when one first breaks the habit. At least one dermatologist recommends shampooing only twice or three times a week.

Water Cane, page 88

If you're wondering why a stick that helps people walk is thought of as a weapon, remember that in parts of Asia, caning is a still form of criminal punishment. It is used much like a whip, meant to flay skin off the caning victim's back. Often in Japanese period dramas, the villains will capture a hero or innocent bystander and cane him or her to try to get information.

Drainage Ditch, page 125

By the side of nearly every road in Japan is a drainage ditch to drain rain water from the road. The ditches are usually covered by small blocks of concrete, but in many rural and some urban settings, the ditches remain uncovered and present something of a hazard to pedestrians since many (if not most) of Japanese streets lack sidewalks.

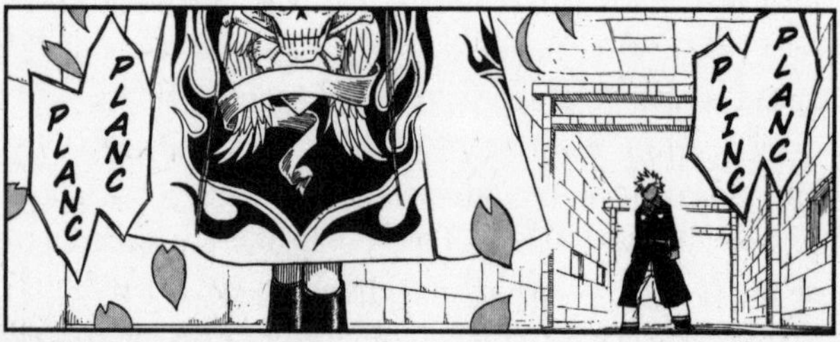
PLANC
PLINC
PLANC
PLANC

Planc and plinc, page 155

This is supposed to be the sound of a shamisen playing traditional music in the background. But since the shamisen isn't a common instrument in the West, the sound effect doesn't come across as well as it does to Japanese readers.

Does it stare at you?...Within the fog bank, page 167

This verse is in the form of a haiku, the form of Japanese poetry that is best known to the Western world. It is descended from the older Japanese poem form, *waka*. But haiku is a form that is more bound by rules (it must be a natural setting; it must have some word indicating the season; etc.), and it is a shorter form of poem at seventeen syllables (5-7-5) to *waka*'s thirty-one (5-7-5-7-7). Although one can generally say more using seventeen syllables of English than one can in seventeen syllables of Japanese, language translation generally takes more words to get the point across—so with some imagination, one can translate haiku into the same number of syllables.

Honorifics Explained

Throughout the Kodansha Comics books, you will find Japanese honorifics left intact in the translations. For those not familiar with how the Japanese use honorifics and, more important, how they differ from American honorifics, we present this brief overview.

Politeness has always been a critical facet of Japanese culture. Ever since the feudal era, when Japan was a highly stratified society, use of honorifics—which can be defined as polite speech that indicates relationship or status—has played an essential role in the Japanese language. When addressing someone in Japanese, an honorific usually takes the form of a suffix attached to one's name (example: "Asuna-san"), is used as a title at the end of one's name, or appears in place of the name itself (example: "Negi-sensei," or simply "Sensei").

Honorifics can be expressions of respect or endearment. In the context of manga and anime, honorifics give insight into the nature of the relationship between characters. Many English translations leave out these important honorifics and therefore distort the feel of the original Japanese. Because Japanese honorifics contain nuances that English honorifics lack, it is our policy at Kodansha not to translate them. Here, instead, is a guide to some of the honorifics you may encounter in Kodansha Comics.

-**san**: This is the most common honorific and is equivalent to Mr., Miss, Ms., or Mrs. It is the all-purpose honorific and can be used in any situation where politeness is required.

-**sama**: This is one level higher than "-san" and is used to confer great respect.

-**dono**: This comes from the word "tono," which means "lord." It is an even higher level than "-sama" and confers utmost respect.

-kun: This suffix is used at the end of boys' names to express familiarity or endearment. It is also sometimes used by men among friends, or when addressing someone younger or of a lower station.

-chan: This is used to express endearment, mostly toward girls. It is also used for little boys, pets, and even between lovers. It gives a sense of childish cuteness.

Bozu: This is an informal way to refer to a boy, similar to the English terms "kid" and "squirt."

Sempai/
Senpai: This title suggests that the addressee is one's senior in a group or organization. It is most often used in a school setting, where underclassmen refer to their upperclassmen as "sempai." It can also be used in the workplace, such as when a newer employee addresses an employee who has seniority in the company.

Kohai: This is the opposite of "sempai" and is used toward underclassmen in school or newcomers in the workplace. It connotes that the addressee is of a lower station.

Sensei: Literally meaning "one who has come before," this title is used for teachers, doctors, or masters of any profession or art.

-[blank]: This is usually forgotten in these lists, but it is perhaps the most significant difference between Japanese and English. The lack of honorific means that the speaker has permission to address the person in a very intimate way. Usually, only family, spouses, or very close friends have this kind of permission. Known as *yobisute*, it can be gratifying when someone who has earned the intimacy starts to call one by one's name without an honorific. But when that intimacy hasn't been earned, it can be very insulting.

Preview of Volume 12

We're pleased to present you with a preview from volume 12, now available from Kodansha Comics. Check out our Web site (www.kodanshacomics.com) for more details!

FAIRY TAIL
12
Hiro Mashima
Creator of Rave Master

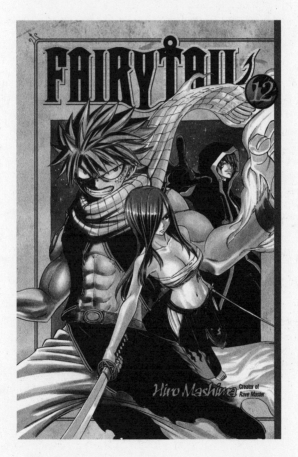

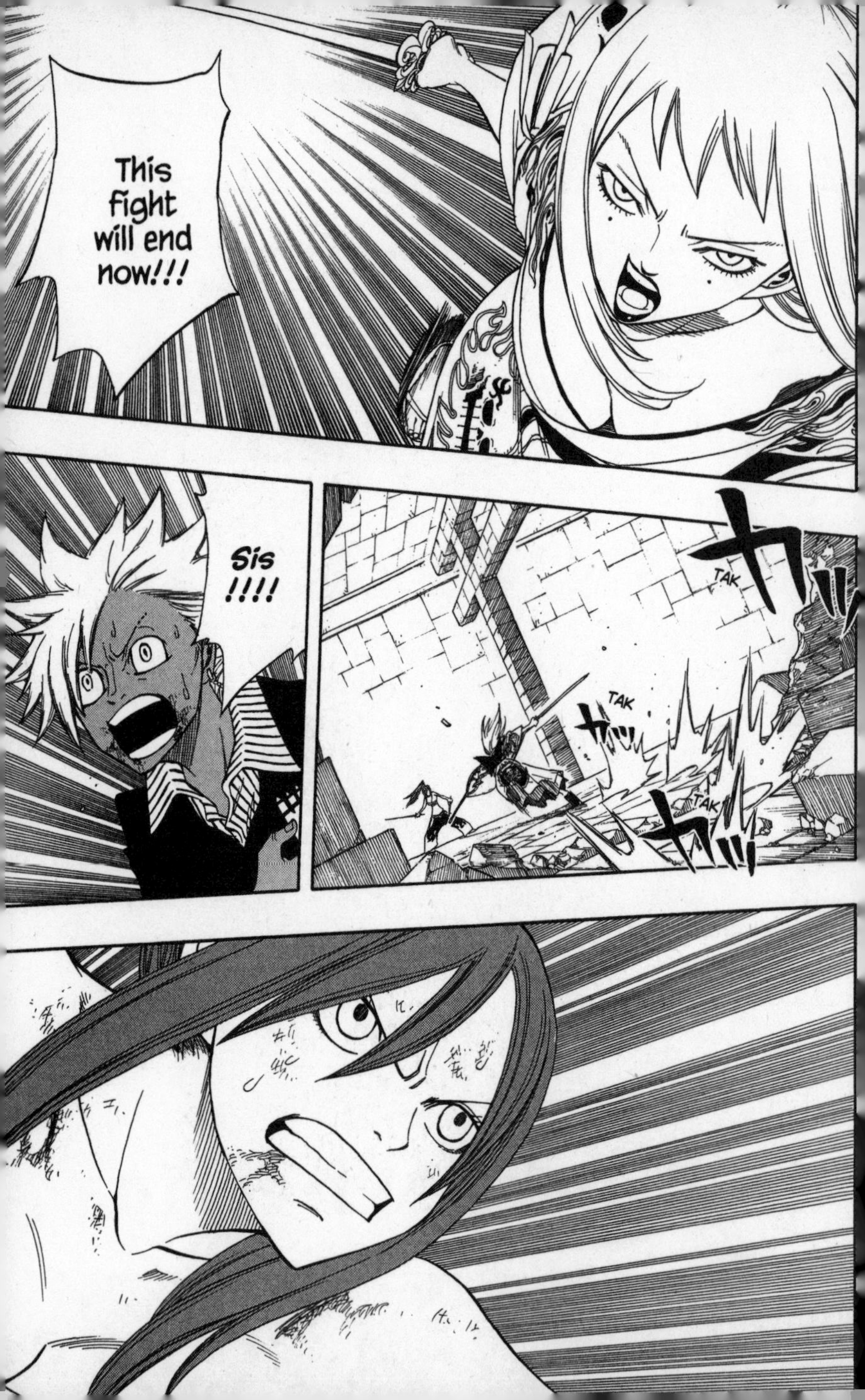
This fight will end now!!!
TAK
TAK
TAK
Sis !!!!

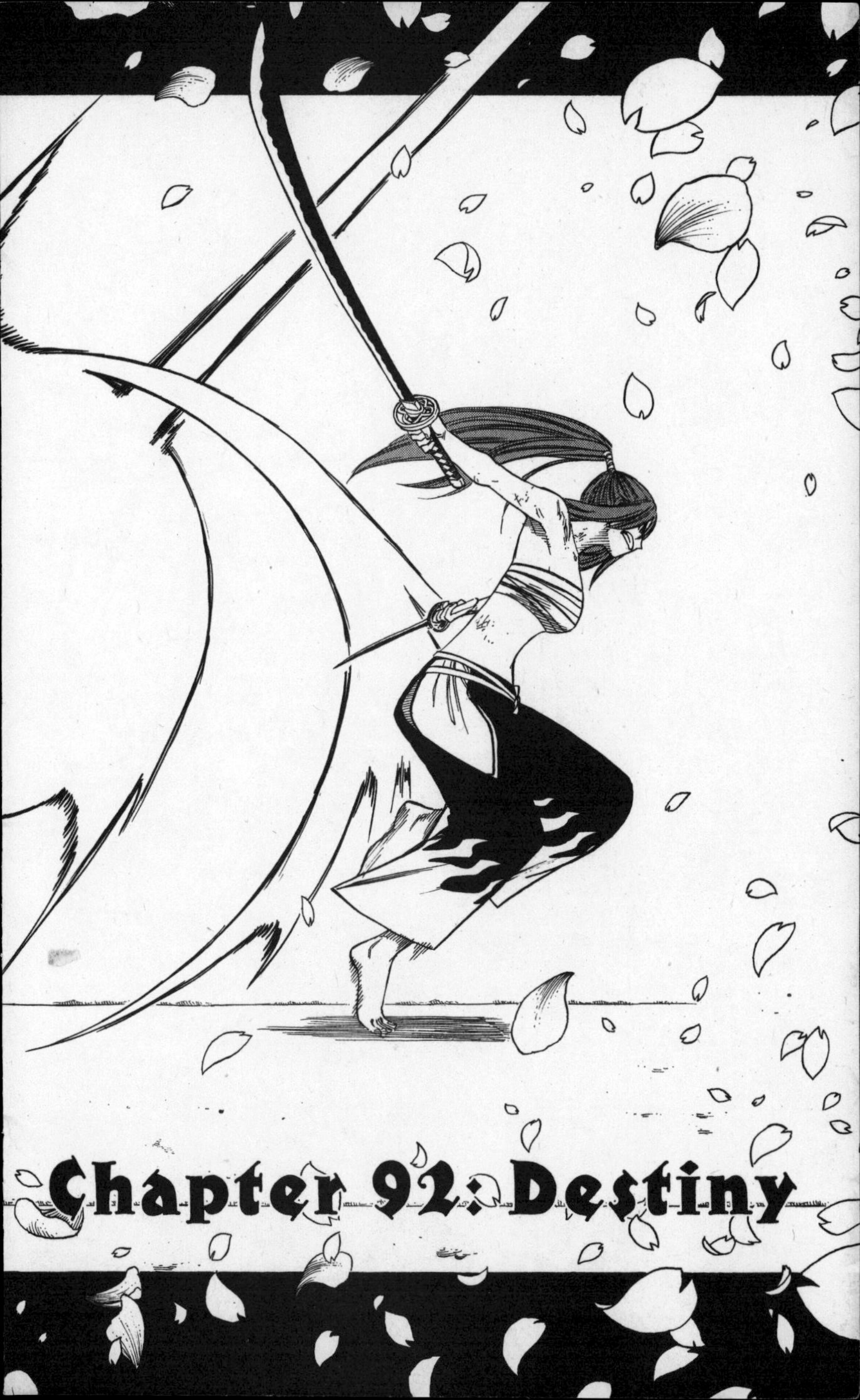
Chapter 92: Destiny

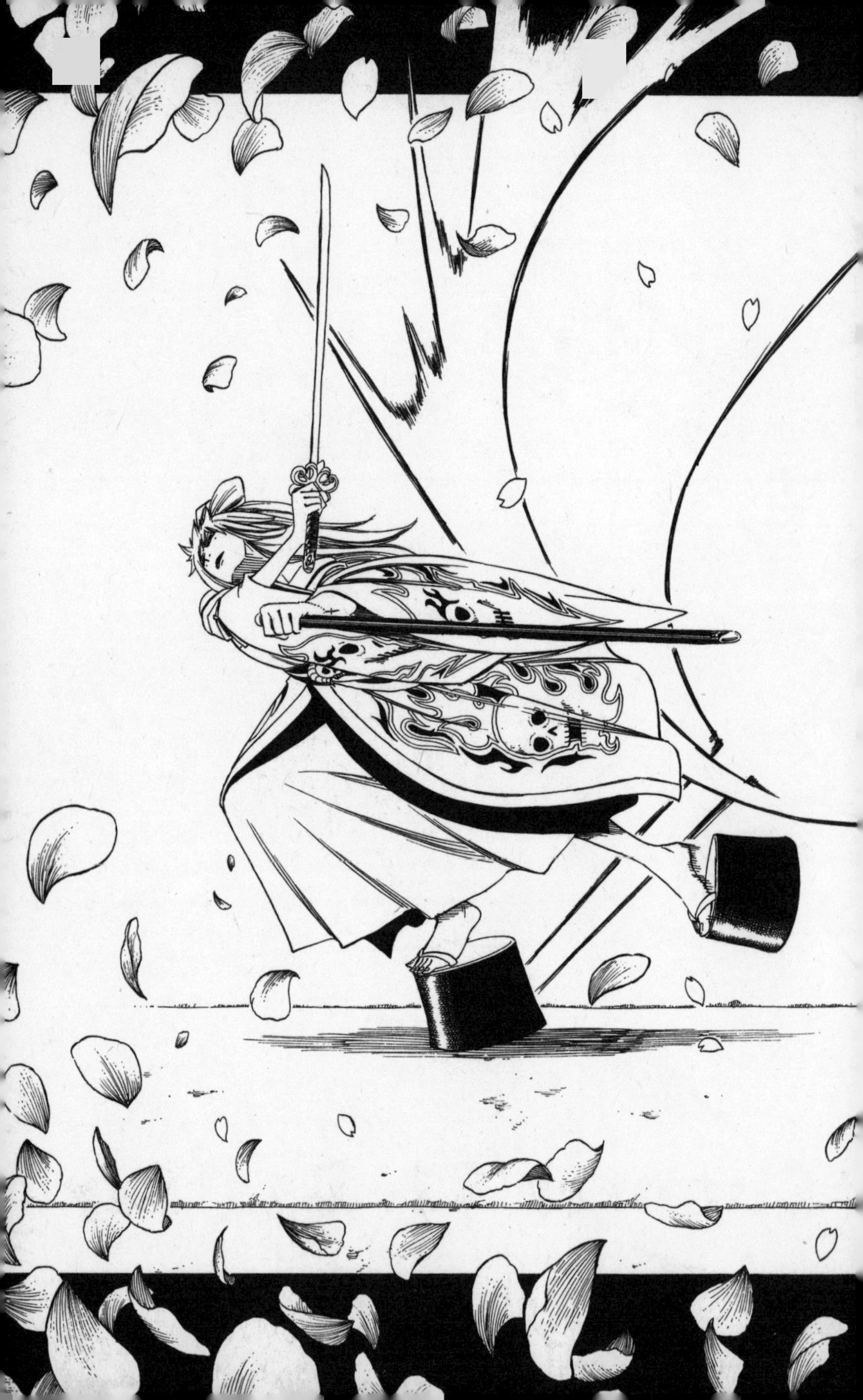

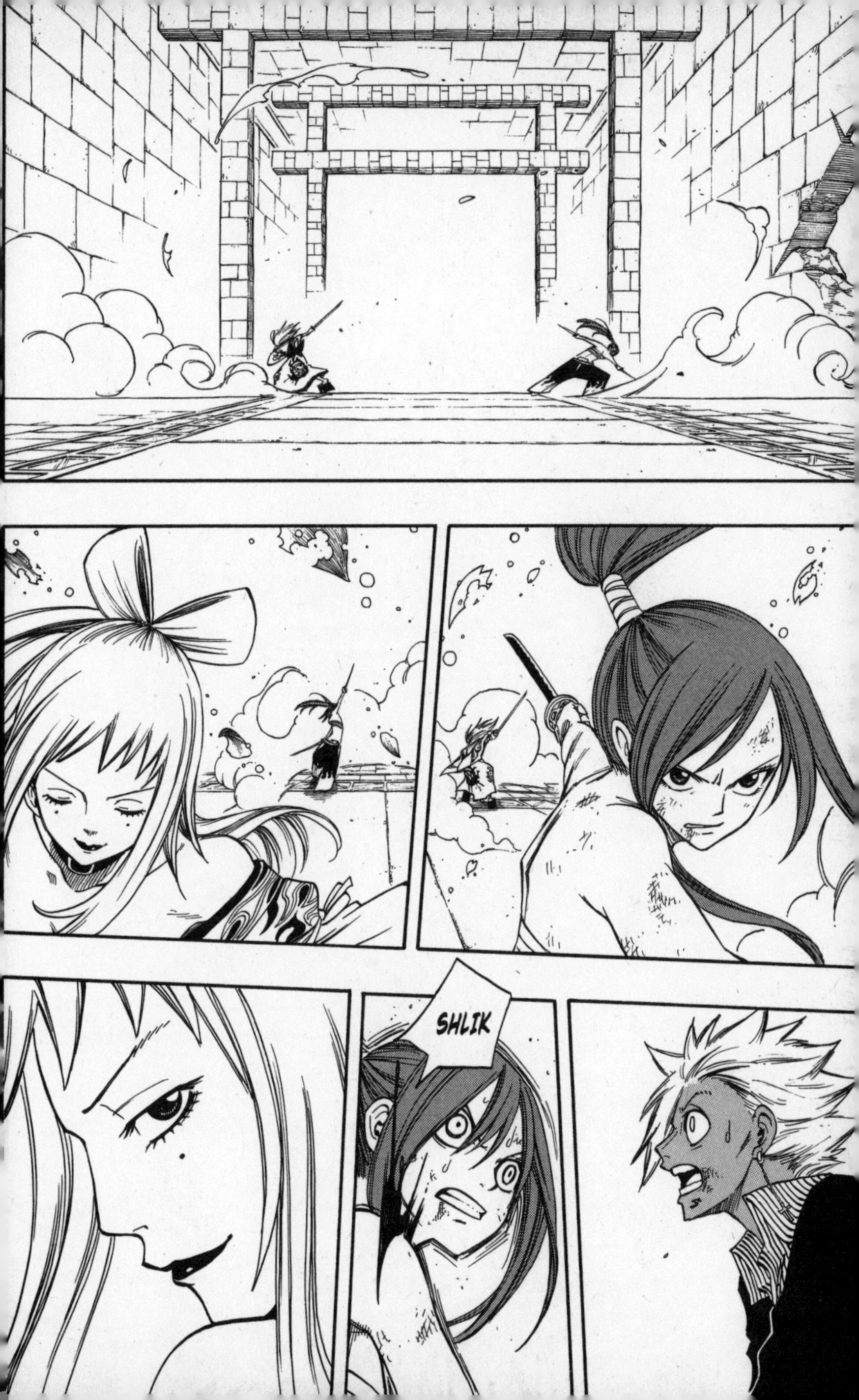
SHLIK

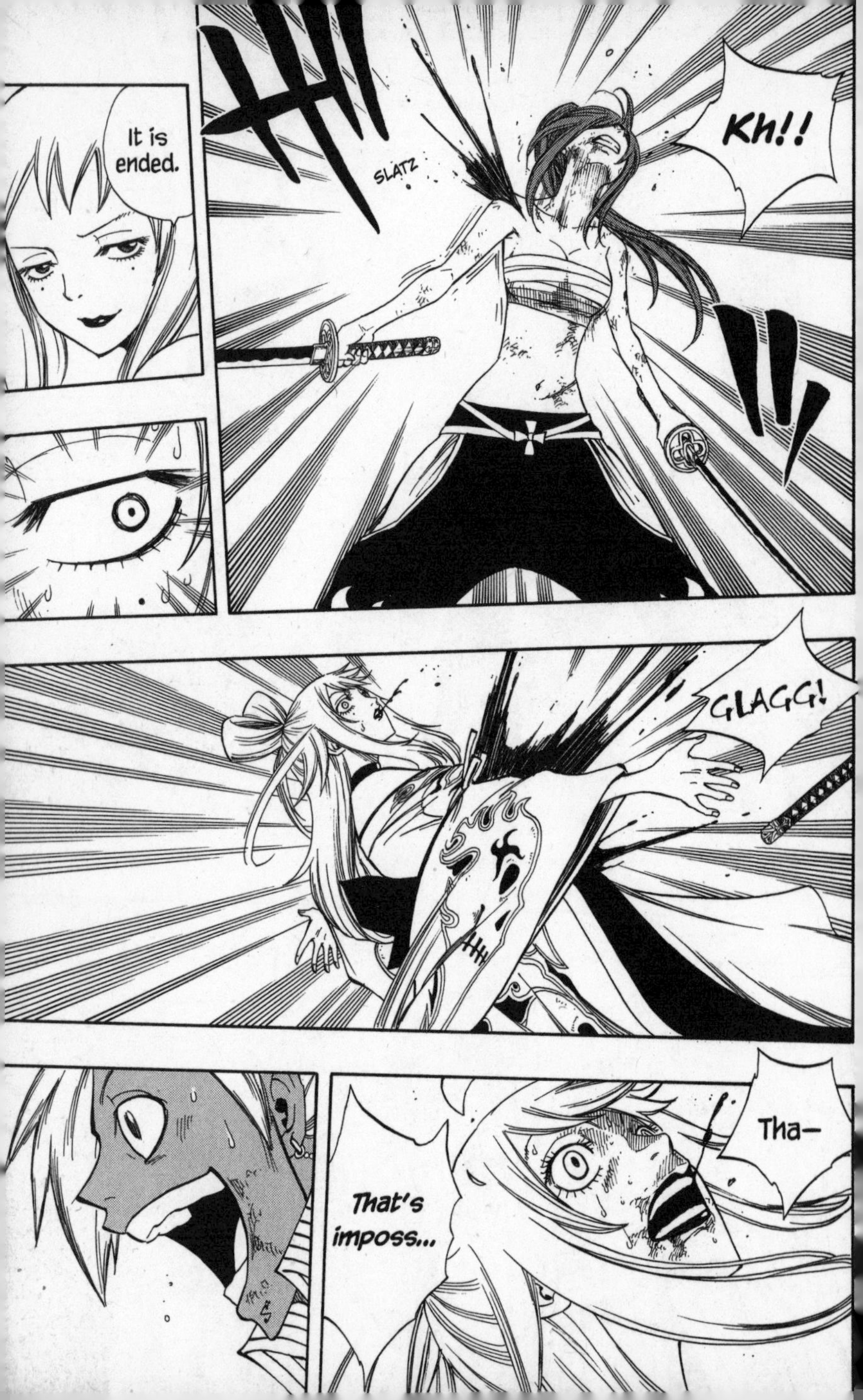

Kh!!
SLATZ
It is ended.
GLAGG!
Tha—
That's imposs...

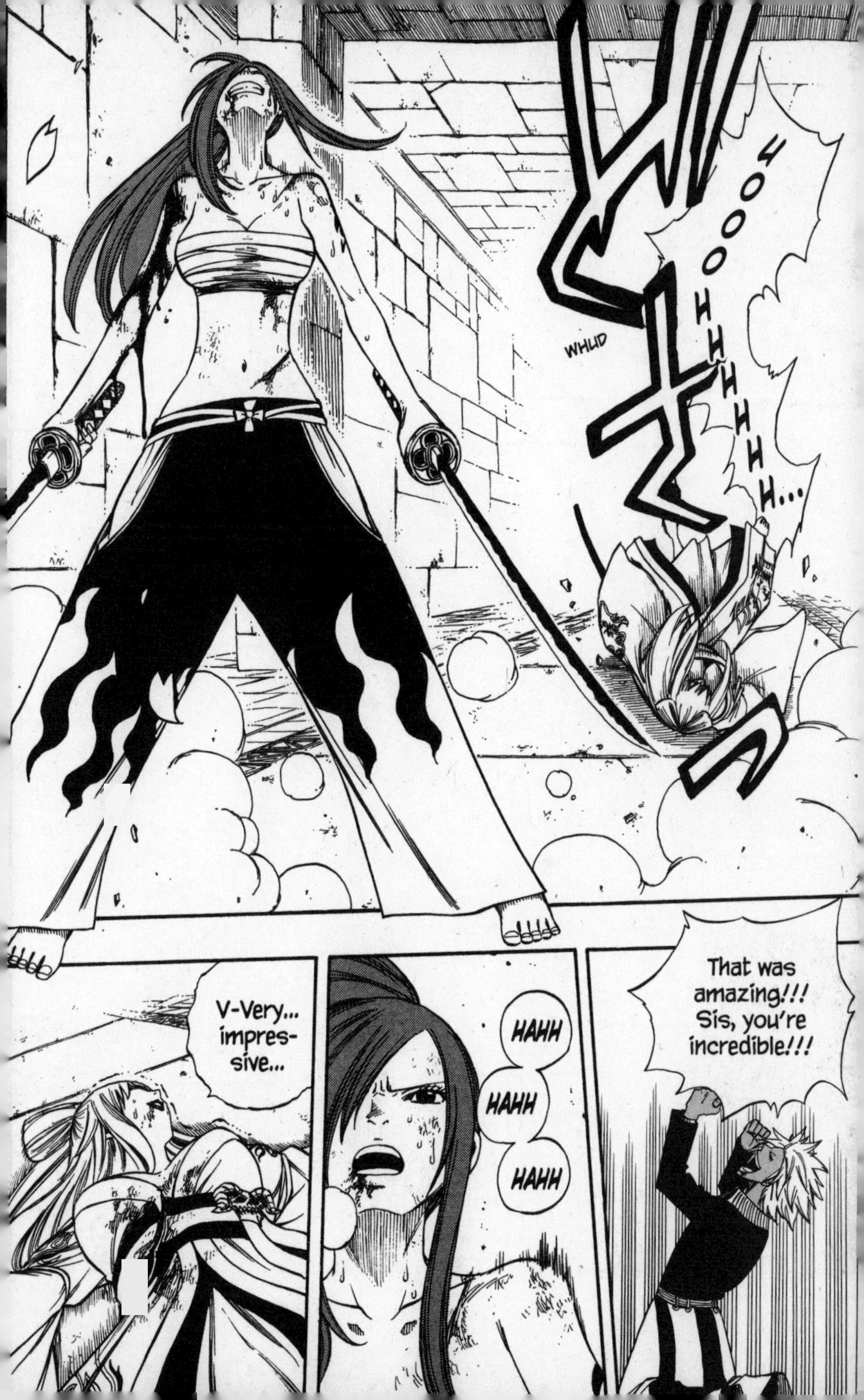
UOOOHHHHHH...
WHUD
That was amazing!!! Sis, you're incredible!!!
HAHH
HAHH
HAHH
V-Very... impres-sive...

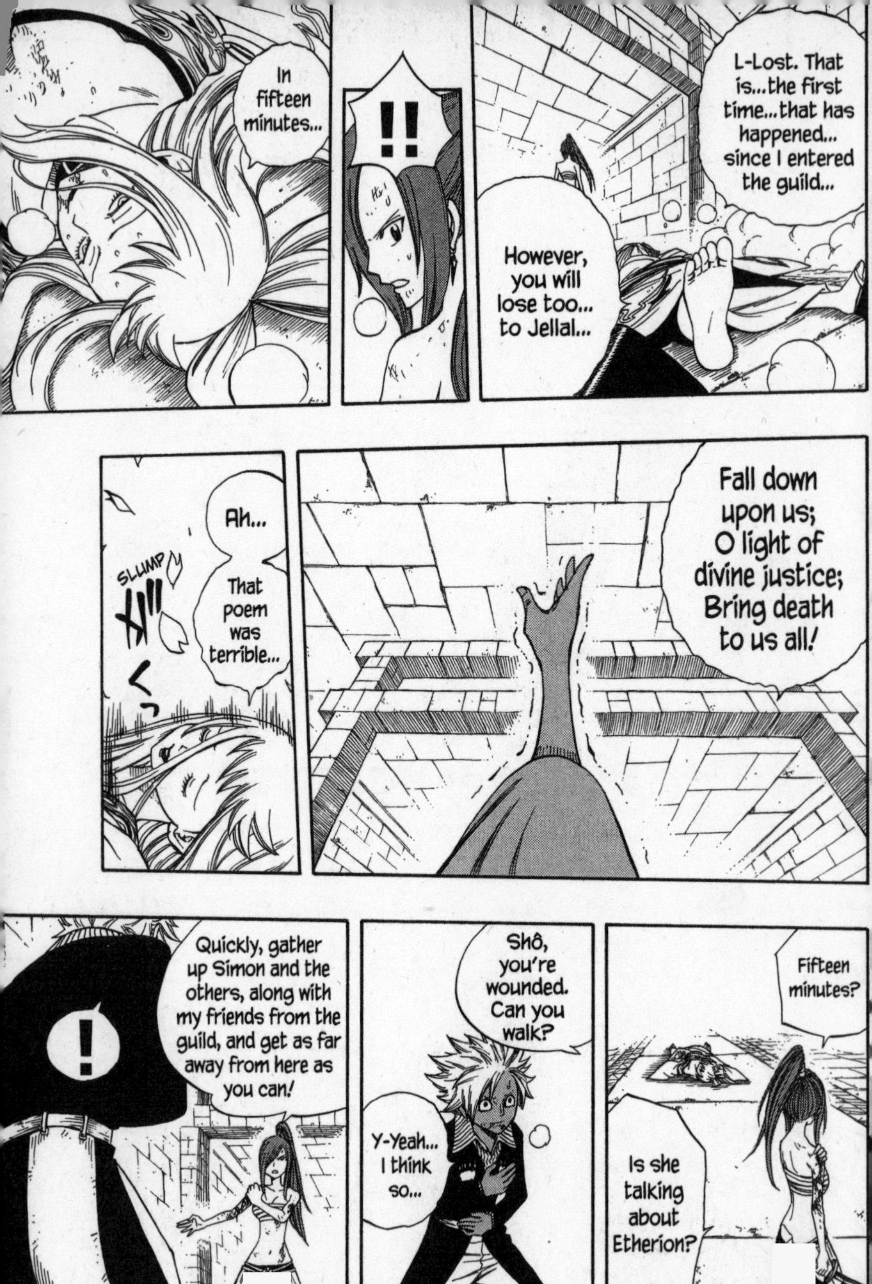
L-Lost. That is...the first time...that has happened... since I entered the guild...
However, you will lose too... to Jellal...
!!
In fifteen minutes...
Fall down upon us; O light of divine justice; Bring death to us all!
Ah...
That poem was terrible...
SLUMP
Fifteen minutes?
Is she talking about Etherion?
Shô, you're wounded. Can you walk?
Y-Yeah... I think so...
!
Quickly, gather up Simon and the others, along with my friends from the guild, and get as far away from here as you can!

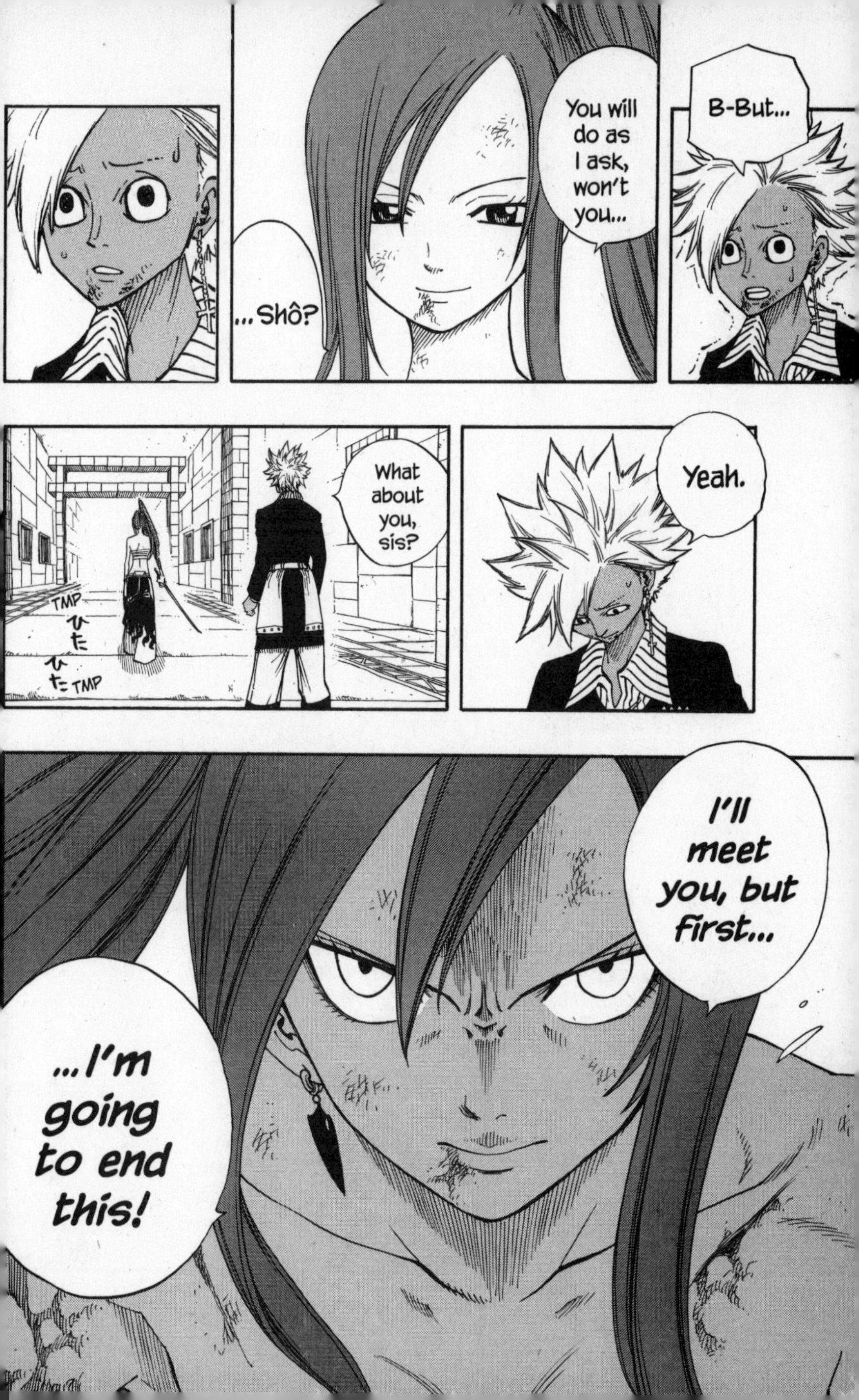
You will do as I ask, won't you...
...Shô?
B-But...
What about you, sis?
TMP ひた
ひた TMP
Yeah.
I'll meet you, but first...
...I'm going to end this!

Fairy Tail volume 11 is a work of fiction. Names, characters, places, and incidents are the products of the author's imagination or are used fictitiously. Any resemblance to actual events, locales, or persons, living or dead, is entirely coincidental.

A Kodansha Comics trade Paperback Original

Fairy Tail volume 11 copyright © 2008 Hiro Mashima
English translation copyright © 2010 Hiro Mashima

All rights reserved.

Published in the United States by Kodansha Comics, an imprint of Kodansha USA Publishing, LLC., New York.

Publication rights for this English edition arranged through Kodansha Ltd., Tokyo.

First published in Japan in 2008 by Kodansha Ltd., Tokyo

ISBN 978-1-612-62282-8

Printed in the United States of America

www.kodanshacomics.com

9   8   7   6   5   4   3

Translator/Adapter: William Flanagan
Lettering: North Market Street Graphics

TOMARE!

止まれ

[STOP!]

HALF HOLLOW HILLS
COMMUNITY LIBRARY
55 Vanderbilt Parkway
Dix Hills, NY 11746

You're going the wrong way!

Manga is a completely different type of reading experience.

To start at the *beginning*,
go to the *end*!

That's right! Authentic manga is read the traditional Japanese way—from right to left, exactly the *opposite* of how American books are read. It's easy to follow: Just go to the other end of the book and read each page—and each panel—from right side to left side, starting at the top right. Now you're experiencing manga as it was meant to be!